LITERATURE IN LETTERS;

OR,

MANNERS, ART, CRITICISM, BIOGRAPHY, HISTORY, AND MORALS,

ILLUSTRATED IN THE

CORRESPONDENCE OF EMINENT PERSONS.

EDITED BY

JAMES P. HOLCOMBE, LL.D.

NEW YORK:
D. APPLETON AND COMPANY, 443 & 445 BROADWAY,
1866.

PREFACE.

"SUCH letters," says Lord Bacon, "as are written from wise men, are, of all the words of man, in my judgment, the best; for they are more natural than orations and public speeches, and more advised than conferences or private ones." The sources of pleasure and instruction to be found in the private correspondence of eminent persons, have never been fully explored; much less have they been rendered accessible to the bulk of the reading public. Our language abounds in letters which contain the most vivid pictures of manners, and the most faithful and striking delineations of character; which are full of wit, wisdom, fancy, useful knowl edge, noble and pious sentiment.

The task of the Editor has been that of selection from many hundreds of volumes, of classification upon some comprehensive system, and of occasional illustration and explanation. Whilst our earlier literature has been freely laid under contribution, much material has been been derived from the more recent. No letter has been introduced to which it was supposed any exception could be taken on the ground of taste or morals. Those only have been selected whose intrinsic merit was preëminent, or which shed light on some great public transaction, or the character of some distinguished person. Scaliger thought it very impertinent in Montaigne to think the world cared which he liked best, white wine or red; but it is nevertheless true, an unfading freshness of interest hangs around these trivial details which brings us, as it were, into the familiar presence of famous men. And probably very few would sympathize with the sentiment of Wordsworth, that if records of Horace and his contemporaries, composed upon "the Boswellian plan," were unearthed from the ruins of Herculaneum, he would regret to hear it, "lest the beautiful ideal of those illustrious persons should be disfigured by incongruous features."

In the distribution of the letters, some have been found which could have been referred to either of several titles. An approximation, however, to an exact classification has, on the whole, seemed to the Editor much preferable to an arrangement on any other plan.

With one or two exceptions, no translations of foreign letters have been introduced. The principal exception has been in the case of Madame de Sévigné, whose letters have given equal pleasure to men of the world like Horace Walpole, and such scholars as Sir James Mackintosh. The selections have been made with the permission of the publishers, Messrs. Mason Brothers, from the American Edition, edited by Mrs. Hale. It is to be hoped that the promised additions to the "Library of Standard Letters" may be soon forthcoming.

JAMES P. HOLCOMBE.

NEW YORK, *December*, 1865.

TABLE OF CONTENTS.

BOOK THE FIRST.

GOSSIP, SOCIETY, AND MANNERS IN LETTERS.

TABLE OF CONTENTS.

BOOK THE SECOND.

LETTERS OF PLEASANTRY, SENTIMENT, AND FANCY.

BOOK THE THIRD.

SKETCHES OF NATURE, ART, AND TRAVEL IN LETTERS.

BOOK THE FOURTH.

PUBLIC HISTORY, ILLUSTRATED BY LETTERS.

BOOK THE FIFTH.

LITERARY BIOGRAPHY, ANECDOTE, AND CRITICISM IN LETTERS.

BOOK THE SIXTH.

LETTERS OF MORAL AND DEVOTIONAL REFLECTION.

BOOK THE FIRST.

Gossip, Society, and Manners in Letters.

BOOK THE FIRST.

GOSSIP, SOCIETY, AND MANNERS IN LETTERS.

I.—COURT OF LOUIS THE FOURTEENTH.

Madame de Sévigné to Madame de Grignan.

PARIS, July 29th, 1676.

WE have a change of the scene here which will gratify you as much as all the world. I was at Versailles last Saturday with the Villarses. You know the Queen's toilet, the mass, and the dinner? Well, there is no need any longer of suffocating ourselves in the crowd to get a glimpse of their majesties at table. At three, the King, the Queen, Monsieur, Madame, Mademoiselle, and every thing else which is royal, together with Madame Montespan and train, and all the courtiers, and all the ladies, all, in short, which constitutes the Court of France, is assembled in that beautiful apartment of the King's, which you remember. All is furnished divinely, all is magnificent. Such a thing as heat is unknown; you pass from one place to another without the slightest pressure. A game at *reversis* gives the company a form and a settlement. The King and Madame de Montespan keep a bank together; different tables are occupied by Monsieur, the Queen, and Madame de Soubise, Dangeau and party, Langlé and party; everywhere you see heaps of *louis d'ors*—they have no other counters. I saw Dangeau play, and thought what fools we all were beside him. He dreams of nothing but what concerns the game; he wins where others lose; he neglects nothing, profits by every thing, never has his attention diverted; in short, his science bids defiance to chance. Two hundred thousand francs in ten days, a hundred thousand crowns in a month; these are the pretty memorandums he puts down in his pocket book. He was kind enough to say that I was partners with him, so I got an excellent seat. I made my obeisance to the King as you told me, and he returned it as if I had been young and handsome. The Queen talked as long to me about my illness, as if it had been a lying-in. The Duke said a thousand kind things, without meaning a word he uttered. Marshal de Lorges attacked me in the name of the Chevalier de Grignan; in short, *tulli quanti* (the whole company). You know what it is to get a word from everybody you meet. Madame de Montespan talked to me of Bourbon, and asked me how I liked Vichi, and whether the place did me good. She said that Bourbon, instead of curing a pain in one of her knees, did mischief to both. Her size is reduced by a good half, and yet her complexion, her eyes, and her lips are as fine as ever. She was dressed all in French point; her hair in a thousand ringlets, the two side ones hanging low on her cheeks, black ribbons on her head, pearls (the same that belonged to Madame de l'Hôpital), the loveliest diamond ear-rings, three or four bodkins—nothing else on the head; in short, a triumphant beauty, worthy the admiration of all the foreign ambassadors. She was accused of preventing the whole French nation from seeing the King; she has restored him, you see, to their eyes; and you cannot conceive the joy it has given all the world, and the splendor it has thrown upon the Court. This charming confusion, without confusion, of all which is the most select, continues from three till six. If couriers arrive, the King retires a moment to read the despatches, and returns. There is always some music going on, to which he listens, and which has an excellent effect. He talks with such of the ladies as are accustomed to enjoy that honor. In short, they leave play at six. There is no trouble in counting, for there is no sort of counters; the pools consist of at least five, perhaps six or seven hundred louis; the bigger ones of a thousand or twelve hundred. At first, each person pools twenty, which is a hundred; and the dealer afterwards pools ten. The person who holds the knave is entitled to four louis; they pass; and when they play before the pool is taken they forfeit sixteen, which teaches them not to play out of turn. Talking is incessantly going on, and there is no end of *hearts*. How many hearts have you? I have two; I have three; I have one; I have four; he has only three then, he has only four; and Dangeau is delighted with all this chatter; he sees through the game, he draws his conclusions, he discovers which is the person he wants. Truly he is your only man for holding the cards. At six, the carriages are at the door. The King is in one of them, with Madame de Montespan, Monsieur and Madame de Thianges, and honest d'Hendicourt in a fool's paradise on the stool. You know how these open carriages are made; they do not sit face to face, but all looking the same way. The Queen occupies another, with the Princess; and the rest come flocking after as it may happen. There are then the gondolas on the canal, and music; and at ten they come back, and then there is a play; and twelve strikes, and they go to supper, and thus rolls round the

Saturday. If I were to tell you how often you were asked after, how many questions were put to me without waiting for answers, how often I neglected to answer, how little they cared, and how much less I did, you would see the *iniqua corte* (wicked Court) before you in all its perfection. However, it never was so pleasant before, and everybody wishes it may last.

II.—THE BIRTHNIGHT BALL.

Lady Wortley Montagu to the Countess of Mar.

October 31, 1723.

I write to you at this time piping-hot from the birthnight; my brain warmed with all the agreeable ideas that fine clothes, fine gentlemen, brisk tunes, and lively dances can raise there. It is to be hoped that my letter will entertain you; at least you will certainly have the freshest account of all passages on that glorious day. First you must know that I led up the ball, which you'll stare at; but what is more, I believe in my conscience I made one of the best figures there: to say truth, people are grown so extravagantly ugly, that we old beauties are forced to come out on show-days, to keep the Court in countenance. I saw Mrs. Murray there, through whose hands this epistle will be conveyed; I do not know whether she will make the same complaint to you that I do. Mrs. West was with her, who is a great prude, having but two lovers at a time; I think those are Lord Haddington and Mr. Lindsay; the one for use, the other for show.

The world improves in one virtue to a violent degree, I mean plain-dealing. Hypocrisy being, as the Scripture declares, a damnable sin, I hope our publicans and sinners will be saved by the open profession of the contrary virtue. I was told by a very good author, who is deep in the secret, that at this very minute there is a bill cooking up at a hunting-seat in Norfolk,* to have NOT taken out of the commandments and clapped into the creed, the ensuing session of Parliament. This bold attempt for the liberty of the subject is wholly projected by Mr. Walpole, who proposed it to the secret committee in his parlor. William Young † seconded it, and answered for all his acquaintance voting right to a man; Doddington ‡ very gravely objected, that the obstinacy of human nature was such, that he feared when they had positive commandments to do so, perhaps people would not commit adultery and bear false witness against their neighbors with the readiness and cheerfulness they do at present. This objection seemed to sink deep into the minds of the greatest politicians at the board, and I don't know whether the bill won't be dropped, though it is certain it might be carried on with great ease, the world being entirely "*revenue du bagatelle*," and honor, virtue, reputation, etc., which we used to hear of in our nursery, as much laid aside and forgotten as crumpled ribands. To speak plainly, I am very sorry for the forlorn state of matrimony, which is as much ridiculed by our young ladies as it used to be by young fellows; in short, both sexes have found the inconvenience of it, and the appellation of rake is as genteel in a woman as a man of quality; it is no scandal to say Miss ——, the maid of honor, looks very well now she is up again, and

* Houghton; Mr. (afterwards Sir Robert) Walpole's, then Prime Minister.

† Sir William Young.

‡ George Bubb Doddington, afterwards Lord Melcomb-Regis, whose Diary has been published.

poor Biddy Noel has never been quite well since her last confinement. You may imagine we married women look very silly; we have nothing to excuse ourselves, but that it was done a great while ago, and we were very young when we did it. This is the general state of affairs; as to particulars, if you have any curiosity for things of that kind, you have nothing to do but to ask me questions, and they shall be answered to the best of my understanding; my time never being passed more agreeably than when I am doing something obliging to you; this is truth, in spite of all the beaus, wits, and witlings in Great Britain.*

M. W. M.

III.—CURIOUS WEDDING AT CHRIST'S HOSPITAL.

Samuel Pepys to Mrs. Steward.

September 20th, 1695.

MADAM: You are very good, and pray continue so, by as many kind messages as you can, and notices of your health, such as the bearer brings you back my thanks for, and a thousand services. Here's a sad town, and God knows when it will be a better, our losses at sea making a very melancholy exchange at both ends of it; the gentlewomen of this, to say nothing of the other, sitting with their arms across,

* This letter has been pronounced by an eminent critic the very best in Lady Montagu's collection. It is refreshing to turn from the picture it presents of female manners and morals in the courtly circles of that age, to the pure and simple home which is brought before us in the letters that follow, written at a somewhat earlier period by Lady Russell. The career of Lady Montagu furnishes abundant evidence that genius, beauty, rank, and fortune cannot confer happiness. Separated in fact from her husband, unfortunate in her child, her letters breathe a restless and unsatisfied spirit, and the finest verses she ever wrote contain an apology for suicide.—H.

without a yard of muslin in their shops to sell, while the ladies they tell me walk pensively by, without a shilling, I mean a good one, in their pockets to buy. One thing there is, indeed, that comes in my way as a governor to hear of, which carries a little mirth with it, and indeed is very odd. Two wealthy citizens are lately dead, and left their estates, one to a Blue-coat boy, and the other to a Blue-coat girl, in Christ's Hospital. The extraordinariness of which has led some of the magistrates to carry it on to a match, which is ended in a public wedding; he in his habit of blue satin, led by two of the girls, and she in blue, with an apron green and petticoat yellow, all of sarsnet, led by two of the boys of the house, through Cheapside to Guildhall Chapel, where they were married by the Dean of St. Paul's, she given by my Lord Mayor. The wedding dinner, it seems, was kept in the Hospital Hall, but the great day will be to-morrow, St. Matthew's; when so much I am sure of, my Lord Mayor will be there, and myself also have had a ticket of invitation thither, and if I can, will be there too; but for other particulars must refer you to my next, and so, dear madam, adieu, S. P.

Bow bells are just now ringing dong, dong, but whether for this I cannot presently tell, but it is likely enough, for I have known them to ring upon much foolisher occasions, and lately too.

IV.—A SLIP BETWEEN CUP AND LIP, OR LOSS OF A ROYAL BRIDE.

*Madame de Sévigné to Madame de Coulanges.**

PARIS, Monday, Dec. 15, 1670.

I am going to tell you a thing the most astonishing, the most surprising, the most marvellous, the most miraculous, the most magnificent, the most confounding, the most unheard of, the most singular, the most extraordinary, the most incredible, the most unforeseen, the greatest, the least, the rarest, the most common, the most public, the most private till to-day, the most brilliant, the most enviable; in short, a thing of which there is but one example in past ages, and that not an exact one either; a thing that we cannot believe at Paris—how then will it gain credit at Lyons? a thing which makes everybody cry, "Lord have mercy upon us!" a thing which causes the greatest joy to Madame De Rohan and Madame De Hauterive; a thing, in fine, which is to happen on Sunday next, when those who are present will doubt the evidence of their senses; a thing which, though it is to be done on Sunday, yet perhaps will not be finished on Monday. I cannot bring myself to tell it you; guess what it is. I give you three times to do it in. What, not a word to throw at a dog? Well, then, I find I must tell you. Monsieur de Lauzun † is to be married next Sunday at the Louvre, to ——, pray guess to whom! I give you four times to do it in, I give you six, I give you a hundred. Says Madame de Coulanges, "It is really very hard to guess; perhaps it is Madame de la

* These letters have been taken from the American edition of Madame de Sévigné's Letters, a work prepared with admirable taste and judgment by Mrs. Hale.

† Antonius Nompar de Caumont, Marquis de Puiguilhem, afterwards Duke de Lauzun.

Vallière." Indeed, madam, it is not. "It is Mademoiselle de Retz, then." No, nor she neither; you are extremely provincial. "Lord bless me," say you, "what stupid wretches we are! it is Mademoiselle de Colbert all the while." Nay, now you are still further from the mark. "Why then it must certainly be Mademoiselle de Crequy." You have it not yet. Well, I find I must tell you at last. He is to be married next Sunday, at the Louvre, with the King's leave, to Mademoiselle, Mademoiselle de ——, Mademoiselle—guess, pray guess her name; he is to be married to Mademoiselle, the great Mademoiselle; Mademoiselle, daughter to the late Monsieur;* Mademoiselle, grand-daughter of Henry the Fourth; Mademoiselle d'Eu; Mademoisellede Dombes; Mademoiselle de Montpensier; Mademoiselle d'Orleans; Mademoiselle, the King's cousin-german; Mademoiselle, destined to the throne; Mademoiselle, the only match in France that was worthy of Monsieur. What glorious matter for talk! If you should burst forth like a bedlamite, say we have told you a lie, that it is false, that we are making a jest of you, and that a pretty jest it is, without wit or invention; in short, if you abuse us, we shall think you quite in the right; for we have done just the same things ourselves. Farewell, you will find by the letters you receive this post, whether we tell you the truth or not.

V.

From the Same to the Same.

PARIS, Friday, Dec. 19, 1670.

What is called "falling from the clouds," happened last night at the Tuileries; but I must go further back. You have

* Gaston of France, Duke of Orleans, brother to Louis XIII.

already shared in the joy, the transport, the ecstacies of the Princess and her happy lover. It was just as I told you, the affair was made public on Monday. Tuesday was passed in talking, astonishment, and compliments. Wednesday, Mademoiselle made a deed of gift to Monsieur de Lauzun, investing him with certain titles, names, and dignities, necessary to be inserted in the marriage-contract, which was drawn up that day. She gave him then, till she could give him something better, four duchies; the first was that of Count d'Eu, which entitles him to rank as first peer of France; the Dukedom of Montpensier, which title he bore all that day; the Dukedom de Saint Fargeau, and the Dukedom de Châtellerault, the whole valued at twenty-two millions of livres. The contract was then drawn up, and he took the name of Montpensier. Thursday morning, which was yesterday, Mademoiselle was in expectation of the King's signing the contract, as he had said that he would do; but, about seven o'clock in the evening, the Queen, Monsieur, and several old dotards that were about him, had so persuaded his majesty that his reputation would suffer in this affair, that, sending for Mademoiselle and Monsieur de Lauzun, he announced to them, before the Prince, that he forbade them to think any further of this marriage. Monsieur de Lauzun received the prohibition with all the respect, submission, firmness, and, at the same time, despair, that could be expected in so great a reverse of fortune. As for Mademoiselle, she gave a loose to her feelings, and burst into tears, cries, lamentations, and the most violent expressions of grief; she keeps her bed all day long, and takes nothing within her lips but a little broth. What a fine dream is here! what a glorious subject for a tragedy or romance, but especially talking and reasoning eternally! This is what we do day and night, morning and evening, without end, and without intermission; we hope you do the same, *E fra tanto vi bacio le mani:* "and with this I kiss your hand."

VI.

From the Same to the Same.

Paris, Wednesday, Dec. 24, 1670.

You are now perfectly acquainted with the romantic story of Mademoiselle and of Monsieur de Lauzun. It is a story well adapted for a tragedy, and in all the rules of the theatre; we laid out the acts and scenes the other day. We took four days instead of four and twenty hours, and the piece was complete. Never was such a change seen in so short a time; never was there known so general an emotion. You certainly never received so extraordinary a piece of intelligence before. M. de Lauzun behaved admirably; he supported his misfortune with such courage and intrepidity, and at the same time showed so deep a sorrow, mixed with such profound respect, that he has gained the admiration of everybody. His loss is doubtless great, but then the King's favor, which he has by this means preserved, is likewise great; so that, upon the whole, his condition does not seem so very deplorable. Mademoiselle, too, has behaved extremely well on her side. She has wept much and bitterly; but yesterday, for the first time, she returned to pay her duty at the Louvre, after having received the visits of every one there; so the affair is all over. Adieu.

VII.

From the Same to the Same.

PARIS, Wednesday, Dec. 31, 1670.

I have received your answers to my letters. I can easily conceive the astonishment you were in at what passed between the 15th and 20th of this month; the subject called for it all. I admire likewise your penetration and judgment, in imagining so great a machine could never support itself from Monday to Sunday. Modesty prevents my launching out in your praise on this head, because I said and thought exactly as you did. I told my daughter on Monday, "This will never go on as it should do till Sunday; I will wager, notwithstanding this wedding seems to be sure, that it will never come to a conclusion." In effect the sky was overcast on Thursday morning, and about ten o'clock, as I told you, the cloud burst. That very day I went about nine in the morning to pay my respects to Mademoiselle, having been informed that she was to go out of town to be married, and that the coadjutor of Rheims* was to perform the cermony. These were the resolves on Wednesday night, but matters had been determined otherwise at the Louvre ever since Tuesday. Mademoiselle was writing; she made me place myself on my knees at her bedside; she told me to whom she was writing, and upon what subject, and also of the fine presents she had made the night before, and the titles she had conferred; and as there was no match in any of the Courts of Europe for her, she was resolved, she said, to provide for herself. She related to me, word for word, a conversation she had had with the King, and appeared overcome with joy to think how happy she should

* Charles Maurice le Tellier.

make a man of merit. She mentioned, with a great deal of tenderness, the worth and gratitude of M. de Lauzun. To all which I made her this answer: "Upon my word, Mademoiselle, your highness seems quite happy; but why was not this affair finished at once last Monday? Do not you perceive that the delay will give time and opportunity to the whole kingdom to talk, and that it is absolutely tempting God, and the King, to protract an affair of so extraordinary a nature as this is to so distant a period?" She allowed me to be in the right, but was so sure of success, that what I said made little or no impression on her at the time. She repeated the many amiable qualities of Monsieur de Lauzun, and the noble house he was descended from. To which I replied in these lines of Corneille's Polyeuctus:

> Du moins on ne la peut blâmer d'un mauvais choix,
> Polyeucte a du nom, et sort du sang des rois.
>
> Her choice of him no one can surely blame,
> Who springs from kings, and boasts a noble name.

Upon which she embraced me tenderly. Our conversation lasted above an hour. It is impossible to repeat all that passed between us, but I may without vanity say that my company was agreeable to her, for her heart was so full that she was glad of any one to unburden it to. At ten o'clock she devoted her time to the nobility, who crowded to pay their compliments to her. She waited all the morning for news from Court, but none came. All the afternoon she amused herself with putting M. de Montpensier's apartment in order, which she did with her own hands. You know what happened at night. The next morning, which was Friday, I waited upon her, and found her in bed; her grief redoubled at seeing me; she called me to her, embraced me, and overwhelmed me with tears.

"Ah!" said she, "you remember what you said to me yesterday? What foresight! what cruel foresight!" In short, she made me weep to see her weep so violently. I have seen her twice since; she still continues in great affliction, but behaves to me as to a person that sympathizes with her in her distress; in which she is not mistaken, for I really feel sentiments for her that are seldom felt for persons of such superior rank. This, however, between us two and Madame de Coulanges; for you are sensible that this chit-chat would appear ridiculous to others.

VIII.—LIFE OF A LADY OF FASHION IN THE COUNTRY.

*Mrs. Bradshaw to Mrs. Howard.**

GOSWORTH HALL, May 28th, 1722.

Our bells have rung ever since four this morning, which is more a proof of Lady Mohun's power than the people's inclination.

I am told you expect from me an account of the manners and customs of this place. It is impossible for me to obey your commands at present, for the weather has been so wet that none of the neighboring nymphs or swains have been able to make their appearance; but if you can be contented with a description of the hall, and the manner of life we lead this Christmas time (for so it is here, I do assure you), take it, as follows:

We meet in the work-room before nine; eat and brake a joke or two till twelve; then we repair to our own chambers

* This lady was afterwards the famous Countess of Suffolk, whose intimacy with both George II. and Queen Caroline was the great court scandal of that day.—H.

and make ourselves ready, for it cannot be called dressing; at noon the great bell fetches us into a parlor, adorned with all sorts of firearms, poisoned *darts*, several pair of old shoes and boots, won from the Tartars by men of might belonging to this castle, with the stirrups of King Charles the First, taken from him at Edge Hill.

Here leave we the historical part of the furniture; and cast your eye (in imagination) upon a table covered with good fish and flesh, the product of our own estate; and such ale!—it would make you stare again, Howard. After your health has gone round (which is always the second glass), we begin to grow witty, and really say things which would make your ears tingle; your court wits are nothing to us for invention (plots only excepted); but being all of a side, we lay no scheme but of getting you amongst us, where, though I say it that should not (because I would have my share in it), you would pass your time very agreeably in our dike, for you must know we have hardly seen dry land since we came.

Mr. Mordaunt has once or twice made an effort to sally out into the gardens, but, finding no rest for the sole of his foot, returns presently to us again; and I must give him his due, always in good humor. Miss had a small ray of hope last night, for Colonel Lawrence and a gentleman with him swam to us; the last was clothed in blue, turned up with red, and adorned with plate buttons; upon which she puts me on her lute-string suit, not omitting all the little flirtations she is mistress of. If she brings it to any thing, you shall be sure to have notice time enough to provide another maid.

Nay, I will assure you, old as I am, I have my little gallantries too. A gentleman of three hundred per annum fancies me extremely, and if he had not been under an engagement before I came, I have some reason to believe I might have kept a chaise of my own; however, I live in hope that a loose man may come, though it will be some time first, for all the best families in the parish are laid up with what they call the yoke—which in England is the itch. We have had a noble captain, who dined in a brave pair of white gloves, to my very great surprise; but it was when I was in my London ignorance.

I am now called upon to see a pond drawn, which will produce carp as big as some of your lords of the bed chamber. Madame Howard, I live in expectation of an epistle from you, which is the only wish I have out of my company, who are all your humble servants; but nobody is more entirely so than your slave, PEGGY.

IX.--DIARY OF A MAN OF FASHION AT BATH.

Lord Chesterfield to the Countess of Suffolk.

BATH, Nov. 2d, 1734.

MADAM: A general history of the Bath since you left it, together with the particulars of Amoretto's (the Hon. William Sawyer Herbert) life and conversation, are matters of too great importance to need any introduction. Therefore, without further preamble, I send you the very minutes, just as I have them down to help my own memory; the variety of events, and the time necessary to observe them, not having yet allowed me the leisure to put them in that style and order in which I propose they shall hereafter appear in public.

Oct. 27.—Little company appeared at the pump; those that were there drank the waters of affliction for the departure of

Lady Suffolk and Mrs. Blount. What was said of them both I need not tell you; for it was so obvious to those that said it, that it cannot be less so to those that deserve it. Amoretto went upon Lansdowne to evaporate his grief for the loss of his Parthenissa (Mrs. Blount), in memory of whom (and the wind being cold into the bargain) he tied his handkerchief over his hat, and looked very sadly.

In the evening, the usual tea-table met at Lyndsey's, the two principal persons excepted, who, it was hoped, were then got safe to Newberry. Amoretto's main action was at our table; but episodically, he took pieces of bread and butter, and cups of tea at about ten others. He laughed his way through the girls out of the long room into the little one, where he *tallied** till he swore, and swore till he went home—and probably some time afterwards.

The Countess of Burlington, in the absence of her Royal Highness, held a circle at Hayes's, where she lost a favorite snuff-box, but unfortunately kept her temper.

Oct. 28.—Breakfast was at Lady Anne's, where Amoretto was with difficulty prevailed upon to eat and drink as much as he had a mind to. At night he was observed to be pleasant with the girls, and with less restraint than usual, which made some people surmise that he comforted himself for the loss of Lady Suffolk and Parthenissa, by the liberty and impunity their absence gave him.

Oct. 29.—Amoretto breakfasted incognito, but appeared at the ball in the evening, where he distinguished himself by his *bon mots.* He was particularly pleased to compare the two Miss

* Played at cards.

Towardins, who are very short, and were a dancing, to a couple of totums set a spinning. The justness and liveliness of this image struck Mr. Marriott to such a degree, that he begged leave of the author to put it off for his own, which was granted him. He declared afterwards to several people, that Mr. Herbert beat the world at similes.

Oct. 30.—Being his Majesty's birthday, little company appeared in the morning, all being resolved to look well at night. Mr. Herbert dined at Mr. Walter's with young Mr. Barnard, whom he rallied to death. Nash gave a ball at Lydnsey's, where Mr. Tate appeared for the first time, and was noticed by Mr. Herbert; he wore his gold-laced clothes on the occasion, and looked so fine, that, standing by chance in the middle of the dancers, he was taken by many at a distance for a gilt garland. He concluded his evening as usual with basset and blasphemy.

Oct. 31.—Amoretto breakfasted at Lady Anne's, where, being now more easy and familiar, he called for a half peck loaf and a pound of butter—let off a great many ideas, and, had he had the same inclination to have let off any thing else, would doubtless have done it. The Countess of Burlington bespoke the play, as you may see by the enclosed original bill; the audience consisted of seventeen souls, of whom I made one.

Nov. 1.—Amoretto took a vomit in the morning, and then with a clear and excellent stomach dined with me, and went to the ball at night, where Mrs. Hamilton chiefly engrossed him. Mrs. Jones gave Sir Humphrey Monoux pain with Mr. Browne, which gave Sir Humphrey the toothach, but Mr. Jones has since made up matters between them.

Nov. 2.—Circular letters are received here from *Miss* Secretary Russell, notifying the safe arrival at London, with many interesting particulars, and with gracious assurances of the continuance of a firm and sincere friendship. It would be as hard to say who received the strongest assurances, as it would be to determine who credited them the worst. Mrs. Hamilton bespoke the play at night, which we all interested ourselves so much to fill, that there were as many people turned back as let in; it was so hot that the Countess of Burlington could not stay it out.

You now see by this week's journal how much you have lost by leaving the Bath so soon; at least I can assure you we feel what we lost by your leaving it before us. We are all disjointed, and so weary that I have prevailed with my brother and Charles Stanhope to start from hence with me on Tuesday se'night, which will just complete the two months I was ordered to stay. We set Mr. Herbert down at Highclere, in our way. This day fortnight I hope to have the pleasure of finding you at St. James's, much the better for the bath; where, over a hot roll with Mrs. Blount, I propose giving you the next week's journal by word of mouth. After having troubled you so long already, it is only in compliance to the form of letters that I add so unnecessary and so known a truth, as the assurance of the respect and attachment with which I am,

Madam, yours, &c., CHESTERFIELD.

X.—HOUSE OF LORDS STORMED BY A MOB OF LADIES.*

Lady Montagu to Lady Pomfret.

———, 1738.

There is no news to be sent you from this place, which has been for this fortnight, and still continues, overwhelmed with

* This curious incident is not without some parallel even in our own day

politics, and which are of so mysterious a nature, one ought to have some of the gifts of Lilly or Patridge to be able to write about them; and I leave all these dissertations to those distinguished mortals who are endowed with the talent of divination; though I am at present the only one of my sex who seems to be of that opinion, the ladies having shown their zeal and appetite for knowledge in a most glorious manner. At the last warm debate in the House of Lords, it was unanimously resolved that there should be no crowd of unnecessary auditors; consequently the fair sex were excluded, and the gallery destined to the sole use of the House of Commons. Notwithstanding which determination, a tribe of dames resolved to show on this occasion that neither men nor laws could resist them. These heroines

The following passage occurs in one of Curran's letters from Paris, in 1814: "We agreed to go to *La Chambre des Députes*. One of the members chanced to have heard of my name, was extremely courteous, lamented that I should be a mere auditor, but he would take care that I should be placed according to my high worthiness. We were accordingly placed *aux premières tribunes*. The question was to be of the liberty of the press and a previous censorship. The baron had some difficulty in working us forward, and said how happy he was in succeeding. I assured him I was greatly delighted by the difficulty, as it marked the just point of solicitude of the public. The chamber is very handsome. The president faces the assembly. Before him is a Tribune, which the orator ascends and reads his speech with his back to the president. We waited anxiously. I thought I shared in the throb of a public heart. We observed some bustle. The seats of the interior, reserved for the members, became crowded to excess by ladies, admitted I know not how. The order for strangers to retire was read, the ladies would not stir. The president could find no remedy, and adjourned the House to next day. I was rather disgusted. The baron asked me what we would have done in England. I said we had too much respect for our ladies to permit them to remain. He shook his head. I did not understand what he meant; but does not this prove what I said a day or two ago to be true; that women here have only a mock respect? If real, would they have dreamed of such a silly termagancy?"—H.

were Lady Huntingdon, the Duchess of Queensbury, the Duchess of Ancaster, Lady Westmoreland, Lady Cobham, Lady Charlotte Edwin, Lady Archibald Hamilton and her daughter, Mrs. Scott, Mrs. Pendarvis, and Lady Francis Saunderson. I am thus particular in their names, since I look upon them to be the boldest assertors, and most resigned sufferers for liberty, I ever read of. They presented themselves at the door at nine o'clock in the morning, where Sir William Saunderson respectfully informed them that the Chancellor had made an order against their admitttance. The Duchess of Queensbury, as head of the squadron, pished at the ill-breeding of a mere lawyer, and desired him to let them up the stairs privately. After some modest refusals, he swore by G— he would not let them in. Her Grace, with a noble warmth, answered by G— they would come in, in spite of the Chancellor and the whole House. This being reported, the peers resolved to starve them out; an order was made that the doors should not be opened till they had raised their siege. These amazons now showed themselves qualified for the duty even of foot soldiers; they stood there till five in the afternoon, without either sustenance or intermission, every now and then playing vollies of thumps, kicks, and raps against the door, with so much violence that the speakers in the House were scarce heard. When the Lords were not to be conquered by this, the two Duchesses (very well apprised of the use of stratagems in war) commanded a dead silence of half an hour; and the Chancellor, who thought this a certain proof of their absence (the Commons also being very impatient to enter), gave order for the opening of the door; upon which they all rushed in, pushed aside their competitors, and placed themselves in the front rows of the gallery. They stayed there till after eleven, when the House rose, and during the debate gave applause, and showed marks of dislike, not only by smiles and winks (which have always been allowed in these cases), but by noisy laughs and apparent contempts; which is supposed the true reason why poor Lord Hervey spoke miserably. I beg your pardon, dear madam, for this long relation; but it is impossible to be short on so copious a subject; and you must own this action to be very well worthy of record, and I think not to be paralleled in any history, ancient or modern.

Yours, &c., ———.

XI.—FAMILY NEWS.

Lady Russell to Lord Russell.

TUNBRIDGE WELLS, 1678.

After a toilsome day, there is some refreshment to be telling our story to our best friends. I have seen your girl well laid in bed, and ourselves have made our suppers upon biscuits, a bottle of white wine, and another of beer, and mingled my uncle's whey with nutmeg and sugar. None are disposing to bed, not so much as complaining of weariness. Beds and things are all very well here; our want is yourself and good weather. But now I have told you our present condition; to say a little of the past, I do really think, if I could have imagined the illness of the journey, it would have discouraged me; it is not to be expressed how bad the way is from Seven Oaks; but our horses did exceeding well, and Spencer very diligent, often off his horse to lay hold of the coach. I have not much more to say this night; I hope the quilt is remembered; and Frances must remember to send more biscuits, either when you come or soon after. I long to hear from you, my dearest soul, and truly think your absence already an age. I have no mind to my gold plate; here is no table to set it on; but if that does not come, I desire you would bid Betty Forster send the silver glass I use every day. In discretion, I haste to bed, longing for Monday, I assure you. From your R. RUSSELL.

Past ten o'clock.—Lady Margaret says we are not glutted with company yet; you will let Northumberland know we are well; and Allie.

XII.—MESSAGE OF LOVE.

Lady Russell to Lord Russell.

STRATTON, 1681—Thursday morning.

A messenger bringing things from Ailesford this morning, gives me the opportunity of sending this by post. If he will leave it at Frimley, it will let you know we are all well; if he does not, it may let such know it as do not care, but satisfy no one's curiosity on any other point; for having said thus much, I am ready to conclude, with this one secret, first, that as thy precious self is the most endearing husband, I believe, in the world, so I am the most grateful wife, and my heart most gladly passionate in its returns. Now you have all for this time,

From your R. RUSSELL.

Boy is asleep, girls singing abed. Lord Marquis sent a compliment yesterday, that he heard one of the girls had the measles; and if I would remove the rest, he would leave his house at an hour's warning. I hope you deliver my service to Mr. James.

For the Lord Russell, to be left at Frimley.

XIII.—ANDREY, AN ADEPT, OR ALCHEMIST—CURIOUS ANECDOTE OF GUSTAVUS ADOLPHUS.

Joseph Spence to his Mother.

TURIN, August 25, 1740.

DEAR MOTHER: If the history of Florio was too melancholy for you (as I fear it was), I am now going to give you an account of some people that may be too mysterious for you, such as some persons will scarce believe ever were, or ever will be in the world; however, one of them I have very lately met with; and I must give you an account of him whilst 'tis fresh in my memory.

Have you ever heard of the people called adepts? They are a set of philosophers superior to whatever appeared among the Greeks and Romans. The three great points they drive at is to be free from poverty, distempers, and death; and if you will believe them, they have found out one secret that is capable of freeing them from all three. There are never more than twelve of these men in the whole world at a time; and we have the happiness of having one of the twelve at this time at Turin. I am very well acquainted with him; and have often talked with him of their secrets, as far as he is allowed to talk to a common mortal, of them.

His name is Andrey, a Frenchman, of a genteel air, but with a certain gravity in his face that I never saw in any Frenchman before. The first time I was in company with him, as I found he had been a great traveller, I asked him whether he had ever been in England, and how he liked the country? He said that he had, and that he liked it more than any country he had ever been in. The last time I was in England, added he, there were eleven philosophers there. I told him I hoped there might be more than eleven in England. He smiled a little and said, " Sir, I don't talk of common philosophers, I talk of adepts ; and of them, I saw in England what I never saw anywhere else : there were eleven at table ; I made the twelfth : and when we began to compare our ages all together, they made somewhat upward of four thousand years." I wondered to hear a grave man talk so strangely, and asked him, as seriously as I could, how old he might be himself. He said that he was not quite 200, but that he was one of the youngest at the table. He said that the secret of carrying on their lives as long as they pleased was known to all of them, and that some of them perhaps might remove out of this world, but that he did not think any one of them would die ; for if they did not like this globe, they had nothing to do but to go into another whenever they pleased. How soon that might be he did not know, but St. John and the travelling Jew, he said, had stayed in it above 1,700 years ; and some of his friends, perhaps, might stay as long. He said the great elixir, of which he had some in his pocket, made him look no older than forty ; that he was afraid of no distemper, for that would cure him immediately ; nor of want, because it would make him as much gold as he pleased. He said many other things as strange and as surprising as what I have told you.

I was talking of him and his gold-making to our Minister here, who, upon this, told me a very odd story, which he had from Marechal Rhebender, General of the King of Sardinia's forces at present. The general, who comes from those parts, says, that when Gustavus Adolphus was going to make war with the emperor, he found himself at a loss for money sufficient for so great an undertaking. He was very melancholy upon it, and every thing was at a stand, when one morning a very old man came to his court, and told the gentleman of the bedchamber in waiting that he wanted to speak to the King. The gentleman desired his name; he refused to tell it, but said he must speak to the King, and that it was on business of the utmost importance to his majesty's affairs. Gustavus, who was incapable of fear, ordered him to be admitted. When they were alone, the old man told him that he knew what straits he was in for money, and that he was come to furnish him with as much as hs should want. He then desired him to send for a crucible full of mercury; he took out a white powder and put in only about the quantity of a pinch of snuff. He then desired him to set by the crucible till the next morning, gave him a large bundle of the white powder, and departed. When Gustavus called for the crucible, the next morning, 'twas all full of one solid piece of gold. He coined this into ducats, and on the coin, in memory of the fact, was struck the chemical marks for mercury and sulphur. Rhebender had several of them thus marked, and gave one of them to our Minister who told me the story.

XIV.—POPULARITY OF THE DUKE OF CUMBERLAND—LORD BATH'S PARSIMONY.

Horace Walpole to Sir Horace Mann.

ARLINGTON STREET, May 24th, 1745.

I have no consequences of the battle of Tournay to tell you but the taking of the town; the Governor has eight days allowed him to consider whether he will give up the citadel. The French certainly lost more men than we did. Our army is still at Lessines, waiting for recruits from Holland and England; ours are sailed. The King is at Hanover. All the letters are full of the Duke's humanity and bravery; he will be as popular with the lower class of men, as he has been for three or four years with the low women; he will be the soldiers' *Great Sir* as well as theirs. I am really glad; it will be of great service to the family if any one of them comes to make a figure.

Lord Chesterfield is returned from Holland; you will see a most simple farewell speech of his in the papers.

I have received yours of the 4th of May, and am extremely obliged to you for your expressions of kindness; they did not at all surprise me, but every instance of your friendship gives me pleasure. I wish I could say the same to good Prince Craon. Yet I must set about answering his letter; it is quite an affair; I have so great a disuse of writing French that I believe it will be very barbarous.

My fears for Tuscany are again awakened. The wonderful march which the Spanish Queen has made Monsieur de Gage take, may probably end in his turning short to the left, for his route to Genoa will be full as difficult as what he has already passed. I watch eagerly every article from Italy, at a time when nobody will read a paragraph but from the army in Flanders.

I am diverted with my Lady's (Lady Walpole, now become Countess of Orford—Ed.) account of the great riches that are now coming to her. She has had so many foolish golden visions, that I should think even the Florentines would not be the dupes of any more. As for her mourning, she may save it if she expects to have it notified. Don't you remember my Lady Pomfret's having a piece of economy of that sort, when she would not know that the Emperor was dead, because my Lord Chamberlain had not notified it to her?

I have a good story to tell you of Lord Bath, whose name you have not heard very lately; have you? He owed a tradesman eight hundred pounds, and would never pay him. The man determined to persecute him till he did, and one morning followed him to Lord Winchilsea's, and sent up word that he wanted to speak with him. Lord Bath came down, and said, "Fellow, what do you want with me?" "My money," said the man, as loud as ever he could bawl, before all the servants. He bade him come the next morning, and then would not see him. The next Sunday the man followed him to church, and got into the next pew; he leaned over, and said, "My money; give me my money!" My lord went to the end of the pew; the man too. "Give me my money!" The sermon was on avarice; and the text, "Cursed are they that heap up riches." The man groaned out, "O Lord!" and pointed to my Lord Bath. In short, he persisted so much, and drew the eyes of all the congregation, that my Lord Bath went out and paid him directly. I assure you this is a fact. Adieu!

XV.—THE EARTHQUAKE *—STORY OF MARIE MIGNOT.

Horace Walpole to Sir Horace Mann.

ARLINGTON STREET, March 11th, 1750.

"Portents and prodigies are grown so frequent,
That they have lost their name."

My text is not literally true; but as far as earthquakes go toward lowering the price of wonderful commodities, to be sure we are overstocked. We have had a second much more violent

* The earthquake is alluded to by Walpole frequently in his letters. Writing to Mann, April 2d, he says: "You will not wonder so much at our

than the first, and you must not be surprised if by next post you hear of a burning mountain sprung up in Smithfield. In the night, between Wednesday and Thursday last (exactly a month since the first shock), the earth had a shivering fit between one and two, but so slight that if no more had followed, I don't be-

earthquakes, as at the effects they have had. All the women in town have taken them up on the footing of *judgments;* and the clergy, who have had no windfalls of a long season, have driven horse and foot into this opinion. There has been a shower of sermons and exhortations. Secker, the Jesuitical bishop of Oxford, began the mode. He heard the women were all going out of town to avoid the next shock, and so, for fear of losing his Easter offerings, he set himself to advise them to await God's good pleasure in fear and trembling. But what is more astonishing, Sherlock, who has much better sense, and much less of the Popish confessor, has been running a race with him for the old ladies, and has written a pastoral letter, of which ten thousand were sold in two days, and fifty thousand have been subscribed for since the two first editions.

"I told you the women talked of going out of town; several families are literally gone, and many more going to day and to-morrow; for what adds to the absurdity is, that the second shock having happened exactly a month after the former, it prevails that there will be a third on Thursday next, a month, which will swallow up London. I am almost ready to burn my letter now I have begun it, lest you should think I am laughing at you. . . I have advised several who are going to keep their next earthquake in the country, to take the bark for it, as it is so periodic. Dick Leveson and Mr. Rigby, who had supped and stayed late at Bedford House the other night, knocked at several doors, and in a watchman's voice cried, "Past four o'clock, and a dreadful earthquake." . . Several women have made earthquake gowns, that is, warm gowns, to sit out of doors all night. These are of the more courageous. One woman, still more heroic, is come to town on purpose; she says all her friends are in London, and she will not survive them. But what will you think of Lady Catherine Pelham, Lady Frances Arundel, and Lord and Lady Galway, who go this evening to an inn ten miles out of town, where they are to play at brag till five in the morning, and then come back. I suppose to look for the bones of their husbands and families under the rubbish." Again, he says, "Turner, a great china man at the corner of the next street, had a jar cracked by the shock; he originally asked ten guineas for the pair, he now asks twenty, because it is the only jar in Europe that has been cracked by an earthquake."—H.

lieve it would have been noticed. I had been awake, and had scarce dozed again—on a sudden I felt my bolster lift up my head; I thought somebody was getting from under my bed, but soon found it was a strong earthquake, that lasted near half a minute, with a violent vibration and great roaring. I rang my bell; my servant came in, frightened out of his senses. In an instant we heard all the windows in the neighborhood flung up. I got up, and found people running into the streets, but saw no mischief done. There has been some: two old houses flung down, several chimneys, and much china-ware. The bells rung in several houses. Admiral Knowles, who has lived long in Jamaica, and felt seven there, says this was more violent than any of them. Francisco prefers it to the dreadful one at Leghorn. The wise say, that if we have not rain soon, we shall certainly have more. Several people are going out of town, for it has nowhere reached above ten miles from London. They say they are not frightened, but that it is such fine weather, "Lord! one can't help going into the country." The only visible effect it has had was on the Ridotto, at which, being the following night, there were but four hundred people. A parson who came into White's the morning of earthquake the first, and heard bets laid on whether it was an earthquake or the blowing up of powder mills, went away exceedingly scandalized, and said: "I protest, they are such an impious set of people, that I believe if the last trumpet was to sound, they would bet puppet-show against Judgment." If we get any nearer still to the torrid zone, I shall pique myself on sending you a present of cedrati and orange-flower water. I am already planning a *terreno* for Strawberry Hill.

The Middlesex election is carried against the court. The

Prince, in a green frock (and I won't swear but in a Scotch plaid waistcoat), sat under the park wall, in his chair, and hallooed the voters on to Brentford. The Jacobites are so transported, that they are opening subscriptions for all boroughs that shall be vacant. This is wise! They will spend their money to carry a few more seats in a Parliament, where they will never have the majority, and so have none to carry the general elections. The omen, however, is bad for Westminster; the high-bailiff went to vote for the opposition.

I now jump to another topic. I find all this letter will be detached scraps; I can't at all contrive to hide the seams; but I don't care. I began my letter merely to tell you of the earthquake, and I don't pique myself upon doing any more than telling you what you would be glad to have told you. I told you, too, how pleased I was with the triumphs of another old beauty, our friend the Princess. Do you know I have found a history that has a great resemblance to hers; that is, that will be very like hers, if hers is but like it. I will tell it you in as few words as I can. Madame la Marechale de l'Hôpital was the daughter of a sempstress; a young gentleman fell in love with her, and was going to be married to her, but the match was broken off. An old fermier-general, who had retired into the province when this happened, hearing the story, had a curiosity to see the victim; he liked her, married her, died, and left her enough not to care for her inconstant. She came to Paris, where the Marechal de l'Hôpital married her for her riches. After the Marechal's death, Casimir, the abdicated King of Poland, who was retired into France, fell in love with the Marechale, and privately married her.* If the event ever happens, I shall cer-

* Mary Mignot, whose third husband is supposed to have been Casimir,

tainly travel to Nancy, to hear her talk of *Ma belle fille la Reine de France.* What pains my Lady Pompret would take to prove that an abdicated king's wife did not take the place of an English countess; and how the Princess herself would grow still fonder of the pretender, for the similitude of his fortune with that of *le Roi mon Mari!* Her daughter, Mirepoise, was frightened the other night with Mrs. Nugent's calling out, *Un voleur! un voleur!* The ambassadress had heard so much of robbing, that she did not doubt but *dans ce pais cy*, they robbed in the middle of an assembly. It turned out to be a thief in the candle! Good night!

XVI.—STRAWBERRY HILL A "PAPHOS."—A GOOD STORY.

Horace Walpole to George Montagu, Esq.

June 2, 1759.

Strawberry Hill is grown a perfect paphos;* it is the land of beauties. On Wednesday the Duchesses of Hamilton and Richmond, and Lady Ailesbury dined there; the two latter stayed all night. There never was so pretty a sight as to see them all three sitting in the shell; a thousand years hence, when I begin to grow old, if that can ever be, I shall talk of that event, and

the ex-king of Poland, who had retired after his abdication to the Monastery of St. Germain des Pres.

* Strawberry Hill and its curiosities became objects of such attraction as to render it a very uncomfortable home. Thus Walpole writes in one of his letters: "My house is full of people, and has been so from the instant I breakfasted, and more are coming; in short, I keep an inn; the sign, 'The Gothic Castle.' Since my gallery was finished, I have not been in it a quarter of an hour together; my whole time is passed in giving tickets for seeing it, and hiding myself while it is seen. Take my advice, never build a charming house for yourself between London and Hampton Court; everybody will live in it but you."—H.

tell young people how much handsomer the women of my time were than they will be then; I shall say, "Women alter now; I remember Lady Ailesbury looking handsomer than her daughter, the pretty Duchess of Richmond, as they were sitting in the shell on my terrace with the Duchess of Hamilton, one of the famous Gunnings." Yesterday t'ther more famous Gunning dined there. She has made a friendship with my charming niece to disguise her jealousy of the new countess' beauty. There were they two, their lords, Lord Buckingham, and Charlotte. You will think that I did not choose men for my parties so well as women. I don't include Lord Waldegrave in this bad election. Loo is mounted to its zenith; the parties last till one and two in the morning. We played at Lady Hertford's last week, the last night of her lying-in, till deep into Sunday morning, after she and her lord were retired. It is now adjourned to Mrs. Fitzroy's, whose child the town called Pam-ela. I proposed that instead of receiving cards for assemblies, one should send in a morning to Dr. Hunter's, the man-midwife, to know where there is loo that evening. I find poor Charles Montagu is dead; is it true, as the papers say, that his son comes into Parliament? The invasion is not half so much in fashion as loo, and the King demanding the assistance of the militia, does not add much dignity to it. The great Pam of Parliament, who made the motion, entered into a wonderful definition of the several sorts of fear, from fear that comes from pusillanimity up to fear from magnanimity. It put me in mind of that wise Pythian, my Lady Londonderry, who, when her sister, Lady Donegal, was dying, pronounced that if it were a fever from a fever she would live, but if it were a fever from death she would die.

Mr. Mason has published another drama called Caractacus;

there are some incantations poetical enough, and odes so Greek as to have very little meaning; but the whole is labored, uninteresting, and no more resembling the manners of Britons than Japanese. It is introduced by a piping elegy; for Mason, in imitation of Gray, "will cry and roar all night," without the least provocation.

Adieu! I shall be glad to hear that your Strawberry tide is fixed.

XVII.—DUKE OF YORK'S VISIT TO STRAWBERRY HILL.

Horace Walpole to G. Montagu.

STRAWBERRY HILL, Oct. 14, 1760.

If you should see in the newspapers that I have offered to raise a regiment at Twickenham, am going with the expedition, and have actually kissed hands, don't believe it, though I own the two first would not be more surprising than the last. I will tell you how the calamity befell me, though you will laugh instead of pitying me. Last Friday morning I was very tranquilly writing my anecdotes of painting; I heard the bell at the gate ring; I called out as usual, "Not at home;" but Harry, who thought it would be treason to tell a lie when he saw red liveries, owned I was, and came running up: "Sir, the Prince of Wales is at the door, and says he has come on purpose to make you a visit." There was I, in the utmost confusion, undressed, in my slippers, and my hair about my ears; there was no help, *insanum vatem aspiciet*, and down I went to receive him. Here was the Duke of York. Behold my breeding of the old court: at the foot of the stairs I kneeled down and kissed his hand. I beg your uncle Algernon Sydney's pardon, but I could not let the second prince of the blood kiss my hand first. He was, as he always is, extremely good-humored, and I, as I am not always, extremely respectful. He stayed two hours, nobody with him but Morrison; I showed him all my castle; the pictures of the Pretender's sons, and that type of the Reformation, Henry the Eighth's—moulded into a weight to the clock he gave Anne Boleyn. But observe my luck, he would have the sanctum sanctorum in the library opened; about a month ago I removed the MSS. in another place. All this is very well, but now for the consequences; what was I to do next? I have not been in a court these ten years, consequently have never kissed hands in the next reign. Could I let a Duke of York visit me, and never go to thank him? I know, if I was a great poet, I might be so brutal, and tell the world in rhyme that rudeness is virtue; or if I was a patriot, I might, after laughing at Kings and Princes for twenty years, catch at the first opening of favor, and beg a place. In truth I can do neither, yet I could not be shocking; I determined to go to Leicester House, and comforted myself that it was not much less meritorious to go there for nothing than to stay quite away; yet I believe I must make a pilgrimage to Saint Liberty of Geneva, before I am perfectly purified, especially as I am dipped even at St. James. Lord Hertford, at my request, begged my Lady Yarmouth to get an order for my Lady Henry to go through the Park, and the countess said so many civil things about me and my suit, and granted it so expeditiously, that I shall be forced to visit, even before she lives here next door to my Lady Suffolk. My servants are transported; Harry expects to see me first minister, like my father, and reckons upon a place in the Custom House. Louis, who drinks like a German, thinks himself qualified for a page of the back stairs.

But these are not all my troubles. As I never dress in summer, I had nothing upon earth but a frock, unless I went in black like a poet, and pretended that a cousin was dead (one of the muses). Then I was in panics lest I should call my Lord Bute Your Royal Highness. I was not, indeed, in much pain at the conjectures the Duke of Newcastle would make on such an apparition, even if he should suspect that a new opposition was on foot, and that I was to write some letters to the Whigs.

Well, but after all do you know that my calamity has not befallen me yet? I could not determine to bounce over head and ears into the drawing room at once, without one soul knowing why I came thither. I went to London on Saturday night, and Lord Hertford was to carry me the next morning; in the mean time I wrote to Morrison, explaining my gratitude to one brother and my unacquaintance with t'other, and how afraid I was it would be thought officious and forward if I was presented now, and begging he would advise me what to do; and all this upon my bended knee, as if Schultz had stood over me and dictated every syllable. The answer was by order from the Duke of York that he smiled at my distress, wished to put me to no inconvenience, but desired that as the acquaintance had begun without restraint, it might continue without ceremony. Now I was in more perplexity than ever! I could not go directly, and yet it was not fit it should be said I thought it an *inconvenience* to wait on the Prince of Wales. At present it is decided by a jury of court matrons, that is courtiers, that I must write to my Lord Bute, and explain the whole, and why I desire to come now; don't fear, I will take care they shall understand how little I come for. In the mean time, you see, it is my fault if I am not a favorite; but alas! I am not heavy enough to be tossed in a blanket like Doddington; I should never come down again; I cannot be driven in a royal curricle to wells and waters; I can't make love now to my contemporary Charlotte Dives; I cannot quit Mufti and my parroquet for Sir William Irby and the prattle of a drawing-room, nor Mrs. Clive for Ælia Lælia Chudleigh; in short, I could give up nothing but an earldom of Eglinton. And yet I foresee that this phantom of a reversion will make me plagued; I shall have Lord Egmont whisper me again, and every tall man and strong woman that comes to town will make interest with me to get the Duke of York to come and see them. Oh! dreadful, dreadful! It is plain I never was a patriot, for I don't find my virtue a bit staggered by this first glimpse of court sunshine.

Mr. Conway has pressed to command the new Quixotism on foot, and been refused. I sing a very comfortable *Te Deum* for it. Kingsley, Crawford, and Keppel are the generals, and Commodore Keppel the admiral. The mob are sure of being pleased, they will get a conquest or a court-martial. A very unpleasant thing has happened to the Keppels; the youngest brother, who had run in debt at Gibraltar and was fetched away to be sent to Germany, gave them the slip at the first port they touched at in Spain, surrendered himself to the Spanish governor, has changed his religion, and sent for a —— that had been taken from him at Gibraltar, *naturam expellas furca*. There's the true blood of Charles II., sacrificing every thing for Popery and a bunter. Lord Bolingbroke, on hearing the name of Lady Coventry at New Market, affected to burst into tears, and left the room, not to hide his crying, but his not crying.

Draper has handsomely offered to go on the expedition, and goes. Ned Finch t'other day, on the conquest of Montreal, wished the King joy of having lost no subjects but those that perished in the *rabbits*. Fitzroy asked him if he thought they crossed the great American in such little boats as one goes to Vauxhall? He replied, "Yes, Mr. Pitt said the *rabbits*"—it was in the falls, the rapids.

I like Lord John almost as well as Fred. Montagu, and I like your letter better than Lord John's. The application of Miss Falkener was charming. Good night.

P. S.—If I had been told in June that I should have the gout, and kiss hands before November, I don't think I should have given much credit to the prophet.

XVIII.—FUNERAL OF GEORGE THE SECOND—HYPOCRISY OF THE DUKE OF NEWCASTLE.

Horace Walpole to George Montagu.

ARLINGTON STREET, Nov. 13, 1760.

Even the honeymoon of a new reign don't produce events every day. There is nothing but the common saying of addresses and kissing hands. The chief difficulty is settled; Lord Gower yields the mastership of the horse to Lord Huntingdon, and removes to the great wardrobe, from whence Sir Thomas Robinson was to have gone into Ellis's place, but he is saved. The city, however, have a mind to be out of humor; a paper has been fixed on the Royal Exchange, with these words, "No petticoat government, no Scotch minister, no Lord George Sackville;" two hints totally unfounded, and the other scarce true. No petticoat ever governed less; it is left at Leicester House; Lord George's breeches are as little concerned; and, except Lady

Susan Stuart and Sir Harry Erskine, nothing has yet been done for any Scots. For the King himself, he seems all good nature, and wishing to satisfy everybody: all his speeches are obliging. I saw him again yesterday, and was surprised to find the levee-room had lost so entirely the air of the lion's den. This sovereign don't stand in one spot, with his eyes fixed royally on the ground, and dropping bits of German news; he walks about, and speaks to everybody. I saw him afterwards on the throne, where he is graceful and genteel, sits with dignity, and reads his answers to addresses well; it was the Cambridge address, carried by the Duke of Newcastle in his doctor's gown, and looking like the *medecin malgrè lui*. He had been vehemently solicitous for attendance, for fear my Lord Westmoreland, who vouchsafes himself to bring the address from Oxford, should outnumber him. Lord Litchfield and several other Jacobites have kissed hands; George Selwyn says, "They go to St. James's, because now there are so many *Stuarts* there."

Do you know I had the curiosity to go to the burying t'other night. I had never seen a royal funeral; nay, I walked as a rag of quality, which I found would be, and so it was, the easiest way of seeing it. It is absolutely a noble sight. The Prince's chamber, hung with purple, and a quantity of silver lamps, the coffin under a canopy of purple velvet, and six vast chandeliers of silver, on high stands, had a very good effect. The ambassador from Tripoli and his son were carried to see that chamber. The procession, through a line of foot-guards, every seventh man bearing a torch, the horse-guards lining the outside, their officers, with drawn sabres and crape sashes, on horseback, the drums muffled, the fifes, bells tolling, and minute guns; all this was very solemn. But the charm was the entrance of the abbey, where we were received by the dean and chapter in rich robes, the choir and almsmen bearing torches, the whole abbey so illuminated, that one saw it to greater advantage than by day; the tombs, long aisles, and fretted roof, all appearing distinctly, and with the happiest *chiara scuro.* There wanted nothing but incense, and little chapels, here and there, with priests saying mass for the repose of the defunct; yet one could not complain of its not being Catholic enough. I had been in dread of being coupled with some boy of ten years old; but the heralds were not very accurate, and I walked with George Grenville, taller and older, to keep me in countenance. When we came to the chapel of Henry the Seventh, all solemnity and decorum ceased; no order was observed, people sat or stood where they could or would; the yeoman of the guard were crying out for help, oppressed by the immense weight of the coffin; the bishop read sadly, and blundered in the prayers; the fine chapter, *Man that is born of a woman*, was chaunted, not read; and the anthem, besides being immeasurably tedious, would have served as well for a nuptial. The real serious part was the figure of the Duke of Cumberland, heightened by a thousand melancholy circumstances. He had a dark brown adonis, and a cloak of black cloth, with a train of five yards. Attending the funeral of a father could not be pleasant; his leg extremely bad, yet forced to stand upon it near two hours; his face bloated and distorted with his late paralytic stroke, which has affected too one of his eyes; and placed over the mouth of the vault, into which, in all probability, he must himself so soon descend; think how unpleasant a situation! He bore it all with a firm and unaffected countenance. This grave scene was fully contrasted by the burlesque Duke of Newcastle. He fell into a fit of crying the moment he came into the chapel, and flung himself back in a stall, the archbishop hovering over him with a smelling-bottle; but in two minutes his curiosity got the better of his hypocrisy, and he ran about the chapel with his glass, to spy who was or was not there, spying with one hand, and mopping his eyes with the other. Then returned the fear of catching cold; and the Duke of Cumberland, who was sinking with heat, felt himself weighed down, and turning round, found it was the Duke of Newcastle standing upon his train, to avoid the chill of the marble. It was very theatric to look down into the vault, where the coffin lay, attended by mourners with lights. Clavering, the groom of the bedchamber, refused to sit up with the body, and was dismissed by the King's order.

I have nothing more to tell you but a trifle, a very trifle. The King of Prussia has totally defeated Marshal Daun. This, which would have been prodigious news a month ago, is nothing to-day; it only takes its turn among the questions, "Who is to be groom of the bedchamber? What is Sir T. Robinson to have?" I have been to Leicester Fields to-day; the crowd was immoderate; I don't believe it will continue so. Good-night. Yours ever.

XIX.--VICTORIES—"YOUNG MR. BURKE."

Horace Walpole to George Montagu.

STRAWBERRY HILL, July 22d, 1761.

For my part, I believe Mademoiselle Scuderi drew the plan of this year. It is all royal marriages, coronations, and victories. They come tumbling so over one another from distant parts of the globe, that it looks just like the handiwork of a lady romance writer, whom it costs nothing but a little false geography to make the great Mogul in love with a Princess of Mecklenburg, and defeat two marshals of France as he rides post on an elephant to his nuptials. I don't know where I am. I had scarce found Mecklenburg-Strelitz with a magnifying glass, before I am whisked to Pondicherri. Well, I take it and rase it. I begin to grow acquainted with Col. Coote, and to figure him packing up chests and diamonds, and sending them to his wife against the King's wedding. Thunder go the tower guns, and behold Broglio and Soubise are totally defeated. If the mob have not much stronger heads and quicker conceptions than I have, they will conclude my Lord Granby is become nabob. How the deuce in two days can one digest all this? Why is not Pondicherri in Westphalia? I don't know how the Romans did, but I cannot support two victories every week. Well, but you will want to know the particulars. Broglio and Soubise, united, attacked our army on the 15th, but were repulsed; the next day, the Prince Mahomet Ali Cawn—no, no, I mean Prince Ferdinand—returned the attack, and the French threw down their arms and fled, run over my Lord Harcourt, who was going to fetch the new Queen; in short, I don't know how it was, but Mr. Conway is safe, and I am as happy as Mr. Conway himself. We have only lost a Lieutenant-Colonel, Keith; Colonel Marlay and Harry Townshend are wounded. I could beat myself for not having a flag ready to display on my round tower, and guns mounted on all my battlements. Instead of that I have been foolishly trying on my new pictures upon my gallery. However, the oratory of our Lady of Strawberry shall be dedicated next year, on the anniversary of Mr. Conway's safety. Think, with his intrepidity and delicacy of honor wounded, what I had to apprehend; you shall absolutely be here on the sixteenth of next July. Mr. Hamilton tells me your King does not set out for his new dominions till the day after the coronation. If you will come to it, I can give you a very good place for the procession; where, is a profound secret, because if known, I should be teased to death, and none but my first friends shall be admitted. I dined with your secretary yesterday; there were Garrick, and a young Mr. Burke, who wrote a book in the style of Lord Bolingbroke that was much admired.* He is a sensible man, but has not worn off his authorism yet, and thinks there is nothing so charming as writers, and to be one. He will know better one of these days. I like Hamilton's little Marly; we walked in the great allée, and drank tea in the arbor of treillage; they talked of Shakspeare and Booth, of Swift and my Lord Bath, and I was thinking of Madame Sévigné. Good-night. I have a dozen other letters to write; I must tell my friends how happy I am, not as an Englishman, but as a cousin.

XX.—LADY WORTLEY MONTAGU—VISIT TO THE COCK LANE GHOST.

Horace Walpole to George Montagu.

ARLINGTON STREET, Feb. 2d, 1762.

I scolded you in my last, but I shall forgive you if you return soon to England, as you talk of doing; for though you are an abominable correspondent, and only write to beg letters, you are good company, and I have a notion I shall still be glad to see you.

Lady Mary Wortley is arrived; I have seen her; I think her avarice, her dirt, and her vivacity are all increased. Her

* Vindication of Natural Society.

dress, like her language, is a galamatias of several countries—the groundwork rags, and the embroidery nastiness. She needs no cap, no handkerchief, no gown, no petticoat, no shoes. An old black laced hood represents the first; the fur of a horseman's coat, which replaces the third, serves for the second; a dimity petticoat is deputy, and officiates for the fourth; and slippers act the part of the last. When I was at Florence, and she was expected there, we were drawing *sortes Virgili-anas* for her. We literally drew:

Insanam vatem aspicies.

It would have been a stronger prophecy now, even than it was then.

You told me not a word of Mr. Macnaughton, and I have a great mind to be as coolly indolent about our famous ghost in Cock lane. Why should one steal half an hour from one's amusements to tell a story to a friend in another island? I could send you volumes on the ghost, and I believe, if I were to stay a little, I might send its *life*, dedicated to my Lord Dartmouth, by the ordinary of Newgate, its two great patrons. A drunken parish clerk set it on foot out of revenge, the Methodists have adopted it, and the whole town of London think of nothing else. Elizabeth Canning and the Rabbit-woman were modest impostors in comparison of this, which goes on without saving the least appearances. The archbishop who would not suffer the Minor to be acted in ridicule of the Methodists, permits this farce to be played every night, and I shall not be surprised if they perform in the great hall at Lambeth. I went to hear it, for it is not an *apparition*, but an *audition*. We set out from the opera, changed our clothes at Northumberland House, the Duke of York, Lady Northumberland, Lady Mary Coke, Lord

Hertford, and I, all in one hackney coach, and drove to the spot; it rained torrents, yet the lane was full of mob, and the house so full we could not get in; at last they discovered it was the Duke of York, and the company squeezed themselves into one another's pockets to make room for us. The house, which is borrowed, and to which the ghost has adjourned, is wretchedly small and miserable. When we opened the chamber, in which were fifty people, with no light but one tallow-candle at the end, we tumbled over the bed of the child to whom the ghost comes, and whom they are murdering by inches in such insufferable heat and stench. At the top of the room are ropes to dry clothes. I asked if we were to have rope-dancing between the acts? We had nothing; they told us, as they would at a puppet-show, that it would not come that night till seven in the morning, that is, when there are only 'prentices and old women. We stayed, however, till half an hour after one. The Methodists have promised them contributions; provisions are sent in like forage, and all the taverns and ale-houses in the neighborhood make fortunes. The most diverting part is to hear people wondering *when it will be found out*, as if there was any thing to find out; as if the actors would make their noises when they can be discovered. However, as this pantomime cannot last much longer, I hope Lady Fanny Shirley will set up a ghost of her own at Twickenham, and that you shall hear one. The Methodists, as Lord Aylesford assured Mr. Chute two nights ago at Lord Dacres', have attempted ghosts three times in Warwickshire. There, how good I am.*

* The history of the Cock lane ghost, which for a considerable time kept all London in commotion, and which was finally exposed in an action for a conspiracy against the authors of the deception, is given in Dr. Mackay's Memoirs of Popular Delusions.—H.

XXI.—BON MOTS.—QUIN AND BISHOP WARBURTON.

Horace Walpole to George Montagu.

ARLINGTON STREET, April 5th, 1765.

I sent two letters t'other day from your kin, and might as well have written then as now, for I have nothing to tell you. Mr. Chute has quitted his bed to-day for the first time for above five weeks, but is still swathed like a mummy. He was near relapsing, for old Mildmay, whose lungs, and memory, and tongue will never wear out, talked to him t'other night from eight till half an hour after ten on the Poor-Bill; but he has been more comfortable with Lord Dacre and me this evening.

I have read the siege of Calais, and dislike it extremely, though there are fine lines, but the conduct is woful. The outrageous applause it has received at Paris was certainly political, and intended to stir up their spirit and animosity against us, their good, merciful, and forgiving allies. They will have no occasion for this ardor; they may smite one cheek and we shall turn t'other.

Though I have little to say, it is worth while to write, only to tell you two *bon mots* of Quin to that turn-coat hypocrite infidel, Bishop Warburton.* That saucy priest was haranguing

* This language may recall an incident related by Pope. The poet and Warburton in the course of a country ramble visited Oxford. It was suggested that the degree of D.D. should be conferred on the divine, and LL.D. on the poet. Through the envy and intrigue of one or two of its members, the University lost the opportunity of decorating with its honors two of the greatest geniuses of the age. The indignant bard, on retiring to Twickenham, consoled himself and his friend with the reflection, "We shall take our degrees together in fame, whatever we do at the University."

The abuse of Walpole will be more than balanced by the well-known declaration of the great Lord Chatham, "that nothing of a private nature, since he had been in office, had given him so much pleasure as bringing Warburton at Bath in behalf of prerogative; Quin said: "Pray, my lord, spare me, you are not acquainted with my principles, I am a Republican; and perhaps I even think the execution of Charles the First might be justified." "Ay," said Warburton, "by what law?" Quin replied: "By all the laws he had left them." The bishop would have got off upon judgments, and bade the player remember that all the regicides came to violent ends; a lie, but no matter. "I would not advise your lordship," said Quin, "to make use of that inference, for if I am not mistaken, that was the case of the twelve apostles." There was great wit *ad hominem* in the latter reply, but I think the former equal to any thing I ever heard. It is the sum of the whole controversy couched in eight monosyllables, and comprehends at once the King's guilt and the justice of punishing it. The more one examines it the finer it proves. One can say nothing after it; so good night. Yours ever.

XXII.—DINNER WITH A FRENCH PARVENU.

Horace Walpole to Lady Suffolk.

PARIS, Dec 5th, 1765—but does not set out till the 13th.

Since Paris has begun to fill in spite of Fontainebleau, I am much reconciled to it, and have seen several people I like. I am established in two or three societies where I sup every

on the bench." It must be admitted that Warburton frequently brought reproach upon the Christian character by the intemperance of his controversial writings and personal conversation; but that he was a sincere, zealous, learned, and able divine, is beyond dispute. Dr. Chalmers refers to him as a man who, beyond Grotius, Cudworth, Chillingworth, Stillingfleet, or Samuel Clarke, had conjoined acquired scholarship with original strength, a Goliath of sacred literature—*capax, profundus, eximius homo et venerabundus*.—H.

5

night, though I have still resisted whist, and am more constant to my old flame loo during its absence than I doubt I have been to my other passions. There is a young Countess, d'Egmont, daughter of Marshal Richelieu, so pretty and pleasing that if I thought it would break anybody's heart in England, I would be in love with her. Nay, madam, I might be so within all the rules here. I am twenty years on the right side of red heels, which her father wears still, and he has still a wrinkle to come before he leaves them off.

The Dauphin is still alive, but kept so only by cordials; yet the Queen and Dauphiness have no doubt of his recovery, having the Bishop of Glandeve's word for it, who got a promise from a vision under its own hand and seal. The Dauphin has certainly behaved with great courage and tranquillity, but is so touched with the tenderness and affection of his family, that he now expresses a wish to live.

Yesterday I dined at La Borde's, the great banker of the court. Lord! madam, how little and poor all your houses in London will look after his! In the first place, you must have a garden half as long as the Mall, and then you must have fourteen windows, each as long as the other half, looking into it, and each window must consist of only eight panes of looking glass; you must have a first and second ante-chamber, and they must have nothing in them but dirty servants. Next must be the grand cabinet, hung with red damask, in gold frames, and covered with eight large and very bad pictures, that cost four thousand pounds. I cannot afford them you a farthing cheaper. Under these, to give an air of lightness, must be hung bas-reliefs in marble; then there must be immense armoires of tortoise shell and ormolu, inlaid with medals; and then you may go into the petit cabinet, and then into the great *salle*, and the gallery, and the billiard room, and the eating room; and all these must be hung with crystal lustres, and looking glasses from top to bottom; and then you must stuff them fuller than they will hold with granite tables and porphyry urns, and bronzes, and statues, and vases, and the Lord or the devil knows what. But for fear you should ruin yourself or the nation, the Duchess de Grammont must give you *this* and Madame de Marsan *that;* and if you have anybody that has any taste to advise you, your eating room must be hung with huge hunting pieces in frames of all colored gold, and at top of one of them you may have a setting dog, who having sprung a wooden partridge, it may be flying a yard off against the wainscot. To warm and light this palace it must cost you eight and twenty thousand livres a year in wood and candles. If you cannot afford that, you must stay till my Lord Clive returns with the rest of the Indies.

The mistress of this Arabian Nights' Entertainments is very pretty, and Sir Lawrence La Borde is so fond of her that he sits by her at dinner, and calls her *Pug* or *Taw*, or I forget what.

Lady Mary Chabot always charges me to mention her to your ladyship with particular attention. There are some to whom I could wish your ladyship would do me the same good office; but I have been too troublesome already, and will only mention Miss Hotham, Mr. Chetwynd, Lady Blandford, and St. James's Square.

Your ladyship's, &c.,

HORACE WALPOLE.

XXIII.—VISIT TO JOHN WESLEY'S "OPERA."

Horace Walpole to John Chute.

BATH, October 10th, 1766.

I am impatient to hear that your charity to me has not ended in the gout to yourself. All my comfort is, if you have it that you have good Lady Brome to nurse you.

My health advances faster than my amusement. However, I have been at one opera, Mr. Wesley's.* They have boys and girls with charming voices, that sing hymns in parts to Scotch ballad tunes, but, indeed, so long that one would think they were already in eternity and knew how much time they had before them. The chapel is very neat, with true Gothic windows (yet I am not converted); but I was glad to see that luxury is creeping in upon them before persecution: they have very neat mahogany stands for benches, and brackets of the same in taste. At the upper end is a broad *haut pas* of four steps, advancing in the middle; at each end of the broadest part are two of my eagles, with red cushions for the parson and clerk. Behind them rise three more steps, in the midst of which is a third eagle for pulpit. Scarlet armed chairs for all three. On either hand is a balcony for elect ladies. The rest of the congregation sit on forms. Behind the pit, in a dark niche, is a plain table within rails; so you see the throne is for the Apostle. Wesley is a

* The idea of adopting the psalms of the church to secular tunes had been put in practice long before Wesley's day. The celebrated Clement Marot wrote a number of psalms to suit the popular airs of his time, for the accommodation of the ladies of the French court, who were devoutly inclined; but he left it to Wesley to assign as a reason for doing so, that there were no just grounds for letting the devil have all the best tunes to himself.—H.

lean elderly man, fresh colored, his hair smoothly combed, but with a *soupçon* of curls at the ends. Wondrous clean, but as evidently an actor as Garrick. He spoke his sermon, but so fast, and with so little accent, that I am sure he has often uttered it, for it was like a lesson. There were parts and eloquence in it; but toward the end he exalted his voice and acted very ugly enthusiasm, decried learning, and told stories, like Latimer, of the fool of his college, who said "I *thanks* my God for every thing." Except a few from curiosity, and *some honorable women*, the congregation was very mean. There was a Scotch Countess of Buchan, who is carrying a fine rosy vulgar face to heaven, and who asked Miss Rich if that wàs the *author of the poets*. I believe she meant me and the Noble Authors. The Bedfords came last night. Lord Chatham was with me yesterday two hours; looks and walks well, and is in excellent political spirits.

Yours ever.*

* This letter is a curious record of the impression made upon a mere man of fashion by the greatest and most truly apostolic divine that England produced in the last century. Great injustice is done to Wesley, who was no ordinary scholar himself, by charging him with hostility to learning. Although frequent exhortations to his preachers to improve themselves by study, are to be found scattered through his writings, he certainly did not look upon profane learning as absolutely essential to the work which his coadjutors were preëminently called on to perform, of reviving pure Christianity in England, and preaching the gospel to the poor. His own explanation of the use of the plainest words is perfectly satisfactory. "Clearness," said he to one of his lay assistants, "is necessary for you and me, because we are to instruct people of the lowest understanding; therefore, we above all, if we think with the wise, must speak with the vulgar. We should constantly use the most common, little, easy words, so they are pure and proper, which our language affords. When first I talked at Oxford to plain people, in the castle or town, I observed they gaped and stared; this quickly obliged me to alter my style, and adopt the language of those I spoke to; and yet there is a dignity in their simplicity which is not disagreeable to those of the highest rank." Let the reader compare with the text the opinion of

XXIV.—VISIT TO STOWE WITH THE PRINCESS AMELIA.

Horace Walpole to H. S. Conway.

ARLINGTON STREET, July 12th, 1770.

Reposing under my laurels! No, no, I am reposing in a much better tent, under the tester of my own bed. I am not obliged to rise by break of day, and be dressed for the drawing-room; I may saunter in my slippers till dinner-time, and not make bows till my back is as much out of joint as my Lord Tem-

Wesley, expressed by another contemporary far more competent and equally disinterested. "At an early age," writes Alexander Knox, "I was a member of Mr. Wesley's society, but my connection with it was not of long duration. Having a growing disposition to think for myself, I could not adopt the opinions which were current among his followers, and before I was twenty years of age my relish for their religious practices had abated. Still my veneration for Mr. Wesley himself suffered no diminution, rather as I became more capable of estimating him without prejudice, my conviction of his excellence and my attachment to his goodness gained fresh strength and deeper cordiality.

"It will hardly be denied that even in this frail and corrupted world, we sometimes meet persons, who, in their very mien and aspect, as well as in the whole habit of life, manifest such a stamp and signature of virtue as to make our judgment of them a matter of intuition, rather than a result of continued examination. I never met a human being who came more perfectly within this description than John Wesley. It was impossible to converse with him, I might say to look at him, without being persuaded, not only that his heart and mind were animated with the purest and most exalted goodness, but that the instinctive bent of his nature accorded so congenially with his Christian principles as to give a pledge for his practical consistency, in which it was impossible not to place confidence.

"It would be far too little to say that it would be impossible to suspect him of any moral taint, for it was obvious that every movement bespoke as perfect a contrariety to all that was earthly or animal, as could be imagined in a mortal being. His countenance as well as conversation expressed an habitual gayety of heart, which nothing but conscious virtue and innocence could have bestowed. He was, in truth, the most perfect specimen of moral happiness I ever saw; and my acquaintance with him has done more to teach me what a heaven upon earth is implied in the maturity of Christian piety, than all I have elsewhere seen or heard, or read, except in the sacred volume."—H.

ple's. In short, I should die of the gout or fatigue, if I was to be Polonius to a Princess for another week. Twice a day we made a pilgrimage to almost every heathen temple in that province they call a garden; and there is no sallying out of the house without descending a flight of steps as high as St. Paul's. My Lord Besborough would have dragged me up to the top of the column to see all the kingdoms of the earth; but I would not, if he could have given them to me. To crown all, because we live under the line, and that we were all of us giddy young creatures of near threescore, we supped in a grotto in the elysian fields, and were refreshed with rivers of dew and gentle showers that dripped from all the trees, and put us in mind of the heroic ages, when kings and queens were shepherds and shepherdesses, and lived in caves, and were wet to the skin two or three times a day. Well! thank heaven, I am emerged from that elysium, and once more in a Christian country! Not but, to say the truth, our pagan landlord and landlady were very obliging, and the party went off much better than I expected. We had no very recent politics, though volumes about the Spanish war; and as I took care to give every thing a ludicrous turn as much as I could, the Princess was diverted. The six days rolled away, and the seventh is my sabbath; and I promise you I will do no manner of work, I, nor my cat, nor my dog, nor any thing that is mine. For this reason, I entreat that the journey to Goodwood may not take place before the 12th of August, when I will attend you. But this expedition to Stowe has quite blown up my intended one to Wentworth Castle; I have not resolution enough left for such a journey. Will you and Lady Ailesbury come to Strawberry before or after Goodwood? I know you like being dragged from home as little as I do; therefore you shall place that visit just when it is most convenient to you. I came to town the night before last, and am just returning. There are not twenty people in all London. Are not you in despair about the summer? It is horrid to be ruined in coals, in June and July. Adieu. Yours ever.

XXV.—THE RICHMOND FIREWORKS, ETC.

Horace Walpole to George Montagu.

ARLINGTON STREET, May 18th, 1749.

DEAR GEORGE: Whatever you hear of the Richmond fireworks that is short of the prettiest entertainment in the world, don't believe it. I really never passed a more agreeable evening. Every thing succeeded; all the wheels played in time; Frederick was fortunate, and all the world in good humor. Then for royalty—Mr. Anstis himself would have been glutted; there were all the Fitzes upon earth, the whole Court of St. Germains, the Duke, the Duke of Modena, and two Anamatoes. The King and Princess Emily bestowed themselves upon the mob on the river; and as soon as they were gone, the Duke had the music into the garden, and himself, with my Lady Lincoln, Mrs. Pitt, Peggy Banks, and Lord Holderness, entertained the good subjects with singing "God save the King" to them, over the rails of the terrace. The Duke of Modena supped there, and the Duke was asked, but he answered it was impossible; in short, he could not adjust his dignity to a mortal banquet. There was an admirable scene; Lady Burlington brought the Violette, and the Richmonds had asked Garrick, who stood ogling and sighing the whole time while my lady kept a most fierce lookout. Sabbatini, one of the Duke of Modena's Court, was asking me who all the people were. And who is that? "C'est miladi Hartington, la belle fille du Duc de Devonshire." "Et qui est cette autre dame?" It was a distressing question. After a little hesitation, I replied, "Mais c'est Mademoiselle Violette?" "Et comment Mademoiselle Violette! j'ai connu une Mademoiselle Violette par exemple." I begged him to look at Miss Bishop.

In the middle of all these principalities and powers was the Duchess of Queensbury, in her forlorn trim, a white apron and a white hood, and would make the Duke swallow all her undress. T'other day she drove post to Lady Sophia Thomas, at Parsons-green, and told her that she was come to tell her something of importance. "What is it?" "Why, take a couple of beef-steaks, clap them together, as if they were for a dumpling, and eat them with pepper and salt; it is the best thing you ever tasted. I could not help coming to tell you this!" and away she drove back to town. Don't a course of folly for forty years make one very sick?

The weather is so hot and the roads so dusty, that I can't get to Strawberry. But I shall begin negotiating with you now about your coming. You must not expect to find it in beauty. I hope to get my bill finished in ten days; I have scrambled it through the Lords; but altogether, with the many difficulties and plagues, I am a good deal out of humor; my purchases hitch, and new proprietors start out of the ground, like the crop of soldiers in the Metamorphosis. I expect but an unpleasant summer; my indolence and inattention are not made to wade through leases and deeds. Mrs. Chenevix brought me one yesterday to sign, and her sister Bertrand, the toy-woman of Bath, for a witness. I showed them my cabinet of enamels instead of treating them with white wine. The Bertrand said, "Sir, I hope you don't trust all sorts of ladies with this cabinet?" What an entertaining assumption of dignity! I must tell you an anecdote that I found t'other day in an old French author, which is a great drawback on beaux sentiments and romantic ideas. Pasquier, in his "Recherches de la France," is giving an account of the Queen of Scots' execution; he says: the night before, knowing her body must be stripped for her shroud, she would have her feet washed, because she used ointment to one of them which was sore. I believe I have told you that in a very old trial of her, which I bought from Lord Oxford's collection, it was said that she was a lame woman. Take sentiments out of their pantoufles, and reduce them to the infirmities of mortality, what a falling off there is? I could not help laughing in myself t'other day, as I went through Holborn, in a very hot day, at the dignity of human nature; all those foul old-clothes women panting without handkerchiefs, and mopping themselves all the way down within their loose jumps. Rigby gave me a strong picture of human nature. He and Peter Bathurst t'other night carried a servant of the latter's, who had attempted to shoot him, before Fielding, who, to all his other vocations, has, by the grace of Mr. Lyttleton, added that of Middlesex Justice. He sent them word he was at supper, that they must come next morning. They could not understand that freedom, and ran up, where they found him banqueting with a blind man, a ——, and three Irishmen, on some cold mutton and a bone of ham, both in one dish, and the dirtiest cloth. He never stirred, nor asked them to sit. Rigby, who had seen him so often come to beg a guinea of Sir C. Williams, and Bathurst, at whose father's he had lived, for victuals, understood that dignity as little, and pulled themselves chairs, on which he civilized. Miller, the bookseller, has done generously by him; finding Tom Jones, for which he had given him six hundred pounds, sell so greatly, he has since given him another hundred. Now I talk to you of authors, Lord Cobham's West has published his translation of Pindar; the poetry is very stiff, but prefixed to it there is a very entertaining account of the Olympic games, and that preceded by an affected inscription to Pitt and Lyttleton. The latter has declared his future match with Miss Rich. George Grenville has been married these two days to Miss Windham. Your friend Lord North is, I suppose you know, on the brink with the Countess of Rockingham, and I think your cousin Rice is much inclined to double the family alliance with her sister Furnese. It went on very currently for two or three days, but last night at Vauxhall his minionette face seemed to be sent to languish with Lord R. Berties's. Was not you sorry for poor Cucumber? I do assure you I was; it was shocking to be hurried away so suddenly, and in such torment. You have heard, I suppose, of Lord Harry Beauclerc's resignation, on his not being able to obtain a respite till November, though the lowest officer in his regiment has got much longer leave. It is incredible how Nolkejumskoi has persecuted this poor man for these four years, since he could not be persuaded to alter his vote at a court-martial for the acquittal of a man whom the Duke would have condemned. Lord Ossulston, too, has resigned his commission.

I must tell you a good story of Charles Townshend. You know his political propensity and importance; his brother George was at supper at the King's Arms, with some more young men. The conversation somehow or other rambled into politics, and it was started that the national debt was a benefit. "I am sure it is not," said Mr. Townshend; "I can't tell why, but my brother Charles can, and I will send to him for arguments." Charles was at supper at another tavern, but so much the dupe of this message, that he literally called for ink and paper, wrote four long sides of arguments, and sent word that when his company broke up he would come and give them more, which he did at one o'clock in the morning. I don't think you will laugh much less at what happened to me. I wanted a print out of a book, which I did not care to buy at Osborn's shop; the next day he sent me the print, and begged that when I had any thing to publish I would employ him. I will now tell you, and finish this long letter, how I shocked Mr. Mackenzie inadvertently at Vauxhall. We had supped there, a great party; and coming out, Mrs. More, who waits at the gate, said, "Gentlemen and ladies, you will walk in and hear the surprising alteration of voice?" I, forgetting Mackenzie's connections, and that he was formally of the band, replied, "No, I have seen patriots enough." I intend this letter shall last you till you come to Strawberry Hill; one might have rolled it out into half a dozen. My best compliments to your sisters.*

XXVI.—THE BISHOP AT COURT.

Bishop Warburton to Dr. Hurd.

GROSVENOR SQUARE, 20th February, 1767.

I have your kind letter of the sixth; and your flattery of me is more delicious to me than that of courts.

* This letter, the last of Walpole's in this book (although prior in time to several others), is amongst the most characteristic. Wordsworth speaks of Walpole as "a cold, false-hearted, Frenchified coxcomb;" but his letters, from the anecdote, gossip, wit, and epigram with which they abound, and their animated pictures of character and society, will always be attractive.—H.

Lord Mansfield called on me as soon as I came to town. The Dedication was received as you supposed it would be.

I brought as usual a bad cold with me to town, and this being the first day I ventured out of doors, it was employed, as in duty bound, at court, it being a levee-day. A buffoon lord in waiting (you may guess whom I mean) was very busy marshalling the circle; and he said to me, without ceremony, "Move forward—you clog up the doorway." I replied with as little: "*Did nobody clog up the King's doorstead more than I, there would be room for all honest men.*" This brought the man to himself.

When the King came up to me he asked, "why I did not come to town before?" I said, "I understood there was no business going forward in the House, in which I could be of service to his Majesty." He replied: "He supposed the severe storm of snow would have brought me up." I replied: "I was under cover of a very warm house."

You see by all this how unfit I am for courts, so let us leave them.

Dr. Balguy is in town, and laments your absence. Mr. Mason called on me the other day; he is grown extremely fat and his wife extremely lean—indeed, in the last stage of a consumption. I inquired after her health; he said she was something better, and that, I suppose, encouraged him to come out; but Dr. Balguy tells me, Heberden says she is irretrievably gone, and has touched upon it to him, and ought to do it to her. Where the terror of such a sentence may impede the doctor's endeavors to save, the pronouncing it would be very indiscreet. But on a consumption confirmed it is a work of charity, as the patient is always deluded with hopes to the very last breath.

Public matters grow worse and worse. When they are at the worst they will mend themselves if (as is the fashionable system) things are left to the care of matter and motion. *Motion* certainly does its part; if there be any failure, it will be in *sluggish matter.*

And now, as you say, let us come to business. It is said that you and I should have no better (as Honest Lopes says in the Spanish Curate),

"Than ringing all—in to a rout of dunces."

I propose to have my visitation between hay and corn harvest. But my officers are so ignorant of this proper vacancy, that I doubt we must have recourse to your brother to acquaint us with the precise interval. I have fixed on this as most commodious to you; for I suppose hay harvest will not be quite ended in Gloucestershire by the 5th of July.

I could not but smile at your putting in a caveat so early against our asking you to return with us to Prior Park. My wife is well, and always yours. I have left half my soul at Claverton in good health, and in such dispositions as I could wish. When any thing befalls me, I not only expect you should be a father to him, but such a father as he shall have lost.

My dearest friend, ever yours, W. GLOUCESTER.

XXVII.—TRIAL OF THE DUCHESS OF KINGSTON.*

Hannah More to her Sister.

ADELPHI, 1776.

I wish it were possible for me to give you the slighest idea of the scene I was present at yesterday. Garrick would make

* The facts connected with this celebrated trial are well known. Whilst a maid of honor to the wife of Frederick, Prince of Wales, Miss Chudleigh,

me take his ticket to go to the trial of the Duchess of Kingston; a sight which, for beauty and magnificence, exceeded any thing which those who were never present at a coronation, or a trial by peers, can have the least notion of. Mrs. Garrick and I were in full dress by seven. At eight we went to the Duke of Newcastle's, whose house adjoins Westminster Hall, in which he has a large gallery, communicating with the apartments in his house. You will imagine the bustle of five thousand people getting into one hall! yet in all this hurry we walked in tranquilly. When they were all seated, and the king-at-arms had commanded silence on pain of imprisonment, which, however, was very ill-observed, the gentleman of the black rod was commanded to bring in his prisoner. Elizabeth, calling herself Duchess-dowager of Kingston, walked in, led by the black rod

who was regarded as one of the most beautiful young women of her time, was privately married to Lord Bristol, then Lieutenant Hervey. A separation, for some reason never clearly explained, took place almost immediately. A child, the fruit of the union, survived its birth but a short time, and the marriage was kept a profound secret from the world. Mrs. Hervey being still young, beautiful, and ambitious, determined to break the chain which bound her to a husband she disliked, and who annoyed her with constant importunities. Ascertaining that the clergyman who married her was dead, she repaired to the parish church where the ceremony was performed, and while a friend engaged the clerk in conversation in another part of the vestry, contrived to abstract the entry of her marriage from the parish register. She soon afterwards became the wife of the Duke of Kingston, with whom, it was believed, she had long carried on an illicit intercourse. On the death of the Duke, his nephew and heir at law, whose suspicions had been aroused, instituted proceedings against the Duchess for bigamy. She was found guilty, but as she claimed the privilege of the peerage, was discharged from custody on payment of the usual fees. Horace Walpole writes thus to Mann, on the 24th April, 1776: "If the Pope expects his Duchess back, he must create her one, for her peers have reduced her to a countess. Her folly and obstinacy now appear in their full vigor, at least her faith in the Ecclesiastical court, trusting to the infalibillity of which she provoked this trial, in the face of every sort of detection. A living wit-

and Mr. La Roche, courtesying profoundly to her judge; when she bent, the lord-steward called out, "Madam, you may rise;" which, I think, was literally taking her up before she was down. The peers made her a slight bow. The prisoner was dressed in deep mourning: a black hood on her head, her hair modestly dressed and powdered, a black silk sack with crape trimmings, black gauze deep ruffles, and black gloves. The counsel spoke about an hour and a quarter each. Dunning's manner is insufferably bad, coughing and spitting at every three words, but his sense and his expression pointed to the last degree; he made her Grace shed bitter tears. I had the pleasure of hearing several of the lords speak, though nothing more than proposals on common things. Among these were Lyttleton, Talbot, Townsend, and Camden. The fair victim had four virgins in

ness of the first marriage; a register of it fabricated long afterwards by herself; the widow of the clergyman who married her; many confidants to whom she had trusted the secret; and even Hawkins, the surgeon, privy to the birth of her child, appeared against her. The Lords were tender, and would not probe the Earl's collusion. The Duchess, who could produce nothing else of consequence in her favor, tried the powers of oratory, and made a long oration, in which she cited the protection of her late mistress. Her counsel would have curtailed this harangue, but she told them they might be good lawyers, but did not understand speaking to the passions. She concluded her rhetoric with a fit, and the trial with rage, when convicted of the bigamy. The Attorney-General labored to have her burnt in the hand, but the judges were hustled into an opinion against it, and it was waived. So all this complication of knavery receives no punishment but the loss of the duchy."

After her trial the Duchess proceeded to Rome, and thence to St. Petersburg, where she was admitted to the friendship of the famous Catharine. An entertainment which she gave to the Empress, is said to have been more magnificent than any which had hitherto been given in that country. Finding herself, however, neglected by the English ambassador and the Russian nobility, she removed to France, where she died in 1778, in the fifty-ninth year of her age.—H.

white behind the bar. She imitated her great predecessor, Mrs. Rudd, and affected to write very often—though I plainly perceived she only wrote as they do their love epistles on the stage, without forming a letter. I must not omit one of the best things: we had only to open a door to get at a very fine cold collation of all sorts of meats and wines, with tea, &c., a privilege confined to those who belonged to the Duke of Newcastle. I fancy the peeresses would have been glad of our places at the trial, for I saw Lady Derby and the Duchess of Devonshire with their workbags full of good things. Their rank and dignity did not exempt them from the "villanous appetites" of eating and drinking.

Foote says that the Empress of Russia, the Duchess of Kingston, and Mrs. Rudd, are the three most extraordinary women in Europe; but the Duchess disdainfully, and I think unjustly, excludes Mrs. Rudd from the honor of deserving to make one in the triple alliance. The Duchess has but small remains of that beauty of which kings and princes were once so enamored; she looked very much like Mrs. Prichard; she is large and ill-shaped; there was nothing white but her face, and had it not been for that, she would have looked like a bale of bombazine. There was a great deal of ceremony, a great deal of splendor, and a great deal of nonsense; they adjourned upon the most foolish pretences imaginable, and did *nothing* with such an air of business as was truly ridiculous. I forgot to tell you the Duchess was taken ill, but performed it badly.

XXVIII.—A ROYAL WEDDING.

Hannah More to Martha More.

FULHAM PALACE, May, 1797.

I am just come from attending the royal nuptials at St. James's. It was, indeed, a most august spectacle. If, indeed, it had been only the spectacle and the procession which I could have seen, I should have had little curiosity; but the bishop, who has the management of the whole chapel, secured me a place with Mrs. Porteous so near the altar that I could hear every word distinctly. The royal bride behaved with great feeling and modesty; the Prince of Wurtemberg had also a very becoming solemnity in his behavior. The King and Queen wept, but took great pains to restrain themselves. As I looked at the sixteen handsome and magnificently dressed royals sitting round the altar, I could not help thinking how many plans were perhaps at that very moment forming for their destruction; for the bad news from Ireland had just arrived. They talk of the number of acknowledged malcontents being 150,000, but I believe not a large part of that number have arms. I forgot to say that the King gave his daughter away, and it was really very affecting. The archbishop read the service with great emphasis and solemnity. The newspapers will have described all the crape, and the foils, and the feathers, and the diamonds, &c. We were four hours in chapel.

Lord Orford's executors, Mrs. Damer and Lord Frederick Campbell, have sent me word they will return all my letters, which they have found carefully preserved. I am also applied to in form to consent to give up such of his letters to me as are fit for publication. I have told them how extremely careful I am as to the publication of letters, and that I cannot make any positive engagement; but if, when I get to Cowslip Green, I should find, in looking them over, that any are quite disencumbered of private history, private characters, &c., I probably shall not withhold those in my possession; but I am persuaded that, after they are reduced as much as will be necessary, there will be little left for publication.

I dined one day at Admiral Gambier's, my kindly-attached friend with whom I spent so many pleasant days at Teston, to meet Sir Charles Middleton, who really brings a comfortable account of Mrs. Bouverie, and I begin to take hope about her.

The "Morning Chronicle" and other *pious newspapers* have labored to throw such a stigma on the association for the better observation of Sunday, that the timid great are sheering off, and very few, indeed, have signed. It has, however, led to so much talk and discussion on the subject as to produce a very considerable effect, and a number of high people have said, that though they will not bind themselves in form, they will conform to the spirit of the resolution. I doubt, however, whether those who show a timidity so little creditable to them, will do much. The Duchess-Dowager of Beaufort, with her usual kindness to me, said if I wished she would certainly sign, otherwise she thought such an old woman could add no credit to it; but I suggested that her high rank might attract others. Friday I dined at the Bishop of London's, and spent the evening at Gloucester House. I know not whether it comes under the act of treason or misprision of treason, to go to a royal house in colors, for people are in such deep mourning as to wear black handkerchiefs and gloves. It is not, however, universal; for, at a small party on Saturday at Mr. M. Montagu's, many were in colors. I met there Lord St. Helens, Mr. King, the American Minister, and others of that stamp.

I was much affected at the death of poor Mason. The Bishop of London was just reading us a sonnet he had sent him on his seventy-second birthday, rejoicing in his unimpaired strength and faculties; it ended with saying that he had still a muse able to praise his Saviour and his God, when the account of his death came. It was pleasing to find his last poetical sentiments had been so devout. I would that more of his writings had expressed the same strain of devotion, though I have no doubt of his having been piously disposed; but the Warburtonian school was not favorable to a devotional spirit. I used to be pleased with his turn of conversation, which was rather of a peculiar cast.

I have been meeting Mr. Smelt, who, at seventy-two, is come up to equip himself for entering into the military. There is patriotism for you! I dined yesterday with Mrs. Goodenough, the accomplished sister of the speaker.

XXIX.—FUNERAL OF GARRICK.

Hannah More to her Sister.

ADELPHI, Feb. 2d, 1779.

We (Miss Cadogan and myself) went to Charing-cross to see the melancholy procession. Just as we got there, we received a ticket from the Bishop of Rochester to admit us into the abbey. No admittance could be obtained but under his hand. We hurried away in a hackney-coach, dreading to be too late. The bell of St. Martin's and the abbey gave a sound that smote upon my very soul. When we got to the cloisters we found multitudes striving for admittance. We gave our ticket, and were let in, but unluckily we ought to have kept it. We followed the man, who unlocked a door of iron, and directly closed it upon us and two or three others, and we found ourselves in a tower, with a dark winding staircase, consisting of half a hundred stone steps. When we got to the top there was no way out; we ran down again, called, and beat the door till the whole pile resounded with our cries. Here we stayed half an hour in perfect agony; we were sure it would be all over; nay, we might never be let out: we might starve; we might perish. At length our clamors brought an honest man—a guardian angel I then thought him. We implored him to take care of us, and get us into a part of the abbey whence we might see the grave. He asked for the Bishop's ticket: we had given it away to the wrong person, and he was not obliged to believe we ever had one; yet he saw so much truth in our grief, that, though we were most shabby, and a hundred fine people were soliciting the same favor, he took us under each arm, carried us safely through the crowd, and put us in a little gallery directly over the grave, where we could see and hear every thing as distinctly as if the abbey had been a parlor. Little things sometimes affect the mind strongly. We were no sooner recovered from the fresh burst of grief, than I cast my eyes, the first thing, on Handel's monument, and read the scroll in his hand, "I know that my Redeemer liveth." Just at three the great doors burst open, with a noise that shook the roof; the organ struck up, and the whole choir, in strains only less solemn than the "archangel's trump," began Handel's fine anthem. The whole choir advanced to the grave, in hoods and surplices, singing all the way; then Sheridan, as chief mourner; then the body (alas! whose body?) with ten noblemen and gentlemen, pall-bearers; then the rest of the friends and mourners; hardly a dry eye—the very players, bred to the trade of counterfeiting, shed genuine tears.

As soon as the body was let down the bishop began the service, which he read in a low but solemn and devout manner. Such an awful stillness reigned, that every word was audible. How I felt it! Judge if my heart did not assent to the wish that the soul of our dear brother now departed was in peace. And this is all of Garrick! Yet a very little while, and he shall "say to the worm, Thou art my brother; and to corruption, Thou art my mother and sister." So passes away the fashion of this world. And the very night he was buried, the playhouses were as full, and the Pantheon was as crowded, as if no such thing had happened; nay, the very mourners of the day partook of the revelries of the night—the same night, too!

As soon as the crowd was dispersed, our friend came to us with an invitation from the bishop's lady, to whom he had related our disaster, to come into the deanery. We were carried into her dressing room, but being incapable of speech, she very kindly said she would not interrupt such sorrow, and left us; but sent up wine, cakes, and all manner of good things, which was really well-timed. I caught no cold, notwithstanding all I went through.

On Wednesday night we came to the Adelphi—to this house! She bore it with great tranquillity; but what was my surprise to see her go alone into the chamber and bed in which he had died that day fortnight. She had a delight in it beyond expression. I asked her the next day how she went through it. She told me very well; that she first prayed with great composure, then went and kissed the dear bed, and got into it with a sad pleasure.

XXX.—EVENING WITH THE TURKISH AMBASSADOR.

Hannah More to her Sister.

LONDON, May 10th, 1786.

I hope our engagements are now pretty well drawing to a close. I was engaged the last four days to Lady Bathurst, Lady Amherst, Lady Cremorne, and Lady Mount Edgecombe. I went through three of them manfully, coughing and creaking with great success.

Sir Joshua is doing a picture for the Empress of Russia, but I do not think he has chosen his subject happily, and so I ventured to tell his friend Burke the other night, though he warmly defended him. The empress left the subject to him, and desired to have a capital work of his in her collection. The story he has taken is Hercules strangling the young serpents. I think he might have chosen better than that stale piece of mythology. Mr. Walpole suggested to Sir Joshua an idea for a picture, which he thought would include something honorable to both nations—the scene Deptford,and the time when the Czar Peter was receiving a ship-carpenter's dress in exchange for his own, to work in the dock. This would be a great idea, and much more worthy of the pencil of the artist than nonsensical Hercules.

I have always had a great curiosity to converse with a disciple of Mahomet, and it was gratified the other day by my being invited to meet the Turkish ambassador. His suite, I think, consisted of six Mussulmans. They took their coffee sitting cross-legged on the floor. I confined my attention entirely to his excellency, who was placed next to me on the sofa, and did not sit cross-legged. His dragoman is a very sensible, agreeable person, and speaks all languages. The ambassador, a good, solemn-looking Turk, was very communicative; his son stood the whole evening behind the sofa on which his father sat. I obtained considerable information about their usages and manners. At my desire they spoke together a little Arabic, which is a very pretty-sounding language. They had, I believe, some hopes of bringing me over to the faith of the prophet, for they recommended me to read Sale's edition of the Alcoran. In return, I think I should have advised them to read White's Sermons. I asked how they contrived to exercise their religion in this country without a mosque. They told me that every great man in their country was both priest and lawyer, and allowed to exercise all the functions of both; that the ambassador did the duties of religion in his own house; and the Turk added, "I do not know how these (pointing to some statesmen who sat at a distance) lords do, but I am not ashamed to own that I retire five times a day to offer prayer and oblation." This he partly explained to me in broken Italian, and the rest was interpreted to me by the secretary.

I believe I have not mentioned Lord Monboddo this winter. I had a memorable quarrel with him one night lately; it was about Shakespeare and John Home. He said Douglas was a better play than Shakespeare could have written. He was angry, and I was pert. I called in Mrs. Montagu to my aid, and very saucy things we did say, which provoked him highly. Lord Mulgrave sat spiriting me up, but kept out of the scrape himself; and Lord Stormont seemed to enjoy the debate, but was shabby enough not to help me out. With his fine, dry humor, he would have had the advantage of us all. I was really very much diverted, though I was angry too; for the prejudiced Scotch critic, by rating Douglas so much above its real merit, made me appear unjust by seeming to undervalue it; but when he said that Shakespeare had no conception of drawing a king or a hero—that there was not so interesting a discovery in the whole of his works as that of Lady Randolph and her son, and that the passions were always vulgarly delineated—it was impossible to be temperate, and difficult to be just. I suppose when, on a former occasion, he declared that no modern could turn a period finely, he meant to make an exception in favor of Scotch authors.

We have had a numerous party to dinner; among others, Mr. and Mrs. Swinburne, the travellers, with whom I am lately become much acquainted; they are people who have been a good deal distinguished in different courts. The lady is the more agreeable of the two, though she has not, like her husband, written three quarto volumes about Spain and Calabria. They live chiefly abroad, and are great bigots to popery. She is the great friend of the Queen of Naples, and not less a favorite of the Queen of France—a singular pair of friendships for an Englishwoman of no rank.

XXXI.—A LONDON THÉ.

Hannah More to her Sister.

LONDON, May 22d, 1788.

I have been pleasantly engaged for a week past, during this fine weather, in going almost every day to some pleasant villa of different friends. Tuesday I dined at Strawberry Hill—a pleasant day, and a good little party. The next day we went to a sweet place which Mr. Montagu has bought on Shorter's Hill. Another day I went to Richmond with Mrs. Boscawen, and came home in the evening to a *thé* at Mrs. Montagu's. Perhaps you do not know what a *thé* is among the stupid new follies of the winter. You are to invite fifty or a hundred people to come at eight o'clock; there is to be a long table, or little parties at small ones; the cloth is to be laid as at breakfast; every one has a napkin; tea and coffee are made by the company, as at a public breakfast; the table is covered with rolls, wafers, bread, and butter; and, what constitutes the very essence of a *thé*, an immense load of hot buttered rolls, muffins, all admirably contrived to create a nausea in persons fresh from the dinner table. Now, of all nations under the sun, as I take it, the English are the greatest fools: because the Duke of Dorset, in Paris, where people dine at two, thought this would be a pretty fashion to introduce, we, who dine at six, must adopt this French translation of an English fashion, and fall into it as if it were an original invention; taking up our own custom at third-hand. This will be a short folly.

Poor Lady Mulgrave, married not a year, a little more than eighteen, good, great, beautiful, and happy, died yesterday in childbirth. It is hard to say whether her poor lord, her father and mother, or the Smelts are in the greatest affliction. I thought she would have proved a pattern to the young women of fashion—so domestic and so discreet! Among my country excursions I must not omit dining with Mrs. Trimmer and her twelve children at Brentford—a scene, too, of instruction and delight. The other day I was at Mr. Langton's; our subject was Abolition; we fell to it with great eagerness, and paid no attention to the wits who were round us, though there were two who were new to me—Mr. Malone, the critic of Shakespeare, and Dr. Gillies, author of the new History of Greece. I go to Mrs

Bouverie's at Teston for a fortnight, and then to Fulham Palace for another fortnight, and then to my own dear cottage.

XXXII.—MEETING MADAME LA CHEVALIERE D'ÆON AT DINNER.

Hannah More to her Sister.

LONDON, May, 1789.

Mr. Wilberforce and his myrmidons are still shut up at Mr. Bouverie's, at Teston, to write; I tell them I hope Teston will be the Runnymede of the negroes, and that the great charter of African liberty will be there completed. It is well that Fulham is so near, so that the bishop will be within reach to forward the work. The fate of Africa now trembles in the balance. On Friday I gratified the curiosity of many years by meeting at dinner, Madame Chevaliere D'Æon; she is extremely entertaining, has universal information, wit, vivacity, and gayety. Something too much of the latter (I have heard) when she has taken a bottle or two of Burgundy; but this being a very sober party, she was kept entirely within the limits of decorum. General Johnson was of the party, and it was ridiculous to hear her military conversation; sometimes it was, *Quand j'étois colonel d'un tel regiment;* then again, *Non c'étois quand c'étois serétaire d'ambassade du Duc de Nivernois*, or *quand je negociois la paix de Paris.* She is, to be sure, a phenomenon in history, and as such, a great curiosity. But *one* D'Æon is enough, and *one slice of her quite sufficient.**

I am expected at Rosedale, at Teston, and at the Bishop of

* These reflections are amusing, when we remember that this celebrated personage, whose beardless face and feminine tact and manners enabled him to pass for many years as a woman in the most distinguished society, in fact belonged to the other sex.—H.

London's, but have given no definite answer, because I do not think I can contrive to see them all. I fear there will be great opposition to the abolition in the Lords. I dined with a party of peers at Lord Ossory's, and there was not one friend to that humane bill. I sat two hours in the evening with Mr. Walpole, who had a pleasant little party—among others, Frederick North, a very agreeable and accomplished young man; so learned, so so pleasant, and with so fine a taste! To-night I go to a little supper at Mrs. Damer's, and to-morrow I take my leave of the pomps and vanities of this town, and go to Fulham Palace. I shall stay a week with the Bishop, from thence I shall go, if possible, for a few days to Mrs. Boscawen, and from thence to Teston.

XXXIII.—ELECTIONEERING AT OLNEY.

William Cowper to Rev. John Newton.

March 29th, 1784.

It being his Majesty's pleasure that I should yet have another opportunity to write before he dissolves the Parliament, I avail myself of it with all possible alacrity. I thank you for your last, which was not the less welcome for coming, like an extraordinary gazette, at a time when it was not expected.

As when the sea is uncommonly agitated the water finds its way into creeks and holes of rocks, which in its calmer state it never reaches, in like manner the effect of these turbulent times is felt even at Orchard-side, where in general we live as undisturbed by the political element as shrimps or cockles that have been accidentally deposited in some hollow beyond the water-mark, by the usual dashing of the waves. We were sitting yesterday after dinner, the two ladies and myself, very composedly, and without the least apprehension of any such intrusion, in our snug parlor, one lady knitting, the other netting, and the gentleman winding worsted, when, to our unspeakable surprise, a mob appeared before the window; a smart rap was heard at the door, the boys hallooed, and the maid announced Mr. Grenville. Puss was unfortunately let out of her box, so that the candidate, with all his good friends at his heels, was refused admittance at the grand entry, and referred to the back door as the only possible way of approach.

Candidates are creatures not very susceptible of affronts, and would rather, I suppose, climb in at the window than be absolutely excluded. In a minute the yard, the kitchen, and the parlor were filled. Mr. Grenville, advancing toward me, shook me by the hand with a degree of cordiality that was extremely seducing. As soon as he and as many as could find chairs were seated, he began to open the intent of his visit. I told him I had no vote, for which he readily gave me credit. I assured him I had no influence, which he was not equally inclined to believe, and the less, no doubt, because Mr. G———, addressing himself to me at that moment, informed me that I had a great deal. Supposing that I could not be possessed of such a treasure without knowing it, I ventured to confirm my first assertion by saying that if I had any, I was utterly at a loss to imagine where it could be or wherein it consisted. Thus ended the conference. Mr. Grenville squeezed me by the hand again, kissed the ladies, and withdrew. He kissed, likewise, the maid in the kitchen, and seemed upon the whole a most loving, kissing, kind-hearted gentleman. He is very young, genteel, and handsome. He has a pair of very good eyes in his head, which not being sufficient, as it should seem, for the many nice and difficult purposes of a senator, he had a third also, which he wore suspended by a riband from his button-hole. The boys halloo'd, the dogs barked, puss scampered, the hero with his long train of obsequious followers withdrew. We made ourselves very merry with the adventure, and in a short time settled into our former tranquillity, never probably to be thus interrupted more. I thought myself, however, happy in being able to affirm truly, that I had not that influence for which he sued, and for which, had I been possessed of it, with my present views of the dispute between the Crown and the Commons, I must have refused him, for he is on the side of the former. It is comfortable to be of no consequence in a world where one cannot exercise any without disobliging somebody. The town, however, seems to be much at his service, and if he be equally successful throughout the country he will undoubtedly gain his election. Mr. Ashburner perhaps was a little mortified, because it was evident that I owed the honor of this visit to his misrepresentation of my importance. But had he thought proper to assure Mr. Grenville that I had three heads, I should not, I suppose, have been bound to produce them.*

* An admirable illustration of the style of an old English canvass, is furnished in the following anecdote of Lord Wharton, the greatest master of the art of electioneering England ever saw—occurring at an earlier period, 1705. "His lordship," says his biographer, "having recommended two candidates to the borough of Wicomb, some of the staunch Churchmen invited two of their own party to oppose them, and money was spent by both sides. A gentleman, a friend of one of the High Church candidates, was desired by him to go down to the borough with him when he went, to make his interest. This gentleman told me the story, and that he was a witness of what past when they came to Wicomb. They found my Lord Wharton was got there before them (of course), and was going up and down the town with his friends to secure votes on their side. The gentleman with his two candidates, and a very few followers, marched on one side of the street; my Lord Wharton's

Mr. Scott, who you say was so much admired in your pulpit, would be equally admired in his own, at least by all capable judges, were he not so apt to be angry with his congregation. This hurts him, and had he the understanding and eloquence of Paul himself, would still hurt. He seldom, hardly ever, indeed, preaches a gentle, well-tempered sermon, but I hear it highly commended; but warmth of temper, indulged to a degree that may be called scolding, defeats the end of preaching. It is a misapplication of his powers, which it also cripples, and teases away his hearers. But he is a good man, and may perhaps outgrow it.

Many thanks for the worsted, which is excellent. We are as well as a spring, hardly less severe than the severest winter, will give us leave to be. With our united love, we conclude ourselves yours, and Mrs. Newton's affectionate and faithful,

W. C.

candidates and a great company on the other. The gentleman not being known to my Lord or the townsmen, joined in with his lordship's men to make discoveries, and was by when my lord, entering a shoemaker's shop, asked '*where Dick was!*' The good women said, '*her husband was gone two or three miles off with some shoes, but his lordship need not fear him—she would keep him tight.*' '*I know that,*' says my lord, '*but I want to see Dick, and drink a glass with him.*' The wife was very sorry Dick was out of the way. '*Well,*' says his lordship, '*how does all thy children? Molly is a brave girl, I warrant, by this time.*' '*Yes, I thank ye, my lord,*' says the woman; and his lordship continued, '*Is not Jemmy breeched yet?*' At this stage the gentleman slipped away to inform his friends that opposition to Wharton was hopeless. Nothing could stand against a great peer who had such a knowledge of the ages of Molly and Jemmy."—H.

XXXIV.—LIFE AT AN ENGLISH COUNTRY PARSONAGE.

Dr. Beattie to Sir William Forbes.

HUNTON (near Maidstone), KENT, July 31st, 1784.

Your last letter having given me the fullest assurance that the unfortunate object of our attention is now in circumstances as comfortable as her condition will admit of, I have been endeavoring to relieve my mind, for a time at least, from that load of anxiety which has so long oppressed it; and I already feel the happy consequences of this endeavor. My health is greatly improved; and, if this rheumatism would let me alone, I might almost say that I am quite well. Certain it is that I have not been so well any time these four years. The tranquillity and beauty, the peace and the plenty, of this charming country, are a continual feast to my imagination; and I must be insensible, indeed, if the kindness, the cheerfulness, the piety, and the instructive conversation, of my excellent friend the Bishop of Chester, and his amiable lady, did not powerfully operate in soothing my mind, and improving my heart. Those people of fashion in the neighborhood, who visit the bishop and are visited by him, are a small but select society, and eminently distinguished for their piety, politeness, literature, and hospitality. Among them I have found some old friends, whom I formerly knew in London, and have acquired some new ones, on whom I set a very high value. Mr. Langton and Lady Rothes have just left us, after a visit of two days. You will readily imagine with what regret we parted with them. Our friend Langton is continually improving in virtue, learning, and every other thing that is good. I always admired and loved him; but now I love and admire him more than ever. We had much conversation about you. I have given the bishop a full account of my family transactions, particularly for the last twelvemonth. He highly approves of every thing that has been done; bestows great commendations on my conduct; and has given me such advices as one would expect from his good sense and knowledge of the world. I have not yet fixed a day for my departure from this paradise; but I fear it must be in the course of next week. My friends urge me to prolong my stay, and I am much disposed to do so; but I must now remember that the year begins to decline, and I have several other visits to make, and things to do, before I leave England. Meanwhile, I shall, from time to time, let you know where I am, and what I am doing. Any letter you may favor me with, you will be pleased to put under the Bishop of Chester's cover.

If I could give you an adequate idea of the way in which we pass our time at Hunton, I am sure you would be pleased with it. This is a rainy day, and I have nothing else to do at present; why, then, should I not make the trial?

Our hour of breakfast is ten. Immediately before it the bishop calls his family together, prays with them, and gives them his blessing; the same thing is constantly done after supper, when we part for the night. In the intervals of breakfast, and in the evening, when there is no company, his lordship sometimes reads to us in some entertaining book. After breakfast, we separate and amuse ourselves, as we think proper, till four, the hour of dinner. At six, when the weather is fair, we either walk, or make a visit to some of the clergy or gentry in the neighborhood, and return about eight. We then have music, in which I am sorry to say that I am almost the only performer. I have got a violoncello, and play Scotch tunes, and perform Handel's, Jackson's, and other songs, as well as I can; and my audience is very willing to be pleased. The bishop and Mrs. Porteus are both fond of music. These musical parties are often honored with the company of the accomplished and amiable Lady Twisden, of whom I gave you some account in my last. Observe, that there are in this part of Kent no fewer than three ladies of that name; but the one I speak of is Lady Twisden of Jennings, in the parish of Hunton; who, in the course of one year, was a maid, a wife, a widow, and a mother; whose husband, Sir Roger, died about five years ago; and who, though possessed of beauty and a large fortune, and not more than twenty-five years of age, has ever since lived in this retirement, employing herself partly in study, but chiefly in acts of piety and beneficence, and in the education of her little daughter, who is indeed a very fine child. I have just now before me Miss Hannah More's Sacred Dramas, which I borrowed from Lady Twisden, and in which I observe that she has marked her favorite passages with a nicety of selection that does great honor to her heart, as well as to her judgment. By the by, Miss More is an author of very considerable merit. My curiosity to see her works were excited by Johnson, who told me, with great solemnity, that she was "the most powerful versificatrix" in the English language.

So much for our week-days. On Sundays, at eleven, we repair to church. It is a small, but neat building, with a pretty good ring of six bells. The congregation are a stout, well-featured set of people, clean and neat in their dress, and most exemplary in the decorum with which they perform the several parts of public worship. As we walk up the area to the bishop's pew, they all make, on each side, a profound obeisance, and the same as we return. The prayers are very well read by Mr. Hill, the curate, and the bishop preaches. I need not tell you now, because I think I told you before, that Bishop Porteus is, in my opinion, the best preacher, in respect both of composition and delivery, I have ever heard. In this capacity, indeed, he is universally admired, and many of the gentry come to hear him from the neighboring parishes. After evening service, during the summer months, his lordship generally delivers from his pew a catachetical lecture, addressed to the children, who, for this purpose, are drawn up in a line before him along the area of the church. In these lectures he explains to them, in the simplest and clearest manner, yet with his usual elegance, the fundamental and essential principles of religion and morality; and concludes with an address to the more advanced in years. This institution of the bishop's I greatly admire. When children see themselves so much attended to, and so much pains taken in instructing them, they cannot fail to look upon religion as a matter of importance; and if they do so, it is not possible for them, considering the advantages they enjoy, to be ignorant of it. The catachetical examinations in the church of Scotland, such of them at least as I have seen, are extremely ill calculated for doing good; being encumbered with metaphysical distinctions, and expressed in a technical language, which to children are utterly unintelligible, and but little understood even by the most sagacious of the common people. The bishop told me that he chose to deliver this lecture from his pew, and without putting on lawn sleeves, that it might make the stronger impression upon the children; having observed, he said, that what is delivered from the pulpit, and with the usual formalities, is too apt to be considered, both by the young and the old, as a thing of course. On

Sunday evening, he sometimes reads to his servants a brief and plain abstract of the Scripture history, somewhat similar to that which was lately published by Mrs. Trimmer, and formerly by Lady Newhaven.

In no other district of Great Britain that I have seen, is there so little the appearance of poverty, and such indications of competence and satisfaction in the countenance and dress of the common people, as in this part of Kent. In this parish there is only one alehouse, the profits whereof are inconsiderable. The people are fond of cricket-matches, at which there is a great concourse of men, women, and children, with good store of ale and beer, cakes, gingerbread, etc. One of these was solemnized a few nights ago in a field adjacent to the parish church. It broke up about sunset, with much merriment, but without drunkenness or riot. The contest was between the men of Hunton and the men of Peckham; and the latter were victorious.

XXXV.—AT DR. FRANKLIN'S WITH MADAME HELVETIUS.

Mrs. Adams to Lucy Cranch.

AUTEUIL, Sept. 5th, 1784.

MY DEAR LUCY: I promised to write to you from the Hague, but your uncle's unexpected arrival at London prevented me. Your uncle purchased an excellent travelling coach in London, and hired a post chaise for our servants. In this manner we travelled from London to Dover, accommodated through England with the best of horses, postilions, and good carriages, clean, neat apartments, genteel entertainment, and prompt attendance. But no sooner do you cross from Dover to Calais than every thing is reversed, and yet the distance is very small between them.

The cultivation is by no means equal to that of England; the villages look poor and mean, the houses all thatched, and rarely a glass window in them; their horses, instead of being handsomely harnessed, as those in England are, have the appearance of so many old cart horses. Along you go, with seven horses tied up with ropes and chains, rattling like two trucks; two ragged postilions, mounted with enormous jack boots, add to the comic scene. And this is the style in which a duke or a count travels through this kingdom. You inquire of me how I like Paris. Why they tell me I am no judge, for that I have not seen it yet. One thing I know, and that is that I have smelt it. I was agreeably disappointed in London; I am as much disappointed in Paris. It is the very dirtiest place I ever saw. There are some buildings and some squares which are tolerable, but in general the streets are narrow, the shops, the houses inelegant and dirty, the streets full of lumber and stone with which they build. Boston cannot boast so many elegant public buildings; but in every other respect it is as much superior in my eyes to Paris, as London is to Boston. To have had Paris tolerable to me, I should not have gone to London. As to the people here, they are more given to hospitality than in England, it is said. I have been in company with but one French lady since I arrived; for strangers here make the first visit, and nobody will know you until you have waited upon them in form.

This lady (the widow of the philosopher Helvetius) I dined with at Dr. Franklin's. She entered the room with a careless, jaunty air; upon seeing ladies who were strangers to her, she bawled out: "Ah! mon Dien, where is Franklin? Why did you not tell me there were ladies here?" You must suppose her speaking all this in French. "How I look!" said she, taking hold of a chemise made of tiffany, which she had on over a blue lute-string, and which looked as much upon the decay as her beauty, for she was once a handsome woman, her hair was frizzled, over it she had a small straw hat, with a dirty gauze half-handkerchief round it, and a bit of dirtier gauze than ever my maid wore was bowed on behind. She had a black gauze scarf thrown over her shoulders. She ran out of the room; when she returned, the doctor entered at one door, she at the other; upon which she ran forward to him, caught him by the hand, "Helas! Franklin," then gave him a double kiss, one upon each cheek and one upon his forehead. When we went into the room to dine, she was placed between the doctor and Mr. Adams. She carried on the chief of the conversation at dinner, frequently locking her hand into the doctor's, and sometimes spreading her arms upon the backs of both the gentlemen's chairs, then throwing her arm carelessly upon the doctor's neck.

I should have been greatly astonished at this conduct if the good doctor had not told me that in this lady I should see a genuine Frenchwoman, wholly free from affectation or stiffness of behavior, and one of the best women in the world. For this I must take the doctor's word; but I should have set her down for a very bad one, although sixty years of age and a widow. I own I was highly disgusted, and never wish for an acquaintance with any ladies of this cast. After dinner she threw herself on a settee, where she showed more than her feet. She had a little lap dog, who was, next to the doctor, her favorite. This she kissed, and when he wet the floor she wiped it up with her chemise. This is one of the doctor's most intimate friends, with whom he dines once in every week, and she with him. She is rich, and is my near neighbor; but I have not yet visited her. Thus, you see, my dear, that manners differ exceedingly in different countries. I hope, however, to find amongst the French ladies manners more consistent with my ideas of decency, or I shall be a mere recluse.

You must write to me and let me know all about you; marriages, births, and preferments, every thing you can think of. Give my respects to the Germantown family; I shall begin to get letters for them by the next vessel. Good night. Believe me,

Your most affectionate aunt,

A. A.

XXXVI.—A LONDON "ROUT."

Mrs. Adams to Mrs. Cranch.

LONDON, April 6th, 1786.

MY DEAR SISTER: Although I was at a stupid rout at the Swedish Minister's last evening, I got home about twelve, and rose early this morning to get a few things ready to send out by Lyde. When a body has attended one of these parties you know the whole of the entertainment. There were about two hundred persons present last evening. Three large rooms full of card-tables; the moment the ceremony of courtesying is past, the lady of the house asks you, "Pray, what is your game; whist, cabbage, or commerce?" And then the next thing is to hunt round the room for a set to make a party; and, as the company are coming and going from eight till two in the morning, you may suppose she has enough to employ her from room to room. The lady and her daughter last night were almost fatigued to death, for they had been out the night before till morning, and were toiling at pleasure for seven hours, in which time they scarcely sat down. I went with a determination not to play, but could not get off; so I was set down to a table with three perfect strangers, and the lady who was against me stated the game at half a guinea apiece. I told her I thought it full high; but I knew she designed to win, so I said no more, but expected to lose. It, however, happened otherwise; I won four games of her. I then paid for the cards, which is the custom here, and left her to attack others; which she did at three other tables, where she amply made up her loss. In short, she was an old experienced hand, and it was the luck of the cards rather than skill, though I have usually been fortunate, as it is termed; but I never play when I can possibly avoid it, for I have not conquered the disagreeable feeling of receiving money for play. But such a set of gamblers as the ladies here are! and such a life as they lead! Good Heavens! were reasonable beings made for this? I will come and shelter myself in America from this scene of dissipation, and upbraid me whenever I introduce the like amongst you. Yet here, you cannot live with any character or consequence unless you give in some measure into the ton.

Mr. Adams is gone to accompany Mr. Jefferson into the country, to some of the most celebrated gardens. This is the first tour he has made since I came abroad; since which time we have lived longer unseparated than we have ever done since we were married. Adieu. Your sister,

A. A.

XXXVII.—LIFE AT THE WELLS—DONKEY RIDING, &c.

Mrs. Barbauld to Miss Taylor.

TUNBRIDGE WELLS, Aug. 7th, 1804.

I may call you dear Susan, may not I? For I can love you, if not better, yet more familiarly and at my ease under that appellation than under the more formal one of Miss Taylor, though you have now a train to your gown, and are, I suppose, at Norwich invested with all the rights of womanhood. I have many things to thank you for; in the first place for a charming letter, which has both amused and delighted us. In the next place I have to thank you for a very elegant veil, which is very beautiful in itself, and receives great additional value from being the work of your ingenious fingers. I have brought it here to parade with upon the Pantiles, being much the smartest part of my dress. O that you were here, Susan, to exhibit upon a *donky!* I cannot tell whether my orthography is right, but a donky is the *monture* in high fashion here; and I assure you, when covered with blue housings and sleek, it makes no bad figure; I mean a lady, if an elegant woman, makes no bad figure upon it, with a little boy or girl behind, who carries a switch, meant to admonish the animal, from time to time, that he is hired to walk on, and not to stand still. The ass is much better adapted than the horse to show off a lady; for this reason, which may perhaps not have occurred to you, that her beauty is not so likely to be eclipsed; for you must know that many philosophers, amongst whom is ——, are decidedly of opinion that a fine *horse* is a much finer animal than a fine woman; but I have not yet heard such a preference asserted in favor of the *ass* —not our English asses at least—a fine Spanish one, or a zebra perhaps.

It is the way to *subscribe* for every thing here—to the library, etc.; and among other things, we were asked on the Pantiles to subscribe for eating fruit, as we pass backwards and forwards. "How much?" "Half a crown." "But for how long a time?" "As long as you please." "But I should soon eat half a crown's worth of fruit." "O, you are upon honor."

There are pleasant walks on the hills here, and picturesque views of the town, which, like Bath, is seen to advantage by lying in a hollow. It bears the marks of having been long a place of resort, from the number of good and rather old built houses, all let for lodgings; and shady walks and groves of old growth. The sides of many of the houses are covered with tiles; but the Pantiles, which you may suppose I saw with some interest, are now paved with freestone.

We were interested in your account of Cambridge, and glad you saw not only buildings but men. With a mind prepared as yours is, how much pleasure have you to enjoy from seeing! That all your improvements may produce you pleasure, and all your pleasures tend to improvement, is the wish of,

Your ever affectionate friend, ———.

XXXVIII.—AN ITALIAN LADY AND SIR HUMPHREY DAVY.

Lord Byron to Mr. Murray.

RAVENNA, May 8th, 1820.

* * * Sir Humphrey Davy was here last fortnight, and I was in his company in the house of a very pretty Italian lady of rank, who, by the way of displaying her learning in presence of the great chemist, then describing his fourteenth ascension of Mount Vesuvius, asked "if there was not a similar volcano in

Ireland?" My only notion of an Irish volcano consisted of the Lake of Killarney, which I naturally conceived her to mean; but on second thoughts, I divined she alluded to Iceland and to Hecla, though she sustained her volcanic topography for some time with all the amiable pertinacity of "the feminine." She soon after turned to me, and asked me various questions about Sir Humphrey's philosophy; and I explained as well as an oracle his skill in gasen safety-lamps, and ungluing the Pompeian MSS. "But what do you call him," said she. "A great chemist," quoth I. "What can he do?" repeated the lady. "Almost any thing," said I. "Oh, then, *mio caro*, pray beg him to give me something to dye my eyebrows black. I have tried a thousand things, and the colors all come off, and besides, they don't grow; can't he invent something to make them grow?" All this with the greatest earnestness, and what you will be surprised at, she is neither ignorant nor a fool, but really well educated and clever. But they speak like children when first out of their convents; and after all, this is better than an English blue-stocking.

I did not tell Sir Humphrey of this last piece of philosophy, not knowing how he might take it. Davy was much taken with Ravenna, and the primitive Italianism of the people, who are unused to foreigners—but he only stayed a day. * * *

XXXIX.—PRESENTATION OF THE SCOTCH COMMISSIONERS TO WILLIAM IV.

Dr. Chalmers to His Daughter.

LONDON, October 28th, 1830.

MY DEAR MARGARET: This is the big and busy day. Got up at seven. Went out to order the loan of a court hat, which is promised me by twelve. A general dressing, and anxiety on all hands to be as *snod* [neat] as possible. A breakfast at which all the members of the deputation were present: Dr. Singer, Dr. Cook, Dr. McKnight, Dr. Lee, and myself; Mr. Paul, Mr. Sinclair, Sir John Connel. We are, besides, to have Sir Henry Jardine, Mr. Pringle of Stair, and Dr. Stewart of Erskine as attendants. A vast deal of conversation anent our movements to and from. We are all on edge. We have to make three bows; and the question is whether we shall all make them on moving toward the throne, or after we have spread ourselves before it; and there is such a want of unanimity and distinct understanding about it, that I fear we shall misbehave. However, time will show, and I now lay down my pen till it is over. We assembled in our hotel at one. The greatest consternation among us about hats, which had been promised at twelve, but had not yet arrived. There were four wanting; and at length only three came, with the promise that we should get the other when we passed the shop. We went in three coaches, and landed at the palace entry at about half-past one. Ascended the stair, passed through a magnificent lobby, between rows of glittering attendants, all dressed in gold and scarlet, ushered into a large anteroom, full of all sorts of company, walking about and collecting there for attendance on the levee; military and naval officers in splendid uniforms; high legal gentlemen with enormous wigs; ecclesiastics, from archbishops to curates and inferior clergy. Our deputation made a most respectable appearance among them, with our cocked three-cornered hats under our arms, our hands upon our breasts, and our gowns of Geneva upon our backs. Mine did not lap so close as I would have liked, so that I was twice as thick as I should be, and it must have been palpable to every eye at the first glance that I was the greatest man there; and that though I took all care to keep my coat unbuttoned, and my gown quite open. However, let not mama be alarmed, for I made a most respectable appearance, and was treated with the utmost attention. I saw the Archbishop of York in the room, but did not get within speech of him. To make up for this, however, I was introduced to the Archbishop of Canterbury, who was very civil; saw the Bishop of London, with whom I had a good deal of talk, and am to dine on Friday; was made up to by Sir Admiral Philip Durham; and was further introduced, at their request, to Sir John Leach, Master of the Rolls, to Lord Chief Justice Tindall, to the Marquis of Bute, etc. But far the most interesting object there was Talleyrand—whom I could get nobody to introduce me to—splendidly attired as the French Ambassador, attended by some French military officers. I gazed with interest on the old shrivelled face of him, and thought I could see there the lines of deep reflection and lofty talent. His moral physiognomy, however, is a downright blank.* He was by far the most important continental personage in the room, and drew all eyes. I was further in conversation with Lord

* Jeffrey, who met Talleyrand at Holland House about this period, describes him thus: "He is more natural, plain, and reasonable than I had expected; a great deal of the repose of high breeding and old age, with a mild and benevolent manner, and great calmness of speech, rather than the sharp, caustic, cutting speech of the practiced utterer of bon mots. He spoke a great deal of old times and old persons, the court of Louis the XVI. when Dauphin, his coronation, Voltaire, Malsherbe, and Turgot, with traditional anecdotes of Massillon and Bossuet, and many women of these days, whose names I have forgotten, and a good deal of diplomatic anecdote, altogether very pleasing and easy. He did not eat much nor talk much about eating, except only that he inquired very earnestly into the nature of *cocky-leekie* (a Scotch soup), and wished very much to know whether *prunes* were essential. He settled at last that they should be boiled in the soup, but not brought up in it. He drank little but iced water."—H.

Melville, Mr. Spencer Percival, and Mr. Henry Drummond. The door in the middle apartment was at length opened for us, when we entered in processional order. The Moderator first, with Drs. Macknight and Cook on each side of him; I and Dr. Lee, side by side, followed; Mr. Paul and Mr. George Sinclair, with their swords and bags, formed the next row; then Sir John Connel and Sir Henry Jardine; and last of all Mr. Pringle, M. P., and Dr. Stewart. We stopped in the middle room—equally crowded with the former, and alike splendid with mirrors, chandeliers, pictures, and gildings of all sorts on the roof and walls—for about ten minutes, when, at length, the folding-doors to the grand state-room were thrown open. We all made a low bow on our first entry, and the King, seated on the throne at the opposite end, took off his hat—putting it on again. We marched up to the middle of the room and made another low bow, when the King again took off his hat; we then proceeded to the foot of the throne, and all made a third low bow, on which the King again took off his hat. After this the Moderator read his address, which was a little long, and the King bowed repeatedly while it was reading. The Moderator then reached the address to the King upon the throne, who took it from him and gave it to Sir Robert Peel on his left hand, who, in his turn, gave the King his written reply, which he read very well. After this the Moderator went up to the stool before the throne, leaned his left knee upon it, and kissed the King's hand. We each, in our turn, did the same thing—the Moderator naming every one of us as we advanced; I went through my kneel and my kiss very comfortably. The King said something to each of us. His first question to me was, "Do you reside constantly in Edinburgh?" I said, "Yes, an't please your majesty." His next question was, "How long do you remain in town?" I said, "Till Monday, an't please your majesty." I then descended the steps leading from the foot of the throne to the floor, and fell into my place in the deputation. After we had all been introduced, we began to retire in a body, just as we had come, bowing all the way, with our faces to the King, and so moving backward, when the King called out, "Don't go away, gentlemen, I shall leave the throne, and the Queen will succeed me." We stopped in the middle of the room, when the most beautiful living sight I ever beheld burst upon our delighted gaze—the Queen, with twelve maids of honor, in a perfect spangle of gold and diamonds, entered the room. I am sorry I cannot go over in detail the particulars of their dresses; only that their lofty plumes upon their heads, and their long sweeping trains upon the floor, had a very magnificent effect.

She took her seat on the throne, and we made the same profound obeisances as before; advancing to the foot of the steps that lead to the footstool of the throne. A short address was read to her as before; and her reply was most beautifully given, in rather a tremulous voice, and just as low as that I could only hear, and no more. We went through the same ceremonial of advancing successively and kissing hands, and then retired with three bows which the Queen returned most gracefully, but with all the simplicity, I had almost said bashfulness, of a timid country girl. She is really a very natural and amiable looking person. The whole was magnificent. On each side of the throne were maids of honor, officers of state, the Lord Chancellor, a vast number of military gentlemen, and among the rest the Duke of Wellington. My next will be to Helen. God bless you, my dear Margaret. I am your affectionate father,

THOMAS CHALMERS.

XL.—DINNER AT THE LORD MAYOR'S.

Dr. Chalmers to his Daughter.

LONDON, October 29th, 1830.

MY DEAR HELEN: I did not finish my description of our interview with the Queen in my letter to Margaret, for, after we left the grand state-room, we remained in the middle room; and after us the corporation of Dublin, a very large body, went with addresses to the King and Queen. There were some very magnificent people among them; and as a great number had to be introduced, it took up a long time, so we had to wait half an hour, at least, in the middle room, till the levee began, when the two inner doors between the middle and great state-rooms were thrown open. The King, instead of being upon the throne, now stood on the floor. There was an immense number of people introduced to him, going in a very close and lengthened column from the outer room by one corner door of the great state-room, passing the King, and retiring through an avenue of state attendants by the other corner door. I kissed his hand the second time, and was named both by him and Sir Robert Peel. After this we remained in the middle room a considerable time, and at length left the palace. We had to wait a long time in the door lobby till our coaches drew up for us. The crowding and calling of coaches had a very animating effect. We got to our hotel at four—waited there half an hour. Our coaches came for us again to take us to the Mansion House, where we were to dine with the Lord Mayor. This is a magnificent house, and has a very noble dining-room. The Lord Mayor himself was unwell, and could not be with us. His chaplain did the honors for him. There were about fifty. We assembled in the drawing-room. There were about six ladies; and I was very graciously received by the Lady Mayoress and the Lady Mayoress elect. The latter of whom I had the honor of leading to the great dining hall. The Lady Mayoress elect will be Lady Mayoress at the great civic feast to their Majesties; so that I had the honor of leading the very lady to dinner whom the King will lead to the great Guildhall dinner in about a fortnight. It was truly a civic feast. I had the honor of sitting second on the right hand from the Lady Mayoress, there being the Lord Mayor elect between me and her, so that I sat between the Lord and Lady Mayor elect—to be Lord and Lady Mayor in a few days. They were both as kind and cordial to me as possible, as was also the Lady Mayoress. There are some venerable customs handed down from very remote antiquity, which I took great delight in witnessing and sharing in. After dinner, one of the portly and magnificent waiters stood behind the Lady Mayoress with a large flagon, having a lid that lifted, and filled with the best spiced wine. He then called out "Silence," and delivered the following speech from behind the Lady Mayoress, with the great flagon in his hand: "Commissioners of the Church of Scotland, the Lord Mayor, the Lady Mayoress, the Lord Mayor elect, the Lady Mayoress elect, my masters the Sheriff and Aldermen of the good city of London, bid you hearty welcome to this our ancient town, and offer you a cup of love and kindness, in token of good feeling and good fellowship." I have not done justice to the speech, for those Aldermen present were named in it, among the rest the famous Alderman Waitman and Sir Claudius Hunter. After this speech by the crier, the cup was given to the Lady Mayoress, who turned round with it to her neighbor, the Lord Mayor elect; he lifted the lid and kept it in his hand till she drank, both standing; she then gave it to him, but not till she wiped with a towel the place she had drunk at; he put on the lid, and turned round to me, who rose; I took off the lid, he drank, wiped, gave the cup to me; I turned round to my next neighbor, the Lady Mayoress elect, she arose and took off the lid, I drank, wiped, and gave the cup to her, who put on the lid, turned to her next neighbor, etc., and so the cup, or great flagon rather, went round the whole company. Another peculiar observance was, that instead of hand glasses for washing, there was put down an immense massive plate of gilt silver, with a little rose water poured into it, and placed before the Lady Mayoress. She dipped the corner of her towel into it, and therewith sponged her face and hands, and said plate went round the table, and each of us did the same. It was most refreshing. Then came toasts and speeches. The Moderator gave one in reply to the Church of Scotland; and the Lady Mayoress declared she would not leave the room till I spoke. So there was a particular toast for me, and I had to make a speech, which I concluded with a toast to the Lady Mayoress. Mr. George Sinclair was asked by her Ladyship to return thanks in her name; which he did with a speech, etc. After the ladies retired, I sat between the Lord Mayor, who took the chair, and Alderman Sir Claudius Hunter, who was particularly kind to me. We drank tea with the ladies, and I had much cordial conversation with the *eminentes* who were there—as Alderman Waitman, Mr. Hartwell Horne, author of the "Introduction," Mr. Alexander Chalmers, author of the "Biographical Dictionary," Sir Peter and Lady Laurie, etc. I should have mentioned that I gave a second little speech in compliment to Mr. Horne, whom I offered as a toast. We went off in our carriages about ten, much delighted with the day's work, and retired to bed soon after our arrival.

XLI.—BARON ROTHSCHILD.

Sir Thomas Fowell Buxton to Miss Buxton.

DEVONSHIRE STREET, Feb. 14th, 1834.

We yesterday dined at Ham House to meet the Rothschilds, and very amusing it was. He (Rothschild) told us his life and adventures. He was the third son of the banker at Frankfort. "There was not," he said, "room enough for us all in that city. I dealt in English goods. One great trader came there who had the market to himself; he was quite the great man, and did us a favor if he sold us goods. Somehow I offended him, and he refused to show us his patterns. This was on a Tuesday. I said to my father, 'I will go to England.' I could speak nothing but German. On the Thursday I started; the nearer I got to England, the cheaper goods were. As soon as I got to Manchester I laid out all my money, things were so cheap; and I made good profit. I soon found that there were three profits—the raw material, the dying, and the manufacturing. I said to the manufacturer, 'I will supply you with material and dye, and you supply me with manufactured goods.' So I got three profits instead of one, and I could sell goods cheaper than anybody. In a short time I made my 20,000*l.* into 60,000*l.* My success all turned on one maxim. I said I can do what another man can, and so I am a match for the man with the patterns, and all the rest of them! Another advantage I had. I was an offhand man; I made a bargain at once. When I was settled in London, the East India Company had £800,000 of gold to sell. I went to the sale and bought it all. I knew the Duke of Wellington must have it; I had bought a great many of his bills at a discount. The Government sent for me, and said they must have it. When they had got it, they did not know how to get it to Portugal. I undertook all that, and I sent it through France, and that was the best business I ever did."

Another maxim, on which he seemed to place great reliance, was never to have any thing to do with an unlucky place or an unlucky man. "I have seen," said he, "many clever men, very clever men, who had not shoes to their feet! I never act with them. Their advice sounds very well, but fate is against them; they cannot get on themselves; and if they cannot do good to themselves, how can they do good to me?" By aid of these maxims he has acquired three millions of money.

"I hope," said ——, "that your children are not too fond of money and business, to the exclusion of more important things. I am sure you would not wish that." Rothschild: "I am sure I should wish that. I wish them to give mind and soul, and heart, and body, and every thing, to business. That is the way to be happy. It requires a great deal of boldness, and a great deal of caution, to make a great fortune; and when you have got it, it requires ten times as much wit to keep it. If I were to listen to all the projects proposed to me, I should ruin myself very soon. Stick to one business young man," said he to Edward; "stick to your brewery, and you may be the great brewer of London. Be a brewer, and a banker, and a merchant, and a manufacturer, and you will soon be in the 'Gazette.' One of my neighbors is a very ill-tempered man; he tries to vex me, and has built a great place for swine close to my walk. So when I go out, I hear first, grunt, grunt, squeak, squeak; but this does me no harm, I am always in good humor. Sometimes, to amuse myself, I give a beggar a guinea. He thinks it is a mistake, and for fear I should find it out, off he runs as hard as he can. I advise you to give a beggar a guinea sometimes; it it is very amusing."

The daughters are very pleasing. The second son is a mighty hunter, and the father lets him buy any horses he likes. He lately applied to the Emperor of Morocco for a first-rate Arab horse. The Emperor sent him a magnificent one, but he died as he landed in England. The poor youth said, very feelingly, "that was was the greatest misfortune he had ever suffered." And I felt strong sympathy with him. I forgot to say that soon after M. Rothschild came here, Bonaparte invaded Germany. "The Prince of Hesse Cassel," said Rothschild, "gave my father his money; there was no time to be lost, he sent it to me. I had £600,000 arrive unexpectedly by the post; and I put it to such good use, that the Prince made me a present of all his wine and linen."

XLII.—A SCOTCH ELECTION.

Francis Jeffrey to Lord Cockburn.

York, April, 1831.

My dear C——: I was duly elected at Malton yesterday. I got there on Tuesday at one o'clock, and, attended by twelve forward disciples, instantly set forth to call on my 700 electors, and solicit the honor of their votes. In three hours and a half I actually called at 635 doors, and shook 494 men by the hand. Next day the streets were filled with bands of music, and flags, and streamers of all descriptions, in the midst of which I was helped up, about eleven, to the dorsal ridge of a tall, prancing steed decorated with orange ribbons, having my reins and stirrups held by men in the borough liveries, and a long range of flags and music moving around me. In this state I paraded through all the streets at a foot pace, stopping at every turning to receive three huzzas, and to bow to all the women in the windows. At twelve I was safely deposited in the market-place, at the foot of a square-built scaffold, packed quite full of people; and after some dull ceremonies, was duly declared elected by a show of hands and fervent acclamations. After which I addressed the multitude, amounting, they say, to near 5,000 persons, in very eloquent and touching terms, and was then received into a magnificent high-backed chair, covered with orange silk, and gay with flags and streamers, on which I was borne on the shoulders of six electors, nodding majestically through all the streets and streetlings, and at length returned safe and glorious to my inn. At five o'clock I had to entertain about 120 of the most respectable of my constituents, and to make divers speeches till near eleven o'clock; having in the mean time sallied out at the head of twenty of my friends, to visit a party of nearly the same magnitude, who were regaling in an inferior inn, and whom we found in a state of far greater exaltation. All the Cayleys, male and female, were kind enough to come in and support me; and about eleven I contrived to get away, with Sir George and his son-in-law, and came out here with a great cavalcade about midnight. The thing is thought to have gone off brilliantly. What it has cost I do not know, but the accounts are to be settled by Lord Milton's agent, and sent to me to London. The place from which I write belongs to a Mr. Worsley, a man of large fortune, who has married one of Sir George Cayley's daughters, and has assembled their whole genealogy in his capacious mansion. You know I always took greatly to the family, and like them if possible better the more I see of them in their family circle. The youngest, who is about sixteen, and I, have long avowed a mutual flame; and the second, who is to be married next month, is nearly a perfect beauty. But it is the sweet blood, and the naturalness and gayety of heart which I chiefly admire in them; and after my lonely journey and tiresome election, the delight of roaming about these vernal valleys, in the idleness of a long sunny day, in the midst of their bright smiles and happy laughs, reconciles me to existence again. It is a strange huge house, built almost eighty years ago, on a sort of Italian model, and full of old pictures and books, and cabinets full of gimcracks, and portfolios crammed with antique original sketches and engravings, and closets full of old plate and rusty china, which would give Thomson and you, and Johnny Clerk in his better days, work enough for a month; though I, who have only a day to spare, prefer talking with living creatures. This is all very childish and foolish I confess, for a careful senator, at a great national crisis. But I have really been so hard worked and bothered of late, that you must excuse me if I enjoy one day of relaxation. I go off to-morrow at six o'clock, etc.

XLIII.—VISIT OF THE QUEEN OF FRANCE TO BRUSSELS.

Hugh S. Legaré to his Sisters.

BRUXELLES, March 24th, 1833.

MY DEAR SISTERS: I have adopted the plan of writing to you both at the same time, that there may be no heart-breaking jealousy between you about so important a matter as my attention.

I told mama I should give you a more particular account of what passed here during the French queen's visit to Brussels, which took place about two weeks ago, and continued until last

Monday afternoon, when she left this city, and arrived in Paris in less than twenty-four hours, having travelled all night. I have repeatedly mentioned how much I admire that great lady, with whom I had the honor of dining at the pretty chateau of Neuilly, near Paris, when I was there last summer. What I saw of her during her stay here, confirmed all those favorable impressions. Her grace, dignity, and affability (*condescenion* it may be, but there is no appearance of that), are really irresistible, and equalled only by her exemplary virtues as a wife and a mother—virtues which happen to shine forth more brilliantly this moment, in contrast with the public infamy of the Duchess of Berry.

The Queen arrived here, accompanied by her second daughter, the Princess Marie, and two ladies of honor, under the protection (as we should say of a *private* person) of her son and heir apparent, the Duke of Orleans, a well-looking young man of some two and twenty years or thereabouts. The day after their arrival was passed in the family circle, but on Sunday (the next day) there was a grand diplomatic dinner of fifty covers at court, at which I had the honor of assisting, with the British ambassador, the French, and their Secretaries of Legation, all the Ministers of State, the Presidents of the Senate and House of Representatives, some generals, the ladies of honor of the two Queens, etc.; and last, but by no means least, the Duke and Duchess d'Arenberg, who are decidedly at the head of society here, and, indeed, are of an *almost royal house.* As soon as all the guests were assembled in the *salle de reception*, and after the Duchess of Arenberg, who had been presented in private audience in another saloon, returned, the royal party made its appearance, the Queen of France leaning upon the arm of her son-in-law, King Leopold;

the Queen of the Belgians on that of her brother, the Duke of Orleans, and the Princess Marie accompanied by her Lady of Honor. The rest of the party only saluted at entering, and stopped near the door, but the Queen of the French went round the whole circle, beginning, of course, with our noble selves, the representatives of foreign nations, who you know are always at the head of every ceremony at least. The British ambassador was first presented. She recognized in him an old acquaintance (Heaven knows how far back!), and reminded him of the occasions on which they met. Her own ambassador, who returned from Paris with her, she soon despatched. Then came my turn; she had seen me not many months ago; hoped I liked my situation; asked after Gen. Wool (an officer sent out on some special errand by our Government last summer, who had been well received by the Court of France, and had afterwards visited Brussels with me, when I first came here), and so forth. In short, she addressed something appropriate to every individual in the circle, except the officers of the King's household, and all with that winning native grace so peculiar to a high-born and perfectly-bred Frenchwoman (by the by, she is an Italian, aunt of the Queen of Spain, who has been lately doing such fine things, and of the Duchess of Berry, who has been doing such naughty ones). The Grand-Marshal then announced to their majesties that dinner was served. They led the way into the banqueting hall (in the *grand apartments*, as they are called), as they had come into the *salle de reception*, except that this time the English Ambassador, as head of the diplomatic body (by *seniority*), gave his arm to the Princess Mary. As I had the third choice, I took the prettiest of our Queen's ladies, and I think the very prettiest woman in all Belgium, although she has three children married, one a daughter almost as old as herself. I was petrified with surprise when I found out the age of my favorite, whom I did not suspect of so many years, almost by half. But that discovery I had made long before this meeting, and I chose her with my eyes open and very deliberately. The lady in question is the Baronne d'Hoogvorst. She was dressed that day in very becoming style, and looked like a blooming wife of thirty. In Europe, you know, that is not old.

At table, the fashion in Europe is not like yours—for the master of the house to sit at one end, and the mistress at the other. The place of honor is at the side, and at the middle of the board. When I dined at Neuille, the Queen sat on one side, and the King opposite to her on the other; but Leopold and Louise are inseparable, at least at dinner, and, judging from their most amiable characters and affectionate dispositions, I should suppose everywhere else. The grand marshal of the palace here always takes his place opposite to their Majesties. And so it was on this occasion. On the right of the King sat the Queen of the French, on her right the Queen of the Belgians, next to her the Duke of Orleans, next the Duchess d'Arenberg, next Count de Latour Maubourg, and on the *left* of the King was the Princess Marie, next the English ambassador, and the grand marshal had on his right the lady of honor handed in by the Duke d'Arenberg, on whose right sat the Duke himself; on the left was Madame d'Hoogvorst, and next to her your humble servant, so that I sat immediately opposite to the Queen of the Belgians, whose sweet, modest face I am never tired of looking upon. The dinner was served with the highest magnificence of the Court, the crowd of servants in waiting being decked out in their most showy liveries (scarlet and gold for some, while others wore a more modest uniform, with swords at their sides), and the table itself covered with gold and silver, and at the dessert with Sèvres china. This last, which is the most beautiful painted china, manufactured near Paris, at a cost of near three hundred francs a *plate*, was a bridal present to the Queen from her father. A grand band of music played the most fashionable and admired pieces of the great German and Italian masters, at intervals during the dinner, which, in all other respects, went off just as Court dinners always do, with the gravest decorum; a conversation confined to two—with no variety except an occasional change from right to left, when one or the other of your neighbors, as it happens, is *run out* of small talk—and carried on, of course, in a sort of whisper. Certainly, however, it must be confessed that a vast table, covered with so much magnificence, and surrounded by ladies and gentlemen—the former sparkling with diamonds, the latter all in court embroidery—presents a very brilliant *coup d'œil.* I was never before so much struck with the effect of precious stones in a lady's toilette, as with the richly colored beams of light that glittered about the neck and head of the Duchess d'Arenberg, a very fine woman about thirty-five, who was arrayed in more than the glory of Solomon. The *worst* of a dinner at Court is that, after having got through the tedious formalities of the reception, and the *execution* (they endure a couple of hours or so), the whole company is marched back into the *salle de reception*, where coffee is served with *liqueurs*, and there are sometimes kept *standing* (for none but the ladies, who take their places at the Queen's round table after dinner, in the middle of the room, are allowed to sit), sometimes for another hour, or hour and a half. For me, whose habit is, and always has been, if possible, to stretch myself off at full length upon a sofa, or at least recline quite at my ease after dinner, this part of my diplomatic duties, aggravated as it is by being buttoned up close in a uniform coat made last summer, when I was by no means in such good case as I am now, is quite a serious task.

But I never suffered so much from it as at a concert given at Court two days after the dinner I speak of. All guests invited to a palace, but especially the members of the diplomatic corps, are expected to be very punctual, for, as Louis XVIII. is said to have remarked, "Punctuality is the politeness of kings." We were invited then to the said concert at three-quarters past seven o'clock, and what with the presentations, the slow progress of the processions through a *suite* of a half dozen rooms, and the musical performance itself, I was standing *four* mortal hours. To be sure I did not suffer alone, there being five or six hundred people present. The ladies had seats on two rows of benches at the two sides of a vast hall, leaving a space between for the circulation of the gentlemen invited, the waiters with refreshments, in short, every thing but *air;* for although it was freezing and snowing out of doors, our artificial atmosphere was so disagreeably heated, that our little Queen, in her delicate situation, could not bear it, and had to leave us amidst our *excruciating* delight at the various performance. The rest of the party exhibited a very tender solicitude at this untoward event, and went out with her but soon after they all returned except the King, and even he after a delay of some time longer. I own I was not *overpowered* by the music, though to be sure I had heard most of the performers before. They were all very good, but a concert is too stupid in itself for any thing but remarkable and exciting talent to make agreeable. * * * And thus ends my long history of the Queen of the French at Brussels.

XLIV.—YOUNG LADIES IN ENGLAND. THE ASCOT RACES.*

William H. Prescott to Miss Prescott.

LONDON, June 24th, 1850.

MY DEAR LIZZIE: As your mother tells me that you are to write to me this week, I will do the same good turn to you. What shall I tell you about? there are so many things that would interest you in this wonderful city. But first of all, I think, on reflection, you judged wisely in not coming. You would have had some lonely hours, and have been often rather awkwardly situated. Girls of your age make no great figure here in society. One never, or very rarely, meets them at dinner parties; and they are not so numerous in the evening parties as with us, unless it be the balls. Six out of seven women whom you meet in society are over thirty, and many of them over forty and fifty, not to say sixty. The older they are the more they are dressed and diamonded. Young girls dress little, and wear very little ornament indeed. They have not much money to spend on such costly luxuries. At the Ascot races yesterday, I happened to be next to Lady ——, a very pleasing girl, the youngest sister of Lord ——. She seemed disposed to bet on the horses; so I told her I would venture anywhere from a shilling to a sovereign. She said she never bet higher than a shilling, but on this occasion would go as high as half a crown. So she did, and lost it. It was quite an exciting race between a horse of Lord Eglinton's, named "Flying Dutchman," and a little mare of Lord Stanley's, named "Canezon." The former had won on several occasions, but the latter had lately begun to

* This letter is taken from the biography of Mr. Ticknor, the most interesting literary biography probably in our language.—H.

make a name in the world, and Lord Stanley's friends were eagerly backing her. It was the most beautiful show in the world.

But I will begin with the beginning. I went with the Lawrences. We went by railway to Windsor, then took a carriage to Ascot, some half dozen miles distant. The crowds of carriages, horses, etc., on the road, filled the air with a whirlwind of dust, and I should have been blinded but for a blue veil which was lent me to screen my hat and face. The Swedish Minister, who furnished these accommodations, set the example by tying himself up. On reaching Ascot we were admitted to the *salon*, which stands against the winning post, and which is occupied by the Queen when there. It was filled with gay company, all in high spirits. Lord Stanley was looking forward to a triumph, though he talked coolly about it. He is one of the ablest, perhaps the ablest debater in Parliament, and next Monday will make a grand assault on the Cabinet. This is the way he relieves himself from the cares of public life. I suspect he was quite as much interested in the result of the race yesterday as he will be in the result of the parliamentary battle on Monday.

The prize, besides a considerable stake of money from subscription, was a most gorgeous silver vase, the annual present of the Emperor of Russia for the Ascot races. It represents Hercules taming the horses of Diomed, beautifully sculptured, making an ornament for a sideboard or a table some five feet in height, and eighteen inches square. What a trophy for the castle of the Earl of Derby or for the Eglinton halls in Scotland!

The horses were paraded up and down before the spectators; betting ran very high—men and women, nobles and commoners, who crowd the ground by thousands, all entering into it. Five horses started on a heat of two miles and a half. The little bay mare led off gallantly—"Flying Dutchman" seemed to lose ground—the knowing ones began to shake—and the odds rose in "Canezon's" favor, when, just as they were within half a mile of the goal, Lord Eglinton's jockey gave his horse the rein, and he went off in gallant style—not running, but touching the ground in a succession of flying leaps that could hardly have brushed the wet from the grass, for it began to rain. There was a general sensation; bets changed; the cry was for the old favorite; and as the little troop shot by us, "Flying Dutchman" came in at the head, by the length of several rods, before all the field. Then there was a shouting and congratulations, while the mob followed the favorite horse as if they would devour him. He was brought directly under our windows, and Lady Eglinton felt, I have no doubt, as much love for him at the moment as for any of her children. It was a glorious triumph, and the race was hers, or her lord's, whom I did not see. Now I do not feel the least excited by all this, but excessively tired, and I would not go to another race if I could do it by walking into the next street; that is, if I had to sit it out, as I did here, for three mortal hours. How hard the English people are driven for amusement!

Coming home, we drove through the Royal Park at Windsor, among trees hundreds of years old, under which troops of deer were lazily grazing, secure from all molestation. The Thames is covered with swans, which nobody would dare to injure. How beautiful all this is! I wish, dear Lizzie, you could have a peep at the English country, with its superb, wide-stretching lawns, its numerous flocks of sheep everywhere dotting the fields, and even the parks in town, and the beautiful white cows, all as clean as if they had been scrubbed down. England, in the country, is without a rival. But in town the houses are all dingy, and most of them as black as a chimney with the smoke. This hangs like a funeral pall over the city, penetrating the houses, and discoloring the curtains and furniture in a very short time. You would be amused with the gay scene which the streets in this part of the town present. Splendid equipages fill the great streets as far as the eye can reach, blazing with rich colors, and silver mountings, and gaudy liveries. Every thing here tells of a proud and luxurious aristocracy. I shall see enough of them to-day, as I have engagements of one kind or another to four houses before bedtime, which is now with me very regularly about twelve, sometimes later, but I do not like to have it later. Why have I no letter on my table from home? I trust I shall find one there this evening, or I shall, after all, have a heavy heart, which is far from gay in this gayety. Your affectionate father,

William H. Prescott.

BOOK THE SECOND.

Letters of Pleasantry, Sentiment, and Fancy.

BOOK THE SECOND.

LETTERS OF PLEASANTRY, SENTIMENT, AND FANCY.

I.—LIFE OF A MAID OF HONOR AT COURT.

*Alexander Pope to Teresa and Martha Blount.**

You cannot be surprised to find him a dull correspondent whom you have known so long for a dull companion. And though I am pretty sensible, if I have any wit, I may as well write to show it as not; yet I will content myself with giving

* This letter, although belonging more appropriately to the first book, has been introduced here, in connection with many others of Pope, that the reader might be able more readily to form a just estimate of this celebrated correspondence. As it is the fashion to depreciate Pope's letters, the editor may be pardoned for introducing a long extract from Thackeray. "With the exception of his love letters, I do not know," says Thackeray, "in the range of our literature, volumes more delightful than the Pope correspondence. You live in them in the finest company in the world. A little stately, perhaps, a little *apprêté*, and conscious that they are speaking to whole generations who are listening; but in the tone of their voices, pitched, as no doubt they are, beyond the mere conversation key, in the expression of their thoughts, their various views and natures, there is something generous, and cheering, and ennobling. You are in the society of men who have filled the greatest parts in the world's story—you are with St. John, the statesman; Peterborough, the conqueror; Swift, the greatest wit of all times; Gay, the kindliest laugher: it is a privilege to sit in that company. Delightful and generous banquet! with a little faith and a little fancy, any one of us here may enjoy it, and conjure up those great figures out of the past and listen to their wit and wisdom. Mind that there is always a certain cachet about great men, they

you as plain a history of my pilgrimage as Purchas himself, or as John Bunyan could do of his *walking through the wilderness of this world.*

First, then, I went by water to Hampton Court, unattended

may be as mean on many points as you or I, but they carry their great air; they speak of common life more largely and generously than common men do, they regard the world with a manlier countenance and see its real features more fairly than the timid shufflers who only dare to look up at life through blinkers, or to have an opinion when there is a crowd to back it; he who reads these noble records of a past age, salutes and reverences the great spirits who adorn it. You may go home now and talk with St. John; you may take a volume from your library and listen to Swift and Pope.

"Might I give counsel to any young hearer I would say to him, try to frequent the company of your betters. In books and life that is the most wholesome society; learn to admire rightly, the great pleasure of life is that. Note what the great men admired: they admired great things; narrow spirits admire basely, and worship meanly. I know nothing in any story more gallant and cheering than the love and friendship which this company of famous men bore toward one another. There never has been a society of men more friendly, as there never was one more illustrious. Who dared quarrel with Mr. Pope, great and famous himself, for liking the society of men great and famous—and for liking them for the qualities which made them so? A mere pretty fellow from White's could not have written the 'Patriot King,' and would very likely have despised little Mr. Pope, the decrepit Papist, whom St. John held to be one of the best and greatest of men. A mere nobleman of the Court could no more have won Barcelona than he could have written Peterborough's letters to Pope, which are as witty as Congreve's; a mere Irish dean could not have written Gulliver; and all these men loved Pope, and Pope loved all these men. To name his friends is to name the best men of his time. Addison had a senate; Pope reverenced his equals. He spoke of Swift with respect and admiration always.

"His admiration for Bolingbroke was so great that when some one said of his friend, 'There is something in that great man which looks as if he was placed here by mistake.' 'Yes,' Pope answered, 'and when the comet appeared to us a month or two ago, I had sometimes an imagination that it might possibly be come to carry him home, as a coach comes to one's door for visitors.' So these great spirits spoke of one another. Show me six of the dullest middle-aged gentlemen that ever dawdled round a club-table, so faithful and so friendly."—H.

by all but my own virtues, which were not of so modest a nature to keep themselves or me concealed; for I met the Prince with all his ladies on horseback coming from hunting. Mrs. B. and Mrs. L. took me into protection (contrary to the laws against harboring Papists), and gave me a dinner with something I liked better, an opportunity of conversation with Mrs. H.* We all agreed that the life of a maid of honor was of all things the most miserable, and wished that every woman who envied it had a specimen of it. To eat Westphalian ham in a morning, ride over hedges and ditches in borrowed hacks, come home in the heat of the day with a fever, and, what is worse a hundred times, with a red mark on the forehead from an uneasy hat; all this may qualify them to make excellent wives for fox-hunters, and bear abundance of ruddy-complexioned children. As soon as they can wipe off the sweat of the day they must simper an hour, and catch cold in the Princess's, from thence (as Shakespeare has it) to dinner, *with what appetite they may*, and after that till midnight, walk, work, or think, which they please. I can easily believe no lone house in Wales, with a mountain and a rookery, is more contemplative than this Court; and as a proof of it, I need only tell you Mrs. L. walked with me three or four hours by moonlight, and we met no creature of any quality but the King, who gave audience to the vice-chamberlain all alone under the garden wall.

In short, I heard of no ball, assembly, basset-table, or any place where two or three were gathered together, except Madam Kilmansegg's; to which I had the honor to be invited and the grace to stay away.

* The three ladies referred to were Mary Bellenden and Mary Lepell, maids of honor to the Princess, and Mrs. Howard, afterwards Countess of Suffolk. It was usual at the time to call unmarried ladies Mistress.

I was heartily tired, and posted to —— Park; there we had an excellent discourse of quackery; Dr. S—— was mentioned with honor. Lady —— walked a whole hour abroad without dying after it, at least in the time I stayed, though she seemed to be fainting, and had convulsive motions several times in her head. I arrived in the forest by Tuesday noon, having fled from the face (I wish I could say the horned face) of Moses, who dined in the midway thither. I passed the rest of the day in those woods, where I have so often enjoyed a book and a friend. I made a hymn as I passed through, which ended with a sigh I will not tell you the meaning of.

Your doctor is gone the way of all his patients, and was hard put to it how to dispose of an estate miserably unwieldy, and splendidly unuseful to him. Sir Samuel Garth says, that for Radcliffe to leave a library, was as if a eunuch should found a seraglio.* Dr. S—— lately told a lady he wondered she could be alive after him; she made answer, she wondered at it for two reasons, because Dr. Radcliffe was dead, and because Dr. S—— was living. I am your, etc.

II.--HUMOR OF WYCHERLEY IN HIS LAST ILLNESS.

Alexander Pope to Edward Blount.

Jan. 21st, 1715–'16.

I know of nothing that will be so interesting to you at present, as some circumstances of the last act of that eminent comic poet, and our friend, Wycherley. He had often told me, as I doubt not he did all his acquaintance, that he would marry as soon as his life was despaired of; accordingly, a few days before

* It was notorious that he had little learning.

his death, he underwent the ceremony; and joined together those two sacraments which, wise men say, should be the last we receive; for, if you observe, matrimony is placed after extreme unction in our Catechism, as a kind of hint of the order of time in which they are to be taken. The old man then lay down, satisfied in the conscience of having by this one act paid his just debts, obliged a woman, who (he was told) had merit, and shown an heroic resentment of the ill usage of his next heir. Some hundred pounds which he had with the lady discharged those debts; a jointure of four hundred a year made her a recompense; and the nephew he left to comfort himself as well as he could, with the miserable remains of a mortgaged estate. I saw our friend twice after this was done, less peevish in his sickness than he used to be in his health; neither much afraid of dying, nor (which in him had been more likely) much ashamed of marrying. The evening before he expired he called his young wife to the bedside, and earnestly entreated her not to deny him one request, the last he should make. Upon her assurances of consenting to it, he told her, "My dear, it is only this, that you will never marry an old man again." I cannot help remarking, that sickness, which often destroys both wit and wisdom, yet seldom has power to remove that talent which we call humor: Mr. Wycherley showed this, even in this half compliment; though I think his request a little hard, for why should he bar her from doubling her jointure on the same easy terms?

So trivial as these circumstances are, I should not be displeased myself to know such trifles, when they concern or characterize any eminent person. The wisest and wittiest of men are seldom wiser or wittier than others in these sober moments;

at least our friend ended much in the character he had lived in; and Horace's rule for a play may as well be applied to him as a playwright,

> "Servetur ad imum,
> Qualis ab inceptu processerit, et sibi constet."

I am, &c.

III.—LORD BOLINGBROKE'S LIFE IN THE COUNTRY.

Alexander Pope to Dr. Swift.

DAWLEY, June 28th, 1728.

I now hold the pen for my Lord Bolingbroke, who is reading your letter between two haycocks; but his attention is somewhat diverted by casting his eyes on the clouds, not in admiration of what you say, but for fear of a shower. He is pleased with your placing him in the triumvirate, between yourself and me; though he says that he doubts he shall fare like Lepidus, while one of us runs away with all the power like Augustus, and another with all the pleasures like Anthony. It is upon a foresight of this that he has fitted up his farm, and you will agree that this scheme of retreat at least is not founded upon weak appearances. Upon his return from the bath all peccant humors, he finds, are purged out of him; and his great temperance and economy are so signal that the first is fit for my constitution, and the latter would enable you to lay up so much money as to buy a bishopric in England. As to the return of his health and vigor, were you here, you might inquire of his hay-makers; but as to his temperance, I can answer that (for one whole day) we have had nothing for dinner but mutton broth, beans and bacon, and a barn-door fowl.

Now his Lordship is run after his cart, I have a moment left to myself to tell you, that I overheard him yesterday agree with a painter for £200 to paint his country hall with trophies of rakes, spades, prongs, etc., and other ornaments, merely to countenance his calling this place a farm. Now turn over a new leaf—

He bids me assure you he should be sorry not to have more schemes of kindness for his friends than of ambition for himself; there, though his schemes may be weak, the motives at least are strong; and he says further, if you could bear as great a fall and decrease of your revenues, as he knows by experience he can, you would not live in Ireland an hour.

The Dunciad is going to be printed in all pomp, with the inscription which makes me proudest. It will be attended with *Prœme*, *Prolegomena*, *Testimonia Scriptorum*, *Index Authorum*, and notes *Variorum*. As to the latter, I desire you to read over the text, and make a few in any way you like best,* whether dry raillery, upon the style and way of commenting of trivial critics; or humorous, upon the authors in the poem; or historical, of persons, of places, times; or explanatory; or collecting the parallel passages of the ancients. Adieu. I am pretty well, my mother not ill, Dr. Arbuthnot vexed with his fever by intervals; I am afraid he declines, and we shall lose a worthy man: I am troubled about him very much.

Am, etc.

IV.—TEMPER AND AMUSEMENTS OF SWIFT.

Dr. Swift to Lord Bolingbroke.

DUBLIN, March 21st, 1729.

You tell me you have not quitted the design of collecting, writing, etc. This is the answer of every sinner who defers his

* Dr. Swift did so.

repentance. I wish Mr. Pope was as great an urger as I, who long for nothing more than to see truth under your hands, laying all detraction in the dust. I find myself disposed every year, or rather every month, to be more angry and revengeful; and my rage is so ignoble, that it descends even to resent the folly and baseness of the enslaved people among whom I live. I knew an old lord in Leicestershire, who amused himself with mending pitchforks and spades for his tenants *gratis*. Yet I have higher ideas left, if I were nearer to objects on which I might employ them; and contemning my private fortune, would gladly cross the channel and stand by, while my betters were driving the boars out of the garden, if there be any probable expectation of such an endeavor. When I was of your age I often thought of death, but now after a dozen years more, it is never out of my mind, and terrifies me less. I conclude that Providence hath ordered our fears to decrease with our spirits; and yet I love *la bagatelle* better than ever; for finding it troublesome to read at night, and the company here growing tasteless, I am always writing bad prose, or worse verses, either of rage or raillery, whereof some few escape to give offence or mirth, and the rest are burnt.

They print some Irish trash in London, and charge it on me, which you will clear me of to my friends, for all are spurious except one* paper, for which Mr. Pope very lately chid me. I remember your lordship used to say, that a few good speakers would in time carry any point that was right; and that the common method of a majority, by calling, To the question, would never hold long, when reason was on the other side. Whether politics do not change like gaming, by the invention of new

* Entitled, *A Libel on Dr. Delany, and a certain great Lord.*

tricks, I am ignorant; but I believe in your time you would never, as a minister, have suffered an act to pass through the H. of Commons, only because you were sure of a majority in the H. of Lords to throw it out; because it would be unpopular, and consequently a loss of reputation. Yet this we are told hath been the case in the qualification bill relating to pensioners. It should seem to me that corruption, like avarice, hath no bounds. I had opportunities to know the proceedings of your ministry better than any other man of my rank; and having not much to do, I have often compared it with these last sixteen years of a profound peace all over Europe, and we running seven millions in debt. I am forced to play at small game, to set the beasts here a madding, merely for want of better game: *Tendanda via est qua me quoque passim*, etc. The d—— take those politics, where a dunce might govern for a dozen years together. I will come in person to England, if I am provoked, and send for the dictator from the plough. I disdain to say, *O mihi præteritos*—but *cruda deo viridisque senectus*. Pray, my lord, how are the gardens? have you taken down the mount, and removed the yew hedges? Have you not bad weather for the spring corn? Has Mr. Pope gone farther in his ethic poem? and is the head-land sown with wheat? and what says Polybius? and how does my lord St. John? which last question is very material to me, because I love Burgundy, and riding between Twickenham and Dawley. I built a wall five years ago, and when the masons played the knaves, nothing delighted me so much as to stand by, while my servants threw down what was amiss: I have likewise seen a monkey overthrow all the dishes and plates in a kitchen, merely for the pleasure of seeing them tumble, and hearing the clatter they made in their fall. I wish you would invite me to such another entertainment; but you think, as I ought to think, that it is time for me to have done with the world, and so I would, if I could get into a better before I was called into the best, and not die here in a rage, like a poisoned rat in a hole. I wonder you are not ashamed to let me pine away in this kingdom while you are out of power.

I come from looking over the *melange* above written, and declare it to be a true copy of my present disposition, which must needs please you, since nothing was ever more displeasing to myself. I desire you to present my most humble respects to my lady.

V.—THE TRUE PHILOSOPHY FOR OLD AGE.

Lord Bolingbroke to Dr. Swift.

March 29th, 1730.

I have delayed several posts answering your letter of January last, in hopes of being able to speak to you about a project which concerns us both, but me the most, since the success of it would bring us together. It has been a good while in my head, and at my heart: if it can be set a-going, you shall hear more of it. I was ill in the beginning of the winter for near a week, but in no danger either from the nature of my distemper, or from the attendance of three physicians. Since that bilious intermitting fever, I have had, as I had before, better health than the regard I have paid to health deserves. We are both in the decline of life, my dear Dean, and have been some years going down the hill; let us make the passage as smooth as we can. Let us fence against physical evil by care, and the use of those means which experience must have pointed out to us; let us fence against moral evil by philosophy. I renounce the alternative you propose; but we may, nay (if we will follow nature, and do not work up imagination against her plainest dictates), we shall of course grow every year more indifferent to life, and to the affairs and interests of a system out of which we are soon to go. This is much better than stupidity. The decay of passion strengthens philosophy; for passion may decay and stupidity not succeed. *Passions* (says Pope, our divine, as you will see one time or other) are the gales of life: let us not complain that they do not blow a storm. What hurt does age do us, in subduing what we toil to subdue all our lives? It is now six in the morning; I recall the time (and am glad it is over) when about this hour I used to be going to bed, surfeited with pleasure, or jaded with business; my head often full of schemes, and my heart as often full of anxiety. Is it a misfortune, think you, that I rise at this hour, refreshed, serene, and calm? that the past, and even the present affairs of life, stand like objects at a distance from me, where I can keep off the disagreeable so as not to be strongly affected by them, and from whence I can draw the others nearer to me? Passions in their force would bring all these, nay, even future contingencies, about my ears at once, and Reason would but ill defend me in the scuffle.

I leave Pope to speak for himself, but I must tell you how much my wife is obliged to you. She says she would find strength enough to nurse you if you was here, and yet, God knows, she is extremely weak. The slow fever works under, and mines the constitution; we keep it off sometimes, but still it returns, and makes new breaches before Nature can repair the old ones. I am not ashamed to say to you, that I admire her more every hour of my life. Death is not to her the King of Terrors; she beholds him without the least. When she suffers much, she wishes for him as a deliverer from pain; when life is tolerable, she looks on him with dislike, because he is to separate her from those friends to whom she is more attached than to life itself. You shall not stay for my next, as long as you have done for this letter; and in every one Pope shall write something much better than the scraps of old philosophers, which were the presents, *munuscula*, that stoical fop Seneca used to send in every epistle to his friend Lucilius.

P. S. My Lord has spoken justly of his lady; why not I of my mother? Yesterday was her birthday, now entering on the ninety-first year of her age; her memory much diminished, but her senses very little hurt, her sight and hearing good; she sleeps not ill, eats moderately, drinks water, says her prayers; this is all she does. I have reason to thank God for continuing so long to me a very good and tender parent, and for allowing me to exercise, for some years, those cares which are now as necessary to her as hers have been to me. An object of this sort daily before one's eyes very much softens the mind, but perhaps may hinder it from the willingness of contracting other ties of the like domestic nature, when one finds how painful it is even to enjoy the tender pleasures. I have formerly made some strong efforts to get and to deserve a friend; perhaps it were wiser never to attempt it, but live extempore, and look upon the world only as a place to pass thro', just pay your hosts their due, disperse a little charity, and hurry on. Yet I am just now writing (or rather planning) a book, to make mankind look upon this life with comfort and pleasure, and put mortality in good humor. And just now too, I am going to see one I love very tenderly; and to-morrow to entertain several civil people, whom if we call friends, it is by the courtesy of England—*Sic, sic juvat ire sub umbras.* While we do live, we must make the best of life,

> "Cantantes licet usque (minus via lædet) eamus,"

as the shepherd said in Virgil, when the road was long and heavy. I am yours.

VI.—ON HIS RECOVERY, AND THE DEATH OF CONGREVE.

Alexander Pope to Mr. Gay.

I am glad to hear of the progress of your recovery; and the oftener I hear it the better, when it becomes easy to you to give it me. I so well remember the consolation you were to me in my mother's former illness, that it doubles my concern at this time not to be able to be with you, or you able to be with me. Had I lost her, I would have been nowhere else but with you during your confinement. I have now past five weeks without once going from home, and without any company but for three or four of the days. Friends rarely stretch their kindness so far as ten miles. My Lord Bolingbroke and Mr. Bethel have not forgotten to visit me; the rest (except Mrs. Blount once) were contented to send messages. I never passed so melancholy a time, and now Mr. Congreve's death touches me nearly. It was twenty years and more that I have known him. Every year carries away something dear with it, till we outlive all tendernesses, and become wretched individuals again, as we begun. Adieu! This is my birthday, and this is my reflection upon it:

> With added days, if life give nothing new,
> But, like a sieve, let every pleasure thro';
> Some joy still lost, as each vain year runs o'er,
> And all we gain, some sad reflection more!
> Is this a birthday?—'Tis, alas! too clear,
> 'Tis but the fun'ral of the former year.

VII.—WRITTEN FROM THE TOWER.

Bishop of Rochester to Alexander Pope.

THE TOWER, April 10th, 1723.

DEAR SIR: I thank you for all the instances of your friendship, both before and since my misfortunes. A little time will complete them, and separate you and me for ever. But in what part of the world soever I am, I will live mindful of your sincere kindness to me, and will please myself with the thought that I still live in your esteem and affection, as much as ever I did, and that no accidents of life, no distance of time, or place, will alter you in that respect. It never can me, who have loved and valued you ever since I knew you, and shall not fail to do it when I am not allowed to tell you so, as the case will soon be. Give my faithful services to Dr. Arbuthnot, and thanks for what he sent me, which was much to the purpose, if any thing can be said to be to the purpose in a case that is already determined. Let him know my defence will be such, that neither my friends need blush for me, nor will my enemies have great occasion to triumph, though sure of the victory. I shall want his advice before I go abroad, in many things; but I question whether I shall be permitted to see him, or anybody, but such as are absolutely necessary towards the dispatch of my private affairs. If so, God bless you both; and may no part of the ill fortune that attends me ever pursue either of you! I know not but I may call upon you at my hearing to say something about my way of spending my time at the deanry, which did not seem calculated towards managing plots and conspiracies. But of that I shall consider. You and I have spent many hours together upon much pleasanter subjects, and, that I may preserve the old custom, I shall not part with you now till I have closed this letter, with three lines of Milton, which you will, I know, readily, and not without some degree of concern apply to your ever affectionate, etc.

> "Some nat'ral tears he dropt, but wip'd them soon:
> The world was all before him, where to choose
> His place of rest, and Providence his guide."

VIII.—IN ANSWER.

Alexander Pope to the Bishop of Rochester.

April 20th, 1723.

It is not possible to express what I think, and what I feel; only this, that I have thought and felt for nothing but you for some time past, and shall think of nothing so long for the time to come. The greatest comfort I had was an intention (which I would have made practicable) to have attended you in your journey, to which I had brought that person to consent who only could have hindered me, by a tie which, though it may be more tender, I do not think more strong than that of friendship. But I fear there will be no way left me to tell you this great truth, that I remember you, that I love you, that I am grateful to you, that I entirely esteem and value you; no way but that one which needs no open warrant to authorize it, or secret conveyance to secure it; which no bills can preclude and no Kings prevent; a way that can reach to any part of the world where you may be; where the very whisper, or even the wish, of a friend must not be heard, or even suspected. By this way I dare tell my esteem and affection of you, to your enemies in the gates, and you, and they, and their sons, may hear of it.

You prove yourself, my Lord, to know me for the friend I

am, in judging that the manner of your defence, and your reputation by it, is a point of the highest concern to me, and assuring me it shall be such that none of your friends shall blush for you. Let me further prompt you to do yourself the best and most lasting justice; the instruments of your fame to posterity will be in your own hands. May it not be that Providence has appointed you to some great and useful work, and calls you to it this severe way? You may more eminently, and more effectually, serve the public even now, than in the stations you have so honorably filled. Think of Tully, Bacon, and Clarendon:* is it not the latter, the disgraced part of their lives, which you most envy, and which you would choose to have lived?

I am tenderly sensible of the wish you express, that no part of your misfortune may pursue me. But, God knows, I am every day less and less fond of my native country (so torn as it is by party rage), and begin to consider a friend in exile as a friend in death; one gone before, where I am not unwilling nor unprepared to follow after, and where (however various or uncertain the roads and voyages of another world may be) I cannot but entertain a pleasing hope that we may meet again.

I faithfully assure you that in the mean time there is no one, living or dead, of whom I shall think oftener or better than of you. I shall look upon you as in a state between both, in which you will have from me all the passions and warm wishes that can attend the living, and all the respect and tender sense of loss that we feel for the dead. And I shall ever depend upon your constant friendship, kind memory, and good offices, though I

* Clarendon, indeed, wrote his best works in his banishment, but the best of Bacon's were written before his disgrace, and the best of Tully's after his return from exile.

were never to see or hear the effects of them; like the trust we have in benevolent spirits, who, though we never see or hear them, we think are constantly serving us and praying for us.

Whenever I am wishing to write to you, I shall conclude you are intentionally doing so to me, and every time that I think of you I will believe you are thinking of me. I never shall suffer to be forgotten (nay, to be but faintly remembered) the honor, the pleasure, the pride, I must ever have, in reflecting how frequently you have delighted me, how kindly you have distinguished me, how cordially you have advised me; in conversation, in study, I shall always want you, and wish for you; in my most lively, and in my most thoughtful hours, I shall equally bear about me the impressions of you; and perhaps it will not be in this life only that I shall have cause to remember and acknowledge the friendship of the Bishop of Rochester.

I am, etc.

IX.—FEELINGS OF AN EXILE.

The Bishop of Rochester to Alexander Pope.

PARIS, NOV. 23, 1731.

You will wonder to see me in print; but how could I avoid it? The dead and the living, my friends and my foes, at home and abroad, called upon me to say something, and the reputation of an* history, which I and all the world value, must have suffered had I continued silent. I have printed it here, in hopes that somebody may venture to reprint it in England, notwithstanding these two frightening words at the close of it.†

* Earl of Clarendon's.

† The Bishop's name, set to his vindication of Bishop Smalridge, Dr. Aldrich, and himself, from the scandalous reflections of Oldmixon, relating to

Whether that happens or not, it is fit you should have a sight of it, who, I know, will read it with some degree of satisfaction, as it is mine, though it should have (as it really has) nothing else to recommend it. Such as it is, *Extremum hoc munus morientis habeto;* for that may well be the case, considering that within a few months I am entering into my seventieth year, after which even the healthy and the happy cannot much depend upon life, and will not, if they are wise, much desire it. Whenever I go you will lose a friend who loves and values you extremely, if in my circumstauces I can be said to be lost to any one, when dead, more than I am already whilst living. I expected to have heard from you by Mr. Morice, and wondered a little that I did not; but he owns himself in a fault for not giving you due notice of his motions. It was not amiss that you forbore writing on a head wherein I promised more than I was able to perform. Disgraced men fancy sometimes that they preserve an influence, where, when they endeavor to exert it, they soon see their mistake. I did so, my good friend, and acknowledge it under my hand. You sounded the coast and found out my error, it seems, before I was aware of it. But enough on this subject.

What are they doing in England to the honor of letters, and particularly what are you doing? *Ipse quid audes? Quæ circumvolitas agilis Thyma?* Do you pursue the moral plan you marked out, and seemed sixteen months ago so intent upon? Am I to see it perfected ere I die, and are you to enjoy the reputation of it while you live? or do you rather choose to leave the marks of your friendship, like the legacies of a will, to be read and enjoyed only by those who survive you? Were I as near

the publication of Lord Clarendon's history. Paris, 1731, 4to, since reprinted in England.

you, as I have been I should hope to peep into the manuscript before it was finished. But alas! there is, and will ever probably be, a great deal of land and sea between us. How many books have come out of late in your parts which you think I should be glad to peruse? Name them; the catalogue, I believe, will not cost you much trouble. They must be good ones indeed to challenge any part of my time, now I have so little of it left. I, who squandered whole days heretofore, now husband hours when the glass begins to run low, and care not to misspend them on trifles. At the end of the lottery of life our last minutes, like tickets left in the wheel, rise in their valuation; they are not of so much worth, perhaps, in themselves as those which preceded, but we are apt to prize them more, and with reason. I do so, my dear friend, and yet think the most precious minutes of my life are well employed in reading what you write. But this is a satisfaction I cannot much hope for, and therefore must betake myself to others less entertaining. Adieu, dear sir; and forgive me engaging with one whom you, I think, have reckoned among the heroes of the Dunciad. It was necessary for me either to accept of his dirty challenge, or to have suffered in the esteem of the world by declining it.

My respects to your mother. I send one of these papers for Dean Swift, if you have an opportunity and think it worth while to convey it. My country at this distance seems to me a strange sight; I know not how it appears to you, who are in the midst of the scene, and yourself a part of it; I wish you would tell me. You may write safely to Mr. Morice, by the honest hand that conveys this, and will return into these parts before Christmas. Sketch out a rough draft of it, that I may be able to judge whether a return to it be really eligible, or whether I should not, like the chemist in the bottle, upon hearing Don Quevedo's account of Spain, desire to be corked up again.

After all, I do and must love my country, with all its faults and blemishes; even that part of the constitution which wounded me unjustly, and itself, through my side, shall ever be dear to me. My last wish shall be like that of Father Paul, *Esto perpetua!* and when I die at a distance from it, it will be in the same manner as Virgil describes the expiring Peloponnesian,

> "Sternitur,
> Et dulces moriens reminiscitur Argos."

Do I still live in the memory of my friends, as they certainly do in mine? I have read a good many of your paper squabbles about me, and am glad to see such free concessions on that head, though made with no view of doing me a pleasure, but merely of loading another. I am, &c.

X.—ON THE EVE OF HIS EXECUTION.*

Mrs. Penruddock to her Husband.

MY DEAR HEART: My sad parting was so far from making me forget you, that I scarce thought upon myself since; but wholly upon you. Those dear embraces, which I yet feel, and shall never lose, being the faithful testimonies of an indulgent husband, have charmed my soul to such a reverence of your remembrance, that, were it possible, I would with my own blood cement your dead limbs to love again, and (with reverence) think

* Steele, in the Lover, publishes the two exquisite letters in the text, which are said to have passed between a husband and his wife on the eve of the latter's execution upon the scaffold. The gentleman was barbarously sentenced to die, at Exeter, during the rebellion.—H.

it no sin to rob heaven a little longer of a martyr. Oh! my dear, you must now pardon my passion, this being my last (oh, fatal words!) that ever you will receive from me; and know that, until the last minute that I can imagine you shall live, I shall sacrifice the prayers of a Christian, and the groans of an afflicted wife. And when you are not (which sure by sympathy I shall know), I shall wish my own dissolution with you that, so we may go hand in hand to heaven. 'Tis too late to tell you what I have, or rather what I have not done for you; how, being turned out of doors because I came to beg mercy. The Lord lay not your blood to their charge. I would fain discourse longer with you, but dare not; passion begins to drown my reason, and will rob me of my *devoirs*, which is all I have left to serve you. Adieu, therefore, ten thousand times, my dearest dear; and since I must never see you more, take this prayer. May your faith be so strengthened that your constancy may continue; and then I know heaven will receive you—whither grief and love will, in a short time (I hope) translate, my dear, your sad but constant wife, even to love your ashes when dead.

Arundel Penruddock.

May 3d, 1665, eleven o'clock at night. Your children beg your blessing, and present their duties to you.

XI.—REPLY TO THE PRECEDING LETTER.

Mr. Penruddock to his Wife.

Dearest, best of Creatures! I had taken leave of the world when I received yours. It did at once recall my fondness to life, and enable me to resign it. As I am sure I shall leave none behind me like you, which weakens my resolution to part from you; so, when I reflect I am going to a place where there are none but such as you, I recover my courage. But fondness breaks in upon me, and as I would not have my tears flow to-morrow, when your husband, and the father of our dear babes, is a public spectacle, do not think meanly of me that I give way to grief now in private, when I see my sand run so fast, and within a few hours I am to leave you helpless, and exposed to the merciless and insolent that have wrongfully put me to a shameless death, and will object the shame to my poor children. I thank you for all your goodness to me, and will endeavor so to die as to do nothing unworthy of that virtue in which we have mutually supported each other, and for which I desire you not to repine that I am first to be rewarded, since you ever preferred me to yourself in all other things. Afford me, with cheerfulness, the precedence in this. I desire your prayers in the article of death; for my own will then be offered for you and yours.

J. PENRUDDOCK.

XII.—CROSSING THE CHANNEL—SEA-SICKNESS.

Lady M. W. Montagu to the Abbé.

DOVER, Oct. 31st, O. S., 1718.

I am willing to take your word for it, that I shall really oblige you by letting you know, as soon as possible, my safe passage over the water. I arrived this morning at Dover, after being tossed a whole night in the packet boat in so violent a manner that the master, considering the weakness of his vessel, thought it proper to remove the mail, and give us notice of the danger. We called a little fishing boat, which could hardly make up to us; while all the people on board us were crying to Heaven. It is hard to imagine one's self in a scene of greater horror than on such an occasion; and yet shall I own it to you? Though I was not at all willing to be drowned, I could not forbear being entertained at the double distress of a fellow passenger. She was an English lady that I had met at Calais, who desired me to let her go over with me in my cabin. She had bought a fine point-head, which she was contriving to conceal from the custom-house officers. When the wind blew high, and our little vessel cracked, she fell very heartily to her prayers, and thought wholly of her soul. When it seemed to abate, she returned to the worldly care of her head-dress, and addressed herself to me: "*Dear madam, will you take care of this point? If it should be lost! Oh, Lord, we shall all be lost! Lord, have mercy on my soul! Pray, madam, take care of this head-dress.*" This easy transition from her soul to her head-dress, and the alternate agonies that both gave her, made it hard to determine which she thought of greatest value. But, however, the scene was not so diverting but I was glad to get rid of it and be thrown into the little boat, but with some hazard of breaking my neck. It brought me safe hither, and I cannot help looking with partial eyes upon my native land. That partiality was certainly given us by nature, to prevent rambling—the effect of an ambitious thirst after knowledge, which we are not formed to enjoy. All we get by it is a fruitless desire of mixing the different pleasures and conveniences which are given to the different parts of the world, and cannot meet in any one of them. After having read all that is to be found in the languages I am mistress of, and having decayed my sight by midnight studies, I envy the easy peace of mind of a ruddy milkmaid, who, undisturbed by doubt, hears the sermon with humility every Sunday, not having confounded the sentiments of natural duty in her head by the vain inquiries of the schools, who may be more learned, but, after all, must remain as ignorant. And after having seen part of Asia and Africa, and almost made the tour of Europe, I think the honest English squire more happy who verily believes the Greek wines less delicious than March beer; that the African fruits have not so fine a flavor as golden pippins; that the Beca figuas of Italy are not so well tasted as a rump of beef; and that, in short, there is no perfect enjoyment of this life out of old England. I pray God I may think so for the rest of my life; and since I must be contented with our scanty allowance of daylight, that I may forget the enlivening sun of Constantinople.

I am, etc.

XIII.—THE DEATH OF TWO LOVERS BY LIGHTNING.

Alexander Pope to Lady M. W. Montagu.

* * * I have a mind to fill the rest of this paper with an accident that happened just under my eyes, and has made a great impression upon me. I have just passed part of this summer at an old romantic seat of my Lord Harcourt's, which he lent me. It overlooks a common field, where, under the shade of a haycock, sat two lovers, as constant as ever were found in romance, beneath a spreading beech. The name of the one (let it sound as it will) was John Hughes, of the other, Sarah Drew. John was a well-set man, about five-and-twenty; Sarah, a brown woman of eighteen. John had for several months borne the labor of the day in the same field with Sarah; when she milked,

it was his morning and evening charge to bring the cows to her pail. Their love was the talk, but not the scandal, of the whole neighborhood; for all they aimed at was the blameless possession of each other in marriage. It was but this very morning that he had obtained her parents' consent, and it was but till the next week that they were to wait to be happy. Perhaps this very day, in the intervals of their work, they were talking of their wedding clothes; and John was now matching several kinds of poppies and field flowers to her complexion, to make her a present of knots for the day. While they were thus employed (it was on the last of July), a terrible storm of thunder and lightning arose and drove the laborers to what shelter the trees or hedges afforded. Sarah, frightened and out of breath, sunk on a haycock, and John (who never separated from her) sate by her side, having raked two or three heaps together to secure her. Immediately there was heard so loud a crack as if heaven had burst asunder. The laborers, all solicitous for each other's safety, called to one another; those that were nearest to our lovers, hearing no answer, stepped to the place where they lay. They first saw a little smoke, and after, this faithful pair; John with one arm about his Sarah's neck, and the other held over her face, as if to screen her from the lightning. They were struck dead, and already grown stiff and cold, in this tender posture. There was no mark or discoloring on their bodies, only that Sarah's eyebrow was a little singed, and a small place between her breasts. They were buried the next day in one grave, in the parish of Stanton-Harcourt, in Oxfordshire, where my Lord Harcourt, at my request, has erected a monument over them. Of the following epitaphs which I made, the critics have chosen the godly one. I like neither, but wish you had been in England to have done this office better; I think 'twas what you could not have refused me on so moving an occasion:

When Eastern lovers feed the fun'ral fire,
On the same pile their faithful fair expire;
Here pitying Heav'n, that virtue mutual found,
And blasted both, that it might neither wound.
Hearts so sincere th' Almighty saw well pleased,
Sent His own lightning, and the victims seized.

Think not, by rig'rous judgment seized,
A pair so faithful could expire;
Victims so pure Heav'n saw well pleased,
And snatched them in celestial fire.

Live well, and fear no sudden fate;
When God calls virtue to the grave,
Alike 'tis justice, soon or late,
Mercy alike to kill or save.
Virtue, unmoved, can hear the call,
And face the flash that melts the ball.

Upon the whole, I can't think these people unhappy. The greatest happiness, next to living as they would have done, was to die as they did. The greatest honor people of this low degree could have, was to be remembered on a little monument, unless you will give them another—that of being honored with a tear from the finest eyes in the world. I know you have tenderness; you must have it, it is the very emanation of sense and virtue; the finest minds, like the finest metals, dissolve the easiest.

But when you are reflecting upon objects of pity, pray do not forget one who had no sooner found out an object of the highest esteem, than he was separated from it; and who is so very unhappy as not to be susceptible of consolation from others, by being so miserably in the right as to think other women what they really are. Such a one can't but be desperately fond of any creature that is quite different from these. * * *

XIV.—IN REPLY.

Lady M. W. Montagu to Alexander Pope.

DOVER, Nov. 1, O. S., 1718.

I have this minute received a letter of yours, sent me from Paris. I believe and hope I shall very soon see both you and Mr. Congreve; but as I am here in an inn, where we stay to regulate our march to London, bag and baggage, I shall employ some of my leisure time in answering that part of yours that seems to require an answer.

I must applaud your good nature in supposing that your pastoral lovers (vulgarly called haymakers) would have lived in everlasting joy and harmony if the lightning had not interrupted their scheme of happiness. I see no reason to imagine that John Hughes and Sarah Drew were either wiser or more virtuous than their neighbors. That a well-set man of twenty-five should have a fancy to marry a brown woman of eighteen, is nothing marvellous; and I cannot help thinking that, had they married, their lives would have passed in the common track with their fellow-parishioners. His endeavoring to shield her from a storm was a natural action, and what he certainly would have done for his horse, if he had been in the same situation. Neither am I of opinion that their sudden death was a reward of their mutual virtue. You know the Jews were reproved for thinking a village destroyed by fire more wicked than those that had escaped the thunder. Time and chance happen to all men. Since you desire me to try my skill in an epitaph, I think the following lines perhaps more just, but not so poetical as yours:

Here lie John Hughes and Sarah Drew;
Perhaps you'll say, What's that to you?
Believe me, friend, much may be said
On this poor couple that are dead.
On Sunday next they should have married,
But see how oddly things are carried!
On Thursday last it rained and lightened,
These tender lovers, sadly frightened,
Sheltered beneath the cocking hay,
In hopes to pass the time away.
But the bold thunder found them out
(Commissioned for that end no doubt),
And, seizing on their trembling breath,
Consigned them to the shades of death.
Who knows if 'twas not kindly done?
For, had they seen the next year's sun,
A beaten wife and cuckold swain
Had jointly cursed the marriage chain.
Now they are happy in their doom,
For Pope has wrote upon their tomb.

I confess these sentiments are not altogether so heroic as yours; but I hope you will forgive them in favor of the last two lines. You see how much I esteem the honor you have done them; though I am not very impatient to have the same, and had rather continue to be your stupid, *living*, humble servant, than to be *celebrated* by all the pens in Europe.

I would write to Congreve, but suppose you will read this to him if he inquires after me.*

* A more interesting and circumstantial account is given by Gay in one of his letters to Pope. That of Pope, borrowed from it, has been selected, as

XV.—HIS DISEASE, "TIME."

Lord Chesterfield to Doctor Monsey.

BATH, Nov. 26th, 1766.

Pray, dear doctor, why must I not write to you? Do you gentlemen of the faculty pretend to monopolize writing in your prescriptions or proscriptions? I will write and thank you for your kind letters; and my writing shall do no hurt to any person living or dying; let the faculty say as much of theirs, if they can. I am very sorry to find that you have not been *vastly* well of late; but it is *vastly* to the honor of your skill to have encountered and subdued almost all the ills of Pandora's box. As you are now got to the bottom of it, I trust that you have found hope—which is what we all live upon, much more than upon enjoyment; and without which we should be, from our boasted reason, the most miserable animals of the creation. I do not think that a physician should be admitted into the college till he could bring proofs of his having cured, in his own person, at least four *incurable* distempers. In the old days of laudable and rational chivalry, a knight could not even present himself to the adorable object of his affections till he had been unhorsed, knocked down, and had two or three spears or lances in his body! but indeed he must be conqueror at last, as you have been. I do not know your goddess Venus or *Vana*,* nor ever heard of her; but, if she is really a goddess, I must know her as soon as ever I see her walk into the rooms; for "*vera incessu*

it elicited the answer of Lady Montagu. The light tone in which the latter touches this truly touching incident, is probably no index to her genuine feelings, and may have been intended to keep her too ardent admirer at a proper distance, by treating every approach to tender sentiments with ridicule.—H.

* A lady who had just made her appearance at Bath.

patuit dea." It is for her sake, I presume, that you now make yourself a year younger than you are; for last year you and I were exactly of an age, and now I am turned of seventy-three. As to my body natural, it is as you saw it last; it labors under no particular distemper but one, which may very properly be called chronical, for it is Χρονος itself, that daily steals away some part of me. But I bear with philosophy these gradual depredations upon myself; and well know, that "*levius fit patientiâ quicquid corrigere est nefas.*" And so good night, dear doctor.

XVI.—CORRESPONDENCE BETWEEN DR. JOHNSON AND MRS PIOZZI, ON HER MARRIAGE.

Mrs. Piozzi to Dr. Johnson.

BATH, June 30.

MY DEAR SIR: The enclosed is a circular letter which I have sent to all the guardians, but our friendship demands something more; it requires that I should beg your pardon for concealing from you a connection which you must have heard of by many, but I suppose never believed. Indeed, my dear sir, it was concealed only to save us both needless pain: I could not have borne to reject that counsel it would have killed me to take, and I only tell it you now because all is irrevocably settled and out of your power to prevent. I will say, however, that the dread of your disapprobation has given me some anxious moments, and though perhaps I am become, by many privations, the most independent woman in the world, I feel as if acting without a parent's consent till you write kindly to

Your faithful servant.

CIRCULAR.

SIR: As one of the executors of Mr. Thrale's will, and guardian to his daughters, I think it my duty to acquaint you that the three eldest left Bath last Friday for their own house at Brighthelmstone, in company with an amiable friend, Miss Nicholson, who has sometimes resided with us here, and in whose society they may, I think, find some advantage, and certainly no disgrace. I waited on them to Salisbury, Wilton, etc., and offered to attend them to the seaside myself; but they preferred this lady's company to mine, having heard that Mr. Piozzi is coming back from Italy, and judging, perhaps, by our past friendship and continued correspondence, that his return would be succeeded by our marriage.

I have the honor to be, sir, your obedient servant.

BATH, June 30th, 1784.

XVII.—ANSWER.

MADAM: If I interpret your letter right, you are ignominiously married: if it is yet undone, let us *once* more *talk* together. If you have abandoned your children and your religion, God forgive your wickedness; if you have forfeited your fame and your country, may your folly do no further mischief. If the last act is yet to do, I who have loved you, esteemed you, reverenced you and *served you*, I who long thought you the first of womankind, entreat that, before your fate is irrevocable, I may once more see you. I was, I once was, madam, most truly yours,

SAM JOHNSON.

July 2d, 1784.

I will come down if you permit it.

XVIII.—IN REPLY.

Mrs. Piozzi to Dr. Johnson.

July 4th, 1784.

SIR: I have this morning received from you so rough a letter in reply to one which was both tenderly and respectfully written, that I am forced to desire the conclusion of a correspondence which I can bear to continue no longer. The birth of my second husband is not meaner than that of my first; his sentiments are not meaner; his profession is not meaner, and his superiority in what he professes acknowledged by all mankind. It is want of fortune, then, that is ignominious; the character of the man I have chosen has no other claim to such an epithet. The religion to which he has been always a zealous adherent will, I hope, teach him to forgive insults he has not deserved; mine will, I hope, enable me to bear them at once with dignity and patience. To hear that I have forfeited my fame is indeed the greatest insult I ever yet received. My fame is as unsullied as snow, or I should think it unworthy of him who must henceforth protect it.

I write by the coach, the more speedily and effectually to prevent your coming hither. Perhaps by my fame (and I hope it is so) you mean only that celebrity which is a consideration of a much lower kind. I care for that only as it may give pleasure to my husband and his friends.

Farewell, dear sir, and accept my best wishes. You have always commanded my esteem, and long enjoyed the fruits of a friendship never infringed by one harsh expression on my part during twenty years of familiar talk. Never did I oppose your will, or control your wish; nor can your unmerited severity itself lessen my regard; but until you have changed your opinion of Mr. Piozzi, let us converse no more. God bless you.

XIX.—RESPONSE.

Dr. Johnson to Mrs. Piozzi.

LONDON, July 8th, 1784.

DEAR MADAM: What you have done, however I may lament it, I have no pretence to resent, as it has not been injurious to me; I therefore breathe out one sigh more of tenderness, perhaps useless, but at least sincere.

I wish that God may grant you every blessing, that you may be happy in this world for its short continuance, and eternally happy in a better state; and whatever I can contribute to your happiness I am very ready to repay, for that kindness that soothed twenty years of a life radically wretched.

Do not think slightly of the advice which I now presume to offer. Prevail upon Mr. Piozzi to settle in England; you may live here with more dignity than in Italy, and with more security; your rank will be higher, and your fortune more under your own eye. I desire not to detail my reasons, but every argument of prudence and interest is for England, and only some phantoms of imagination seduce you to Italy.

I am afraid, however, that my counsel is vain, yet I have eased my heart by giving it.

When Queen Mary took the resolution of sheltering herself in England, the Archbishop of St. Andrew's attempting to dissuade her, attended on her journey, and when they came to the irremeable stream that seperated the two kingdoms, walked by her side into the water, in the middle of which he seized her bridle, and with earnestness proportioned to her danger and his own affection pressed her to return. *The* Queen went forward. If the parallel reaches thus far, may it go no further. The tears stand in my eyes.

I am going into Derbyshire, and hope to be followed by your good wishes, for I am, with great affection,

Yours, etc.

Any letters that may come for me hither will be sent me.*

XX.—AMUSEMENTS IN TOWN—REFLECTIONS ON RICHES.

Mr. Gray to Dr. Wharton.

CAMBRIDGE, Dec. 11th, 1746.

I would make you an excuse (as indeed I ought) if they were a sort of thing I ever gave any credit to myself, in these cases; but I know they are never true. Nothing so silly as indolence, when it hopes to disguise itself; every one knows it by its saunter, as they do his Majesty (God bless him!) at a masquerade, by the firmness of his tread, and the elevation of his chin. However, somewhat I had to say that has a little shadow of reason in it. I have been in town (I suppose you know) flaunting about at all kinds of public places with two friends lately

* The reader, who is no doubt familiar with the harsh strictures of Macaulay on this marriage, should bear in mind a more kindly criticism. In the Recollections of the Table Talk of Samuel Rogers, it is said that he was very intimate with the Piozzis, and thought the world most unjust in blaming Mrs. Thrale for marrying Piozzi. "He was a very handsome, gentlemanly, and amiable person, and made her a very good husband. In the evening he used to play to us most beautifully on the piano. Her daughters never would see her after that marriage; and (poor woman) when she was at a very great age, I have heard her say that she would go down on her knees to them, if they would only be reconciled to her."—H.

returned from abroad. The world itself has some attractions in it to a solitary of six years' standing; and agreeable, well-meaning people of sense (thank Heaven there are so few of them!) are my peculiar magnet. It is no wonder then if I felt some reluctance at parting with them so soon; or if my spirits, when I returned back to my cell, should sink for a time, not indeed to storm and tempest, but a good deal below changeable. Besides, Seneca says (and my pitch of philosophy does not pretend to be much above Seneca), *Nunquam mores, quos extuli, refero. Aliquid ex eo quod composui, turbatur; aliquid ex his, quæ fugavi, redit.* And it will happen to such as us, mere imps of science. Well it may, when wisdom herself is forced often

> In sweet retired solitude
> To plume her feathers, and let grow her wings,
> That in the various bustle of resort
> Were all too ruffled, and sometimes impaired.

It is a foolish thing that without money one cannot either live as one pleases, or where and with whom one pleases. Swift somewhere says, that Money is Liberty; and I fear money is Friendship too and Society, and almost every external blessing. It is a great, though an ill-natured comfort, to see most of those who have it in plenty, without Pleasure, without Liberty, and without Friends. I am not altogether of your opinion as to your historical consolation in time of trouble; a calm melancholy it may produce a stiller sort of despair (and that only in some circumstances, and in some constitutions); but I doubt no real comfort or content can ever arise in the human mind, but from Hope.

I take it very ill you should have been in the twentieth year of the War,* and yet say nothing of the retreat before Syracuse;

* Thucydides.

is it, or is it not, the finest thing you ever read in your life? And how does Xenophon or Plutarch agree with you? For my part I read Aristotle, his Poetics, Politics, and Morals—though I do not know well which is which. In the first place, he is the hardest author by far I ever meddled with. Then he has a dry conciseness which makes one imagine one is perusing a table of contents rather than a book; it tastes for all the world like chopped hay, or rather like chopped logic, for he has a violent affection to that art, being, in some sort, his own invention; so that he often loses himself in little trifling distinctions and verbal niceties; and what is worse, leaves you to extricate him as well as you can. Thirdly, he has suffered vastly from the transcribblers, as all authors of great brevity necessarily must. Fourthly and lastly, he has abundance of fine uncommon things, which make him well worth the pains he gives one. You see what you are to expect from him.

XXI.—ON THE PRESENT OF A BUSTARD.—IO PÆAN.

William Cowper to John Johnson.

Jan. 31st, 1793.

MY DEAREST JOHNNY: Even as you foretold, so it came to pass. On Tuesday I received your letter, and on Tuesday came the pheasants: for which I am indebted in many thanks, as well as Mrs. Unwin, both to your kindness and to kind friend Mr. Copeman.

In Copeman's ear, this truth let echo tell,
"Immortal bards like mortal pheasants well;"
And when his clerkship's out, I wish him herds
Of golden clients for his golden birds.

Our friends the Courtenays have never dined with us since their marriage, *because* we have never asked them; and we have never asked them *because* poor Mrs. Unwin is not so equal to the task of providing for and entertaining company as before this last illness. But this is no objection to the arrival here of a bustard; rather it is a cause for which we shall be particularly glad to see the monster. It will be a handsome present to *them*. So let the bustard come, as the Lord Mayor of London said of the hare, when he was hunting, "Let her come, a' God's name! I am not afraid of her!" Adieu, my dear cousin and caterer. My eyes are terribly bad, else I had much more to say to you.

Ever affectionately yours, W. C.

XXII.—APPEAL IN BEHALF OF HIS RACE.

Ignatius Sancho to Mr. Sterne.

1776.

Reverend Sir: It would be an insult on your humanity (or perhaps look like it) to apologize for the liberty I am taking. I am one of those people whom the vulgar and illiberal call negroes. The first part of my life was rather unlucky, as I was placed in a family who judged ignorance the best and only security for obedience. A little reading and writing I got by unwearied application. The latter part of my life has been, through God's blessing, truly fortunate, having spent it in the service of one of the best and greatest families in the kingdom.* My chief pleasure has been books; philanthropy I adore. How

* The family of the Duke of Manchester. Such was the esteem in which the duke held the author of this letter, who had been a slave in the West Indies, that he left him an annuity in his will.—H.

very much, good sir, am I (amongst millions) indebted to you for the character of your amiable uncle Toby? I declare I would walk ten miles in the dog-days to shake hands with the honest corporal. Your sermons have touched me to the heart, and I hope have amended it; which brings me to the point. In your tenth discourse is this very affecting passage: "Consider how great a part of our species, in all ages down to this, have been trod under the feet of cruel and capricious tyrants, who would neither hear their cries nor pity their distresses! Consider slavery, what it is; how bitter a draught, and how many millions are made to drink of it!" Of all my favorite authors, not one has drawn a tear in favor of my miserable black brethren, excepting yourself and the humane author of Sir Geo. Ellison. I think you will forgive me, I am sure you will applaud me, for beseeching you to give one half-hour's attention to slavery, as it is this day practised in our West Indies. That subject, handled in your striking manner, would ease the yoke perhaps of many; but if only of one, gracious God! what a feast to a benevolent heart! and sure I am you are an epicurean in acts of charity. You, who are universally read, and as universally admired, you could not fail. Dear Sir, think in me you behold the uplifted hands of thousands of my brother Moors. Grief (you pathetically observe) is eloquent; figure to yourself their attitudes, hear their supplicating addresses! Alas! you cannot refuse. Humanity must comply; in which hope I beg permission to subscribe myself, Reverend sir,

I. S.

XXIII.—HUMANITY KNOWS NO SHADES OF COLOR.

Mr. Sterne to Ignatius Sancho.

COXWOULD, July 27th, 1776.

There is a strange coincidence, Sancho, in the little events as well as in the great ones of this world; for I had been writing a tender tale of the sorrows of a friendless poor negro girl, and my eyes had scarce done smarting with it, when your letter of recommendation, in behalf of so many of her brethren and sisters, came to me. But why her brethren? or yours, Sancho, any more than mine? It is by the finest tints and most insensible gradations that nature descends from the fairest face about St. James's to the sootiest complexion in Africa. At which tint of these is it that the ties of blood are to cease? and how many shades must we descend lower still in the scale, ere mercy is to vanish with them? But 'tis no uncommon thing, my good Sancho, for one-half of the world to use the other half of it like brutes, and then endeavor to make them so. For my own part, I never look *westward* (when I am in a pensive mood at least) but I think of the burdens which our brothers and sisters are *there* carrying; and, could I ease their shoulders from one ounce of them, I declare I would set out this hour upon a pilgrimage to Mecca for their sakes; which, by the bye, Sancho, exceeds your walk of ten miles in about the same proportion that a visit of humanity should one of mere form. However, if you meant my uncle Toby, more, he is your debtor. If I can weave the tale I have wrote into the work I am about, 'tis at the service of the afflicted; and a much greater matter, for, in serious truth, it casts a sad shade upon the world, that so great a part of it are, and have been, so long bound in chains of darkness and in chains of misery; and I cannot but both respect and felicitate you, that, by so much laudable diligence, you have broke the one, and that, by falling into the hands of so good and merciful a family, Providence has rescued you from the other.

And so, good-hearted Sancho, adieu! and believe me I will not forget your letter. Yours,

L. STERNE.

XXIV.—DESCRIPTION OF HIS WIFE.

Robert Burns to Mrs. Dunlop.

ELLISLAND, June 13th, 1788.

* * * Your surmise, madam, is just. I am, indeed, a husband. * * * To jealousy and infidelity I am an equal stranger. My preservation from the first is the most thorough consciousness of her sentiments of honor, and of her attachment to me; my antidote against the last is my long and deep-rooted affection for her.

In housewife matters, of aptness to learn, and activity to execute, she is eminently mistress; and during my absence in Nithsdale, she is regularly and constantly apprentice to my mother and sisters in their dairy and other rural business.

The muses must not be offended when I tell them the concerns of my wife and family will, in my mind, always take the *pas;* but I assure them their ladyships will ever come next in place.

You are right that a bachelor state would have insured me more friends; but, from a cause you will easily guess, conscious peace in the enjoyment of my own mind, and unmistrusting confidence in approaching my God, would seldom have been of the number.

I found a once much loved, and still much loved female, literally and truly, cast out to the mercy of the naked elements; but I enabled her to purchase a shelter; there is no sporting with a fellow-creature's happiness or misery.

The most placid good nature, and sweetness of disposition; a warm heart, gratefully devoted with all its powers to love me; vigorous health, and sprightly cheerfulness, set off to the best advantage by a more than commonly handsome figure; these, I think, in a woman, may make a good wife, though she should have never read a page but the Scriptures of the Old and New Testaments, nor have danced in a brighter assembly than a penny-pay wedding. R. B.

XXV.—LEGENDS OF ALLOWAY KIRK.

Robert Burns to Francis Grose.

DUMFRIES, 1792.

Among the many witch stories I have heard relating to Alloway Kirk, I distinctly remember only two or three.

Upon a stormy night, amid whistling squalls of wind and bitter blasts of hail—in short, on such a night as the devil would choose to take the air in—a farmer, or farmer's servant, was plodding and plashing homeward, with his plough irons on his shoulder, having been getting some repairs on them at a neighboring smithy. His way lay by the Kirk of Alloway, and being rather on the anxious lookout in approaching a place so well known to be a favorite haunt of the devil, and the devil's friends and emissaries, he was struck aghast by discovering through the horrors of the storm and stormy night a light, which, on his nearer approach, plainly showed itself to proceed from the haunted edifice. Whether he had been fortified from above, on his devout supplication, as is customary with people when they suspect the immediate presence of Satan, or whether, according to another custom, he had got courageously drunk at the smithy, I will not pretend to determine; but so it was that he ventured to go up to, nay into, the very kirk. As luck would have it, his temerity came off unpunished.

The members of the infernal junto were all out on some midnight business or other, and he saw nothing but a kind of kettle or cauldron, depending from the roof over the fire, simmering some heads of unchristened children, limbs of executed malefactors, etc., for the business of the night. It was in for a penny in for a pound, with the honest ploughman; so, without ceremony, he unhooked the cauldron from off the fire, and pouring out the damnable ingredients, inverted it on his head, and carried it fairly home, where it remained long in the family, a living evidence of the truth of the story.

Another story, which I can prove to be equally authentic, was as follows:

On a market day, in the town of Ayr, a farmer from Carrick, and consequently whose way lay by the very gate of Alloway Kirkyard, in order to cross the river Doon at the old bridge, which is about two or three hundred yards farther on than the said gate, had been detained by his business, till by the time he reached Alloway it was the wizard hour, between night and morning.

Though he was terrified with a blaze streaming from the kirk, yet it is a well-known fact that to turn back upon these occasions is running by far the greatest risk of mischief; he prudently advanced on his road. When he had reached the gate of the kirkyard he was surprised and entertained through the ribs and arches of an old gothic window, which still faces the highway, to see a dance of witches, merrily footing it round their old sooty blackguard master, who was keeping them all alive with the power of his bagpipe. The farmer, stopping his horse to observe them a little, could plainly descry the faces of many old women of his acquaintance and neighborhood. How the gentleman was dressed tradition does not say, but that the ladies were all in their smocks; and one of them, happening unluckily to have a smock which was considerably too short to answer all the purposes of that piece of dress, our farmer was so tickled that he involuntarily burst out with a loud laugh: "Weel luppen, Maggy wi' the short sark!" and recollecting himself, instantly spurred his horse to the top of his speed. I need not mention the universally known fact, that no diabolical power can pursue you beyond the middle of a running stream. Lucky it was for the poor farmer that the River Doon was so near, for, notwithstanding the speed of his horse, which was a good one, against he reached the middle of the arch of the bridge, and consequently the middle of the stream, the pursuing vengeful hags were so close at his heels, that one of them actually sprung to seize him; but it was too late, nothing was on her side of the stream but the horse's tail, which immediately gave way at her infernal grip, as if blasted by a stroke of lightning; but the farmer was beyond her reach. However, the unsightly, tailless condition of the vigorous steed was, to the last hour of the noble creature's life, an awful warning to the Carrick farmer not to stay too late in Ayr markets.

The last relation I shall give, though equally true, is not so well identified as the two former with regard to the scene; but as the best authorities give it for Alloway, I shall relate it.

On a summer's evening, about the time that nature puts on her sable to mourn the expiring of the cheerful day, a shepherd boy, belonging to a farmer in the immediate neighborhood of Alloway Kirk, had just folded his charge and was returning home. As he passed the kirk in the adjoining field, he fell in with a crew of men and women, who were busy pulling stems of the plant ragwort. He observed that as each person pulled a ragwort, he or she got astride of it, and called out, "Up, horsee," on which the ragwort flew off, like Pegasus, through the air, with its rider. The foolish boy likewise pulled his ragwort, and cried with the rest, "Up, horsee," and, strange to tell, away he flew with the company. The first stage at which the cavalcade stopped was a merchant's wine-cellar in Bordeaux, where, without saying by your leave, they quaffed away at the best the cellar could afford, until the morning, foe to the imps and works of darkness, threatened to throw light on the matter, and frightened them from their carousals.

The poor shepherd lad being equally a stranger to the scene and the liquor, heedlessly got himself drunk; and when the rest took horse he fell asleep, and was found so next day by some of the people belonging to the merchant. Somebody that understood Scotch, asking him who he was, he said such-a-one's herdboy in Alloway, and by some means or other getting home again, he lived long to tell the world the wondrous tale.*

I am, etc., R. B.

* This letter, says Allan Cunningham, must be interesting to all who desire to see how a poet works beauty and regularity out of a vulgar tradition.

XXVI.—ADVICE TO AN EDITOR.

Dr. Franklin to Francis Hopkinson.

PASSY, Dec. 24th, 1782.

I thank you for your ingenious paper in favor of the trees. I own I now wish we had two rows of them in every one of our streets. The comfortable shelter they would afford us in walking, from our burning summer suns, and the greater coolness of our walls and pavements, would, I conceive in the improved health of the inhabitants, amply compensate the loss of a house now and then by fire, if such should be the consequence; but a tree is soon felled, and as axes are at hand in every neighborhood, may be down before the engines arrive.

You do well to avoid being concerned in the pieces of personal abuse, so scandalously common in our newspapers, that I am afraid to lend any of them here, 'till I have examined and laid aside such as would disgrace us, and subject us among strangers to a reflection like that used by a gentleman in a coffee-house to two quarrellers, who, after a mutually free use of the words rogue, villain, rascal, etc., seemed as if they would refer their dispute to him. "I know nothing of you, or your affairs," said he. "I *only perceive that you know one another.*"

The conductor of a newspaper should, methinks, consider himself as, in some degree, the guardian of his country's reputation, and refuse to insert such writings as may hurt it. If people will print their abuses of one another, let them do it in little pamphlets, and distribute them where they think proper. It is absurd to trouble all the world with them; and unjust to subscribers in distant places, to stuff their paper with matters so unprofitable and so disagreeable. With sincere esteem and affection, I am, my dear friend,

Ever yours, B. FRANKLIN.

XXVII.—RETROSPECT OF LIFE.

Dr. Franklin to Mrs. Hewson.

PASSY, January 27th, 1783.

The departure of my dearest friend,* which I learn from your last letter, greatly affects me. To meet with her once more in this life was one of the principal motives of my proposing to visit England again before my return to America. The last year carried off my friends Dr. Pringle and Dr. Fothergill, and Lord Kaimes and Lord Le Despencer; this has begun to take away the rest, and strikes the hardest. Thus the ties I had to that country, and indeed to the world in general, are loosened one by one; and I shall soon have no attachment left to make me unwilling to follow.

I intended writing when I sent the eleven books, but lost the time in looking for the first. I wrote with that; and hope it came to hand. I therein asked your counsel about my coming to England; on reflection, I think I can, from my knowledge of your prudence, foresee what it will be; viz., not to come too soon, lest it should seem braving and insulting some who ought to be respected. I shall, therefore, omit that journey till I am near going to America, and then just step over to take leave of my friends, and spend a few days with you. I purpose bringing Ben† with me, and perhaps may leave him under your care.

* Refers to Mrs. Hewson's mother.

† Benjamin Franklin Bache, a grandson of Dr. Franklin, by his daughter.

At length we are in peace, God be praised; and long, very long, may it continue. All wars are follies, very expensive and very mischievous ones: when will mankind become convinced of this, and agree to settle their difficulties by arbitration? Were they to do it, even by the cast of a die, it would be better than by fighting and destroying each other.

Spring is coming on, when travelling will be delightful. Can you not, when your children are all at school, make a little party and take a trip hither? I have now a large house, delightfully situated, in which I could accommodate you and two or three friends; and I am but half an hour's drive from Paris.

In looking forward, twenty-five years seem a long period; but, in looking back, how short! Could you imagine that it is now full a quarter of a century since we were first acquainted? It was in 1757. During the greatest part of the time I lived in the same house with my dear deceased friend, your mother, of course you and I saw and conversed with each other much and often. It is to all our honors, that, in all that time, we never had among us the smallest misunderstanding. Our friendship has been all clear sunshine, without any, the least, clouds in its hemisphere. Let me conclude by saying to you, what I have had too frequent occasions to say to my other remaining old friends, *the fewer we become, the more let us love one another*. Adieu, etc.

XXVIII.—MODE OF TELLING A STORY.

Dr. Franklin to Mrs. Mecom, Boston.

PHILADELPHIA, Nov. 26, 1788.

I never see any Boston newspapers. You mention there being often something in them to do me honor. I am obliged to them. On the other hand, some of our papers here are endeavoring to disgrace me. I have long been accustomed to receive more blame, as well as more praise, than I deserved. 'Tis the lot of every public man, and I have one account to balance the other. As you observe, there was no d——n your souls in the story of the poker when I told it. The late dresser of it was probably the same, or perhaps of kin to him, who, in relating a dispute that happened between Queen Anne and the Archbishop of Canterbury, concerning a vacant mitre, which the Queen was for bestowing on a person the Archbishop thought unworthy, made both the Queen and the Archbishop swear three or four thumping oaths in every sentence of the discussion; and the Archbishop at last gained his point. One present at the tale, being surprised, said, "But did the Queen and the Archbishop swear so at one another?" "O! no, no," said the relater, "that is only my way of telling the story."

Yours, etc., B. FRANKLIN.

XXIX.—ADIEU ON LEAVING EUROPE.

Dr. Franklin to David Hartley.

PASSY, July 5, 1785.

I cannot quit the coasts of Europe, without taking leave of my ever dear friend Mr. Hartley. We were long fellow laborers in the best of all works, the work of peace. I leave you still in the field; but, having finished my day's task, I am going home *to go to bed!* Wish me a good night's rest, as I do you a pleasant evening. Adieu! And believe me ever yours most affectionately,

B. FRANKLIN.

XXX.—RENEWAL OF ACQUAINTANCE.

Mrs. Leadbetter to Rev. George Crabbe.

BALLITORE, 7th of 11th month, 1816.

I believe it will surprise George Crabbe to receive a letter from an entire stranger, whom most probably he does not remember to have ever seen or heard of, but who cannot forget having met him at the house of Edmund Burke, Charles Street, James's Square, in the year 1784. I was brought thither by my father, Richard Shackleton, the friend from their childhood, of Edmund Burke. My dear father told thee that "Goldsmith's would now be the *deserted village.*" Perhaps thou dost not remember this compliment, but I remember the ingenious modesty which disclaimed it. He admired the "Village," the "Library," and the "Newspaper" exceedingly; and the delight with which he read them to his family could not but be acceptable to the author, had he known the sound judgment and the exquisite taste which that excellent man possessed. But he saw no more of the productions of the Muse he had admired, whose originality was not the least charm. He is dead; the friend whom he loved and honored, and to whose character thou dost so much justice in the preface to the "Parish Register," is also gone to the house appointed for all living. A splendid constellation of poets arose in the literary horizon. I looked around for Crabbe. "Why does not he, who shines as brightly as any of these, add his lustre?" I had not long thought thus, when in an Edinburgh Review I met with reflections similar to my own, which introduced the "Parish Register." Oh! it was like the voice of a long-lost friend, and glad was I to hear that voice again in "The Borough;" still more in the "Tales" which appear to me excelling all that preceded them. Every work is so much in unison with our own feelings, that a wish for information concerning them and their author, received into our hearts, is strongly excited. One of our friends, Dykes Alexander, who was in Ballitore in 1810, I think, said he was personally acquainted with thee, and spoke highly of thy character. I regretted I had not an opportunity of conversing with him on this subject, as perhaps he would have been able to decide arguments which have arisen; namely, whether we owe to truth, or to fiction, that "ever new delight" which thy poetry affords us? Thy characters, however singular some of them may be, are never unnatural; and thy sentiments, so true to domestic and social feelings as well as to those of a higher nature, have the convincing power of reality over the mind; and I maintain that all thy pictures *are drawn from life*. To inquire whether this be the case, is the excuse which I make to myself for writing this letter. I wish the excuse may be accepted by thee; for I greatly fear I have taken an unwarrantable liberty in making the inquiry. Though advanced in life, yet from an education of peculiar simplicity, and from never having been long absent from my retired native village, I am too little acquainted with decorum. If I have now transgressed the rules it prescribes, I appeal to the candor and liberality of thy mind to forgive a fault caused by strong enthusiasm. I am thy sincere friend,

MARY LEADBETTER.

P. S. Ballitore is the village in which Edmund Burke was educated by Abraham Shackleton, whose pupil he became in 1741, and from whose school he entered the college of Dublin in 1744. The school is still flourishing.

XXXI.—RESPONSE TO "THE CHILD OF SIMPLICITY."

Rev. George Crabbe to Mrs. Leadbetter.

TROWBRIDGE, 1st of 12th month, 1816.

Mary Leadbetter! yes, indeed, I do well remember you! Not Leadbetter then, but a pretty, demure lass, standing a timid auditor, while her own verses were read by a kind friend, but a keen judge. And I have in my memory your father's person and countenance, and you may be sure my vanity retained the compliment which he paid me in the moment when he permitted his judgment to slip behind his good humor and desire of giving pleasure. Yes, I remember all who were present; and of all, are not you and I the only survivors? It was the day, was it not, when I introduced my wife to my friend? And now both are gone! And your father and Richard Burke who was present (yet again, I must ask, was he not?) and Mrs. Burke? All departed—and so, by-and-by, they will speak of us. But, in the mean time, it was good of you to write. Oh very—very good!

But are you not your father's own daughter? Do you not flatter after his manner? How do you know the mischief you may do in the mind of a vain man, who is but too susceptible of praise, even while he is conscious of so much to be placed against it? I am glad that you like my verses; it would have mortified me much if you had not, for you can judge as well as write. * * * Yours are really very admirable things; and the morality is as pure as the literary merit is conspicuous. I am not sure that I have read all that you have given us, but what I have read, has really that rare and all but undefinable quality, genius; that is to say, it seizes on the mind and commands attention, and on the heart and compels its feelings.

How could you imagine that I could be otherwise than pleased—delighted rather—with your letter? And let me not omit the fact, that I reply the instant I am at liberty, for I was enrobing myself for church. You are a child of simplicity, I know, and do not love robing; but you are a pupil of liberality, and look upon such things with a large mind, smiling in charity. Well, I was putting on the great black gown, when my servant—(you see I can be pompous, to write of gowns and servants with such familiarity)—when he brought me a letter first directed, the words yet legible, to "George Crabbe, at Belvoir Castle," and then by Lord Mendip, to the "Reverend," at Trowbridge; and at Trowbridge I hope again to receive these welcome evidences of your remembrance, directed in all their simplicity, and written, I trust, in all their sincerity. The delay was occasioned by a change in my place of residence. I now dwell in the parsonage of a busy, populous, clothing town, sent thither by ambition and the Duke of Rutland. It is situated in Wiltshire, not far from Bath.

There was a Suffolk family of Alexanders, one of whom you probably mean; and as he knew very little of me, I see no reason why he should not give me a good character. Whether it was merited is another point, and that will depend upon our ideas of good character. If it means, as it generally does, that I paid my debts, and was guilty of no glaring, world-defying immorality—why, yes! I was so far a good character. But before the Searcher of Hearts what are our good characters?

But your motive for writing to me was your desire of knowing whether my men and women were really existing creatures or beings of my own imagination. Nay, Mary Leadbetter, yours was a better motive; you thought that you should give me pleasure by writing, and yet—you will think me very vain—you felt some pleasure yourself in renewing the acquaintance that commenced under such auspices! Am I not right? My heart tells me that I am, and hopes that you will confirm it. Be assured that I feel a very cordial esteem for the friend of my friend—the virtuous, the worthy character whom I am addressing. Yes, I will tell you readily about my creatures, whom I endeavored to paint as nearly as I could and dared, for in some cases I dared not. This you will readily admit; besides, charity bade me be cautious. Thus far you are correct; there is not one of whom I had not in my mind the original, but I was obliged in some cases to take them from their real situations; in one or two instances to change even the sex, and in many the circumstances. The nearest to real life was the proud, ostentatious man in the "Borough," who disguises an ordinary mind by doing great things; but the others approach to reality at greater or less distances. Indeed, I do not know that I could paint merely from my own fancy, and there is no cause why we should. Is there not diversity sufficient in society? And who can go, even but a little, into the assemblies of our fellow wanderers from the way of perfect rectitude, and not find characters so varied and so pointed that he need not call upon his imagination?

Will *you* not write again? Write *to* thee, or *for* the public? wilt thou not ask. *To* me, and *for* as many as love and can discern the union of strength and simplicity, purity and good sense. *Our* feelings and *our* hearts is the language you can adopt. Alas! I cannot with propriety use it; *our* I too once could say, but I am alone now, and since my removing into a busy town, among the multitude, the loneliness is but more apparent and more melancholy. But this is only at certain times;

and then I have, though at considerable distances, six female friends, unknown to each other, but all dear, very dear, to me. With men I do not much associate, not as deserting, and much less disliking, the male part of society, but as being unfit for it; not hardy nor grave; not knowing enough; not sufficiently acquainted with the every day concerns of men. But my beloved creatures have minds with which I can better assimilate. Think of you I must, and of me I must entreat that you would not be unmindful. Thine, dear lady, very truly,

George Crabbe.

XXXII.—DESCRIPTION OF A DROUGHT—"MANNERS OF THE GREAT."

Hannah More to Mr. Harford.

Barley Wood

My dear Friend: I have been much entertained with your picturesque letter. Scotland is a country I should particularly like to visit, as its scenes retain so much of their original character, and have not been spoiled by art and industry, which, though very good things in themselves, yet efface the old ideas that contribute to the pleasant romance of life. I particularly envy you the sight of Staffa's cave. Its laird, or, as he styles himself, *Staffa* only, has visited me, and I remember his account of his little empire was very amusing. But if these scenes have my admiration, Dumblane would have my homage. Of Leighton I could almost say with Burnet, "And I am not the better for that man; I shall have to answer for it at the day of judgment." What sacrilege to demolish his cathedral!

The heat here is almost tropical. Not a blade of grass left.

The complexion of my field is hardly distinguishable from the gravel walk. I believe the farmers, like Milton's Satan, "never see the sun except to tell him how they hate his beams." What a fine description there is in the 11th of Jeremiah of a drought: "And the nobles sent their little ones to the water; they came to the pits and found none; they returned with their vessels empty, and were ashamed and confounded. And the ploughmen were ashamed, for there *was no grass*. And the asses snuffed up the wind, for there was no grass," etc. Pray turn to the chapter.

I have just had a visit from a very old and interesting friend, Mrs. ———. We had not met for twenty-seven years. We lived much together when I lived in the great and gay world. She told me when my little book of "Manners of the Great" was first published (anonymously), she was sitting with the Queen, who was reading it. When Her Majesty came to the passage which censured the practice of ladies in sending on Sundays for a hair-dresser, she exclaimed, "This, I am sure, is Hannah More; she is in the right, and I will never send for one again." She did not mean she would not have her hair dressed on a Sunday, but she would not compel a poor tradesman to violate the Sabbath, but rather employ one of her own household.

A letter from ——— tells me that Mrs. ——— is doing well after her confinement. They still feel the loss of their son. I never saw a lovelier youth, or one better disposed. *Oh vita humana chi est si bella in vista!* etc., etc. What a sweet passage in Petrarca follows! With kind love to Mrs. H——, believe me, my dear friend,

Yours very sincerely,

H. MORE.

XXXIII.—LITTLE USE MEN MAKE OF THEIR ADVANTAGES.

Miss Berry to Joanna Baillie.

WIMPOLE, Nov., 1809.

MY DEAR JOANNA: What are you doing? and where are you going? Troth, say you, if you had wanted to know, you would have inquired sooner; and troth, if I had been doing better myself, so I should, answer I. I have been here a month, with people that I love, in a comfortable family-circle, surrounded by every comfort and every luxury of life, and sitting in a library—such a library as would

> "Make those read now, who never read before,
> And those who always read, now read the more."

Yet even thus situated, with the perfect command of my own time, and nothing to fatigue me, if I were to tell you how little use I have been able to make of all these advantages—if I were to reckon up how many days in this month I have enjoyed the free and unembarrassed use of my own faculties—I should make you, as well as myself, melancholy, and therefore, as this is a good day with me, I will say no more about it.

My last and only letter from you was on the 8th, from Cotswold. You had been seeing Oxford, which I was delighted to find had impressed your mind exactly as it had always done mine. During my stay here I have been to Cambridge, which I had seen in a slight manner so long ago as to have almost entirely forgotten. It cannot vie with the magnificent groups of Oxford. But it has one college which may rival, if not surpass Christ's Church in picturesque beauty, and one point of view in which it appears singularly adapted for the seat of calm contemplation and learned ease. I fear the evil-minded will say, the calm is often unaccompanied by contemplation, and the ease unaccompanied by learning. Still I must ever love to see such great means brought together, and such assistance offered to both, and must ever feel a degree of exaltation of mind in places dedicated for so many centuries to the cultivation of the noblest and most distinguished faculty of human nature; perhaps, too, a little spark of sexual vanity creeps in with the wonder one cannot help feeling at *men* enjoying such advantages and doing so little, and women laboring under such disadvantages doing so much. This, my dear Joanna, regards *you* more than any other female now living. Go on, then, and prove to them that poetry, at least, is as independent of sex as of rule; that it is a spark of ethereal fire kindled on earth once in an age, which Shakspeare alone has described, and with which you are enlightened. M. B.

XXXIV.—A LADY'S EXPERIENCE AT THE "OLD BAILEY."

Lady Dufferin to Miss Berry.

HAMPTON HALL, DORCHESTER, 1846.

Your kind little note followed me here, dear Miss Berry, which must account for my not having answered it sooner. As you guessed, I was obliged to follow my "*things*" (as the maids always call their raiment) into the very jaws of the law. I think the Old Bailey is a charming place. We were introduced to a live Lord Mayor, and I sat between two sheriffs. The common sergeant talked to me familiarly, and I am not sure that the Governor of Newgate did not call me "Nelly." As for the Rev. Mr. Carver (the ordinary), if the inherent vanity of my sex does not mislead me, I *think* I have made a deep impression there. Altogether, my Old Bailey recollections are of the most pleasing and gratifying nature. It is true that I have only got back three pairs and a half of stockings, one gown, and two shawls; but that is but a trifling consideration in studying the glorious institutions of our country. We were treated with the greatest respect, and ham sandwiches; and two magistrates handed us down to the carriage. For my part, I could not think we were in the *criminal* court, as the law was so uncommonly *civil.* But I will reserve any observations I may have made in those pleasant and polite regions until we meet, which I hope will be soon after I leave Hampton, and I shall make it a point to call on the hermits of Curson street as soon as I go to town. I was so glad to hear such excellent accounts of your health and looks from Frederick Pigou, for you were very unwell when I left England about this time two years ago. * * * * * * * * I began a little note to you the other day to thank you for your kind remembrance of me, and for your coming so far to see me (which opportunity I was *very* sorry to have missed); but my note, in the agitating agonies of packing up, disappeared, and I have not strength of mind to begin another. My mother and I have returned to this place for a few days, in order to make an ineffectual grasp upon any *remaining* property that we may have in the world. Of course, you have heard that we were robbed and murdered the other night by a certain soft-spoken cook, who headed a storming party of banditti through my mother's kitchen window; if not, you will see the full, true, and dreadful particulars in the papers, as we are to be "had up" at the Old Bailey on Monday next for the trial. We have seen a great deal of life, and learned a great deal of the criminal law of England this week—knowledge cheaply purchased at the cost of all my wardrobe and all my mother's plate.

We have gone through two examinations in court; they were very hurrying and agitating affairs, and I had to kiss either the Bible or the magistrate, I don't recollect which, but *it* smelt of thumbs. The magistrates seemed to take less interest in my clothes than in my mother's spoons—I suppose from secret *affinity* or *congeniality*, which they were conscious of, *similis gaudet*, something (I have lost my Latin with the rest of my property). When I say "similis," I don't so much allude to the purity of the metal, as to its particular form.

I find that the idea of *personal property* is a fascinating illusion, for our goods belong in fact to our country and not to us; and that the petticoats and stockings I have fondly imagined *mine*, are really the petticoats of Great Britain and Ireland. I am now and then indulged with a distant glimpse of my most necessary garments in the hands of different policemen; but "in this stage of the proceedings" may do no more than wistfully recognize them. Even on such occasions, the words of Justice are, "Policeman B, 25, produce *your* gowns." "Letter A, 36, identify *your* lace." "Letter C, tie up *your* stockings." All this is harrowing to the feelings, but one cannot have every thing in this life. We have obtained *justice*, and can easily wait for a change of linen. Hopes are held out to us, that at some vague period in the lapse of time we may be allowed a *wear* out of our raiment—at least so much of it as may have resisted the wear and tear of justice; and my poor mother looks confidently forward to being restored to the bosom of her silver teapot. But I don't know! I begin to look upon all property with a philosophic eye, as unstable in its nature, and liable to all sorts of pawn-brokers; moreover, the police and I have so long had my clothes in common, that I shall never feel at home in them again. To a virtuous mind the idea that "Inspector Dousett" examined into all one's hooks and eyes, tapes and buttons, etc., is inexpressibly painful. But I cannot pursue that view of the subject. Let me hope, dear Miss Berry, that you feel for us as we really deserve, and that you wish me well "thro' my clothes" on Monday next! If I were sure you are at Richmond still, I might endeavor to return your kind visit; but at present our costumes are too *light* and our hearts too heavy for the empty forms and ceremonies of social intercourse. I hope, however, to see you ere very long; and with very kind remembrances to your sister, believe me, yours very truly.

XXXV.—BARLEY WOOD "NO HERMITAGE."

Hannah More to Mr. Wilberforce.

Barley Wood, 1816.

My dear Friend: I was glad to receive even your promissory note, though it was not followed by the prompt payment it announced. I do not mean your half bank-note of £50, which came safe, but your letter. The papers told us of—not your honors, but those of the regent—for surely he never did himself so much credit as in seeking your society; and though it does you no good, yet it will do good in too many ways for me to specify.

I have been ill since my last attack of fever, my nights being not only wakeful, but harassing and distressing. I am getting better, though I thought I was rapidly breaking up. The fever has left me a wholesome warning. Like Barzillai, I have long ceased "to hear any more the voice of singing men and singing women;" but now, though I hope I can still "discern between good and evil," "thy servant cannot taste what I eat or what I drink;" that is, I have lost the two senses of smell and taste completely, for six weeks. It has given me an excellent lesson not to overlook common mercies, for I forgot to value these blessings till I had lost them; the loss, too, is a good corrective of sensuality, as I know not bread from meat.

You bid me not be silent under the pretence of living in a hermitage. Alas! Barley Wood is nothing less. Thinking it right, almost twenty years ago, to gain a little interval between the world and the grave, when I renounced the society of the great and the gay, the learned and the witty, I fully made up my mind to associate only with country people. Yet it so happens that the retirement I sought I have never yet been able to find; for though we neither return visits nor give invitations, I think, except when quite confined by sickness, I never saw more people, known and unknown, in my gayest days. They come to me as to the witch of Endor; and I suppose I shall soon be desired to tell fortunes and cast nativities. I do little or no good to their minds, and they do much harm to my body, as talking so much inflames my chest.

In spite of our inability to attend in winter, our schools are very flourishing. We have pious, faithful teachers, who have served us twenty years; and we have reason to believe that many young persons, especially at Chedder, are living in the fear of God. The evening sermons are well attended, and many seem seriously impressed.

I rejoice to hear that Mrs. Stephen is better. I have but just received his masterly pamphlet.

Adieu, my very dear friend. Do not forget sometimes to include in your prayers not the least affectionate of your friends,

H. MORE.

XXXVI.—FELICITY IN METAPHOR—THIRD MARRIAGES.

Sir W. W. Pepys to Hannah More.

WIMPOLE STREET, March 31, 1813.

MY DEAR FRIEND: You are too well acquainted with the ceremonial between the judge and the elephant, who came both at the same time into a circuit town, which the judge settled by waiting first on the elephant, not to follow, as you have done, so good an example. I have long been in hopes of a letter from you, but as I considered your kind present on "Christian Morality" in the light of an apostolic epistle, I was not sure that you might not intend it to supply the place of a letter. I have read it with great pleasure, and, I trust, with advantage; though I confess the sensation of self-dissatisfaction, which all your writings leave upon my mind, however salutary, is rather humiliating and painful. I approve the style in which it is written, as less redundant in metaphor than your former work, and therefore better adapted, perhaps, to the solemnity of the subject; though, at the same time, I am sorry to lose the delight which I never fail to receive from your use of the metaphor, which *never* changes in your hands, as it does in those of some conjurers I know, from a ring to a purse, from a knife to a guinea. You and Burke are the only *two* persons I know who can safely be trusted with a metaphor; and it may be said of you, as I once heard a man say of him, while he was pouring forth torrents of eloquence in the House of Commons, "How closely that fellow reasons in metaphor!"

It is very pleasant to see by your letter that we have been for some time past reading exactly the same books; and I do not see why two friends may not enjoy the consciousness of both being employed at a distance on the same book, as well as two lovers that of both looking at the same time on the moon. Your observations, too, on them correspond exactly with my own.

Many thanks for your kind congratulations on my dear S——'s marriage. She is really a charming creature, with one of the best hearts and most cultivated minds I have ever known. What you say of Lady O. S. has raised in me a strong desire to be acquainted with her; but I have not yet arrived at that happy state of confidence which would enable me to say, as a Frenchman once said to me, *J'ai con que vous senez charmé de ma compagnie*, a sentence which I much question whether the vainest Englishman could pronounce.

Your complaint of the dampness of churches is not only well founded, but of so important and serious a nature that I think you cannot do a better service to religion, or at least to religious people, than to take an opportunity in some of your next publications (which are sure of being universally read) of descanting on that subject, and recommending, as somebody well said, that the old alliance between the *Aris* and the *Focis* should be restored. In recommending to you this subject, I do full as well, methinks, as a gentleman I know, who, when I asked him how he liked the subject of a sermon which was very abstruse, answered that he had rather hear him preach against the crime of putting alum into bread. Apropos of abstruse subjects for sermons, I shall certainly, at your recommendation, read some more of Horsley's; but must own that I have been deterred from it upon finding that one of them was upon the place in which our Saviour passed the interval between his crucifixion and his resurrection. Such subjects as those are better left untouched, because every one sees that the most learned theologian and the convert of yesterday must be equally informed upon them. I did read, and did, I confess, experience great disappointment in reading, his attempt to "show what part of our Saviour's discourses applied to the destruction of Jerusalem, and what to his coming at the end of the world." His disposing of the principal difficulty, by applying it to Judas Iscariot, appears to me very forced and improbable. Horsley was, however, the right sort of man to grapple with those and similarly difficult passages, and I am truly sorry that I could not obtain from him more satisfaction, for you cannot rank him among

> "Those commentators who dark meanings shun,
> But hold their farthing candle to the sun."

As to his explanation of the 45th Psalm, as I have no better to offer, I must be content with it, though the meaning which he annexes to it does seem very strange. I have often lamented that, instead of giving the *whole* book of Psalms, to be read in churches, which habituates the people, as well as the priest, to repeat daily what they no more understand than if it were Arabic, our ancestors did not make a copious *selection* of those divine passages, so feelingly adapted to every state of mind, and so expressive of the most pure and most exalted devotion.

I hear from Mrs. Dickenson, and indeed from everybody, how delightfully you are situated, and how hospitably you receive your friends; so that, were I ever to be within reach of you, I should make no more scruple of presenting myself at your gate, than a pilgrim would have had in throwing himself upon the hospitality of my lady abbess.

Pray convey my congratulations to Dr. —— when you see him, upon his marriage, though they will have but little effect, he is so used to them; as a lady once said to me, when I was going to give her away to her *third* husband, and told her that she ought not to appear in such high spirits, but look timid and apprehensive: "Matrimony is like a cold bath, very formidable the first time, but when you have tried it often, you become used to it."

Cadell promises two more volumes of Mrs. M——'s letters; but from what I can learn, they will not come out immediately. If I had had to advise on the former publication, I should have suggested that as some of the letters could have been written by very few except Mrs. Montagu, none ought to have been admitted which *anybody* could have written as well as Mrs. Montagu. But the editor is under great difficulties, for it often happens that some brilliant passages are so intermixed with headaches, etc., which occupy the rest of the letter, that it is hardly possible to detach the embroidery from the cloth. You, therefore, whose letters hereafter will be sought after with great avidity, should so write that the subjects, though familiar, should be always interesting; and though it might spoil your letters were you to write them with a view to publication, yet I would not have you totally lose sight of the possibility of such a thing taking place. "Why don't you wear your ring, my dear?" says a father in some play to his daughter. "Because, papa, it hurts me when any body squeezes my hand." "What business have you to have your hand squeezed?" "Certainly not; but still you know, papa, one would like to keep it in *squeezeable order!*"

As I trust you never fail to repeat every day, every year, my favorite lines in the beginning of Dryden's "Flower and the Leaf," I will say nothing about this delicious spring weather, but will only add, which I am sure you feel with me, that nothing excites in me so strong an emotion of gratitude as that sense of the gracious and beneficent protection of Providence, which has permitted me once more, in health and prosperity, to see the reminiscences of these His glorious works. Remember Beattie, and the beautiful apostrophe in the Minstrel, and

Believe me always most faithfully yours,

W. W. Pepys.

XXXVII.—BILL OF FARE FOR CAMP DINNER.

George Washington to Dr. John Cochran.

Dear Doctor: I have asked Mrs. Cochran and Mrs. Livingston to dine with me to-morrow; but am I not in honor bound to apprise them of their fare? As I hate deception, even where the imagination only is concerned, I will. It is needless to premise that my table is large enough to hold the ladies. Of this they had ocular proof yesterday. To say how it is usually covered is more essential, and this shall be the purport of my letter. Since our arrival at this happy spot, we have had a ham, sometimes a shoulder of bacon, to grace the head of the table; a piece of roast beef adorns the foot, and a dish of beans or greens almost imperceptible decorates the centre. When the cook has a mind to cut a figure, which I presume will be the case to-morrow, we have two beefsteak pies, or dishes of crabs, in addition, one on each side of the centre dish, dividing the space, and reducing the distance between dish and dish to about six feet, which, without them, would be about twelve feet apart. Of late he has had the surprising sagacity to discover that apples will make pies; and it is a question if, in the violence of his efforts, we do not get one of apples instead of having both of beefsteaks. If the ladies can put up with such entertainment, and will submit to partake of it on plates, once tin, but now iron (not become so by the labor of scouring), I shall be happy to see them.*

XXXVIII.—ON THE EVE OF HIS DEPARTURE AS A PRISONER TO EUROPE.

George Washington to Lt.-Gen. Burgoyne (then a prisoner).

HEADQUARTERS, March 11th, 1778.

SIR: Your indulgent opinion of my character, and the polite terms in which you are pleased to express it, are peculiarly flattering; and I take pleasure in the opportunity you have offered me of assuring you that, far from suffering the views of the national opposition to be embittered and debased by personal animosity, I am ever ready to do justice to the merit of the man and soldier, and to esteem, where esteem is due, however the idea of a public enemy may interpose. You will not think it the language of unmeaning ceremony if I add, that sentiments of personal respect are in the present instance reciprocal.

Viewing you in the light of an officer contending against what I conceive to be the rights of my country, the reverses you experienced in the field cannot be unacceptable to me; but abstracted from considerations of national advantage, I can sincerely sympathize with your feelings as a soldier, the unavoidable difficulties of whose situation forbade his success; and as a man, whose lot combines the calamity of ill health, the anxieties of captivity, and the painful sensibility for a reputation exposed where he most values it to the assaults of malice and detraction.

* Mr. Irving states that this is almost the only instance of sportive writing in Washington's correspondence.

Wishing you a safe and agreeable passage, with a perfect restoration of your health, I have the honor to be

Very respectfully, etc.

XXXIX.—APPEAL IN BEHALF OF HER SON.

Lady Asgill to Count De Vergennes.

LONDON, July 18th, 1782.

SIR: If the politeness of the French Court will permit an application of a stranger, there can be no doubt but one, in which all the tender feelings of an individual can be interested, will meet with a favorable reception from a nobleman, whose character does honor not only to his own country, but to human nature. The subject, sir, on which I presume to implore your assistance, is too heart-piercing for me to dwell on, and common fame has, most probably, informed you of it; it, therefore, renders the painful task unnecessary.

My son (an only son), as dear as he is brave, amiable as he is deserving to be so, only nineteen, a prisoner under the articles of capitulation at Yorktown, is now confined in America, an object of retaliation. Shall an innocent suffer for the guilty? Represent to yourself, sir, the situation of a family under these circumstances; surrounded, as I am, by objects of distress, distracted with fear and grief, no words can express my feelings, or paint the scene. My husband, given over by his physicians a few hours before the news arrived, and not in a state to be informed of the misfortune; my daughter, seized with a fever and delirium, raving about her brother, and without one interval of reason, save to hear heart-rending circumstances.

Let your feelings, sir, suggest and plead for my inexpressible misery. A word from you, like a voice from heaven, will save us from distraction and wretchedness. I am well informed General Washington reveres your character; say but to him you wish my son to be released, and he will restore him to his distracted family, and render him to happiness. My son's virtue and bravery will justify the deed. His honor, sir, carried him to America. He was born to affluence, independence, and the happiest prospects. Let me again supplicate your goodness; let me respectfully implore your high influence in behalf of innocence; in the cause of justice, of humanity, that you would, sir, despatch a letter to General Washington from France, and favor me with a copy of it, to be sent from hence.

I am sensible of the liberty I have taken in making this request; but I am sensible that, whether you comply with it or not, you will pity the distress that suggests it; your humanity will drop a tear on the fault, and efface it. I will pray that Heaven may grant you may never want the comfort it is in your power to bestow on ASGILL.

XL.—ANSWER TO THE SAME.

Count de Vergennes to General Washington.*

VERSAILLES, 29th July, 1782.

SIR: It is not in quality of a king, the friend and ally of the United States (though with the knowledge and consent of his Majesty), that I now have the honor to write to your Exellency. It is as a man of sensibility, and a tender father, who feels all the force of paternal love, that I take the liberty to address to your Excellency

* The letter of Count de Vergennes, enclosing that of Lady Asgill, in connection with other circumstances, led to the release of young Asgill.

my earnest solicitations in favor of a mother and family in tears. Her situation seems the more worthy of notice on our part, as it is to the humanity of a nation at war with her own, that she has recourse for what she ought to receive from the impartial justice of her own generals.

I have the honor to enclose to your Excellency a copy of a letter which Lady Asgill has just written. I am not known to her, nor was I acquainted that her son was the unhappy victim destined by lot to expiate the odious crime that a formal denial of justice obliges you to avenge. Your Excellency will not read this letter without being extremely affected; it had that effect upon the King and Queen, to whom I communicated it. The goodness of their Majesties' hearts induces them to desire that the inquietudes of an unfortunate mother may be calmed, and her tenderness reassured. I felt, sir, that there are cases where humanity exacts the most extreme rigor—perhaps the one now in question may be of the number—but allowing reprisals to be just, it is not less horrid to those who are the victims; and the character of your Excellency is too well known for me not to be persuaded that you desire nothing more than to be able to avoid the disagreeable necessity.

There is one consideration, sir, which, though it is not decisive, may have an influence on your resolution. Captain Asgill is doubtless your prisoner; but he is among those whom the arms of the King contributed to put into your hands at Yorktown. Although this circumstance does not operate as a safeguard, it justifies the interest I permit myself to take in this affair. If it is in your power, sir, to consider and have regard to it, you will do what is agreeable to their Majesties; the danger of young Asgill, the tears, the despair of his mother, affect them sensibly;

and they will see with pleasure the hope of consolation shine out for those unfortunate people.

In seeking to deliver Mr. Asgill from the fate which threatens him, I am far from engaging you to secure another victim; the pardon to be perfectly satisfactory must be entire. I do not imagine it can be productive of any bad consequences. If the English General has not been able to punish the horrible crime you complain of, in so exemplary a manner as he should, there is reason to think he will take the most efficacious measure to prevent the like in future.

I sincerely wish, sir, that my intercession may meet success; the sentiment which dictates it, and which you have not ceased to manifest on every occasion, assures me that you will not be indifferent to the prayers and the tears of a family which has recourse to your clemency through me. It is rendering homage to your virtue to implore it. I have the honor to be, with the most perfect consideration, sir, Yours, etc.,

De Vergennes.

XLI.—DESCRIPTON OF MISS WORDSWORTH.

S. T. Coleridge to Joseph Cottle.

Stoway, 1797.

My dear Cottle: Wordsworth and his exquisite sister are with me. She is a woman indeed! in mind I mean, and heart; for her person is such, that if you expected to see a pretty woman, you would think her rather ordinary; if you expected to see an ordinary woman, you would think her rather pretty; but her manners are simple, ardent, impressive. In every motion her innocent soul outbeams so brightly, that who saw, would say,

"Guilt was a thing impossible in her."

Her information various. Her eye watchful in minutest observation of nature; and her taste a perfect electrometer. It bends, protrudes, and draws in at subtlest beauties and most recondite faults.

She and W. desire their kindest respects to you.

Your ever affectionate friend, S. T. C.

XLII.—MODE OF MAKING A DOCTOR OF LAW.

Robert Southey to Bertha, Kate, and Isabel Southey.

June 26th, 1820.

Bertha, Kate, and Isabel, you have been very good girls, and have written me very nice letters, with which I was much pleased. This is the last letter which I can write in return; and as I happen to have a quiet hour to myself, here at Streatham, on Monday noon, I will employ that hour in relating to you the whole history and manner of my being ell-ell-deed at Oxford by the Vice-Chancellor.

You must know, then, that because I had written a great many good books, and more especially the Life of Wesley, it was made known to me by the Vice-Chancellor, through Mr. Heber, that the University of Oxford were desirous of showing me the only mark of honor in their power to bestow, which was that of making me an LL.D.—that is to say, a doctor of law. Now you are to know that some persons are ell-ell-deed every year at Oxford, at the great annual meeting, which is called the Commemoration. There are two reasons for this: first, that the University may do itself honor by bringing persons of distinction to receive the degree publicly as a mark of honor; and, secondly, that certain persons in inferior offices may share in the fees paid by those upon whom the ceremony of ell-ell-deeing is performed. For the first of these reasons the Emperor Alexander was made a Doctor of Laws at Oxford, the King of Prussia, and old Blucher and Platoff; and for the second, the same degree is conferred upon noblemen, and persons of fortune and consideration who are any ways connected with the University, or city, or county of Oxford.

The ceremony of ell-ell-deeing is performed in a large circular building called the theatre, of which I will show you a print when I return; and this theatre is filled with people. The undergraduates (that is, the young men who are called Cathedrals at Keswich) entirely fill the gallery. Under the gallery there are seats, which are filled with ladies in full dress, separated from the gentlemen. Between these two divisions of the ladies are seats for the heads of houses, and the doctors of law, physic, and divinity. In the middle of these seats is the vice-chancellor's, opposite the entrance, which is under the orchestra. On the right and left are two kinds of pulpits, from which the prize essays and poems are recited. The area, or middle of the theatre, is filled with bachelors and masters of arts, and with as many strangers as can obtain admission. Before the steps which lead up to the seats of the doctors, and directly in front of the Vice-Chancellor, a wooden bar is let down, covered with red cloth, and on each side of this the beadles stand in their robes.

When the theatre is full, the vice-chancellor and the heads of houses and the doctors enter. Those persons who are to be ell-ell-deed remain without in the divinity schools, in their robes, till the convocation have signified their assent to the ell-ell-deeing, and then they are led into the theatre one after another, in a line, into the middle of the area, the people first making a lane for them. The professor of civil law, Dr. Phillimore, went before, and made a long speech in Latin, telling the vice-chancellor and the dignissimi doctores what excellent persons we were who were now to be ell-ell-deed. Then he took us one by one by the hand, and presented each in his turn, pronouncing his name aloud, saying who and what he was, and calling him many laudatory names, ending in issimus. The audience then cheered loudly to show their approbation of the person; the vice-chancellor stood up, and repeating the first words in issime, ell-ell-deed him; the beadles lifted up the bar of separation, and the new made doctor went up the steps and took his seat among the dignissimi doctores.

Oh, Bertha, Kate, and Isabel, if you had seen me that day! I was like other issimis, dressed in a great robe of the finest scarlet cloth, with sleeves of rose-colored silk, and I had in my hand a black velvet cap like a beef-eater, for the use of which dress I paid one guinea for that day. Dr. Phillimore, who was an old school-fellow of mine, and a very good man, took me by the hand in my turn, and presented me; upon which there was a great clapping of hands and huzzaing at my name. When that was over, the vice-chancellor stood up and said these words, whereby I was ell-ell-deed: "*Doctissime et ornatissime vir, ego, pro auctoritate meâ et totius universitatis hujus, admitto te ad gradum doctores in jure civili, honoris causâ.*" These were the words which ell-ell-deed me; and then the bar was lifted up, and I seated myself among the doctors.

Little girls, you know it might be proper for me now to wear a large wig, and to be called Dr. Southey, and to become very severe, and leave off being a comical papa. And if you find that ell-ell-deeing has made this difference in me, you will not be surprised. However, I shall not come down in a wig; neither shall I wear my robes at home. God bless you all!

Your affectionate father,

R. Southey.

XLIII.—HOW TO TREAT A BORE.

Sir Walter Scott to Mrs. Walter Scott.

Abbottsford, March 23d, 1825.

My Dearest Jane: I am afraid you will think me a merciless correspondent, assailing you with so close a fire of letters; but having a frank I thought it as well to send you an epistle, though it can contain nothing more of interest excepting that we are all well. I can, however, add more particularly than formerly, that I learn from Mrs. Bayley that Mrs. Jobson's health is not only good but her spirits are remarkably so, so as to give the greatest pleasure to all friends. I can see, I think, a very good reason for this; for after the pain of the first separation from so dear an object, and after having brought her mind to believe that your present situation presented to you a fair chance for happiness, I can easily suppose that her maternal anxiety is greatly relieved from fears and apprehensions which formerly distressed her. Nothing can be more kind and more handsome than the way in which Mrs. Jobson speaks of Walter, which I mention because it gives me sincere pleasure, and will, I am sure, afford the same to you, or rather much more.

My troops here are sadly diminished. I have only Anne to parade for her morning walk, and to domineer over for going in thin slippers and silk stockings through dirty paths, and in lace veils through bushes and thorn brakes. I think Jane sometimes came in for a share of the lecture on these occasions. So I walk my solitary round—generally speaking—look after my laborers, and hear them regularly inquire, "If I have heard from the Captain and his Leddy!" I wish I could answer them *yes*, but have no reason to be impatient. This is the 23d, and I suppose Walter will be at Cork this evening to join the 15th, and that you are safe at Edgeworthstown to spend your first short term of widowhood. I hope the necessary hospitality to his mess will not occasion his dissipating too much; for, to be a very strong young man, I know no one with whom hard living agrees so ill. A happy change in the manners of the times fortunately renders such abuse of the good creature, wine, much less frequent and less fashionable than it was in my days and Sir Adam's. Drinking is not now the vice of the times, whatever vices and follies they may have adopted in its stead.

I had proceeded thus far in my valuable communication, when, lo! I was alarmed by the entrance of that terrific animal, a two-legged boar—one of the largest size and most tremendous powers. By the way, I learned, from no less an authority than George Canning, what my own experience has since made good, that an efficient bore must always have something respectable about him, otherwise no one would permit him to exercise his occupation. He must be, for example, a very rich man (which perhaps, gives the greatest privilege of all)—or he must be a man of rank and condition too important to be treated *sans ceremonie*—or a man of learning (often a dreadful bore)—or of talents undoubted, or of high pretensions to wisdom and experience, or a great traveller; in short, he must have some tangible privilege to sanction his profession. Without something of this kind one would treat a bore as you do a vagrant mendicant, and send him off to the workhouse if he presumed to annoy you. But when properly qualified the bore is more like a beggar with a badge and pass from his parish, which entitles him to disturb you with his importunity whether you will or no. Now, my bore is a complete gentleman and an old friend, but, unhappily for those who know him, master of all Joe Miller's stories of sailors and Irishmen, and full of quotations from the classics as hackeneyed as the post-horses of Melrose. There was no remedy; I must either stand his shot within doors or turn out with him for a long walk, and for the sake of elbow-room I preferred the last. Imagine an old gentleman, who has been handsome, and has still that sort of pretension which leads him to wear tight pantaloons and a smart half-boot, neatly adapted to show off his leg; suppose him as upright and straight as a poker, if the poker's head had been by some accident bent to one side; add to this that he is as deaf as a post; consider that I was writing to Jane, and desired not to be interrupted by much more entertaining society. Well, I was *had*, however—fairly caught—and out we sallied to make the best we could of each other. I felt a sort of necessity to ask him to dinner; but the invitation, like Macbeth's *amen*, stuck in my throat. For the first hour he got the lead, and kept it; but opportunities always occur to an able general, if he knows how to make use of them. In an evil hour for him and a happy one for me, he started the topic of our intended railroad; *there* I was a match for him, having had, on Tuesday last, a meeting with Harden, the two Torwoodlees, and the engineer, on this subject, so that I had at my finger-end every *cut*, every lift, every degree of elevation or depression, every pass in the country, and every possible means of crossing them. So I kept the whip-hand of him completely, and never permitted him to get off the railway again to his own ground. In short, so thoroughly did I bore my bore that he sickened and gave in, taking a short leave of me. Seeing him in full retreat I *then* ventured to make the civil offer of a dinner. But the railroad had been breakfast, luncheon, dinner, and supper to boot; he hastily excused himself and left me at double-quick time, sick of railroads, I dare say, for six months to come. But I must not forget that I am perhaps abusing the privilege I have to bore you, being that of your affectionate papa.

How nicely we could manage without the said railroad, now the great hobby of our Teviotdale lairds, if we could, by any process of conjuration, waft to Abbottsford some of the coal and lime from Lochore; though, if I were to wish for such impossibilities, I would rather desire Prince Houssein's tapestry in the Arabian Nights, to bring Walter and Jane to us now and then, than I would wish for "Fife and all the lands about it."*

By the by, Jane, after all, though she looks so demure, is a very sly girl, and keeps her accomplishments to herself. You would not talk with me about planting and laying out ground; and yet, from what you had been doing at Kochore, I see what a pretty turn you have for these matters. I wish you were here to advise me about the little pond which we passed, where, if you remember, there is a new cottage built. I intend to plant it with aquatic trees, willows, alders, poplars, and so forth, and put trouts and perches into the water, and have a preserve of wild ducks on the pond, with Canadian geese and some other water-fowl. I am to get some eggs from Lord Traquair of a curious species of half-reclaimed wild ducks which abound near his solitary old chateau, and nowhere else in Scotland that I know of;

* A song of Dr. Blacklock's.

and I can get the Canadian geese, curious painted animals, that look as if they had flown out of a figured Chinese paper, from Mr. Murray, of Broughton. The foolish folks, when I was absent, chose to improve on my plan by making an island in the pond, which is exactly the size and shape of a Stilton cheese. It will be useful, however, for the fowl to breed in.

Mamma drove out your pony and carriage to-day. She was (twenty years ago) the best *lady-whip* in Edinburgh, and was delighted to find that she retained her dexterity. I hope she will continue to exercise the rein and whip now and then, as her health is much improved by moderate exercise.

Adieu, my dear Jane. Mamma and Anne join in the kindest love and best wishes, I please myself with the idea that I shall have heard you are well and happy long before this reaches you. Believe me always your affectionate father,

WALTER SCOTT.

I hope you will take my good example, and write without caring or thinking either what you have got to say or in what words you say it.

XLIV.—WHIMSICAL DESCRIPTION OF A BAD COLD.*

Charles Lamb to Bernard Barton.

January 9th, 1824.

DEAR B. B.: Do you know what it is to succumb under an insurmountable day-mare—" a whoreson lethargy," Falstaff calls it—an indisposition to do any thing, or to be any thing; a total deadness and distaste; a suspension of vitality; an indiffer-

* Dr. James Alexander, describing a visit to the India House, says he inquired for Charles Lamb of the doorkeeper. He replied he had been there

ence to locality; a numb, soporifical, good-for-nothingness; an ossification all over; an oysterlike insensibility to the passing events; a mind-stupor; a brawny defiance to the needles of a thrusting-in conscience? Did you ever have a very bad cold, with a total irresolution to submit to water-gruel processes? This has been for many weeks my lot, and my excuse; my fingers drag heavily over this paper, and to my thinking, it is three and twenty furlongs from here to the end of this demi-sheet. I have not a thing to say; nothing is of more importance than another; I am flatter than a denial or a pancake; emptier than Judge ——'s wig when the head is in it; duller than a country stage when the actors are off it; a cipher, an O! I acknowledge life at all only by an occasional convulsional cough, and a permanent phlegmatic pain in the chest. I am weary of the world; life is weary of me. My day is gone into twilight, and I don't think it worth the expense of candles. My wick hath a thief in it, but I can't muster courage to snuff it. I inhale suffocation; I can't distinguish veal from mutton; nothing interests

since he was sixteen years old, and had never heard of any Mr. Lamb. But the doorkeeper of the museum remembered him well. "Oh yes, sir, he was a very little man, with such small legs, and wore knee breeches." He directed me to a private stair, which would take me down to the accounts. I went into a place below like a bank, and was shown to a principal person, Mr. W. It was the room in which Lamb wrote many years, but had been altered. Mr. W. showed me his window and where his desk was. I looked out at the high blank wall, not five feet beyond, and understood Lamb's "India House." Mr. W. showed me a quarto volume of *Interest* Tables, with such remarks as these, in Lamb's fine, round hand on the fly-leaf: "A book of much interest.—Ed. Rev." "A work in which the interest never flags.—Q. Rev." "We may say of this volume that the interest increases from the beginning to the end.—Monthly Rev." Mr. W. knew Lamb well. "He was a small man, smaller than you, and always wore shorts and black gaiters. Sometimes his puns were poor. He often came late, and then he would say, "Well, I will make up for it by going away early."—H.

me. 'Tis twelve o'clock and Thurtell is just now coming out upon the New Drop, Jack Ketch alertly tucking up his greasy sleeves to do the last office of mortality, yet cannot I elicit a groan or a moral reflection. If you told me the world will be at an end to-morrow, I should just say, "Will it?" I have not volition enough left to dot my i's, much less to comb my eyebrows; my eyes are set in my head; my brains are gone out to see a poor relation in Moorfields, and they did not say when they'd come back again; my skull is a Grub street attic to let—not so much as a joint-stool or a crack'd jordan left in it; my hand writes, not I, from habit, as chickens run about a little when their heads are off. O for a vigorous fit of gout, colic, toothache—an earwig in my auditory, a fly in my visual organs. Pain is life—the sharper the more evidence of life; but this apathy, this death! Did you ever have an obstinate cold—a six or seven weeks' unintermitting chill and suspension of hope, fear, conscience, and every thing? Yet do I try all I can to cure it; I try wine and spirits, and smoking, and snuff in unsparing quantities; but they all only seem to make me worse instead of better. I sleep in a damp room, but it does me no good; I come home late o' nights, but do not find any visible amendment! Who shall deliver me from the body of this death? It is just fifteen minutes after twelve; Thurtell is by this time a good way on his journey, baiting at Scorpion perhaps! Ketch is bargaining for his cast-coat and waistcoat; the Jew demurs at first at three half-crowns, but on consideration that he may get somewhat by showing them in the town, finally closes.

C. Lamb.

XLV.—TRAVELLING WITH "A WELL-INFORMED MAN"—ECCENTRIC BARRISTER.

Charles Lamb to Mrs. Haslett.

May 24th, 1830.

"Mary's love? Yes. Mary Lamb is quite well."

DEAR SARAH: I found my way to Northan on Thursday, and saw a very good woman behind a counter, who says also that you are a very good lady. I did not accept her offered glass of wine (homemade I take it), but craved a cup of ale, with which I seasoned a slice of cold lamb, from a sandwich box, which I ate in her back parlor, and proceeded for Berkhampstead, etc.; lost myself over a heath, and had a day's pleasure. I wish you could walk as I do, and as you used to do. I am sorry to find you are so poorly; and, now I have found my way, I wish you back at Goody Tomlinson's. What a pretty village 'tis. I should have come sooner, but was waiting a summons to Bury. Well, it came, and I found the good parson's lady (he was from home) exceedingly hospitable.

Poor Emma, the first moment we were alone, took me into a corner, and said: "Now, pray, don't *drink;* do check yourself after dinner, for my sake, and when we get home to Enfield you shall drink as much as ever you please, and I won't say a word about it." How I behaved you may guess, when I tell you that Mrs. Williams and I have written acrostics on each other, and she hoped that she should have "no reason to regret Miss Isola's recovery, by its depriving her of our begun correspondence." Emma stayed a month with us, and has gone back (in tolerable health) to her long home, for she comes not again for a twelvemonth. I amused Mrs. Williams with an occurrence on our road to Enfield. We travelled with one of those troublesome fellow-passengers in a stage-coach, that is called a well-informed man. For twenty miles we discoursed about the properties of steam, probabilities of carriages by ditto, till all my science, and more than all, was exhausted, and I was thinking of escaping my torment by getting up on the outside, when getting into Bishop's Stortford, my gentleman, spying some farming land, put an unlucky question to me: "What sort of a crop of turnips I thought we should have this year?" Emma's eyes turned to me to know what in the world I could have to say, and she burst into a violent fit of laughter, maugre her pale, serious cheeks, when, with the greatest gravity, I replied, that "it depended, I believed, upon boiled legs of mutton." This clenched our conversation, and my gentleman, with a face half wise, half in scorn, troubled us with no more conversation, scientific or philosophical, for the remainder of the journey. S—— was here yesterday, and as learned to the full as my fellow-traveller. What a pity that he will spoil a wit, and a most pleasant fellow (as he is) by wisdom. N. Y—— is as good, and as odd as ever. We had a dispute about the word "heir," which I contended was pronounced like "air;" he said that it might be in common parlance, or that we might so use it speaking of the "Heir at Law," a comedy: but that in the law courts it was necessary to give it a full aspiration, and to say *hayer*; he thought it might even vitiate a cause if a counsel pronounced it otherwise. In conclusion, he would consult Sergeant Wilde, who gave it against him. Sometimes he falleth into the water; sometimes into the fire. He came down here and insisted on reading Virgil's Æneid all through with me (which he did), because a counsel must know Latin. Another time he read out all the Gospel of St. John, because Biblical quotations are very emphatic in a court of justice.

A third time, he would carve a fowl, which he did very ill favoredly, because " we did not know how indispensable it was for a barrister to do all those sort of things well! Those little things were of more consequence than we supposed!" So he goes on, harassing about the way to prosperity, and losing it. With a long head, but somewhat a wrong one—harum-scarum. Why does not his guardian angel look to him? He deserves one; maybe he has tired him out. I am done with this long scrawl, but I thought in your exile you might like a letter. Commend me to all the wonders in Derbyshire, and tell the devil I humbly kiss—my hand to him.

Yours ever, C. LAMB.

ENFIELD, Saturday.

XLVI.—EFFECT OF PRESENT OF A WATCH ON HIS BETROTHED.

Charles Lamb to Mr. Moxon.

July 24th, 1833.

For God's sake give Emma no more watches; one has turned her head. She is arrogant and insulting. She said something very unpleasant to our old clock in the passage, as if he did not keep time, and yet he had made her no appointment. She takes it out every instant to look at the moment-hand. She lugs us out into the fields, because there the bird-boys ask you, " Pray, sir, can you tell us what's o'clock?" and she answers them punctually. She loses all her time looking to see " what the time is." I overheard her whispering, " Just so many hours, minutes, etc., to Tuesday;" I think St. George's goes too slow! This little present of Time!—why—'tis Eternity to her!

What can make her so fond of a gingerbread watch? She has spoiled some of the movements. Between ourselves, she has kissed away "half-past twelve," which I suppose to be the canonical hour in hanover Square.

Well, if "love me, love my watch" answers, she will keep time to you. "It goes right by the Horse Guards."

DEAREST M.: Never mind opposite nonsense.* She does not love you for the watch, but the watch for you. I will be at the wedding, and keep the 30th July as long as my poor months last me, as a festival gloriously.

Yours ever, ELIA.

We have not heard from Cambridge, I will write the moment we do.

Edmonton, 24th July, twenty minutes past three by Emma's watch.

XLVII.—NO AFFECTION BEYOND 78° OR BELOW 20° FAHRENHEIT.

Rev. Sydney Smith to Mrs. ——.

July, 1836.

DEAR MRS. ——: I shall have great pleausre in calling for you to go to Mrs. Charles Buller, on Wednesday. Mrs. Sydney's arm is rather better, many thanks for the inquiry. Very high and very low temperature extinguishes all human sympathy and relations. It is impossible to feel affection beyond 78° or below 20° of Fahrenheit; human nature is too solid or too liquid beyond these limits. Man only lives to shiver or to perspire. God send that the glass may fall and restore me to my regard for you, which, in the temperate zone, is invariable.

SYDNEY SMITH.

* Written on the opposite page to that in which the previous affectionate letter appears.

XLVIII.—THE GOUT—VALUE OF EASY-CHAIRS.

Sydney Smith to Lady Dufferin.

COMBE FLOREY (No date).

I am just beginning to get well from that fit of gout, at the beginning of which you were charitable enough to pay me a visit, and I said the same Providence that inflicts gout creates Dufferins! We must take the good and the evils of life.

I am charmed, I confess, with the beauty of this country. I hope some day you will be charmed with it too. It banished, however, every Arcadian notion to see —— walk in at the gate to-day. I seemed to be transported instantly to Piccadilly, and the innocence went out of me.

I hope the process of furnishing goes on well. Attend, I pray you, to the proper selection of an easy-chair, where you may cast yourself down in the weariness and distresses of life, with the absolute certainty that every joint of the human frame will receive all the comfort which can be derived from easy position and soft materials; then the glass, on which your eyes are so often fixed, knowing that you have the great duty imposed on the Sheridans, of looking well. You may depend upon it, happiness depends mainly on these little things.

I hope you remain in perfect favor with Rogers, and that you are not omitted in any of the dress breakfast parties. Remember me to the Norton. Tell her I am glad to be sheltered from her beauty by the insensibility of age; that I shall not live to see its decay, but die with that unfaded image before my eyes. But don't make a mistake and deliver the message to ——, instead of your sister.

I remain, dear Lady Dufferin,

Very sincerely yours, SYDNEY SMITH.

XLIX. — INVITATION ACCEPTED.

Sydney Smith to Charles Dickens.

May 14th, 1842.

My dear Dickens: I accept your obliging invitation conditionally. If I am invited by any man of greater genius than yourself, or one by whose works I have been more completely interested, I will repudiate you, and dine with the more splendid phenomenon of the two.

Ever yours sincerely, Sydney Smith.

L.—APOLOGY FOR DECLINING A DINNER PARTY.

Sydney Smith to Lord Mahon.

July 4th, 1843.

My dear Lord Mahon: I am only half recovered from a violent attack of gout in the knee, and I could not bear the confinement of dinner without getting up and walking between the courses, or thrusting my foot on somebody else's chair, like the Archbishop of Dublin. For these reasons I have been forced for some time, and am still forced, to decline dinner engagements. I should, in a sounder state, have had great pleasure in accepting the very agreeable party you are kind enough to propose to me; but I shall avail myself, in the next campaign, of your kindness. I consider myself as well acquainted with Lady Mahon and yourself, and shall hope to see you here, as well as elsewhere. Pray present my benediction to your charming wife, who I am sure would bring any plant in the garden into full flower by looking at it and smiling upon it. Try the experiment from mere curiosity.

Ever yours, Sydney Smith.

LI.—A HUNDRED PERSONS STARVED BY HIS VORACITY.

Sydney Smith to Lord Murray.

COMBE FLOREY, Sept. 29th, 1843.

MY DEAR MURRAY; Jeffrey has written to me to say he means to dedicate his essays to me. This I think a very great honor, and it pleases me very much. I am sure he ought to resign. He has very feeble health; a mild climate would suit the state of his throat. Mrs. Jeffrey thinks he could not employ himself. Wives know a great deal about husbands, but if she is right I should be surprised. I have thought he had a canine appetite for books, though this sometimes declines in the decline of life. I am beautifying my house in Green street; a comfortable house is a great source of happiness. It ranks immediately after health and a good conscience. I see your religious war is begun in Scotland. I suppose Jeffrey will be at the head of the Free Church troops. Do you think he has any military talents?

You are, I hear, attending more to diet than heretofore. If you wish for any thing like happiness in the fifth act of life, eat and drink about one-half what you could eat and drink. Did I ever tell you my calculation about eating and drinking? Having ascertained the weight of what I could live upon, so as to preserve health and strength, and what I did live upon, I found that, between ten and seventy years of age, I had eaten and drunk forty-four horse wagon loads of meat and drink more than would have preserved me in life and health! The value of this mass of nourishment I considered to be worth seven thousand pounds sterling. It occurred to me that I must, by my voracity, have starved to death fully a hundred persons. This is a frightful calculation, but irresistibly true; and I think, dear Murray, your wagons would require an additional horse each!

Lord and Lady Lansdowne, who are rambling about this fine country, are to spend a day here next week. You must really come to see the west of England. From Combe Florey we will go together to Linton and Lynmouth—than which there is nothing finer in this island. Two of our acquaintances died this week—Stewart Mackenzie and Bell. We must close our ranks. God bless you, my dear Murray!

SYDNEY SMITH.

LII.—REFLECTIONS ON THE LOSS OF FRIENDS.

Lady Blessington to Walter Savage Landor.

GORE HOUSE, KENSINGTON GORE, March 10th, 1836.

I write to you from my new residence in what I call the country, being a mile from London. I have not forgotten that your last letter announced the pleasing intelligence that you were to be in London in April, and I write to request that you will take up your residence at my house. I have a comfortable room to offer you, and, what is better still, a cordial welcome. Pray bear this in mind, and let me have the pleasure of having you under my roof. Have you heard of the death of poor Sir William Gell? He expired at Naples on the 4th of February, literally exhausted by his bodily infirmity.

Poor Gell! I regret him much; he was gentle, kind-hearted, and good-tempered, possessed a great fund of information, which was always at the service of any one requiring it, and if free from passion (not always, in my opinion, a desirable thing), totally exempt from prejudice, which I hold to be most desirable.

How much more frequently we think of a friend we have lost than when he lived! I have thought of poor Gell continually since I got Mr. Craven's melancholy letter announcing his demise, yet when he lived I have passed weeks without bestowing a thought on him. Is not this a curious fact in all our natures, that we only begin to know the value of friends when they are lost to us forever? It ought to teach us to turn with increased tenderness to those that remain; and I always feel that my affection for living friends is enlivened by the reflection that they too may pass away.

If we were only half as lenient to the living as we are to the dead, how much happiness might we render them, and from how much vain and bitter remorse might we be spared, when the grave, the all-atoning grave, has closed over them. I long to read your book; it will be to me like water in the desert to the parched pilgrim. Let me hear from you, and, above all, tell me that you will take up your abode with me, where quiet and friendship await you.

M. Blessington.

LIII.—COMPLIMENTS—ARABIAN NIGHTS.

Walter Savage Landor to Lady Blessington.

January 13th, 1835.

Arnold is so mischievous as to show me, at this moment, the portrait of the Duchess of ——, and to say she ought to have been put in the index or notes. Sure enough she never was a beauty. The Duke had so little idea of countenance, that he remarked a wonderful resemblance between me and ——. Perhaps he thought to compliment both parties. Now you had better find a ghost than a resemblance. If an ugly woman is compared to a beautiful one, she will tell you, "This is the first time I was ever taken for an idiot." If a sensible woman is compared to Madame de Stael, she shows you her foot and thanks God she has not yet taken to rouge.

I have been reading Beckford's Travels and Vatheck. The last pleases me less than it did forty years ago, and yet the Arabian Nights have lost none of their charms for me. All the learned and wiseacres in England cried out against this wonderful work upon its first appearance—Gray among the rest. Yet I doubt whether any man, except Shakespeare, has afforded so much delight, if we open our hearts to receive it. The author of the Arabian Nights was the greatest benefactor the East ever had, not excepting Mohammed. How many hours of pure happiness has he bestowed upon six-and-twenty millions of hearers? All the springs of the desert have less refreshed the Arabs than those delightful tales, and they cast their gems and genii over our benighted and foggy regions.

B——, in his second letter, says that two or three of Rosa da Tivoli's landscapes merit observation, and in the next he scorns P. Potter. Now all Rosa da Tivoli's works are not worth a blade of grass from the hand of P. Potter. The one was a consummate artist; the other one of the coarsest that ever bedaubed a canvas. He talks of "the worst roads that ever pretended to be made use of," and of a *dish* of tea, without giving us the ladle or the carving knife for it. When I read such things I rub my eyes and awaken my recollections. I not only fancy that I am older than I am in reality (which is old enough, in all conscience), but that I have begun to lose my acquaintance with our idiom. Those who desire to write upon light matters gracefully, must read with attention the writings of

Pope, Lady M. W. Montagu, and Lord Chesterfield—three ladies of the first water.

I am sorry you sent my "Examination" by a private hand. Nothing affects me but pain and disappointment. Hannah More says "there are no evils in the world but sin and bile." They fall upon me very unequally. I would give a good quantity of bile for a trifle of sin, and yet my philosophy would induce me to throw it aside. No man ever began so early to abolish hopes and wishes. Happy he who is resolved to walk with Epicurus on his right and Epictetus on his left, and to shut his ears to every other voice along the road.

W. S. Landor.

LIV.—DETERMINATION NOT TO WRITE AFTER SEVENTY.

Walter Savage Landor to Lady Blessington.

P. M.—Bath, Nov. 5th, 1844.

Always kind and considerate. I have indeed had a touch of the rheumatism—a mere touch; not a blow—and the rheumatism you know (or rather I hope you do *not* know) always comes with a heavy cudgel. It was caused by my imprudence in rising up in my bed to fix a thought on paper; night is not the time to pin a butterfly on a blank leaf. Four hot baths have now almost buoyed up this monster from oppressing me. Of its four legs I feel only one upon me, and, indeed, just the extremity of the hoof. At Gore House I should forget it; there I forgot the plague when I had it. But Bath air is the best air in the world; in twenty minutes we can have three climates.

I hope in the spring I may be able to pay you my respects. Where else can I find so much wit and so much wisdom? The rest of the earth may pretend it can collect (but I doubt it) as much beauty. Do not whisper a word of this to a certain pair of sisters. I hope I myself shall be in full bloom when we meet again; indeed, I have little doubt of it. I have youth on my side; I shall not see seventy for nearly three months to come. I am very busy collecting all I have written. It may, perhaps, be published in another eight or ten months. Once beyond seventy I will never write a line, in verse or prose, for publication. I will be my own Gil Blas. The wisest of us are unconscious when our faculties begin to decay. Knowing this, I fixed my determination many years ago. I am now plucking out my weeds all over the field, and will leave only the strongest shoots of the best plants standing. W. S. L.

LV.—PICTURE OF THE PRINCE OF DARKNESS.

Robert Southey to Grosvenor C. Bedford.

January 21st, 1799.

My dear Grosvenor: You ask me why the devil rides on horseback. The Prince of Darkness is a gentleman, and that would be reason enough; but, moreover, the history doth aver that he came on horseback for the old woman, and rode before her, and that the color of the horse was black.* Should I falsify the history, and make Apollyon a pedestrian? Besides, Grosvenor, Apollyon is cloven-footed; and I humbly conceive that a biped—and I never understood his dark majesty to be otherwise—that a biped, I say, would walk clumsily upon cloven feet. Neither hath Apollyon wings, according to the best representations; and, indeed, how should he? For, were they of feathers, like the angels', they would be burned in the everlasting fire;

* The allusion is to the ballad of "The Old Woman of Berkeley."

and were they of leather, like a bat's, they would be shrivelled. I conclude, therefore, that wings he hath not. Yet do we find, from sundry reputable authors and divers histories, that he transporteth himself from place to place with exceeding rapidity. Now, as he cannot walk fast or fly, he must have some conveyance. Stage-coaches to the infernal regions there are none, though the road be much frequented. Balloons would burst at setting out, the air would be so rarefied with the heat; but horses he may have of a particular breed.

I am learned in Dæmonology, and could say more, but this sufficeth. I should advise you not to copy the ballad, because the volume will soon be finished. I expect to bring it with me on Ash-Wednesday to town. . . . . .

I am better, but they tell me that constant exercise is indispensable, and that, at my age and with my constitution, I must either throw off the complaint now, or it will stick to me forever. Edith's health requires care; our medical friend dreads the effect of London upon both. When my time is out at our present house (at Midsummer), we must go to the sea a while. I thought I was like a Scotch fir, and could grow anywhere, but I am sadly altered, and my nerves are in a vile state. I am almost ashamed of my own feelings; but they depend not upon volition. These things throw a fog over the prospect of life. I cannot see my way; it is time to be in an office, but the confinement would be ruinous. You know not the alteration I feel. I could once have slept with the seven sleepers without a miracle; now the least sound awakes me, and with alarm. However, I am better. . . . God bless you.

Yours affectionately,

R. SOUTHEY.

BOOK THE THIRD.

Sketches of Nature, Art, and Travel, in Letters.

BOOK THE THIRD.

SKETCHES OF NATURE, ART, AND TRAVEL IN LETTERS.

I.—THE MORNING.

Daniel Webster to Mrs. J. W. Page.

RICHMOND, April 29, 1841.—Five o'clock A. M.

Whether it be a favor or an annoyance, you owe this letter to my habit of early rising. From the hour marked at the top of the page you will naturally conclude that my companions are not now engaging my attention, as we have not calculated on being early travellers to-day.

This city has a "pleasant seat." It is high, the James River runs below it, and when I went out an hour ago nothing was heard but the roar of the falls. The air is tranquil and its temperature mild.

It is morning, and a morning sweet and fresh and delightful. Everybody knows the morning in its metaphorical sense, applied to so many objects and on so many occasions. The health, strength, and beauty of early years lead us to call that period the "morning of life." Of a lovely young woman we say, she is "bright as the morning;" and no one doubts why Lucifer is called " son of the morning." But the morning itself few people, inhabitants of cities, know any thing about. Among all our good people of Boston, not one in a thousand sees the sun rise once a year. They know nothing of the morning. Their idea of it is, that it is that part of the day which comes along after a cup of coffee and a beefsteak, or a piece of toast. With them morning is not a new issuing of light, a new bursting forth of the sun, a new waking up of all that has life, from a sort of temporary death, to behold again the works of God, the heavens and the earth; it is only a part of the domestic day, belonging to breakfast, to reading the newspapers, answering notes, sending the children to school, and giving orders for dinner. The first faint streak of light, the earliest purpling of the east which the lark springs up to greet, and the deeper and deeper coloring into orange and red, till at length the " glorious sun is seen, Regent of day;" this they never enjoy, for this they never see.

Beautiful descriptions of the morning abound in all languages, but they are the strongest perhaps in those of the east, where the sun is so often an object of worship. King David speaks of taking to himself " the wings of the morning." This is highly poetical and beautiful. The " wings of the morning" are the beams of the rising sun. Rays of light are wings. It is thus said that the Sun of Righteousness shall arise, " with healing in his wings;" a rising sun which shall scatter light, and health, and joy, throughout the universe.

Milton has fine descriptions of morning, but not so many as Shakespeare, from whose writings pages of the most beautiful images, all founded on the glory of the morning, might be filled.

I never thought that Adam had much advantage of us from

having seen the world while it was new. The manifestations of the power of God, like His mercies, are "new every morning" and "fresh every evening." We see as fine risings of the sun as Adam ever saw, and its risings are as much a miracle now as they were in his day, and I think a good deal more, because it is now a part of the miracle that for thousands and thousands of years he has come to his appointed time, without the variation of a millionth part of a second. Adam could not tell how this might be!

I know the morning; I am acquainted with it and I love it, fresh and sweet as it is; a daily new creation, breaking forth and calling all that have life, and breath, and being, to new adoration, new enjoyments, and new gratitude.*

* * * To-morrow we leave for Raleigh, at an hour which the world calls "morning." The air is fine, quite cool enough, and dry. What struck me last evening was the dryness of the night air. Of all the cities of the Atlantic, south, this is probably the finest for elevation, situation, handsome houses and public buildings, and prospects of growth.

Be kind enough to give or send our love to your husband and children. Yours affectionately, DANIEL WEBSTER.

* Mr. Webster's correspondence is full of evidence of the genuineness of his appreciation of morning. The following passage occurs in a letter to Mr. Blatchford (Vol. 2, Private Correspondence, p. 262):

MARSHFIELD, Tuesday morning, five o'clock, Dec. 7, 1847.

It is a beautiful, clear, cold, still morning. I rose at four o'clock, and have looked forth. The firmament is glorious. Jupiter and Venus are magnificent, "and stars unnumbered gild the glowing pole." I wish I could once see the constellations of the South, though I do not think they can excel the heavens which are over our heads. An hour or two hence we shall have a fine sunrise. The long twilights of this season of the year make the sun's rising a slow and beautiful progress. About an hour hence these lesser lights will begin to pale their ineffectual fires.

II.—DESCRIPTION OF OXFORD.

Dr. James Alexander to Dr. Hall.

OXFORD, September 26th, 1851.

I came here to dinner yesterday from Liverpool, 176 miles. We touched Rugby village, about a mile from the school. It is vacation here, which is bad; but the claustral silence, and venerable solitude, and regal ecclesiastical state of this monastic city of palaces, is surely unique. The impression is that of an awful dream. You have read so long and so much about Oxford that I should think it idle to repeat what is in a score of books. I will set down some incoherences not in print.

Oxford is larger, greater, and lordlier than Cambridge. It has more colleges—more large colleges—and an aggregate of architectural glories beyond Cambridge; but Oxford has nothing like King's College, Cambridge, and little like Trinity, and no grounds like those of the last named. There is a family-likeness in the two towns, but Oxford is more antique, civic, mediæval, and proud. Cambridge has incomparably the more beautiful site. There is no chapel in Oxford, or the world, like King's at Cambridge. There is no hall at Cambridge like Christ Church here.

The turf is close-shaven, cut every few days, rolled and swept; and is unlike any thing known among us, the moist climate favoring grass. Flowers abound, not only in the landscape gardening of the immense college greens, but in the windows of fellows. Some of the quadrangles here are not green, but gravelled. Christ Church meadow is surrounded by a walk of a mile, and elms three centuries old. You may lose yourself in the groves and thickets of some of those river-gardens. I learn that the "men" seldom prefer them to the streets. The halls or refectories are, as a whole, less regal than at Cambridge, except only Christ Church, where they daily provide for three hundred in term. Around these are portraits, generally full length, of great members. The painted glass windows in the chapels are by far the best I have met with, especially five Flemish windows in New College chapel (William of Wyckham's). The feeling in these cloisters, "quods," and parks (where deer come to your hand), is that of absolute sequestration from the world. Pusey's house, in one of the inner corners of Christ Church, is just the spot to generate such fancies as his. The system here, though inexpressibly fascinating, is out of harmony with the age. In every buttery-entrance where you look to espy a monk under the black honey-combed arches, you see the placards of "Time Tables of N. W. Railway." The present warden of All Souls (where there are none not fellows), is the first married warden. The pressure of the age will certainly bring collapse on these outworn cenobitic shells. I feel it every moment in a country where steam affects every inch, and trains thunder by some places twenty in a day. The agitation about exclusive privileges and overgrown foundations every year, shakes down part of the old pile, as in regard to the income of bishops, by the late act. A clergyman here is regarded everywhere with a deference unknown anywhere else. But as a class, they evidently feel very fully that they are on their good behavior, and that public opinion cannot be disregarded. Some, I believe many, are laboring to gain good will to the church in the best of all ways.

It would consume pages, and emulate guide-books, to tell of college chapel after chapel, halls, gardens, portraits, statues, libraries, and cloisters. Books of great size are taken up with this. Dr. Routh, author of the Reliquiæ Sacræ, Master of Magdalen College, has his portrait in the Bodleian, aet. 96. He is the oldest living Oxonian. The general effect produced by Oxford is soothing to my mind in a high degree. Such self-contained wealth of learning, such seclusion from the stir of life, such yielding of every thing to learned honors, such architectural glory, such libraries, such lawns, such trees, such prizes held out to studious ambition, such histories of past genius, such mighty and beloved names, such costly display of taste, such approaches to what Rome was and would again be, exist here only and at Cambridge, and more here than there. But it all strikes me as a tree whose root is dead in the earth, vast, green, and lovely, but destined to die presently. I doubt whether the glory has not already passed away. The true Oxonian spirit is that of Newman and Pusey; but it is not of the age. Such a chapel as Christ College, which has lately been repaired at an expense of $90,000, is fitted to absorb a young man in reveries, but they are of an age which cannot live again. My hopes rise beyond what I am able to report during this rapid tour; that God is working by new agencies, and a new *zeitgeist*, and our new world, to bring in a new kingdom. So far from letting my intense and scarce excusable fondness for the relics of darker ages tempt me to wish them back again, or try to imitate them, I am even more filled with a sense of the gigantic progress of the modern arts and civilization. One day at the exhibition, one day at Birmingham and Manchester, or one day on any one trunk of English railways, is worth volumes to awaken expectation. I have meditated, I trust not unusefully, amidst objects which have the odor of past ages. My reigning sentiment, after a hurrying and exciting travel among the thousands of this unspeakably teeming population of Europe, is an impression that men and generations pass away like the herb of the field, but the word of the Lord abideth forever; His kingdom is coming; His house is going up; His plan is unfolding; old traditionary things which vain men call eternal, are crumbling; new things predicted, but not expected, are rolling in like a flood; our life and that of our children is but a link in the great chain. I trust I can sometimes add, "Thy kingdom come! Thy will be done!"

III.—SOUTHAMPTON—NETTLELY ABBEY.

Thomas Gray to Mr. Nicholls.

I received your letter at Southampton; and as I would wish to treat everybody according to their own rule and measure of good breeding, have, against my inclination, waited till now before I answered it, purely out of fear and respect, and an ingenuous diffidence of my own abilities. If you will not take this as an excuse, accept it at least as a well-turned period, which is always my principal concern.

So I proceed to tell you that my health is much improved by the sea: not that I drank it, or bathed in it, as the common people do; no! I only walked by it and looked upon it. The climate is remarkably mild, even in October and November; no snow has been seen to lie there for these thirty years past; the myrtles grow in the ground against the houses, and Guernsey lilies bloom in every window; the town, clean and well-built, surrounded by its old stone walls, with their towers and gateways, stands at the point of a peninsula, and opens full south to an arm of the sea, which, having formed two beautiful bays on each hand of it, stretches away in direct view, till it joins the British Channel; it is skirted on either side with gentle rising grounds, clothed with thick wood, and directly across its mouth rise the high lands of the Isle of Wight at a distance, but distinctly seen. In the bosom of the woods (concealed from profane eyes) lie hid the ruins of Nettely Abbey; there may be richer and greater houses of religion, but the abbot is content with his situation. See there, at the top of that hanging meadow, under the shade of those old trees that bend into a half circle about it, he is walking slowly (good man!) and telling his beads for the souls of his benefactors, interred in that venerable pile that lies beneath him. Beyond it (the meadows still descending) nods a thicket of oaks that mask the building, and have excluded a view too garish and luxuriant for a holy eye; only on either hand they leave an opening to the blue glittering sea. Did you not observe how, as that white sail shot by and was lost, he turned and crossed himself to drive the tempter from him that had thrown that distraction in his way? I should tell you that the ferryman who rowed me, a lusty young fellow, told me that he would not for all the world pass a night at the Abbey (there were such things seen near it) though there was a power of money hid there. From thence I went to Salisbury, Wilton, and Stonehenge; but of these things I say no more, they will be published at the University press.

P. S. I must not close my letter without giving you one principal event of my history, which was, that (in the course of my late tour) I set out one morning before five o'clock, the moon shining through a dark and misty autumnal air, and got to the seacoast time enough to be at the sun's levee. I saw the clouds and dark vapors open gradually to right and left, rolling over one another in great smoky wreaths, and the tide (as it flowed gently in upon the sands) first whitening, then slightly tinged with gold and blue; and all at once a little line of insufferable brightness that (before I can write these five words) was grown to half an orb, and now to a whole one, too glorious to be distinctly seen.* It is very odd it makes no figure on paper, yet I shall remember it as long as the sun, or at least as long as I endure. I wonder whether anybody ever saw it before? I hardly believe it.

IV.—PARIS—BURIAL OF THE DUKE DE TRESMES.

Horace Walpole † *to Richard West.*

PARIS, April 21, N. S., 1739.

DEAR WEST: You figure us in a set of pleasures, which, believe me, we do not find: cards and eating are so universal, that they absorb all variation of pleasures. The operas indeed are much frequented three times a week; but to me they would be a greater penance than eating maigre: their music resembles a gooseberry tart as much as it does harmony. We have not yet been at the Italian playhouse; scarce any one goes there.

* This puts me in mind of a similar description written by Dr. Jeremy Taylor, which I shall here beg leave to present to the reader, who will find by it that the old divine had occasionally as much power of description as even our modern poet. "As when the sun approaches toward the gates of the morning, he first opens a little eye of heaven, and sends away the spirits of darkness; gives light to the cock, and calls up the lark to mattins; and by and by gilds the fringes of a cloud, and peeps over the eastern hills, thrusting out his golden horns * * *; and still (while a man tells the story) the sun gets up higher till he shows a fair face and a full light."—J. TAYLOR'S *Holy Dying*, p. 17.—M.

† Walpole's letters are full of society, but have little of nature or art.

Their best amusement, and which in some parts beats ours, is the comedy; three or four of the actors excel any we have: but then to this nobody goes, if it is not one of the fashionable nights, and then they go, be the play good or bad—except on Molière's nights, whose pieces they are quite weary of. Gray and I have been at the Avare to-night: I cannot at all commend their performance of it. Last night I was in the Place de Louis le Grand (a regular octagon, uniform, and the houses handsome, though not so large as Golden Square), to see what they reckoned one of the finest burials that ever was in France. It was the Duke de Tresmes, Governor of Paris and Marshal of France. It began on foot from his palace to his parish church, and from thence in coaches to the opposite end of Paris, to be interred in the church of the Celestins, where is his family vault. About a week ago we happened to see the grave digging, as we went to see the church, which is old and small, but fuller of fine ancient monuments than any except St. Denis, which we saw on the the road, and excels Westminster; for the windows are all painted in mosaic, and the tombs as fresh and well preserved as if they were of yesterday. In the Celestins' church is a votive column to Francis II., which says that it is one assurance of his being immortalized, to have had the martyr Mary Stuart for his wife. After this long digression, I return to the burial, which was a most vile thing. A long procession of flambeaux and friars; no plumes, trophies, banners, led horses, scutcheons, or open chariots; nothing but

> Friars,
> White, black, and gray, with all their trumpery.

This goodly ceremony began at nine at night, and did not finish 'till three this morning; for, each church they passed, they stopped for a hymn and holy water. By the by, some of these choice monks, who watched the body while it lay in state, fell asleep one night, and let the tapers catch fire of the rich velvet mantle, lined with ermine, and powdered with gold flower-de-luces, which melted the lead coffin, and burnt off the feet of the deceased before it wakened them. The French love show; but there is a meanness reigns through it all. At the house where I stood to see this procession, the room was hung with crimson damask and gold, and the windows were mended in ten or a dozen places with paper. At dinner they give you three courses; but a third of the dishes is patched up with salads, butter, puff-paste, or some such miscarriage of a dish. None but Germans wear fine clothes; but their coaches are tawdry enough for the wedding of Cupid and Psyche. You would laugh extremely at their signs; some live at the Y grec, some at Venus's toilette, and some at the sucking cat. You would not easily guess their notions of honor; I'll tell you one; it is very dishonorable for any gentleman not to be in the army, or in the King's service, as they call it, and it is no dishonor to keep public gaming houses; there are at least a hundred and fifty people, of the first quality in Paris, who live by it. You may go into their houses at all hours of the night, and find hazzard, pharaoh, etc. The men who keep the hazzard-table at the Duke de Gesvres' pay him twelve guineas each night for the privilege. Even the princesses of the blood are dirty enough to have shares in the banks kept at their houses. We have seen two or three of them; but they are not young, nor remarkable but for wearing their red of a deeper die than other women, though all use it extravagantly.

The weather is still so bad that we have not made any excursions to see Versailles and the environs, not even walked in the Tuileries; but we have seen almost every thing else that is worth seeing in Paris, though that is very considerable. They beat us vastly in buildings, both in number and magnificence. The tombs of Richelieu and Mazarine at the Sorbonne and the College de Quatre Nations are wonderfully fine, especially the former. We have seen very little of the people themselves, who are not inclined to be propitious to strangers, especially if they do not play, and speak the language readily. If we did not remember there was such a place as England, we should know nothing of it; the French never mention it, unless it happens to be in one of their proverbs. Adieu! Yours ever.

V.—VISIT TO THE LOUVRE IN 1814 WITH MRS. SIDDONS.

Thomas Campbell to Dr. Beattie.

I was one of the many English who availed themselves of the first short peace to get a sight of the continent. The Louvre was at that time in possession of its fullest wealth. In the statuary-hall of that place I had the honor of giving Mrs. Siddons my arm the first time she walked through it, and the first in both our lives that we saw the Apollo Belvidere. From the farthest end of that spacious room, the god seemed to look down like a president on that chosen assembly of sculptured forms; and his glowing marble, unstained by time, appeared to my imagination as if he had stepped freshly from the sun. I had seen casts of the glorious statue with scarcely any admiration; and I must undoubtedly impute that circumstance in part to my inexperience in art, and to my taste having till then laid torpid. But still I prize the recollected impressions of that day too dear to call them fanciful. They seemed to give my mind a new sense of the harmony of Art—a new visual power of enjoying beauty. Nor is it mere fancy that makes the difference between the Apollo himself and his plaster casts. The dead whiteness of the stucco copies is glaringly monotonous, whilst the diaphonous surface of the original seems to soften the light which it reflects. Every particular of that hour is written indelibly on my memory. I remember entering the Louvre with a latent suspicion on my mind that a good deal of the rapture expressed at the sight of superlative sculptures was exaggerated or affected; but as we passed through the vestibule of the hall there was a Greek figure, I think that of Pericles, with a chlamys and helmet, which John Kemble desired me to notice; and it instantly struck me with wonder at the gentlemanlike grace which art could give to a human form in so simple a vesture. It was not, however, until we reached the grand saloon that the first sight of the god overawed my incredulity. Every step of approach to his presence added to my sensations; and all recollections of his name in classic poetry swarmed on my mind as spontaneously as the associations that are conjured up by the sweetest music. * * * *

Engrossed as I was with the Apollo, I could not forget the honor of being before him in the company of so august a worshipper; and it certainly increased my enjoyment to see the first interview between the paragon of Art and that of Nature. Mrs. Siddons was evidently much struck, and remained a long time before the statue; but like a true admirer she was not loquacious. I remember she said: "What a great idea it gives us of God, to think that he has made a human being capable of fashioning so divine a form!" When we walked around to other sculptures

I observed almost every eye in the hall was fixed upon her and followed her; yet I could perceive that she was not known, as I could hear the spectators say, "Who is she? Is she not an Englishwoman?" At this time, though in her fifty-ninth year, her looks were so noble, that she made you proud of English beauty—even in the presence of Grecian sculpture.*

* In another place Campbell states that Joanna Baillie has left an almost perfect picture of Mrs. Siddons in the following passage:

Page.—Madam, there is a lady in your hall,
Who begs to be admitted to your presence.
Lady.—Is it not one of our invited friends?
Page.—No; far unlike to them. It is a stranger.
Lady.—How looks her countenance?
Page.—So queenly, so commanding, and so noble,
I shrunk at first in awe; but when she smiled
Methought I could have compassed sea and land
To do her bidding.
Lady.—Is she young or old?
Page.—Neither, if right I guess; but she is fair,
For time has laid his hand so gently on her,
As he too had been awed,
So stately and so graceful is her form.
I thought at first her statue was gigantic,
But, on a near approach, I found in truth
She scarcely does surpass the middle size.
Lady.—What is her garb?
Page.—I cannot well describe the fashion of it;
She is not decked in any gallant trim,
But seems to me clad in the usual weeds
Of high habitual state.
Lady.—Thine eyes deceive thee, boy,
It is an apparition thou hast seen.
Friberg.—It *is* an apparition he has seen,
Or Jane de Montford.

Jane de Montford, Act 2.—S. 1.

This description will not seem extravagant to those who read the letters of Dr. Beattie or Washington Irving, recording the impression made upon them by this wonderful woman, when far advanced in life. Dr. Johnson, when asked whether he did not think her finer on the stage, where she was adorned by art, replied, "On the stage art does not adorn her; nature adorns her there, and art glorifies her."

VI.—THE GRANDE CHARTREUSE.

Mr. Gray to Mr. West.

TURIN, NOV. 16, N. S., 1739.

After eight days' journey through Greenland, we arrived at Turin—you approach it by a handsome avenue of nine miles long, and quite straight. The entrance is guarded by certain vigilant dragons, called Douaniers, who mumbled us for some time. The city is not large, as being a place of strength, and consequently confined within its fortifications; it has many beauties and some faults; among the first are streets all laid out by the line, regular uniform buildings, fine walks that surround the whole, and in general a good, lively, clean appearance; but the houses are of brick, plastered, which is apt to want repairing; the windows of oiled paper, which is apt to be torn; and every thing very slight, which is apt to tumble down. There is an excellent opera, but it is only in the carnival: balls every night, but only in the carnival: masquerades too, but only in the carnival. This carnival lasts only from Christmas to lent; one-half of the remaining part of the year is past in remembering the last, the other in expecting the future carnival. We cannot well subsist upon such slender diet, no more than upon an execrable Italian comedy, and a puppet show, called Rappresentazione d'un'anima dannata, which, I think, are all the present diversions of the place; except the Marquise de Cavaillac's conversazione, where one goes to see people play at ombre and taroc, a game with 72 cards all painted with suns, and moons, and devils, and monks. Mr. Walpole has been at court; the family are at present at a country palace, called La Venerie. The palace here in town is the very quintessence of gilding and looking glass; inlaid floors, carved panels, and painting, wherever they could stick a brush. I own I have not, as yet, anywhere met with those grand and simple works of art, that are to amaze one, and whose sight one is to be the better for; but those of nature have astonished me beyond expression. In our little journey up to the Grande Chartreuse, I do not remember to have gone ten paces without an exclamation, that there was no restraining. Not a precipice, not a torrent, not a cliff, but is pregnant with religion and poetry. There are certain scenes that would awe an atheist into belief, without the help of other argument. One need not have a very fantastic imagination to see spirits there at noonday. You have death perpetually before your eyes; only so far removed, as to compose the mind without frighting it. I am well persuaded St. Bruno was a man of no common genius, to choose such a situation for his retirement; and perhaps should have been a disciple of his, had I been born in his time. You may believe Abelard and Heloise were not forgot upon this occasion: if I do not mistake, I saw you too every now and then at a distance among the trees; il me semble, que j'ai vu ce chien de visage la quelque part. You seemed to call to me from the other side of the precipice, but the noise of the river below was so great that I really could not distinguish what you said; it seemed to have a cadence like verse. In your next you will be so good as to let me know what it was. The week we have since passed among the Alps has not equalled the single day upon that mountain, because the winter was rather too far advanced, and the weather a little foggy. However, it did not want its beauties; the savage rudeness of the view is inconceivable without seeing it. I reckoned, in one day, thirteen cascades, the least of which was, I dare say, one hundred feet in height. I had Livy in the chaise with me, and beheld his "Nives cœlo prope immistæ, tecta informia imposita rupibus, pecora jumentaque torrida frigore, homines intonsi et inculti, animalia inanimaque omnia rigentia gelu; omnia confragosa, præruptaque." The creatures that inhabit them are, in all respects, below humanity, and most of them, especially women, have the tumidum guttur, which they call goscia. Mont Cenis, I confess, carries the permission mountains have of being frightful rather too far, and its horrors were accompanied with too much danger to give one time to reflect upon their beauties. There is a family of the Alpine monsters I have mentioned, upon its very top, that in the middle of winter calmly lay in their stock of provisions and firing, and so are buried in their hut for a month or two under the snow. When we were down it, and got a little way into Piedmont, we began to find "Apricos quosdam colles, rivosque prope silvas, et jam humano cultu digniora loca." I read Silius Italicus too, for the first time, and wished for you, according to custom. We set out for Genoa in two days' time.

VII.—SWITZERLAND.

William Wordsworth to the Earl of Lonsdale.

LUCERNE, Aug. 19th, 1820.

MY LORD: You did me the honor of expressing a wish to hear from me during my continental tour. Accordingly, I have great pleasure in writing from this place, where we arrived three days ago. Our route has lain through Brussels, Namur, along the banks of the Meuse to Liege; thence to Aix la Chapelle, Cologne, and along the Rhine to Mayence, to Frankfort, Heidelburg (a noble situation at the point where the Neckar issues from steep lofty hills into the plain of the Rhine), Carlsruhe, and through the Black Forest to Schaff hausen; thence to Zurich, Berne, Thun, Interlachen. Here our Alpine tour might be said to commence, which has produced much pleasure thus far, and nothing that deserves the name of difficulty, even for the ladies. From the valley of Lautertrunnen, we crossed the Wiegern Alp to Grindelwald, and then over the grand Shiedech to Meyringen. This journey led us over high ground, and for fifteen leagues along the base of the loftiest Alps, which reared their bare or snowclad ridges and pikes, in a clear atmosphere, with fleecy clouds now and then settling upon and gathering round them. We heard and saw several avalanches; they are announced by a sound like thunder, but more metallic and musical. This warning naturally makes one look about, and we had the gratification of seeing one falling, in the shape and appearance of a torrent or cascade of foaming water, down the deep worn crevices of the steep or perpendicular granite mountains. Nothing can be more awful than the sound of these cataracts of ice and snow thus descending, unless it be the silence which succeeds. The elevations from which we beheld these operations of nature, and saw such an immense range of primitive mountains stretching to the east and west, were covered with rich pasturage and beautiful flowers, among which was abundance of the Monkshood, a flower which I had never seen but in the trim borders of our gardens, and which here grew not so much in patches as in little woods or forests, towering above the other plants. At this season, the herdsmen are with their cattle in still higher regions than those which we trod, the herbage where we travelled being reserved till they descend in the autumn. We have visited the Abbey of Engelberg, not many leagues from the borders of the lake of

Lucerne. The tradition is, that the site of the Abbey was appointed by angels, singing from a lofty mountain that rises from the plain of the valley, and which, from having been thus honored, is called Engelberg, or the Hill of the Angels. It is a glorious position for such beings, and I should have thought myself repaid for the trouble of so long a journey by the impression made upon my mind when I first came in view of the vale in which the convent is placed, and of the mountains that enclose it. The light of the sun had left the valley; and the deep shadows spread over it heightened the splendor of the evening light, and spread upon the surrounding mountains, some of which had their summits covered with pure snow, and others were half hidden by vapors rolling round them; and the Rock of Engelberg could not have been seen under more fortunate circumstances, for masses of cloud glowing with the reflection of the rays of the setting sun were hovering round it, like choirs of spirits preparing to settle upon its venerable head. To-day we quit this place to ascend the mountain Righi. We shall be detained in this neighborhood till our passports are returned from Berne, signed by the Austrian Minister, which we find absolutely necessary to enable us to proceed into the Milanese. At the end of five weeks, at the latest, we hope to reach Geneva, returning by the Simplon Pass. There I might have the pleasure of hearing from your Lordship; and may I beg that you would not omit to mention our Westmoreland politics? The diet of Switzerland is now sitting in this place. Yesterday I had a long conversation with the Bavarian envoy, whose views of the state of Europe appear to me very just. This letter must unavoidably prove dull to your Lordship; but when I have the pleasure of seeing you, I hope to make some amends, though I feel this is a very superficial way of viewing a country, even with reference merely to the beauties of nature. We have not met with many English; there is scarcely a third part as many in the country as there was last year. A brother of Lord Gray is in the house where we now are, and Lord Ashburton left yesterday. I must conclude abruptly, with kindest remembrances to Lady Lonsdale and Lady Mary. Believe me, my Lord, most faithfully,

Your Lordship's WM. WORDSWORTH.

VIII.—LAKE OF COMO AND ITS AMUSEMENTS.

Lady Morgan to Lady Clarke.

LAKE OF COMO (VILLA FONTANA), June 26th, 1817.

The attentions of the Milanese increase with our residence among them, and persons of all parties, Guelphs and Ghibellines, have united to pay us attention. The ex-Minister of the Interior made a splendid entertainment for us at his beautiful villa, as did the Trivulgis, and a Marquis de Sylvas, of whose villa and gardens there are many printed accounts. We were told there was no hospitality in Italy. We not only dined out three times a week on an average, but we have had carriages and horses so much at our service, that, though we have made several excursions of twenty and thirty miles into the country, we never had occasion to hire horses but once, and that was to go to Pavia, where we spent a few days, and made the acquaintance of old Volta, the inventor of the Voltaic battery. We went with the Count and Countess Confalonieri to see Monza and its magnificent cathedral, where the iron crown of Lombardy is kept. The difficulty and ceremonies attending on this, convince me that the travellers (not even Eustace, who mentions so lightly having seen this relic) have never seen it at all. We had an order, expedited the night before, from the Archduke to the chanoines of Monza, who received us in grand pontificals at the gates of the church, as did the Grand Master of the imperial suite at the palace of Monza, where the Archduke resides. We have also been to see the Grand Chartreuse, and in all my life I was never so entertained; but as to churches, and pictures, and public edifices, and institutions, my head is full of nothing else. To tell the truth, we became latterly quite overcome and exhausted by the life we led, for we never knew one moment's quiet, nor had time to do any thing. We had been offered the use of two beautiful villas on the Lake of Como for nothing; one of them, the Villa Someriva, one of the handsomest palaces in Lombardy. We left Milan ten days back, and have since lived in a state of enchantment, and I really believe in fairy land. I know not where to refer you for an account of the Lake of Como, except to Lady M. W. Montagu's letters. The lake is fifty miles long, and the stupendous and magnificent mountains which embosom it are strewn along their edges with the fantastic villas of the nobility of Milan, to which, as there is no road, there is no approach but by water. We took boat at the pretty antique town of Como, and literally landed in the drawing-room of the Villa Tempi. The first things I perceived were the orange and lemon trees, laden with fruit, growing in groves in the open air; the American aloes, olive trees, vines, and mulberries, all in blossom or fruit, covering the mountains almost to their summits. The blossoms and orange flowers, with the profusion of roses and wild pinks, were almost too intoxicating for our vulgar senses. The next day we set off on our aquatic excursions through regions the mildest, the loveliest, the most romantic that can be conceived. We landed at all the curious and classical points—at Pliny's fountain, the site of his villa, etc., and after a course of twenty-five miles reached my villa of Someriva, which we found to be a splendid palace, all marble, surrounded by groves of orange trees, but so vast, so solitary, so imposing, and so remote from all medical aid, that I gave up the idea of occupying it, and we rowed off to visit other villas, and at last set up our boat at a pretty inn on the lake, where we sat up half the night watching the arrival of boats and listening to the choruses of the boatmen. The next day we returned, and after new voyages found a beautiful little villa on the lake, ten minutes' row from Como, which we have taken for two months, at six pounds a month. The Villa Fontana consists of two pavilions, as they are called here, or small houses of two stories, which are separated by a garden. In one reside the signor and signora, our hosts, with a charming family; in the other reside the Signor and Signora Morgan, with an Italian valet-de-chambre. These pavilions are on the lake in a little pyramid, the vines and grapes festooned from tree to tree, and woven into a canopy above. The lake spreads before us with all its mountain beauties and windings. To the right lies the town of Como, with its Gothic cathedral. Immediately behind us, on every side, rise the mountains which divide Italian Switzerland from Lombardy, covered with vines, olives, and lime trees, and all this is lighted by a brilliant sun and canopied by skies bright, and blue, and cloudless. We have already made some excursions into these enchanting mountains, which are like cultivated gardens raised into the air, and walked within a mile of the Swiss frontier, We have a boat belonging to the villa anchored in the garden, into which we jump and row off. But of all the delights, imagine that shoals of foolish fish float on the surface of the lake in the evening, and that Morgan, who ambitioned nothing but a nibble on the Liffey line, here catches the victims of his art by dozens! Our villa consists of seven pretty rooms on the upper floor, and four below. The floors are stone, sprinkled with water two or three times a day; the walls painted in fresco, green jalousies, and muslin draperies, and yet, with all these cooling precautions, the heat obliges us to sit still all day. There is only one circumstance which reconciles me to your not sharing our pleasures, and that is a small matter of lightning and thunder, which comes about two days out of three, and is sometimes a little too near and too loud for the nerves of some of my friends. At this present moment it shakes the house, and the rain is falling as if Cox of Kilkenny was coming again. If, by the time we return, I don't make "Les serpens d'envie sifler dans votre cœur" with my Spanish guitar, my name is not Oliver! Morgan is making great progress on the guitar. I think it would amuse you to witness the life we lead here. We rise early, and as our house is a perfect smother, we open the blinds (the sashes are never shut), and paradise bursts on us with a sun and sky that you never dreamt of in your philosophy. We breakfast under our arcade of vines, and the table is covered with peaches and nectarines, while the fish literally pop their heads out of the lake to be fed, though Morgan, like a traitor, takes them by hundreds. Except you saw him in a yellow muslin gown and straw hat, on the Lake of Como, you have no idea of human felicity! All day we are shut up in our respective little studies, in which the light scarcely penetrates, for the intolerable heat obliges every one to remain shut up during the middle of the day, and the houses and villages look as if they were *uninhabited. At two o'clock we dine, at five drink tea*, and then we are off to the mountains, and frequently don't come back till night, or else we are on the lake; but in either instance we are in scenes which no pencil could delineate nor pen describe. The mountains, with their valleys and glens, are covered with fig trees, chestnuts, and olive trees, and with the lovely vineyards which are formed into festoons and arcades, and have quite another appearance from the stunted vineyards of France. The other day after dinner we walked on till we came to some barriers, where we were stopped by donaniers. We asked where we were, and found it was Switzerland. So, having walked through a pretty Swiss village, and admired a sign, "William Tell," we walked back to Italy to tea.

We are by no means destitute of society; some of our Milanese nobles come occasionally to their villas on the lake, and we are always asked to join the party. The Commandant de la Ville continues to give us tea parties, and we have three very nice English families, of whom we see a good deal (that is, as much as we like). One consists of three sisters, heiresses and nieces to the Bishop of Rochester, the Misses King. They are sensible, off-handed women, travel about with no protection but a Newfoundland dog, though still youngish, and are equally independent in every other respect. They are so anxious to know us, and so fearful of intruding, that the youngest (drôle de corps) was coming in disguise as an Italian lady (because English women, they said, have no right to force themselves on one), with some story to get admittance! Another family, Mr. Lawrie's, English people of fashion, with seven children, a French governess, an Irish tutor, and an English houskeeper. Our last and most delightful is Mrs. Locke and three charming daughters;

she is aunt to the Duke of Leinster, being the old Duchess's daughter by Ogilvie. She is connected with all the first and cleverest people in England, and smacks of all that's best in the best way. She was, she said, a long time negotiating the business of an introduction to me, and at last effected it by getting a dinner made on the lake, to which we were invited. Since then we are in constant correspondence, either by voyages on the lake or by notes. We dined there the other day, and by way of amusing the sweet girls, who are shut up in the loveliest but most solitary site, I announced a party in my vineyard; and there were the Kings, and my Austrian commandant, and some of his officers and Spanish guitars, and a little band of music, and fireworks, provided by the young signori of my host's family; there was tea, and cakes, and all sorts of things laid on the terrace by the lake, and Mrs. Locke's boat approached in view, and the heavens looked transcendently bright, when lo! up rose one of the lake hurricanes; the lightning flashed, the thunder rolled, tea, cakes, and fireworks were carried into the air, and poor Mrs. Locke, after tossing for five hours in a boat, which at every moment threatened to be overset, was too happy to land at midnight, two miles off, at a wretched little village, and pass the night at a cabaret, or miserable public house. So much for my Como news!

The weather has been splendid; the heat was at ninety degrees of our thermometer for some days. In the midst of the glories of this beautiful clime these sudden storms burst forth, and while they last spoil all. Among our Comesque amusements, one is going to the festivals of the saints on the mountains, and to the churches. To-morrow we are to have an opera in Como, with a company from Milan, and the Commandant has given us his box. There has been an imperial fête at Milan, called a carousal, for which we had an imperial invitation; but as court dresses were necessary, we thought it not worth the expense. We are delighted with the good family of our host here; they are Don Giongo and Donna Teresa, the heads: he is ready for the "Padrone," and excellent in his way; she, the best woman in the world; but as they speak Milanese, and very little Italian, we get on as it pleases heaven. The chief beau is the eldest son, a Major in the army, and aide-de-camp to his uncle, a General; he is "Don Gallias," and "my poor servant ever," for he absolutely watches our looks and anticipates our wishes. Then two younger sons, handsome lads, come home for their college vacation, and two pretty, brown, black-eyed girls, Donna Giovana and Donna Rosina; nothing can equal their gayety and noise. They live in the garden, and the young men are delightfully musical. The talent for music here is as common as speech. The children walk hand-in-hand and sing in parts almost from the cradle. On Sundays the recreation of the peasantry is to get into boats and float on the lake, and sing in chorus, which they do wonderfully; but you never hear a solo, though there is nothing but singing from morning till night. Such is our life, circle, and society here! Considering the remoteness of our habitation *ce n'est pas mal.* I forgot to mention we have an ex-Ambassador and his gay French wife, and some Capuchin friars, and that I was most gallantly received by the monks of a most famous college here; one of them the finest head I ever beheld. Nothing can equal the beauty of some of the fine heads here, of our young hosts in particular; but there is also the most hideous race, called Cretins, that ever nature sent into the world to disgrace her handiworks; they are precisely the figure of nut-crackers that we have in toy-shops, not above two feet high, with the head almost on the knees, but monstrously gay and self-conceited.

I labor, as usual, four or five hours a day. I think I shall do the best that I have done yet, and that my great glory is to come. Lord Byron is, I hear, at Bologna. We have read his Don Juan. It is full of good fun, excellent hits, and *à mourir de rire*. His blue-stocking lady is sketched off wickedly well, but his shipwreck is horrible bad taste, bad feeling, and bad policy. I see they have put in the French papers that I have left Italy for Vienna. I don't know the motive. What is to be done about Moore? We were going to write to Byron about him, poor fellow.

Love to Clarke; kisses to the children. *Sans adieu!*

L. M.

IX.—VERONA, VENICE, AND TRAVEL IN ITALY.

Charles Dickens to Lady Blessington.

MILAN, Wednesday, November 20th, 1844.

Appearances are against me. Don't believe them. I have written you, in intention, fifty letters, and I can claim no credit for any one of them (though they were the best letters you ever read), for they all originated in my desire to live in your memory and regard.

Since I heard from Count D'Orsay I have been beset in I don't know how many ways. First of all I went to Marseilles, and came back to Genoa. Then I moved to the Peschiere. Then some people, who had been present at the Scientific Congress here, made a sudden inroad on that establishment, and overran it. Then they went away. I shut myself up for one month, close and tight, over my little Christmas book, "The Chimes." All my affections and passions got twined and knotted up in it, and I became as haggard as a murderer long before I wrote "The End." When I had done that, like "The Man of Thessaly," who, having scratched his eyes out in a quickset hedge, plunged into a bramble-bush to scratch them in again, I fled to Venice to recover the composure I had disturbed. From thence I went to Verona and to Mantua. And now I am here; just come up from under ground, and earthy all over, from seeing that extraordinary tomb in which the dead saint lies in an alabaster case, with sparkling jewels all about him to mock his dusky eyes, not to mention the twenty-franc pieces which devout votaries were ringing down upon a sort of skylight in the Cathedral pavement above, as if it were the counter of his heavenly shop.

You know Verona? You know every thing in Italy, I know. I am not learned in geography, and it was a great blow to me to find that Romeo was only banished five-and-twenty miles. It was a greater blow to me to see the old house of the Capulets, with their cognizance still carved in stone over the gateway of the court-yard. It is a most miserable little inn, at this time ankle deep in dirt, and noisy vetturini and muddy market carts were disputing possession of the yard with a brood of geese, all splashed and bespattered as if they had their yesterday's white trowsers on. There was nothing to connect it with the beautiful story but a very unsentimental middle-aged lady (the Padrona I suppose) in the doorway, who resembled old Capulet in the one particular of being very great indeed in the family-way.

The Roman amphitheatre delighted me beyond expression. I never saw any thing so full of solemn, ancient interest. There are the four-and-forty rows of seats, as fresh and perfect as if their occupants had vacated them but yesterday; the entrances, passages, dens, rooms, corridors, the numbers over some of the arches. An equestrian troop had been there some days before, and had scooped out a little ring at one end of the arena, and had their performances in that spot. I should like to have seen it, of all things, for its very dreariness.

Fancy a handful of people sprinkled over one corner of the great place (the whole population of Verona wouldn't fill it), and a spangled cavalier bowing to the echoes and the grass-grown walls! I climbed to the topmost seat and looked away at the beautiful view for some minutes; when I turned round and looked down into the theatre again, it had exactly the appearance of an immense straw hat, to which the helmet in the Castle of Otranto was a baby; the rows of seats representing the different plaits of straw, and the arena the inside of the crown.

I had great expectations of Venice, but they fall immeasurably short of the wonderful reality. The short time I passed there went by me in a dream. I hardly think it possible to exaggerate its beauties, its sources of interest, its uncommon novelty and freshness. A thousand and one realizations of the thousand and one nights could scarcely captivate and enchant me more than Venice.

Your old house at Albaro—Il Paradiso—is spoken of as yours to this day. What a gallant place it is! I don't know the present inmate, but I hear that he bought and furnished it not long since with great splendor, in the French style, and that he wishes to sell it. I wish I were rich, and could buy it. There is a third-rate wine shop below Byron's house, and the place looks dull, and miserable, and ruinous enough.

Old ——— is a trifle uglier than when I first arrived. He has periodical parties, at which there are a great many flower-pots and a few ices; no other refreshments. He goes about constantly, charged with extemporaneous poetry, and is always ready, like tavern dinners, on the shortest notice and the most reasonable terms. He keeps a gigantic harp in his bedroom, together with pen, ink, and paper, for fixing his ideas as they flow; a kind of profane King David, but truly good-natured and very harmless.

Pray say to Count D'Orsay every thing that is cordial and loving from me. The travelling purse he gave me has been of immense service; it has been constantly opened. All Italy seems to yearn to put its hand in it. I think of hanging it, when I come back to England, on a nail as a trophy, and of gashing the brim like the blade of an old sword, and saying to my son and heir, as they do upon the stage, "You see this notch, boy? Five hundred francs were laid low on that day for post-horses. Where this gap is, a waiter charged your father treble the correct amount—and got it. This end, worn into teeth like the rasped edge of an old file, is sacred to the custom-houses, boy, this passport, and the shabby soldiers at town gates, who put an open hand and a dirty coat-cuff into the coach windows of all Forestieri. Take it, boy, thy father has nothing else to give!"

My desk is cooling itself in a mail-coach somewhere down at the back of the cathedral, and the pens and ink in this house are so detestable that I have no hope of your ever getting to this portion of my letter. But I have the less misery in this state of mind, from knowing that it has nothing in it to repay you for the trouble of perusal. CHARLES DICKENS.

X.—MILAN—CORRESPONDENCE OF LUCRETIA BORGIA.

Lord Byron to Mr. Murray.

MILAN, Oct. 15th, 1816.

I hear that Mr. Davies has arrived in England, but that, of some letters committed to his care by Mr. Hobhouse, only *half* have been delivered. This intelligence naturally makes me feel a little anxious for mine, and among them for the MS. which I wished to have compared with them sent by me through the hands of Mr. Shelley. I trust that *it* has arrived safely; and, indeed, not less so that some little crystals from Mont Blanc, for my daughter and niece, have reached their address. Pray have the goodness to ascertain from Mr. Davies that no accident (by custom-house or loss) has befallen them, and satisfy me on this point at your earliest convenience.

If I recollect rightly, you told me that Mr. Gifford had kindly undertaken to correct the press (at my request) during my absence; at least I hope so. It will add to my many obligations to that gentleman.

I wrote to you on my way here a short note, dated Martigny. Mr. Hobhouse and myself arrived here a few days ago, by the Simplon and Lago Maggiore routes. Of course, we visited the Borromean islands, which are fine, but too artificial. The Simplon is magnificent in its nature and its art; both God and man have done wonders, to say nothing of the Devil, who must certainly have had a hand (or a hoof) in some of the rocks and ravines, through and over which the works are carried.

Milan is striking; the cathedral superb. The city altogether reminds me of Seville, but a little inferior. We had heard divers bruits and took precautions on the road, near the frontier, against some worthy fellows (*i. e.*, felons) that were "out," and had ransacked some preceding travellers a few weeks ago, near Sesto, or Cesto, I forget which, of cash and raiment, besides putting them in bodily fear, and lodging about twenty slugs in the retreating part of a courier belonging to Mr. Hope. But we were not molested, nor I think in any danger, except in the way of making mistakes in cocking and priming, whenever we saw an old house or an ill-looking thicket, and now and then suspecting the true men, who have very much the appearance of the thieves of other countries. What the thieves may look like I know not, nor desire to know, for it seems they come upon you in bodies of thirty (in buckram and Kendal green) at a time, so that voyagers have no great chance. It is something like poor dear Turkey in that respect, but not so good, for there you can have as great a body of rogues to match the regular banditti; but here the gens-d'armes are said to be no great things, and as for one's own people, one can't carry them about, like Robinson Crusoe, with a gun on each shoulder.

I have been to the Ambrosian library; it is a fine collection, full of manuscripts, edited and unedited. I enclose you a list of the former, recently published. These are matters for your *literati*. For me, in my simple way, I have been most delighted with a correspondence of letters, all original and amatory, between *Lucretia Borgia and Cardinal Bembo*, preserved there. I have pored over them and a lock of her hair, the prettiest and fairest imaginable; I never saw fairer, and shall go repeatedly to read the epistles over and over, and if I can obtain some of the hair by fair means I shall try. I have already persuaded the librarian to promise me copies of the letters, and I hope he will not disappoint me. They are short but very simple, sweet and to the purpose.* There are some copies of verses in Spanish, also by her. The tress of her hair is long, and, as I said before, beautiful. The Brera gallery of paintings has some fine pictures, but nothing of a collection. Of painting I know nothing, but I like a Guercino, a picture of Abraham putting away Hagar and Ishmael, which seems to me natural and goodly. The Flemish school, such as I saw it in Flanders, I utterly detested, despised, and abhorred; it might be painting, but it was not nature. The Italian is pleasing, and their ideal very noble.

The Italians I have encountered here are very intelligent and agreeable. In a few days I am to meet Monti. By the way, I have just heard an anecdote of Beccaria, who published such admirable things against the punishment of death. As soon as his book was out, his servant having read it I presume, stole his watch, and his master, while correcting the press of a second edition, did all he could to have him hanged, by way of advertisement.

I forgot to mention the triumphal arch begun by Napoleon as a gate to this city; but the part completed worthy of another age, and the same country. The society here is very oddly carried on, at the theatre and the theatre only, which answers to our opera. People meet there, but as at a rout, and in very small circles. From Milan I shall go to Venice. If you write, write to Geneva, as before. The letter will be forwarded.

Yours ever.

* The existence of this correspondence is mentioned by Mr. Roscoe in his life of Leo X., but he had not seen it.

XI.—ROME, AND REMAINS OF ANCIENT ART.

Lord Dudley to the Bishop of Llandaff.

ROME, Jan. 14th, 1815.

I begin upon this monstrous sheet of long paper not with the malicious design of inflicting the whole of it upon you, covered with my cramped handwriting, but because, as far as a single letter goes, it is always well to give oneself room enough, in order to prepare against any sudden influx of ideas; and also, what is far more to the purpose, because at this moment my portfolio does not afford any thing of less unreasonable dimensions. I wrote to you before from Rome, but I said nothing about it, because at that time I had not taken even the most cursory view of what it contains. Since that I have been pretty nearly over it. One is always desirous to collect as many opinions as one can with respect to a great man or a celebrated place, from those that have seen them; and I shall therefore explain to you, as well as I can, the sort of impression that Rome has made upon my mind. In the first place, I am bold enough to think, and rash enough to say—with deference, however, to better judgments—that the merit of the ancient buildings here has been a good deal exaggerated. No doubt they deserve a great deal of praise and admiration, but they have received a double share of both from fancy, affectation, and that blind attachment to classical antiquity which swayed the minds of artists and scholars for some centuries after the revival of learning. There are two ways of considering these objects—as what they are, or as what they have been. Now there are not above four or five of the ancient monuments that are still perfect enough to give much pleasure, except to a very enthusiastic eye. First, and much before any thing else, comes the Pantheon, complete, beautiful, and of the purest age. I really think it deserves all that has been said in its praise, though one's pleasure in seeing it is in part to be attributed to the satisfaction and surprise one feels at the singular good fortune which has preserved it entire amidst the wreck of almost every thing else. Besides, one is a good deal awed by Agrippa and the Augustan age. Still I will fairly own, that if it stood at Turnham Green and had been finished yesterday by a man from Birmingham, it would still strike one as a noble and beautiful work. Its size, however, which in architecture is a very material point, is (as I need not tell you) not by any means remarkable. It is surpassed by all the great modern churches. Then comes the Coliseum, which, though sadly ruined, it is impossible to look at without being very much struck with its enormous mass. Then the triumphant arches, Trajan's pillar, and the little temple of Vesta. This is pretty nearly all that actually pleases the eye. The Obelisks, indeed, are numerous and perfect, but they are curious rather than beautiful. What else remains of antiquity consists of unsightly ruins. There are, perhaps, some few exceptions which I ought to have made, but not many. You may find a great many pretty bits and scraps, but nothing else sufficiently entire to be admired as a whole. I am sensible, however, that the present beauty and perfectness of these monuments is not the most interesting subject of consideration. They are to be looked at chiefly as traces, in which, by the help of history, we may discover the state of ancient art, wealth, and power. And certainly in every part of Rome there are abundant proofs of its having been the capital of a great, rich, enlightened, and victorious people. Yet I own that, when I recollect how long and how completely the Romans were masters of the world, how severely they governed it, how unmercifully they plundered it, and how much of their greatness and authority was concentrated in this single city, I am not at all surprised at the extent or splendor of their public works. All that they did, when compared with the vastness of their empire, is very much inferior, indeed, to what was accomplished by the little republics both of Greece and its colonies. Indeed, there is no point upon which travellers seem now to be more agreed than on the preference that is due to the remaining monuments of Grecian architecture. Those that have seen Greece first—and there are several of that description here now—speak of the Roman buildings much less respectfully than I have ventured to do. Something must be ascribed to the strength of first impressions, and to the vanity which induces people almost always to overrate what they have seen, particularly if it is at all difficult of access; but still their opinion is so decisive and so universal, that I am persuaded it is founded in truth.

The greatest part of the distinguished modern buildings are. of course, churches, which are everywhere scattered about with pious profusion. At first their immense number fatigues the eye and oppresses the recollection, but still one cannot but be struck with their size and splendor. The ancient monuments have, indeed, been heavily taxed to adorn them. They are full of columns taken from the temples and palaces of the Romans. In many instances these have been employed with more liberality than taste—chiefly in the older churches. You see Ionic and Corinthian, granite and white marble, huddled together with an ignorance not only of the nicer rules of architecture, but of the effect which uniformity seems universally calculated to produce, that in this age is hardly conceivable. It is but justice, how ever, to observe that some of the finest specimens are more judiciously disposed of. It is probable, too, that the buildings from which they were taken were already in a state of irretrievable ruin, and it is only by being transplanted into holy ground that they were saved from being thrown down and mutilated.

There are, I apprehend, but few specimens of completely pure architecture among the Roman churches. Many of them are positively ugly; "St. Paul's without the walls," for instance, which on the outside looks like a huge barn. In others, even of those that have just pretensions to beauty, the defects are still obvious enough to strike the eye even of an unskilful beholder. However, they are all worth seeing at least once, either for what they are or what they contain; and on the whole, they give one a very high notion of the riches, taste, and liberality of papal Rome—even exclusively of St. Peter's, which forms a class by itself.

I suppose I should, generally speaking, be reckoned among those that are inclined to undervalue Rome, both ancient and modern. But whatever praise I have subtracted from other objects I am disposed to heap upon this one. My expectations were of course great, but they have been more than fulfilled. Indeed, I had no notion that such an effect could be produced by a mere building. There is no getting accustomed to its grandeur and beauty. I see it every day, but my admiration and delight are as great as ever. The "Duomo" at Milan has not even prepared you for it. You have, I dare say, often seen and heard the common remark, that owing to the accuracy of its proportions, people are not aware of its prodigious size when they first enter it. This observation, however, has not been confirmed by my own experience. Its size was what struck me most at the first moment, and before I had time to attend to the symmetry of its form and the richness and exquisite workmanship of its ornaments. It has, too, another quality, which one should not, perhaps, have expected to find united to so much grandeur and magnificence—that of being remarkably cheerful. But it is a decent-tempered cheerfulness, which is, perhaps, quite as well suited to its destination as the awful gloom of the Gothic churches. I say this though I am extremely fond of Gothic architecture. Indeed, if I could imagine any thing finer than St. Peter's, it would be a Gothic church of the same enormous dimensions, in as pure a taste and as finely executed as the cathedral at York.

You have seen a great many fine palaces at Genoa. They can hardly be upon a grander scale than those at Rome, which are by much the most magnificent habitations I ever saw for private persons, in point both of size and exterior decoration.

But now comes the drawback upon the splendid and interesting objects in Rome, and which, I own, diminishes their effect, to my eye at least, to a wonderful degree. It is the extreme filth and shabbiness of the wretched town that surrounds them. Regular streets of lofty, well-built houses, are not at all necessary in order to set off fine public buildings. Oxford is a sufficient proof of that, where there is hardly a single handsome private house, and yet where every thing appears to the best advantage. But cleanliness, neatness, space, and a tolerable state of repair, are quite indispensable.

In Rome you search in vain for any one of these advantages. There is not a single wide street, and but one handsome square (Piazza di Savona). Poverty and dirt pursue you to the gates of every monument, ancient or modern, public or private. You never saw any place so nasty and so beggarly, nor I, except one. Lisbon is a little worse than Rome, and only a little; and it is a disgrace to civilized man. The description of dirt is no very pleasant thing, and therefore, for your sake and my own, I will not make one. But if you ever come to Rome, you must prepare yourself for having your senses outrageously offended wherever you go. The dignity of a palace, the sanctity of a church, the veneration that is due to the remains of ancient greatness, nothing commands the smallest attention to decency or cleanliness. One of our earliest and most natural associations is that of purity with a fountain. Rome has destroyed that in my mind forever. It contains an incredible number of beautiful fountains, most abundantly supplied with water, but they are all so surrounded by every object that is calculated to excite disgust as to be absolutely unapproachable. So much dirt implies negligence and sloth. Accordingly, every thing is kept in a careless, slovenly way—not a trace of that neatness and attention to details which gives so much additional beauty to the splendid scene you have beheld from the "Place de Louis XV.," and which in England is quite universal. In every thing here, and in every body, you see symptoms of that sort of foolish laziness of which, among us, none but children and very bad servants are guilty. You meet with it on all occasions, great and small. When they repair a church, the rubbish remains to spoil the roof and encumber the steps. When they cut a garden-hedge, they leave the clippings to stop up the walk. The effect of this disposition upon the buildings is quite deplorable. Nothing looks its best, and most things look their worst—except St. Peter's; for, to do them justice, they have the grace to keep that in good order. All the rest looks as if it had been thrown into chancery for the last twenty years. I believe the *substantial repairs* (as our builders speak) are in general pretty well attended to, but in spite of that they contrive to preserve all the effect of incipient ruin. Rome is like a beautiful woman slip-shod, in a dirty gown, with her hair "en papillote." It requires great enthusiasm, or great powers of abstraction, to prevent disgust from being the prevalent feeling, even while one is looking at some of the most considerable objects. It has been observed that the Spaniards *finish* nothing. The Italians *take care* of nothing. They have suffered more fine things to go to ruin in Rome, from mere neglect, than almost any other modern capital ever possessed. Some of the finest works of Raphael, of Domenichino and Guido, have been destroyed for want of the most trifling expense or trouble. One half of Rome is to me invisible.

With respect to the fine arts, I am in a state of total, irrecoverable blindness. I have caused myself to be carried round to all the fine pictures and statues, and placed in the full blaze of their beauty; but scarce a ray has pierced the film that covers my eyes. Statues give me no pleasure, pictures very little; and when I am pleased, it is uniformly in the wrong place, which is enough to discourage one from being pleased at all. In fact, I believe that if people in general were as honest as I am, it would be found that the works of the great masters are in reality much less admired than they are now supposed to be. Not that I am at all sceptical about their merit, but I believe that merit to be of a sort which it requires study, habit, and perhaps even some practical knowledge of the principles of the fine arts, to perceive and relish. You remember that Sir Joshua tells us that he was at first incapable of tasting all the excellency of Raphael and Michael Angelo. And if he, already no mean artist, was still uninitiated in some of the higher mysteries of his art, and obliged at first to take upon trust much of that which was afterwards made clear to him by further study and labor; what shall we say about the sincerity of those who, knowing so much less, pretend to feel so much more? For my part, I think of them very much as I should think of anybody who, being just able to pick out the meaning of a Latin sentence, should affect to admire the language and versification of the Georgics. So much by way of apology, "pro me ipso et pro omni *Mummiorum* domo!" I learn from others that the riches in all that belongs to the fine arts, which Rome still contains, are quite prodigious. They have been a good deal diminished by the robbery of the French, and by the poverty of Prince Giustiniani, and the baseness of Prince Borghese, who both sold their collections. But what remains is sufficient to afford an inexhaustible subject of admiration to artists and connoisseurs. It is but justice to the French to say, that though they deprived Rome of some of its greatest ornaments, yet in other respects they rendered it great service. My good friend Eustace wrote under the influence of a most childish prejudice when he represented them as enemies to the fine arts. Napoleon was beginning to improve Rome with the same magnificence and good taste of which he has left such monuments at Paris. By his orders immense accumulations of earth and rubbish were removed from some of the ancient ruins, an operation by which, in all instances, the appearance of them was much improved, and in some, curious discoveries were made. From what I have said (and, indeed, from what you well know already), you must be aware that what is wanted here is not any new buildings. All that is necessary, is to take care of those that already exist, and to set them off to advantage, and above all, to cleanse away the Augean filth of this imperial city. He had already directed his attention to all these objects, and in a few years Rome would have assumed quite a new aspect, and, in my opinion at least, the loss of all that was taken away would have been more than compensated by the improvement of what remains. Consider, for instance, if you happen to have a plan of Rome, what an effect would have been produced, in one single instance, by throwing down the wretched houses that now come up to the colonnade of St. Peter's, and opening a magnificent street to the Castle of St. Angelo and the Tiber. But the whole spirit of improvement is gone, and indeed the power. The Pope is too poor to employ money in building. Indeed, if they don't give him back the March, he will hardly have enough to carry on his government even on its present frugal plan.

The mention of His Holiness puts me in mind that there are several English Catholics here: Milner represents the violent party, but those of moderate sentiments have prevailed. Milner is not at all in favor, and the Pope has declared plainly and without reserve in favor of the veto. He says the King of Prussia has it, and he sees no reason why the King of England should not have it. I wonder what effect this will have on the red-hot Irish. Will they pretend to be better Papists than the Pope? I know that in France they used to complain "que le Roi n'etoit pas assez royaliste." What I have seen does not incline me to think very highly either of society or of learning at Rome. But then I have not seen a great deal. I fancy there are several pretty good Latin scholars here. In fact, it is the language both of the law and the religion of the place, and the Pope's correspondence is still carried on in it. No unfavorable specimen of pontificial Latin appeared the other day in a letter of His Holiness. * * * * * *

The winter here is a great deal better than it is in England, but still it is winter. The few last days have been particularly bad—thunder, lightning, rain, hail, and snow. But this is everywhere on our hemisphere the worst month of the year. I shall not stir till February, and then go to Naples. Our English society here is quite excellent. The Italian post is everywhere execrably irregular. I am quite persuaded that several letters to me must have been lost. I shall send this by a private hand as far as Paris, so that it will probably reach you.

I see there has been an unusually active session before Christmas—my old friends the Whigs all alive again, and in Castlereagh's absence making minced-meat of Van & Co. I am not sorry for it. A government should never have things entirely its own way. Direct me at Perregeaux, or, if there is any difficulty of sending a foreign letter from Oxford, under cover, to John Benbow, Esq., Stone Buildings, Lincoln's Inn.

Believe me, my dear Copleston, ever most sincerely yours,

G. W. W.

XII.—POMPEII.

Percy B. Shelley to T. L. P.

POMPEII.*

* * * * * *

Since you last heard from me we have been to see Pompeii, and are waiting now for the return of spring weather, to visit,

* Pompeii, says Lord Dudley, "may be considered as a town *potted* about seventeen hundred years ago for the use of the antiquarians of the present century. You may easily conceive how much one's notions of the state of things in the ancient world are helped by a mere glimpse of this singular remain. When, in the course of their labors, the workmen had got to any spot which seemed to be particularly interesting, notice was sent to the court, which generally attended to watch the result."

first, Pæstum, and then the islands; after which we shall return to Rome. I was astonished at the remains of this city; I had no conception of any thing so perfect yet remaining. My idea of the mode of its destruction was this: first, an earthquake shattered it, and unroofed almost all its temples, and split its columns; then a rain of light, small pumice-stones fell; then torrents of boiling water, mixed with ashes, filled up all its crevices. A wide, flat hill, from which the city was excavated, is now covered by thick woods, and you see the tombs and the theatres, the temples and the houses, surrounded by the uninhabited wilderness. We entered the town from the side towards the sea, and first saw two theatres; one more magnificent than the other, strewn with the ruins of the white marble which formed their seats and cornices, wrought with deep, bold sculpture. In the front, between the stage and the seats, is the circular space occasionally occupied by the chorus. The stage is very narrow, but long, and divided from this space by a narrow enclosure parallel to it, I suppose for the orchestra. On each side are the consuls' boxes, and below, in the theatre at Herculaneum, were found two equestrian statues of admirable workmanship, occupying the same place as the great bronze lamps did at Drury Lane. The smallest of the theatres is said to have been comic, though I should doubt. From both you see, as you sit on the seats, a prospect of the most wonderful beauty.

You then pass through the ancient streets; they are very narrow, and the houses rather small, but all constructed on an admirable plan, especially for this climate. The rooms are built round a court, or sometimes two, according to the extent of the house. In the midst is a fountain, sometimes surrounded with a portico, supported on fluted columns of white stucco; the floor is paved with mosaic, sometimes wrought in imitation of vine-leaves, sometimes in quaint figures, and more or less beautiful, according to the rank of the inhabitant. There were paintings on all, but most of them have been removed to decorate the royal museums. Little winged figures, and small ornaments of exquisite elegance, yet remain. There is an ideal life in the forms of these paintings of an incomparable loveliness, though most are evidently the work of very inferior artists. It seems as if, from the atmosphere of mental beauty which surrounded them, every human being caught a splendor not his own. In one house you see how the bed-rooms were managed: a small sofa was built up, where the cushions were placed; two pictures, one representing Diana and Endymion, the other Venus and Mars, decorate the chamber; and a little niche, which contains the statue of a domestic god. The floor is composed of a rich mosaic of the rarest marbles, agate, jasper, and porphyry; it looks to the marble fountain and the snow-white columns, whose entablatures strew the floor of the portico they supported. The houses have only one story, and the apartments, though not large, are very lofty. A great advantage results from this, wholly unknown in our cities. The public buildings, whose ruins are now forests, as it were, of white fluted columns, and which then supported entablatures loaded with sculptures, were seen on all sides over the roofs of the houses. This was the excellence of the ancients. Their private expenses were comparatively moderate: the dwelling of one of the chief senators of Pompeii is elegant indeed, and adorned with most beautiful specimens of art, but small. But their public buildings are everywhere marked by the bold and grand designs of an unsparing magnificence. In the little town of Pompeii (it contained about twenty thousand inhabitants), it is wonderful to see the number and the grandeur of their public buildings. Another advantage, too, is that, in the present case, the glorious scenery around is not shut out, and that, unlike the inhabitants of the Cimmerian ravines of modern cities, the ancient Pompeians could contemplate the clouds and the lamps of heaven; could see the moon rise high behind Vesuvius, and the sun set in the sea, tremulous with an atmosphere of golden vapor, between Inarime and Misenum.

We next saw the temples. Of the temple of Æsculapius little remains but an altar of black stone, adorned with a cornice imitating the scales of a serpent. His statue, in terra-cotta, was found in the cell. The temple of Isis is more perfect. It is surrounded by a portico of fluted columns, and in the area around it are two altars, and many ceppi for statues, and a little chapel of white stucco, as hard as stone, of the most exquisite proportion; its panels are adorned with figures in bas-relief, slightly indicated, but of a workmanship the most delicate and perfect that can be conceived. They are Egyptian subjects, executed by a Greek artist, who has harmonized all the unnatural extravagances of the original conception into the supernatural loveliness of his country's genius. They scarcely touch the ground with their feet, and their wind-uplifted robes seem in the place of wings. The temple in the midst, raised on a high platform and approached by steps, was decorated with exquisite paintings, some of which we saw in the museum at Portici. It is small, of the same materials as the chapel, with a pavement of mosaic, and fluted Ionic columns of white stucco, so white that it dazzles you to look at it.

Thence, through other porticos and labyrinths of walls and columns (for I cannot hope to detail every thing to you), we came to the Forum. This is a large square, surrounded by lofty porticos of fluted columns, some broken, some entire, their entablatures strewed under them. The temple of Jupiter, of Venus, and another temple, the Tribunal, and the Hall of Public Justice, with their forests of lofty columns, surround the Forum. Two pedestals or altars of an enormous size (for, whether they supported equestrian statues, or were the altars of the temple of Venus, before which they stand, the guide could not tell), occupy the lower end of the Forum. At the upper end, supported on an elevated platform, stands the temple of Jupiter. Under the colonnade of its portico we sat, and pulled out our oranges, and figs, and bread, and medlars (sorry fare, you will say), and rested to eat. Here was a magnificent spectacle. Above and between the multitudinous shafts of the sun-shining columns was seen the sea, reflecting the purple heaven of noon above it, and supporting, as it were, on its line the dark lofty mountains of Sorrento, of a blue inexpressibly deep, and tinged toward their summits with streaks of new-fallen snow. Between was one small green island. To the right was Capreæ, Inarime, Prochyta, and Misenum. Behind was the single summit of Vesuvius, rolling forth volumes of thick white smoke, whose foam-like column was sometimes darted into the clear dark sky, and fell in little streaks along the wind. Between Vesuvius and the nearer mountains, as through a chasm, was een the main line of the loftiest Apennines, to the east. The ay was radiant and warm. Every now and then we heard the ubterranean thunder of Vesuvius; its distant deep peals seemed) shake the very air and light of day, which interpenetrated our rames, with the sullen and tremendous sound. This scene was hat the Greeks beheld (Pompeii, you know, was a Greek city). hey lived in harmony with nature; and the interstices of their incomparable columns were portals, as it were, to admit the spirit of beauty which animates this glorious universe to visit those whom it inspired. If such is Pompeii, what was Athens? What scene was exhibited from the Acropolis, the Parthenon, and the temples of Hercules, and Theseus, and the Winds?—the islands and the Ægean sea, the mountains of Argolis, and the peaks of Pindus and Olympus, and the darkness of the Bœotian forests interspersed?

From the Forum we went to another public place; a triangular portico, half enclosing the ruins of an enormous temple. It is built on the edge of the hill overlooking the sea. That black point is the temple. In the apex of the triangle stand an altar and a fountain, and before the altar once stood the statue of the builder of the portico. Returning hence, and following the consular road, we came to the eastern gate of the city. The walls are of enormous strength, and enclose a space of three miles. On each side of the road beyond the gate are built the tombs. How unlike ours! They seem not so much hiding-places for that which must decay, as voluptuous chambers for immortal spirits. They are of marble, radiantly white; and two, especially beautiful, are loaded with exquisite bas-reliefs. On the stucco-wall that encloses them are little emblematic figures, of a relief exceedingly low, of dead and dying animals, and little winged genii, and female forms bending in groups in some funereal office. The higher reliefs represent, one a nautical subject, and the other a bacchanalian one. Within the cell stand the cinerary urns sometimes one, sometimes more. It is said that paintings were found within; which are now, as has been every thing movable in Pompeii, removed, and scattered about in royal museums. These tombs were the most impressive things of all. The wil woods surround them on either side; and along the broad stones of the paved road which divides them, you hear the late leaves of autumn shiver and rustle in the stream of the inconstant wind, as it were like the step of ghosts. The radiance and magnificence of these dwellings of the dead, the white freshness of the scarcely finished marble, the impassioned or imaginative life of the figures which adorn them, contrast strangely with the simplicity of the houses of those who were living when Vesuvius overwhelmed them.

I have forgotten the amphitheatre, which is of great magnitude, though much inferior to the Coliseum. I now understand why the Greeks were such great poets; and, above all, I can account, it seems to me, for the harmony, the unity, the perfection, the uniform excellence, of all their works of art. They lived in a perpetual commerce with external nature, and nourished themselves upon the spirit of its forms. Their theatres were all open to the mountains and the sky. Their columns, the ideal types of a sacred forest, with its roof of interwoven tracery, admitted the light and wind; the odor and the freshness of the country penetrated the cities. Their temples were mostly upaithric; and the flying clouds, the stars, or the deep sky, were seen above.

* * * * * *

XIII. — BULL-FIGHT AT LISBON.

Robert Southey to Lieut. Southey.

LISBON, June 22d, 1800.

MY DEAR TOM: We are just returned from a bull-feast, and I write to you while the feelings occasioned by this spectacle are fresh. I had never before seen one. The buffoonery of teazing bullocks at Madrid was rather foolish than cruel, and its extreme folly excited laughter, as much at the spectators as the thing itself. This is widely different. The hand-bill was pompous: "Antonio de Cordeiro, who had so distinguished himself last year, was again to perform. The entertainment would deserve the approbation of a generous public. Ten bulls were to be killed, four to be tormented; they were picked bulls, of the Marquis de ——'s breed (I forget his name), and chosen out for their courage and ferocity." Yesterday the bull-fighters paraded the streets, as you may have seen rope-dancers and the "equestrian troop" at Bristol fair. They were strangely disfigured with masques: one fellow had a paunch and a Punch-humpback, and all were dressed in true tawdry style. Hot weather is always the season, and Sunday always the day, the amusement being cool and devout! At half after four it began; the hero was on horseback, and half a dozen men on foot to assist him; about ten more sat with pitchforks to defend themselves, ready when wanted. The bulls were all in the area till the amusement opened. They were not large, and not the same breed as in England; they had more the face of the cow than the short, sulky look of gentlemen—quiet, harmless animals, whom a child might safely have played with, and a woman would have been ashamed to fear. So much for their *ferocity!* Courage, indeed, they possessed; they attacked only in self-defence, and you would, like me, have been angry to see a fellow with a spear provoking a bull whose horns were tipped with large balls, the brave beast, all bleeding with wounds, still facing him with reluctant resistance. Once I saw crackers stuck into his neck to irritate him, and heard them burst in his wounds: you will not wonder that I gave the Portuguese a hearty and honest

English curse. It is not an affair of courage; the horse is trained, the bull's horns muffled, and half a dozen fellows, each ready to assist the other, and each with a cloak, on which the poor animal wastes his anger; they have the rails to leap over, also, and they know that when they drop the cloak he aims always at that; there is, therefore, little danger of a bruise, and none of any thing else. The amusement is, therefore, as cowardly as cruel. I saw nine killed; the first wound sickened Edith, and my own eyes were not always fixed upon the area. My curiosity was not, perhaps, strictly excusable, but the pain which I endured was penalty enough. The fiercest of the whole was one of the four who were only tormented; two fellows on asses attacked him with goads, and he knocked them over and over with much spirit; two more came on, standing each in the middle of a painted horse, ridiculously enough—and I fancy those fellows will remember him for the next fortnight whenever they turn in bed—and their sham horses were broken to pieces. Three dogs were loosed at another bull, and effectually sickened. I hate bull-dogs; they are a surly, vicious breed, ever ready to attack, mischievous and malicious enough to deserve Parliamentary praise from Mr. Wyndham and Mr. Canning. A large theatre was completely full; men, women, and children were clapping their hands at every wound, and watching with delight the struggles of the dying beasts. It is a damnable sport! and much to the honor of the English here, they all dislike it; very rarely does an Englishman or Englishwoman witness it a second time.

You will find in Thalaba one accurate image which I observed this evening: a death-sweat *darkening the dun hide* of the animal. This amusement must have mischievous effects; it makes cruelty familiar; and as for the assertion that bull-baiting or bull-butchering keeps up the courage of the nation, only Wyndham and Canning could have been absurd enough and unfeeling enough to believe it; if it were true, the Spaniards ought to be the bravest nation in the world, because their amusement is the most cruel, and a butcher ought to make the best soldier.

On Thursday we go to Cintra; this, therefore, will be my last letter of Lisbon anecdote. In Africa a Portuguese saw an orang-outang, the most human beast that has yet been discovered, walking quietly with a stick in his hand; he had the wickedness to shoot him, and was not, as he ought to have been, hung for wilful murder. The head and hands were sent here; I have seen them in the Museum, in spirits. I have seen many an uglier fellow pass for a man, in spite of the definition that makes him a reasoning animal: he has eyebrows and a woolly head, almost like a negro's, but the face not black.

Fielding died and was buried here. By a singular fatality, four attempts have been made to erect a monument, and all have miscarried. A Frenchman set on foot a subscription for this purpose, and many of the factory engaged for one, two, or three moidores; circumstances took him from Lisbon, and this dropped. Another Frenchman had a monument made at his own expense, and paid for it; there was a fine French inscription, that, as his own countrymen had never given the great Fielding a monument, it was reserved for a Frenchman to honor his country by paying that respect to genius; he also went away, and is now following the French Pretender; and his monument lies among masonry and rubbish, where I have sought for it in vain. Then De Visme undertook the affair; and the bust of

Fielding, designed for this purpose, is still in the house which belonged to him here. I know not what made this scheme abortive. Last, the Prince of Brazil went to work, and the monument was made. The Lady Abbess of the New Convent wished to see it: it was sent to her; she took a fancy to it, and there it has remained ever since; and Fielding is still without a monument.

De Visme introduced the present fashion of painting rooms in stucco, with landscapes on the walls, and borders of flowers or arabesque; the fashion is, I believe, Italian. The workmen whom he employed had taste enough to be pleased with it, and it is general in all new houses. The ceilings are now painted; thus, instead of the huge layer of boards which was usual, nothing can look more cool, or be more convenient, for a cloth and soap clean it.

In the larger old houses, here and in Spain, in the country, there is usually a room with no windows, but, instead, arches quite open to the air. The appearance is strange and picturesque, and I should esteem it one of the inconveniences of Lisbon that the intolerable dust prevents the enjoyment of these open rooms there: the dust is a huge evil. * * * We had the hot wind for three days this week; a detestable burning blast, a bastard sort of siroc, tamed by crossing the sea and the land, but which parches the lips, and torments you with the Tantalus plague of fanning your cheek and heating it at the same time. The sea-breeze is, on the other hand, as delightful: we feel it immediately; it cools the air, and freshens up all our languid feelings. In the West Indies they call this wind the doctor—a good seamanly phrase for its healing and comfortable effect.

At the time the aqueduct was built, a large reservoir was made for its waste water. In winter much water runs to waste; in summer more is wanted, and the watermen wait a long time round the fountain before they can in turn fill their barrels; but these people, in building the reservoir, never calculated the weight of the water till the building was finished; so it stands still uncovered, a useless pile, and a rare monument of the national science. I saw a funeral from the country pass the window at night, the attendants holding torches, and the body in the trunk-coffin carried upon a litter (that is, like a sedan chair carried by mules instead of men).

The servants here, in marketing, think it a part of their fair profits to cheat you as much as they can, and have no idea that it is dishonesty; it is a sort of commission they think they are entitled to. This is so much the case that one of these fellows, when he was stipulating about wages, thought them too little, and inquired if he was to go to market; he was told yes, and then he said he would come. * * *

The queen's stables serve as an asylum. Rogues and murderers go there, and do the work for nothing. They are safe by this means, and the people, whose business it is to hire and pay the servants, pocket the money, so that they infest the neighborhood. They quarrelled with our dragoons, who broke into the stables, and thrashed them heartily, to the great satisfaction of the people near.

God bless you! Edith's love.

Yours, R. S.

XIV.—THE PRADO OF MADRID.*

Washington Irving to Mrs. Paris.

1845.

* * * My evening drives, though lonely, are pleasant. You can have no idea of the neighborhood of Madrid from that of other cities. The moment you emerge from the gates you enter upon a desert; vast wastes as far as the eye can reach of undulating, and in part hilly country, without trees or habitations, green in the early part of the year, and cultivated with grain, but burnt by the summer sun into a variety of browns, some of them rich, though sombre. A long picturesque line of mountains closes the landscape to the west and north, on the summits of some of which the snow lingers even in midsummer. The road I generally take, though a main road, is very solitary. Now and then I meet a group of travellers on horseback, roughly clad, with muskets slung behind their saddles, and looking very much like the robbers they are armed against; or a line of muleteers from the distant provinces, with their mules hung with bells, and tricked out with worsted bobs and tassels; or a goatherd driving his flock of goats home to the city for the night, to furnish milk for the inhabitants. Every group seems to accord with the wild, half-savage scenery around; and it is difficult to realize that such scenery and such groups should be in the midst of a populous and ancient capital. Some of the sunsets behind the Guadarrama mountains, shedding the last golden rays over this vast melancholy landscape, are really magnificent.

I have had much pleasure in walking on the Prado on bright

* From the Life and Letters of Irving, by his nephew, Pierre M. Irving.

moonlight nights. This is a noble walk within the walls of the city, and not far from my dwelling. It has alleys of stately trees, and is ornamented with five fountains, decorated with statuary and sculpture. The Prado is the great promenade of the city. One grand alley is called the saloon, and is particularly crowded. In the summer evening there are groups of ladies and gentlemen seated in chairs and holding their *tertulias*, or gossiping parties, until a late hour. But what most delights me are the groups of children, attended by their parents or nurses, who gather about the fountains, take hands, and dance in rings to their own nursery songs. They are just the little beings for such a fairy moonlight scene. I have watched them night after night, and only wished I had some of my own little nieces or grandnieces to take part in the fairy ring. These are all the scenes and incidents I can furnish you from my present solitary life.

I am looking soon for the return of the Albuquerques to Madrid, which will give me a family circle to resort to. Madame Albuquerque always calls me uncle, and I endeavor to cheat myself into an idea that she is a niece; she certainly has the kindness and amiableness of one, and her children are most entertaining companions for me.

Your letter from the cottage brings with it all the recollections of the place; its trees and shrubs, its roses, and honeysuckles, and humming-birds. I am glad to find that my old friend the cat-bird still builds and sings under the window. You speak of Vaney's barking too; it was like suddenly hearing a well-known but long-forgotten voice, for it is a long time since any mention was made of that most meritorious little dog. * *

XV.—CONSTANTINOPLE—ITS MOSQUES AND PALACES.

Lady M. W. Montagu to the Countess of Bute.

At length I have heard from my dear Lady B—— for the first time. I am persuaded you have had the goodness to write before, but I have had the ill-fortune to lose your letters. Since my last, I have stayed quietly at Constantinople, a city that I ought in conscience to give your ladyship a right notion of, since I know you can have none but what is partial and mistaken from the writings of travellers. 'Tis certain there are many people that pass years here in Pera without having ever seen it, and yet they all pretend to describe it. Pera, Tophana, and Galata, wholly inhabited by French Christians (and which, together, make the appearance of a very fine town), are divided from it by the sea, which is not above half so broad as the broadest part of the Thames; but the Christian men are loath to hazard the adventures they sometimes meet with amongst the Levents or seamen (worse monsters than our watermen), and the women must cover their faces to go there, which they have a perfect aversion to do. 'Tis true they wear veils in Pera, but they are such as only serve to show their beauty to more advantage, and would not be permitted in Constantinople. These reasons deter almost every creature from seeing it; and the French ambassadress will return to France, I believe, without ever having been there. You'll wonder, madam, to hear me add that I have been there very often. The Asmack, or Turkish veil, is become not only very easy, but agreeable to me; and if it was not, I would be content to endure some inconvenience to gratify a passion that is become so powerful with me as curiosity. And, indeed, the pleasure of going in a barge to Chelsea is not comparable to that of rowing upon the canal of the sea here, where, for twenty miles together down the Bosphorus, the most beautiful variety of prospects present themselves. The Asian side is covered with fruit-trees, villages, and the most delightful landscapes in nature; on the European stands Constantinople, situated on seven hills. The unequal heights make it seem as large again as it is (though one of the largest cities in the world), showing an agreeable mixture of gardens, pine and cypress trees, palaces, mosques, and public buildings, raised one above another, with as much beauty and appearance of symmetry as your ladyship ever saw in a cabinet adorned by the most skilful hands, where jars show themselves above jars, mixed with canisters, babies, and candlesticks. This is a very odd comparison; but it gives me an exact idea of the thing. I have taken care to see as much of the seraglio as is to be seen. It is on a point of land running into the sea; a palace of prodigious extent, but very irregular. The gardens take in a large compass of ground, full of high cypress trees, which is all I know of them. The buildings are all of white stone, headed on top with gilded turrets and spires, which look very magnificent; and, indeed, I believe there is no Christian king's palace half so large. There are six large courts in it, all built round and set with trees, having galleries of stone; one of these for the guard, another for the slaves, another for the officers of the kitchen, another for the stables, the fifth for the divan, and the sixth for the apartment destined for audiences. On the ladies' side there are at least as many more, with distinct courts belonging to their eunuchs and attendants, their kitchens, etc.

The next remarkable structure is that of St. Sophia, which 'tis very difficult to see. I was forced to send three times to the

Caimairam (the Governor of the town), and he assembled the chief Effendis, or heads of the law, and inquired of the Mufti whether it was lawful to permit it. They passed some days in this important debate; but I insisting on my request, permission was granted. I can't be informed why the Turks are more delicate on the subject of this mosque than on any of the others, where what Christian pleases may enter without scruple. I fancy they imagine that, having been once consecrated, people, on pretence of curiosity, might profane it with prayers, particularly to those saints who are still very visible in mosaic work, and no other way defaced but by the decays of time; for it is absolutely false, though so universally asserted, that the Turks defaced all the images that they found in the city. The dome of St. Sophia is said to be one hundred and thirteen feet diameter, built upon arches, sustained by vast pillars of marble, the pavement and staircase marble. There are two rows of galleries, supported with pillars of party-colored marble, and the whole roof mosaic-work, part of which decays very fast and drops down. They presented me a handful of it; the composition seems to me a sort of glass, or that paste with which they make counterfeit jewels. They show here the tomb of the Emperor Constantine, for which they have a great veneration.

This is a dull, imperfect description of this celebrated building; but I understand architecture so little, that I am afraid of talking nonsense in endeavoring to speak of it particularly. Perhaps I am in the wrong, but some Turkish mosques please me better. That of Sultan Solyman is an exact square, with four fine towers in the angles; in the midst is a noble cupola, supported with beautiful marble pillars; two lesser at the ends, supported in the same manner; the pavement and gallery round the mosque of marble; under the great cupola is a fountain, adorned with such fine-colored pillars that I can hardly think them natural marble; on one side is the pulpit of white marble, and on the other the little gallery for the Grand Signior. A fine staircase leads to it, and it is built up with gilded lattices. At the upper end is a sort of altar, where the name of God is written; and before it stand two candlesticks, as high as a man, with wax candles as thick as three flambeaux. The pavement is spread with fine carpets, and the mosque illuminated with a vast number of lamps. The court leading to it is very spacious, with galleries of marble, of green columns, covered with twenty-eight leaded cupolas on two sides, and a fine fountain of basins in the midst of it.

This description may serve for all the mosques in Constantinople. The model is exactly the same, and they only differ in largeness and richness of materials. That of the Sultana Valida is the largest of all, built entirely of marble, the most prodigious, and, I think, the most beautiful structure I ever saw, be it spoke to the honor of our sex, for it was founded by the mother of Mahomet the Fourth. Between friends, Paul's Church would make a pitiful figure near it; as any of our squares would do near the Atlerdan, or place of horses (*at* signifying a horse in Turkish). This was the hippodrome in the reign of the Greek Emperors. In the midst of it is a brazen column of three serpents twisted together, with their mouths gaping. 'Tis impossible to learn why so old a pillar was erected; the Greeks can tell nothing but fabulous legends when they are asked the meaning of it, and there is no sign of its having ever had any inscription. At the upper end is an obelisk of porphyry, probably brought from Egypt, the hieroglyphics all very entire, which I look upon as mere ancient puns. It is placed on four little brazen pillars, upon a pedestal of square freestone full of figures in bass-relief on two sides; one square representing a battle, another an assembly. The others have inscriptions in Greek and Latin; the last I took in my pocket-book, and it is as follows:

> Difficilis quondam, dominis parere serenis
> Jussus, et extinctis palmam portare tyrannis
> Omnia Theodosio cedunt, sobolique perenni.

Your lord will interpret these lines. Don't fancy they are a love-letter to him.

All the figures have their heads on—and I cannot forbear reflecting again on the impudence of authors, who all say they have not; but I dare swear the greatest part of them never saw them, but took the report from the Greeks, who resist with incredible fortitude the conviction of their own eyes whenever they have invented lies to the dishonor of their enemies. Were you to believe them, there is nothing worth seeing in Constantinople but Sancta Sophia, though there are several larger, and, in my opinion, more beautiful mosques in that city. That of Sultan Achmet has this particularity, that its gates are of brass. In all these mosques there are little chapels, where are the tombs of the founders and their families, with wax candles burning before them.

The exchanges are all noble buildings, full of fine alleys, the greatest part supported with pillars, and kept wonderfully neat. Every trade has its distinct alley, where the merchandise is disposed in the same order as in the New Exchange at London. The Bisisten, or jewellers' quarter, shows so much riches, such a vast quantity of diamonds, and all kinds of precious stones, that they dazzle the sight. The embroiderers' is also very glittering, and people walk here as much for diversion as business. The markets are most of them handsome squares, and admirably well provided, perhaps better than in any other part of the world.

I know you'll expect I should say something particular of the slaves; and you will imagine me half a Turk, when I don't speak of it with the same horror other Christians have done before me. But I cannot forbear applauding the humanity of the Turks to these creatures; they are never ill used, and their slavery is, in my opinion, no worse than servitude all over the world. 'Tis true they have no wages, but they give them yearly clothes to a higher value than our salaries to our ordinary servants. But you'll object that men buy women *with an eye to evil.* In my opinion, they are bought and sold as publicly and as infamously in all our Christian great cities.

I must add to the description of Constantinople, that the historical pillar is no more. It dropped down about two years before I came to this part of the world. I have seen no other footsteps of antiquity except the aqueducts, which are so vast that I am apt to believe they are yet more ancient than the Greek Empire. The Turks, indeed, have clapped in some stones with Turkish inscriptions, to give the natives the honor of so great a work; but the deceit is easily discovered. The other public buildings are the hans and monasteries; the first are very large and numerous; the second, few in number and not at all magnificent. I had the curiosity to visit one of them, and to observe the devotions of the dervises, which are as whimsical as any at Rome. These fellows have permission to marry, but are confined to an odd habit, which is only a piece of coarse white cloth, wrapped about them, with their legs and arms naked. Their order has few other rules, except that of performing their fantastic rites every Tuesday and Friday, which is done in this manner: They meet together in a large hall, where they all stand with their eyes fixed on the ground, and their arms across, while the imaum or preacher reads part of the Alcoran from a pulpit placed in the midst; and when he has done, eight or ten of them make a melancholy concert with their pipes, which are no unmusical instruments. Then he reads again, and makes a short exposition on what he has read; after which they sing and play, till their superior (the only one of them dressed in green) rises and begins a sort of solemn dance. They all stand about him in a regular figure, and while some play, the others tie their robe (which is very wide) fast round their waist, and begin to turn round with an amazing swiftness, and yet with great regard to the music, moving slower or faster as the tune is played. This lasts above an hour, without any of them showing the least appearance of giddiness, which is not to be wondered at when it is considered they are all used to it from their infancy; most of them being devoted to this way of life from their birth. There turned amongst them some little dervises of six or seven years old, who seemed no more disordered by that exercise than the others. At the end of the ceremony they shout out: "There is no other God but God, and Mahomet his Prophet;" after which they kiss the superior's hand and retire. The whole is performed with the most solemn gravity. Nothing can be more austere than the form of these people; they never raise their eyes, and seem devoted to contemplation. And as ridiculous as this is in description, there is something touching in the air of submission and mortification they assume. This letter is of a horrible length; but you may burn it when you have read enough, etc.

XVI.—JERUSALEM.

E. D. Clarke to the Rev. William Otter.

CONVENT OF ST. SALVADOR, JERUSALEM, July 10th, 1801.

The date! the date's the thing! You will thank me for a letter dated Jerusalem; more for that little local honor stuck in its front than for all the fine composition and intelligence it may contain. I hardly yet feel the reality of my being here, and when I reflect, and look back on the many years in which I vainly hoped for this happiness—on my fatigue, and fevers, and toil—I am ready to sink beneath the weight of an accomplishment possessing so much influence on my life; for all my hopes centered here; all my plans, speculations, wishes, were concerned in travels, and without visiting Egypt, Syria, and Greece, my travels, however extensive, would have appeared to me to want that nucleus which, like the heart, is necessary to give life and sensation to the body. If I could repose a little, I should now, I think, be found more quiet for my future life. A stillness must succeed to the gratification of desires which have so long irritated my mind and body. I have done my portion, and am satisfied. If I set down in old England's meadows, I may hope to listen no more to schemes of enterprise, but leave it to younger and stronger men to visit those regions, which I have no longer the wish nor the power to explore.

Do not fear that I shall give you a new edition of old Sandys, or Maundrell, or Ranwolff. I came not here in an age of credulity, though sufficiently an enthusiast. But what blind or wilful ignorance has caused the Christians of this place, through several ages, to show a spot as the house of Dives, and another of the Samaritan? converting the parables of our Saviour to realities, and giving the lie to the Gospels. It matters not, there are antiquities of the highest character around the city. We have been falsely taught to believe that nothing was to be seen here but monks, and monasteries, and relics, and pilgrims, and ignorance, and folly. It is not true! Jerusalem is, of all the cities in the East, one of the most interesting to which our historic traveller can resort for information. Leaving apart the common mummery which occupies its daily visitants, there is enough yet untouched and undescribed to bring pilgrims of a very different description from the universities of Europe to pursue the most important inquiries. If you find that what I shall write is new, and worthy your attention, it will prove what might be discovered here by men having more time and better talents. To me it appears as though the eyes of former travellers had been entirely shut upon their coming here, or that they were so occupied by the monks and their stories that they neglected to go out of the walls.

To those interested in evangelical history, no spectacle can be more mortifying than Jerusalem in its present state. The mistaken zeal of early Christians in their attempts to preserve, has for the most part annihilated those testimonies which might have remained at this day to establish the authenticity of the Gospel, and for which such expense and danger was encountered. Their labors are only calculated to excite regret, if not indignation; and, sighing over the havoc made by the pious hands of the Crusaders, of the Empress Helena, and Godfrey of Bouillon, you would lament that the Holy Land was ever rescued from the hands of Saracens, far less barbarous than their conquerors.

"Quanto praestantius esset
Numen aquae viridi si margine clauderet undas;
Herba, nec ingenuum violarent marmora tophum."

The absurdity of hewing the rocks of Mount Calvary into gilded chapels, and disguising the Holy Sepulchre by coverings of marble and painted domes, has so effectually removed or concealed all that might have borne witness to the history of the Crucifixion, that a visit to Jerusalem has often weakened, instead of fortifying the faith of pilgrims, many of whom have returned worse Christians than they came. This may be the case with those who seek for guidance in the works and relations of ignorant monks; but Jerusalem will be no source of incredulity to men who, with the Gospel in their hands, and a proper attention to history, tread over the ground, shutting their ears and opening their eyes.

More pleasing is the prospect from the summit of Mount Olivet, Mount Sion, or the insulated top of Tabor, in the plains of Esdraelon. Thence all Jerusalem is presented to your view, and such confirmation of the accuracy of the Scriptures, that the earliest records to which history can refer appear the most authentic. The wild Arab, journeying with his immense family, with his camels, his oxen, his mules, and his asses, is still the picture of patriarchal manners. Customs that were thought peculiar to people who have disappeared in the lapse of ages, characterize, at this moment, the inhabitants of the same countries. Novelty, so adored in Europe, has few charms in Asia. The same habits are transmitted invariably from father to son. A thousand years may pass away, and future travellers find the descendants of Abraham watering their camels by the well of Nahor, while another Rebecca, with the daughters of the men of the city, come down, with pitchers on their shoulders and draw waters from the well; wearing ear-rings of half a shekel weight, and bracelets ten shekels weight of gold. Visit ing their tents, he will find a second Sarah, kneading three measures of fine meal, to make cakes upon the hearth, and to offer it for his refreshment beneath a tree, in the plains of Mamre; while Amraphel, King of Shinar; Arioch, King of Ellasar; Chedorlaomer, King of Elam; and Tidal, King of Nations, are at war with Beza, King of Sodom; and with Birsha, King of Gomorrah; Shinab, King of Admah; and Shemeber, King of Zeboim; and the King cf Belas, which is Zoar. Such wars were raging as we passed from Jerusalem to Joppa, and we once saw a circle of such kings and princes seated on the ground, holding council whether we should be smitten, as were the Rephaims in Ashteroth, Karnaim, and the Horites in Mount Seir.

But the antiquities to which I particularly wish to call your attention, I found in descending from Mount Sion to the valley of Jehoshaphat. I forget whether, in my letter to you describing the antiquities in the Gulf of Glaucus, I mentioned some remarkable sepulchres hewn in the rocks there, and which, I said, so exactly answered the description given of the tomb of Jesus Christ, that I was convinced, could I visit Jerusalem, I should find similar antiquities there. Having visited the sepulchre supposed to have been that of Christ, I was not satisfied with its appearance. It is now so disguised with marble that no one can judge, from its appearance, of its original state. I found no rock in which it seemed to have been hewn, but its sides were of that sort of marble called verd-antique, and all the rocks of Jerusalem are a very hard limestone. Add to this, it is only forty paces distant from the spot on which they pretend the cross stood, and almost on a level with it, both being beneath the roof of the same church. Finding it difficult to reconcile the topography of modern Jerusalem, and the situation of the places shown there, with its ancient history, I began to extend my researches without the walls. Coming down from the gate of Mount Sion, I perceived the sides of the opposite hill perforated with sepulchres, exactly resembling those among the ruins of Telmessus, in the Gulf of Glaucus, and fulfilling my prediction most completely. One of these, facing Mount Sion, so exactly corresponds with the description of the sepulchre of our Saviour, that you would be at once disposed to pronounce the hill on which it has been cut Mount Calvary, and this, or at least one of the other tombs, the precise place in which his body was laid. It is hewn in the rock. To look into it, it is necessary "to stoop down" (see St. John, chap. xx., 5). The stone which filled its mouth was of such size that it could only be rolled to its place, and when once there would have astonished any person to find it had been removed (Mark, chap. xvi., 3). It is natural to suppose that a hill for the execution of malefactors would be placed as this is, out of the walls of the city. But there is a stronger reason to suppose the body of Jesus was placed there, and that exactly upon this mount, and no other, Joseph of Arimathea would construct his tomb. It is this: that from time immemorial the Karaean Jews (a sect of all others the most correct in the observance of ancient ceremonies, and whose traditions, extending to the remotest periods, are the least corrupted) have been accustomed to bring their dead for interment to this mount. They bury them there at this hour, but having no longer the power to execute such prodigious works of art, are contented to cover the bodies of their relations with more simple works. * * *

The two strongest arguments to prove that the sepulchre of Christ was one of these, is that Joseph of Arimathea, being a

Jew, must necessarily have constructed his tomb in the Jewish cemetery; and, secondly, to prove that this was the place of burial of the ancient Jews, it is sufficient to have shown that the Karaean, a sect the most obstinate in adhering to ancient customs, have beyond memory buried their dead there. It is on the south side of the city, facing Mount Sion.

These discussions are no otherwise of moment than as they serve to show that the writers of the Gospels, in the most minute circumstances, respecting the manners of the age whose events they celebrate, have been entirely exact. It is for the same reason that I beheld with very great satisfaction, from our windows in Nazareth, two women grinding at the mill, exactly as mentioned by our Saviour: and the machine they use for this purpose is the most ancient mill of which we have any knowledge; it is the same as the *quern* of the Scottish Highlands. I have seen it also in Lapland, and in the Isle of Cyprus, countries sufficiently in their primeval state to afford the first view of those arts which are called forth by the necessities of life.

The Druses are a people inhabiting Mount Lebanon, with whom our patron and preserver, the Pacha of Acre, is at war. We were escorted by his guards from Mount Carmel, over all Galilee, to Nazareth and Jerusalem, and narrowly escaped falling into the hands of the Arabs established on Mount Tabor. I had an opportunity to converse with some of the Druses, near the Lake of Gennesaret. They are the most extraordinary people on earth, singular in the simplicity of their lives, by their strict integrity and virtue. They will only eat what they earn by their own labor, and preserve at this moment the superstitions brought by the Israelites out of Egypt. What will your surprise be to learn that, every Thursday, they elevate the molten calf, before which they prostrate themselves, and, having paid their adoration, each man selects, among the women present, the wife he likes the best, with whom the ceremony ends. The calf is of gold, silver, or bronze. This is exactly that worship at which Moses was so incensed in descending from Mount Sinai. The cow was the Venus of the Egyptians, and of course the calf, a personification of animal desire, or Cupid, before which the sacrifices so offensive to Moses were held. For it is related that they set up a molten calf, which Aaron had made from the ear-rings of the Israelite women; before which similar sacrifices were made. And certainly the Druses on Mount Lebanon are a detachment of the posterity of those Israelites who are so often represented in Scripture as deserters from the true faith, falling back into the old superstitions and pagan worship of the country from whence they came. I could not visit Mount Lebanon, but I took every method necessary to ascertain the truth of this relation; and I send it to you as one of the highest antiquities and most curious relics of remote ages, which has yet been found upon earth.

From the mountains near Bethlehem, the Dead Sea, with the river Jordan, appeared as if I could walk down to it in two hours. It is a most extraordinary place. I shall show you, I hope, some of its productions. The plants were almost all withered, and the heat of the sun so great, that it threw me into one of my fevers—which alarmed us, as the plague raged both in Nazareth and Bethlehem, and it began with such symptoms as are usually deemed pestilential. I have recovered in this convent, among the fattest friars who ever fed on the milk and honey of Canaan. You will imagine what sufferings accompany travels in such climates, where one looks in vain for shade; where the wind is hotter than the sun's rays; and where Fahrenheit's thermometer, not being exposed to either, rises to 105. Lord Keith told me that, in the tents of the English, near Cairo, it had risen to 120. An umbrella is but a mockery of woe, for the reflected heat from the ground is full as insupportable as the direct rays of the sun.

Besides the antiquities I have mentioned to you, on the south side of the city, Jerusalem is entirely surrounded with others, which bear no features to indicate in what age or by whom they were left. They are, for the most part, of the same character, and consist of subterraneous excavations of a magnitude and beauty without parallel. They are not like the catacombs at Naples or Rome, though the greatest part of them appear sepulchral. In riding without the walls of the city, sometimes a small aperture like the mouth of a well, at others the whole side of a rock, cut like a quarry, with wide openings, beautifully sculptured and adorned with columns, lead to numberless chambers of different dimensions, all hewn in the solid rock, where you may wander as in a labyrinth, and find no end to your research. The most considerable of them are the only ones to which the inhabitants have given even a name; and they are, the Sepulchre of the Virgin Mary, and all her family, of the Saints Joachim, Anne, and Joseph; and some prodigious excavations, on the north side of Jerusalem, called the Sepulchre of its ancient kings. I can form no conjecture respecting their origin, but have found them all over the Holy Land, as well as on the coast of Asia Minor. Even on the summit of the Mount of Olives are some of these subterranean works; and one there, in particular, is deserving of notice, as it differs from all the rest in being lined with a very hard antique stucco, similar to some subterranean works which I found on the Isle of Bequieres, in the bay of Aboukir, on the coast of Egypt. It is also of a very remarkable form; being a cone, or funnel, whose vertex, rising to the surface of the summit of the mountain, affords a small opening to admit light, as well as the only entrance; below this hole, the sides of the cone extend to such a width and depth that I could not determine the immense size of the cavern they contained.

I cannot conclude this letter, already swelled to a volume (which convinces me of the impossibility of writing half I wish to add), without mentioning our travels in Galilee, by much the most pleasing part of our journey. I know of no travellers who have visited this portion of the Holy Land, as it lies out of the usual pilgrimage of persons bound merely to Jerusalem. Our plan was to pursue the history of Jesus Christ from His nativity to His death; following His footsteps, with the Gospel in our hands, and reading, at every spot mentioned in it, the passage which had rendered it sacred. For this purpose we went first to Nazareth; from thence into Galilee, visiting Cana, the Lake of Gennesaret, and even the borders of the Desert, to which He retired in His earliest years. Galilee affords the highest satisfaction, because its objects are among the features of nature, and are not liable to receive injury from the barbarous zeal of monks. The scenery there is very grand. The Lake of Gennesaret, or Sea of Tiberias, is more beautiful than the Lake of Locarno, which it resembles; at the same time, it has that grandeur which is ever found where water of such extent is surrounded by high mountains, and hardly yields the palm to the Lake of Geneva. I had the happiness of swimming in its crystal waters; buoyed above its waves by all those emotions which local enthusiasm, when called forth by piety as well as memory in scenery so dignified, cannot fail to excite.

Returning from Galilee, we took a road by Mount Tabor, passing through the country in which His disciples are said to have plucked the ears of corn on the Sabbath day, and came again to Cana and to Nazareth. At Cana we saw, still in use, those "stone water-pots" which are described, John, chap. ii., 5, 6, as "containing two or three firkins apiece." We then crossed the beautiful plain of Erzelon, or Esdraelon, more fertile than the richest gardens; in the midst of which Mount Tabor rises insulated to a great height, of a conic form, and offers a retreat to the wildest bands of Arab robbers. The cavalry of the Pacha of Acre were encamped on this plain, and they received us into their tents, feeding us after the Eastern custom, all out of one dish, seated on the ground, and teaching us to eat pilau and sour milk with our fingers. They afterwards escorted us to a fortress in the mountains, under the government of the Pacha of Damascus, our train consisting of thirty-three armed men on horseback; while our Arabs kept skirmishing, practising all those feats of horsemanship for which they are so celebrated, firing their pieces, and engaging in sham fights around us, that the distant enemy might not count our numbers, nor be able to survey our strength.

Some of the princes of the robbers, Arab chiefs, such as were of old times shepherd kings, came down from the mountains to enter into a league with the general of the cavalry in the plain, and dined by our side, beneath the same tent, but would not eat out of the same dish. The Arabs then encamped had already taken from some of the neighboring tribes 20,000 oxen, 12,000 camels, 10,000 sheep, 8,000 asses, besides horses, prisoners, arms, etc. One hundred of the oxen have been given to the captain of our frigate, Captain Culverhouse, of the Romulus, to take back to the fleet at Aboukir.

The whole country is a succession of hills and plains. The former are cultivated to their tops, with uncommon industry, and covered with olive and fig trees. The plains produce the richest harvest, except in the perturbed dominions of the Pacha of Acre. Nazareth alone seems to preserve its old character of wretchedness and sterility, the hills around being a bleak, incorrigible rock, and its inhabitants in the greatest poverty; so that one would still exclaim, "Can any thing good come out of Nazareth?" Of the Holy Land in general, the valley watered by the Jordan and the rich plains of Canaan, it is still but truth to style it "a land flowing with milk and honey." The eye ranges over an extent of corn, wine, oil, rice, tobacco, figs, melons, and whatever the earth can yield to fill the granaries of men or gratify their palates. Among these are seen swarms of partridges, wild deer, wild boars, which hardly move at your approach; while the stately camel, moving with dignified step in the long caravans, bearing wealth and power, lifts his tall head above the harvest, and seems with his eye to command immeasurable distance. Such is the Holy Land, or, rather, such the only account I can now give you. Since I wrote last to you I have visited Cyprus, being conveyed there in the Ceres frigate, Captain Russell. I have no time now to enter upon the subject of that island. I had hardly been two days back to the fleet, when the captain of the Romulus offered us a passage to Acre. These are favorable moments for travellers in the Levant, when frigates are daily sailing in all directions, and the English name is so much respected. I can tell you nothing of affairs in Egypt till I get back, but believe things are much as they were when I sent you my last letter. Cripps unites in remembrance. God bless you. I must beg of you to let my mother see this letter, and also G. Stracey, if you have an opportunity, as you will see the impossibility of writing to all friends in the midst of such fatigue and occupation.

XVII.—FIRST IMPRESSIONS OF INDIA.

Bishop Heber to Hon. C. W. W. Wynn.

BARRACKPOOR, Oct. 29th, 1823.

MY DEAR WYNN: The first quiet morning which I have had since my arrival in India I cannot employ more agreeably than in writing to those dear and kind friends, the recollection of whom I feel binding me still more strongly to England the farther I am removed from it.

The first sight of India has little which can please even those who have been three months at sea. The coast is so flat as only to be distinguished when very near it by the tall cocoa trees which surround the villages; and Juggernaut, which is a conspicuous sea mark, shows merely three dingy conical domes, like glass houses. The view of Saugor is still worse, being made up of marshes and thick brushwood on the same level line of shore, and conveying at once the idea, which it well deserves, of tigers, serpents, and fevers. During the night of our anchoring under its lee, however, few of us went to bed without reluctance; since, besides the interest which men feel in looking at land at all after so long an absence, I never saw such magnificent sheet lightning in my life as played over it all night. When coupled with the unhealthy and dangerous character of the place, and the superstitions connected with it as the favorite abode of Rali, it was impossible to watch the broad, red, ominous light which flickered without more intermission than just served to heighten its contrast with darkness, and not to think of Southey's Padalon; and it luckily happened that "Kehama" was on board, and that many of the party, at my recommendation, had become familiar with it during the voyage. By the way, what a vast deal of foolish prejudice exists about Southey and his writings. Of the party on board, some had been taught to think him a Jacobin, some an ultra-Tory, some a Methodist, some an enemy to all religion, and some a madman. None had read a line of his works, but all were inclined to criticize him; and yet all, when they really tried the formidable volume, were delighted both with the man and the poetry. Nor is he the only poet for whom I succeeded in obtaining some justice. I repeated, at different times, some parts of the "Ancient Mariner," without telling whose it was, and had the pleasure to find that its descriptions of nature in tropical countries were recognized by the officers and more experienced passengers as extremely vivid, and scarcely exaggerated. The chief-mate, a very hard-headed Scotchman, a grandson of Lord Monboddo's, was peculiarly struck and downright affected with the shrinking of the planks of the devoted ship when becalmed under the line, the stagnation and rolling of the deep, and the diminished size and terrible splendor of the noon-day sun right over the mast-head, "in a hot and copper sky." He foretold that we should see something like this when the Grenville came to anchor in the Hooghly; and verily he fabled not. The day after our arrival off Saugor the sun was, indeed, a thing of terror, and almost intolerable; and the torrent, carrying down trees, sugar-canes, and corpses past us every five minutes, and boiling as it met the tide-stream like milled chocolate, with its low banks of jungle or of bare sand, was as little promising to a new-comer as could well be conceived. Of these different objects, the corpses, as you are aware, are a part of the filthy superstition of the country, which throws the dead, half roasted over a scanty fire, into the sacred river; and such objects must always be expected and perceived by more senses than one. The others, though also usual at the termination of the rains, were this year particularly abundant, from the great height to which the river had risen, and the consequent desolation which it had brought on the lower plantations and villages.

We arrived in Fort William on the evening of the 10th. The impression made by the appearance of the European houses which we passed in Gardenreach, by our own apartments, by the crowd of servants, the style of carriages and horses sent to meet us, and almost all the other circumstances which meet our eyes, was that of the extreme similarity of every thing to Russia; making allowance only for the black instead of the white faces, and the difference of climate, though even in Russia, during summer, it is necessary to guard against intense heat. This impression was afterwards rather confirmed than weakened. The size of the houses, their whiteness and Palladian porticos, the loftiness of the rooms, and the scanty furniture, the unbounded hospitality and apparent love of display, all reminded me of Petersburg and Moscow; to which the manner in which the European houses are scattered, with few regular streets, but each with its separate courtyard and gateway, and often intermixed with miserable huts, still more contributed. I caught myself several times mixing Russian with my newly-acquired

Hindoostanee, talking of rubles instead of rupees, and bidding the attendants come and go in what they of course mistook for English, but which was Sclavonic. I was surprised to find how little English is understood by them; out of upwards of forty servants, there are only two who have the least smattering of it, and they know a few of the commonest words, without the power of putting together or understanding a sentence. The Sircar, indeed, is a well-educated man, but of him we see comparatively little, so that we have abundant opportunity and necessity for the acquisition of the native languages. After a manner, indeed, everybody speaks them, but we find (I must say) our previous instructions in grammar from Gilchrist extremely valuable, both as facilitating our progress and as guarding us from many ridiculous equivoques and blunders into which other griffins fall. * * * * * My situation here is extremely pleasant—as pleasant as it can be at a distance from such friends as those whom I have left behind; and I have a field of usefulness before me so vast, that my only fear is lest I should lose my way in it. The attention and the kindness of the different members of government, and the hospitality of the society of Calcutta, have been every thing we could wish, and more. The arrears of business which I have to go through, though great, and some of a vexatious nature, are such as I see my way through. My own health, and those of my wife and child, have rather improved than otherwise since our landing; and the climate, now that we have lofty rooms, and means of taking exercise at proper times of the day, is any thing but intolerable. * * * * * Of what are called in England "the luxuries of the East," I cannot give a very exalted description; all the fruits now in season are inferior to those of England. The oranges, though pleasant, are small and acid; the plantain is but an indifferent mellow pear; the shaddock has no merit but juiciness and a slight bitter taste, which is reckoned good in fevers; and the guava is an almost equal mixture of raspberry jam and garlic. Nor are our artificial luxuries more remarkble than our natural. They are, in fact, only inventions (judicious and elegant certainly) to get rid of real and severe inconveniences; while all those circumstances in which an Englishman mainly places his ideas of comfort or splendor, such as horses, carriages, glass, furniture, etc., are, in Calcutta, generally paltry and extravagantly dear. In fact, as my shipmate, Colonel Pennington, truly told me, "the real luxuries of India, when we can get them, are cold water and cold air." But though the luxury and splendor are less, the society is better than I expected. The state in which the high officers of government appear, and the sort of deference paid to them in society are great, and said to be necessary in conformity with native ideas, and the example set by the first conquerors, who took their tone from the Mussulmans whom they supplanted. All members of council, and others, down to the rank of puisne judges inclusive, are preceded by two men with silver sticks, and two others with heavy silver maces; and they have in society some queer regulations, which forbid any person to quit a party before the lady or gentleman of most rank rises to take leave. * * *

There are some circumstances in Calcutta dwellings which at first surprise and annoy a stranger. The lofty rooms swarm with cockroaches and insects; sparrows and other birds fly in and out all day, and, as soon as the candles are lighted, large bats flutter on their indented wings, like Horace's cura, round our *laqueata tecta*, if this name could be applied to roofs without any ceiling at all, where the beams are left naked and visible, lest the depredations of the white ant should not be seen in time.

* * * * * * *

On the whole, however, you will judge from my description that I have abundant reason to be satisfied with my present comforts and my future prospects, and that in the field which seems open to me for extensive usefulness and active employment, I have more and more reason to be obliged to the friends who have placed me here.

The country round Calcutta is a perfect flat, intersected by pools and canals, natural and artificial, teeming with population like an ant-hill, and covered with one vast shade of fruit trees, not of low growth, like those of England, but, generally speaking, very lofty and majestic. To me it has great interest; indeed, such a scene as I have described, with the addition of a majestic river, may be monotonous, but cannot be ugly.

Barrackpoor, the governor's country house, is really a beautiful place, and would be thought so in any country. It has what is here unexampled—a park of about 150 acres of fine turf, with spreading scattered trees, of a character so European that, if I had not been on an elephant, and had not from time to time seen tall cocoa trees towering above all the rest, I could have fancied myself on the banks of the Thames instead of the Ganges. It is hence that I date my letter, having been asked to pass two days here. Our invitation was for a considerably longer period, but it is as yet with difficulty that I can get away even for a few hours from Calcutta. * * * * *

Of the religious state of India I have little as yet to say. I have bestowed the archdeaconry, much to my satisfaction, on the senior resident chaplain, Mr. Corrie, who is extremely popular in the place, and one of the most amiable and gentlemanly men in manners and temper I ever met with.

In the schools which have been lately established in this part of the empire, of which there are at present nine established by the Church Missionary, and eleven by the Christian Knowledge Societies, some very unexpected facts have occurred. As all direct attempts to convert the children are disclaimed, the parents send them without scruple. But is no less strange than true that there is no objection made to the use of the Old and New Testaments as a class-book; that so long as the teachers do not urge them to eat what will make them lose their caste, or to be baptized, or to curse their country's gods, they readily consent to every thing else, and not only Mussulmans, but Brahmins, stand by with perfect coolness, and listen sometimes with apparent interest and pleasure, while the scholars by the roadside are reading the stories of the creation and of Jesus Christ. Whether the children themselves may imbibe Christianity by such means, or whether they may suffer these truths to pass from their minds as we allow the mythology which we learn at school to pass from ours, some further time is yet required to show; but this, at least, I understand has been ascertained, that a more favorable opinion, both of us and our religion, has been, apparently, felt of late by many of those who have thus been made acquainted with its leading truths, and that some have been heard to say that they did not know till now that the English had "a caste or a shaster." You may imagine with what feelings I have entered the huts where these schools are held, on seeing a hundred poor little children seated on the ground, writing their letters in sand, or their copies on banana leaves, coming out one after another to read the history of the good Samaritan, or of Joseph, proud of showing their knowledge, and many of them able to give a very good account of their studies.

I have been even much gratified at seeing the confidence and respect evidently shown by the elder villagers toward the clergy who superintend these schools. I yesterday saw a man follow a German missionary to request that he would look at his little boy's copy; and Mr. Hawtayne, the secretary to the society for promoting Christian knowledge, seems as well known and received in the vicinity of his schools, as any English clergyman in his parish. I have not as yet received any visits from the wealthy natives, though some of them have made inquiries through my Sircar, whether such visits would be agreeable to me, to which I of course answered, "Extremely so." Their progress in the imitation of our habits is very apparent, though still the difference is great. None of them adopt our dress (indeed their own is so much more graceful and so much better adapted to the climate that they would act very absurdly in doing so). But their houses are adorned with verandahs and Corinthian pillars; they have very handsome carriages, often built in England; they speak tolerable English, and they show a considerable liking for European society, where (which unfortunately is not always the case) they are encouraged or permitted to frequent it on terms of any thing like equality. Few of them, however, will eat with us; and this opposes a bar to familiar intercourse, which must, even more than fashion and John Bullism, keep them at a distance.

They are described, especially the Hindoos, as not ill affected to a government under which they thrive, and are allowed to enjoy the fruits of their industry, while many of them still recollect the cruelties and exactions of their former rulers.

This is, I feel, an unreasonable letter, but I know your friendship will not be indifferent to details in which I am so much interested; and I have not been sorry, while the novelty yet remained, to communicate to you my first impressions of a country in all respects so unlike our own, and yet so important to an Englishman. Lord Hastings appears to have been very popular here, and to have done much good. The roads which he made in different parts of Calcutta and its neighborhood, his splendor and his extreme courtesy, made him liked both by natives and Europeans.

Adieu, dear Wynn. Present our mutual best regards to Mrs. Williams Wynn and young folk, and believe me ever,

Your obliged and affectionate friend,

REGINALD CALCUTTA.

XVIII.—VISIT TO A BRAHMIN—TALK ABOUT FRANKLIN, AND NATURAL PHILOSOPHY.

Bishop Heber to Hon. C. W. W. Wynn.

FORT WILLIAMS, Dec. 1st, 1823.

MY DEAR WYNN: I hope you will, ere this reaches you, have received a long letter from Barrackpoor, giving an account of my first impressions of India. By all which I have yet seen, I do not think they were too favorable. The climate since I wrote is very materially improved, and is now scarcely hotter, and to the full as pleasant as our finest August weather. The mornings and evenings are particularly agreeable, and the sun during the day time, though still too hot to admit of taking exercise, is any thing but oppressive to those who are setting still under a roof or driving in a carriage. The only plague, and a sore plague too, are the musquitoes.

I am constantly and sometimes intensely occupied, insomuch that I have as yet had no time whatever for my usual literary pursuits, and scarcely any time for the study of Hindoostanee and Persian, or the composition of sermons, of which last, unluckily owing to a mistake, my main stock was sent by another ship, which has not yet arrived, so that I have more trouble in this way than I expected, or than is very consistent with my other duties.

Since my last letter I have become acquainted with some of the wealthy natives of whom I spoke, and we are just returned from passing the evening at one of their country houses. This is more like an Italian villa than what one should have expected as the residence of Baboo Hurree Mohun Thakoor. Nor are his carriages, the furniture of his house, or the style of his conversation, of a character less decidedly European. He is a fine old man, who speaks English well, is well informed on most topics of general discussion, and talks with the appearance of much familiarity on Franklin, chemistry, natural philosophy, etc. His family is Brahminical, and of singular purity of descent; but about 400 years ago, during the Mohammedan invasion of India, one of his ancestors having become polluted by the conquerors intruding into his Zennanah, the race is conceived to have lost claim to the knotted cord, and the more rigid Brahmins will not eat with them. Being, however, one of the principal landholders in Bengal, and of a family so ancient, they still enjoy to a great degree the veneration of the common people, which the present head of the house appears to value, since I can hardly reconcile in any other manner his philosophical studies and imitation of many European habits, with the daily and austere devotion which he is said to practise toward the Ganges (in which he bathes three times every twenty-four hours), and his veneration for all the other duties of his ancestors. He is now said, however, to be aiming at the dignity of Raja, a title which at present bears pretty much the same estimation here as a peerage in England, and is conferred by Government in almost the same manner.

The house is surrounded by an extensive garden, laid out in formal parterres of roses, intersected by straight walks, with some fine trees, and a chain of tanks, fountains, and summer-houses, not ill adapted to a climate where air, water, and sweet smells are almost the only natural objects which can be relished during the greater part of the year. The whole is little less Italian than the façade of his house; but on my mentioning this similarity he observed that the taste for such things was brought into India by the Mussulmans. There are also swings, whirligigs, and other amusements for the females of his family, but the strangest was a sort of "Montagne Russe" of masonry, very steep, and covered with plaster, down which, he said, the ladies used to *slide*. Of these females, however, we saw none; indeed, they were all staying at his town-house in Calcutta. He himself received us, at the head of a whole tribe of relations and descendants, on a handsome flight of steps, in a splendid shawl by way of mantle, with a large rosary of coral set in gold, leaning on an ebony crutch with a gold head. Of his grandsons, four very pretty boys, two were dressed like English children of the same age, but the round hat, jacket, and trowsers by no means suited their dusky skins so well as the splendid brocade caftans and turbans covered with diamonds, which the two elder wore. On the whole, both Emily and I have been greatly interested with the family, both now and during our previous interviews. We have several other Eastern acquaintance, but none of equal talent, though several learned Moolahs, and one Persian doctor, of considerable reputed sanctity, have called on me. The Raja of Calcutta, and one of the sons of Tippoo Sultan, do not choose, I am told, to call till I have left the fort, since they are not permitted to bring their silver sticks, led horses, carriages, and armed attendants, within the ramparts. In all this nothing strikes me more than the apparent indifference of these men to the measures employed for extending Christianity, and rendering it more conspicuous in Hindoostan. They seem to think it only right and decent that the conquering nation should have its hierarchy and establishment on a handsome scale, and to regard with something little short of approbation the means we take for educating the children of the poor. One of their men of rank has absolutely promised to found a college at Burdwan, with one of our missionaries at its head, and where little children should be clothed and educated under his care. All this is very short indeed of embracing Christianity themselves, but it proves how completely those feelings are gone by, in Bengal at least, which made even the presence of a single missionary the occasion of tumult and alarm. I only hope that no imprudence or overforwardness on our part will revive these angry feelings. Believe me, dear Charles, ever your obliged friend, REGINALD CALCUTTA.

BOOK THE FOURTH.

Public History, Illustrated by Letters.

BOOK THE FOURTH.

PUBLIC HISTORY, ILLUSTRATED BY LETTERS.

I.—PRAYER FOR A FAIR TRIAL.

Queen Anne Boleyn to Henry the Eighth.

SIR: Your grace's displeasure and my imprisonment are things so strange unto me, as what to write, or what to excuse, I am altogether ignorant. Whereas you send unto me (willing me to confess a truth, and so obtain your favor) by such an one whom you know to be mine ancient professed enemy, I no sooner received this message by him than I rightly conceived your meaning; and if, as you say, confessing a truth indeed may procure my safety, I shall, with all willingness and duty, perform your command.

But let not your grace ever imagine that your poor wife will ever be brought to acknowledge a fault where not so much as a thought thereof preceded. And, to speak a truth, never prince had wife more loyal in all duty, and in all true affection, than you have ever found in Anne Boleyn; with which name and place I could willingly have contented myself, if God and your grace's pleasure had been so pleased. Neither did I at any time so far forget myself in my exaltation, or received queenship, but that I always looked for such an alteration as now I find; for th ground of my preferment being on no surer foundation than you grace's fancy, the least alteration I know was fit and sufficien to draw that fancy to some other subject. You have chosen m from a low estate to be your queen and companion, far beyonc my desert and desire. If, then, you found me worthy of such honor, good your grace let not any light fancy, or bad counsel of mine enemies, withdraw your princely favor from me; neither let that stain, that unworthy stain, of a disloyal heart toward your good grace, ever cast so foul a blot on your most dutiful wife, and the infant princess, your daughter. Try me, good King, but let me have a lawful trial; and let not my sworn enemies sit as my accusers and judges; yea, let me receive an open trial (for my truth shall fear no open shame); then shall you see either mine innocence cleared, your suspicion and conscience satisfied, the ignominy and slander of the world stopped, or my guilt openly declared. So that whatsoever God or you may determine of me, your grace may be freed from an open censure, and mine offence being so lawfully proved, your grace is at liberty, both before God and man, not only to execute worthy punishment on me as an unlawful wife, but to follow your affection, already settled on that party, for whose sake I am now as I am, whose name I could some good while since have pointed unto your grace, being not ignorant of my suspicion therein. But if you have already determined of me, and that not only my death, but an infamous slander must bring you the enjoying of your desired happiness, then I desire of God that he will pardon your great sin therein, and likewise mine enemies the instruments thereof; and that he will not call you to a strict account for your unprincely and cruel usage of me, at his general judgment-seat, where both you and myself must shortly appear, and in whose judgment, I doubt not (whatsoever the world may think of me), mine innocence shall be openly known and sufficiently cleared. My last and only request shall be, that myself may only bear the burthen of your grace's displeasure, and that it may not touch the innocent souls of those poor gentlemen who, as I understand, are likewise in strait imprisonment for my sake. If ever I found favor in your sight, if ever the name of Anne Boleyn hath been pleasing in your ears, then let me obtain this request, and I will so leave to trouble your grace any farther with my earnest prayers to the Trinity to have your grace in his good keeping, and to direct you in all your actions. From my doleful prison in the Tower, the 6th of May. Your most loyal and ever faithful wife.*

* "This letter contains so much nature, and even elegance," says Hume, "as to deserve to be transmitted to posterity without any alteration in the expression." The original manuscript was partly destroyed by fire in 1731. It is now to be seen in the British Museum, with the marks of its partial mutilation by the flames. "It is not wonderful," says Sir James Mackintosh, "that the excitement of such a moment, if it left Anne calmness enough to write, should raise her language to an energy unknown in her other writings. If this explanation from Lord Herbert should be deemed inadequately to account for the singular exactness and elegance of the composition, why may we not suppose, consistently with its substantial authenticity, that a compassionate confessor, or one lingering friend, may have secretly lent his hand to refine and elevate the diction? Sir Thomas Wyatt, one of the fathers of English poetry (to take an instance), could not have forgotten that his heart had once been touched by her youthful loveliness, and if he had been moved by a generous remembrance of affection to lend his help 'at her utmost need,' he would assuredly not have disturbed any of the inimitable strokes of nature which she could scarcely avoid, but which it is unlikely that he with all his genius could have invented."—H.

II.—QUEEN ELIZABETH'S SPEECH AT TILBURY FORT.

Dr. Sharpe to the Duke of Buckingham.

I remember, in eighty-eight, waiting upon the Earl of Leicester at Tilbury camp, and in eighty-nine going into Portugal with my noble master, the Earl of Essex, I learned somewhat fit to be imparted to your grace.

The Queen, lying in the camp one night, guarded with her army, the old Lord Treasurer Burleigh came thither, and delivered to the Earl the examination of Don Pedro, who was taken and brought in by Sir Francis Drake, which examination the Earl of Leicester delivered unto me to publish to the army in my next sermon. The sum of it was this:

Don Pedro being asked, What was the intent of their coming? stoutly answered the lords, What, but to subdue your nation and root it out!

Good, said the lords; and what meant you then to do with the Catholics? He answered, We meant to send them (good men) directly unto heaven, as all you that are heretics to hell. Yea, but said the lords, What meant you to do with your whips of cord and wire? (whereof they had great store in their ships). What? said he; we meant to whip you heretics to death, that have assisted my master's rebels, and done such dishonors to our Catholic King and people. Yea, but what would you have done, said they, with their young children? They, said he, which were above seven years old, should have gone the way their fathers went; the rest should have lived, branded in the forehead with the letter L., for Lutheran, to perpetual bondage.

This, I take God to witness, I received of those great lords upon examination taken by the council, and by commandment delivered it to the army.

The Queen the next morning rode through all the squadrons of her army, as armed Pallas, attended by noble footmen, Leicester, Essex, and Norris, then Lord Marshal, and divers other great lords, where she made an excellent oration to her army, which the next day after her departure I was commanded to redeliver to all the army together, to keep a public fast. Her words were these:

"My loving people, we have been persuaded by some that are careful of our safety, to take heed how we commit ourself to armed multitudes for fear of treachery; but I assure you I do not desire to live to distrust my faithful and loving people. Let tyrants fear; I have always so behaved myself that, under God, I have placed my chiefest strength and safeguard in the loyal hearts and good will of my subjects. And, therefore, I am come amongst you as you see at this time, not for my recreation and disport, but being resolved, in the midst and heat of the battle, to live or die amongst you all, to lay down for my God, and for my kingdom, and for my people, my honor, and my blood, even in the dust. I know I have the body but of a weak and feeble woman, but I have the heart and stomach of a king, and of a king of England too; and think foul scorn, that Parma, or Spain, or any prince in Europe should dare to invade the borders of my realm, to which, rather than any dishonor should grow by me, I myself will take up arms, I myself will be your general, judge, and rewarder of every one of your virtues in the field. I know already for your forwardness you have deserved rewards and crowns; and we do assure you, in the word of a prince, they shall be duly paid you. In the mean time, my Lieutenant-General shall be in my stead, than whom never prince commanded a more noble or worthy subject; not doubting but by your obedience to my general, by your concord in the camp, and your valor in the field, we shall shortly have a famous victory over those enemies of my God, of my kingdoms, and of my people." *

* This speech of Elizabeth (as a piece of martial rhetoric) has never been surpassed. It was splendidly commemorated by Sir James Mackintosh in his defence of Peltier, when he describes the resistance which Queen Elizabeth offered to the schemes of universal domination that were attempted by Phillip II. "That wise and magnanimous Princess," says he, "placed herself in the front of the battle for the liberties of Europe. Though she had to contend at home with the fanatical faction of Phillip, which almost occupied Ireland, which divided Scotland, and was not of contemptible strength in England, she aided the oppressed inhabitants of the Netherlands in their just and glorious resistance to his tyranny; she aided Henry the Great in suppressing the abominable rebellion which anarchical principles had excited, and Spanish arms had supported in France; and after a long reign of various fortune, in which she preserved her unconquered spirit through great calamities and still greater dangers, she at length broke the strength of the enemy, and reduced his power within such limits as to be compatible with the safety of England and of all Europe. Her only effectual ally was the spirit of her people, and her policy flowed from that magnanimous nature which in the hour of peril teaches better lessons than those of cold reason. Her great heart inspired her with a higher and a nobler wisdom, which disdained to appeal to the low and sordid passions of her people, even for the protection of their low and sordid interests, because she knew, or rather she felt, that these are effeminate, creeping, cowardly, short-sighted passions which shrink from conflict even in defence of their own mean objects. In a righteous cause, she roused those generous affections of her people which alone teach boldness, constancy, and foresight, and which are, therefore, the only safe guardians of the lowest as well as highest interests of a nation. In her memorable address to her army, when the invasion of the kingdom was threatened by Spain, this woman of heroic spirit disdained to speak to them of their ease, and their commerce, and their wealth, and their safety. No; she touched another chord—she spoke of their national honor, of their dignity as Englishmen, of 'the *foul* scorn that Parma or Spain should dare invade the borders of her realms;' she breathed into them those grand and powerful sentiments which exalt vulgar men into heroes, which led them into the battle of their country armed with holy and irresistible enthusiasm, which even cover with their shield all the ignoble in-

This I thought would delight your grace, and no man hath it but myself, and such as I have given it to; and therefore I made bold to send it unto you, if you have it not already.

III.—ON THE EVE OF THE BATTLE OF DUNBAR.

Oliver Cromwell to Sir Arthur Heselrig.

DUNBAR, 2d September, 1650.

DEAR SIR: We are upon an engagement very difficult. The enemy hath blocked up our way at the Pass at Copperspath, through which we cannot get without almost a miracle. He lieth so upon the Hills that we know not how to come that way without great difficulty; and our lying here daily consumeth our men, who fall sick beyond imagination.

I perceive your forces are not in a capacity for present release. Wherefore, *whatever becomes of us*, it will be well for you to get what forces you can get together: and the South to help what they can. The business nearly concerneth all Good People. If your forces had been in a readiness to have fallen upon the back of Copperspath, it might have occasioned supplies to have come to us. But the only wise God knows what is best. All shall work for Good. Our spirits are comfortable, praised be the Lord—though our present condition be as it is. And indeed we have much hope in the Lord; of whose mercy we have had large experience.

Indeed, do you get together what forces you can against them. Send to friends in the South to help with more. Let H. Vane know what I write. *I would not make it public lest danger*

terests that base calculation and cowardly selfishness tremble to hazard, but shrink from defending."—H.

should accrue thereby. You know what use to make hereof. Let me hear from you. I rest, your servant,

OLIVER CROMWELL.*

IV.—PLAGUE IN LONDON.

Samuel Pepys to Lady Carteret.

WOOLWICH, Sept. 4, 1665.

DEAR MADAM: Your Ladyship will not, I hope, imagine I expected to be provoked, by letters from you, to think of the duty I ought, and should long since have paid your ladyship, by mine, had it been fit for me (during my indispensable attendance alone in the city) to have ventured the affrighting you with any thing from thence. But now that, by the despatch of the fleet, I am at liberty to retire wholly to Woolwich, where I have been purging my ink horn and papers these six days, your Ladyship shall find no further cause to reproach me my silence. And in amends for what is past, let me conjure you, madam, to believe that no day hath passed since my last kissing your hands, without my most interested wishes for your health, and the uninterrupted prosperity of your Ladyship and family.

I took care for the present disposal of what were enclosed in your Ladyship's to me; and in answer to that to Dagenham's, return these from my Lady Wright, who, in hers to myself, gives assurance of my Lord Hinchingbroke's being got up, and the health of the rest of her family.

* Cromwell wrote this letter, in the full expectation that the morrow might terminate his victories and his life. It was the next morning, at the first charge of the cavalry, that as the clouds rolled away, and the sun shone out, "I heard Noll say," says Hodgson, "'Let God arise,—let His enemies be scattered!'" A more sublime, and yet more simple war-cry than even the celebrated watchword of Napoleon from the foot of the Pyramids.

My Lord Sandwich has gone to sea with a noble fleet, in want of nothing but a certainty of meeting the enemy. My best Lady Sandwich, with the flock at Hinchingbroke, was by my last letters very well.

The absence of the court and emptiness of the city, takes away all occasion of news, save only such melancholy stories as would rather sadden than find your Ladyship any divertisement in the hearing; I, having stayed in the city till above 7,400 died in one week, and of them, above 6,000 of the plague, and little noise heard day or night but tolling of bells; till I could walk Lumber street, and not meet twenty persons from one end to the other, and not fifty upon the Exchange; till whole families, ten and twelve together, have been swept away; till my very physician, Dr. Burnet, who undertook to secure me against any infection, having survived the month of his own house being shut up, died himself of the plague; till the nights, though much lengthened, are grown too short to conceal the burials of those that died the day before, people being thereby constrained to borrow daylight for that service; lastly, till I could find neither meat nor drink safe—the butcheries being everywhere visited, my brewer's house shut up, and my baker with his whole family dead of the plague.

Yet, madam, through God's blessing, and the good humors begot in my attendance upon our late amours,* your poor servant is in a perfect state of health, as well as resolution of employing it as your Ladyship and family shall find work for it.

How Deptford stands, your Ladyship is, I doubt not, informed from nearer hands.

Greenwich begins apace to be sickly; but we are, by com-

* The marriage of Lady Carteret's son to the daughter of Lord Sandwich.

mand of the King, taking all the care we can to prevent its growth; and meeting to that purpose yesterday, after sermon, with the town officers, many doleful informations were brought us, and among others this, which I shall trouble your Ladyship with the telling. Complaint was brought us against one in the town for receiving into his house a child, newly brought from an infected house in London. Upon inquiry, we found that it was the child of a very able citizen in Gracious street, who, having lost already all the rest of his children, and himself and wife being shut up and in despair of escaping, implored only the liberty of using the means for the saving of this only babe, which with difficulty was allowed, and they suffered to deliver it, stripped naked, out at a window, into the arms of a friend, who, shifting into fresh clothes, conveyed it thus to Greenwich, where, upon this information from Alderman Hooker, we suffer it to remain. This, I tell your Ladyship, as one instance of the miserable streights our poor neighbors are reduced to.

But, madam, I'll go no farther in this disagreeable discourse, hoping, from the coolness of the last seven or eight days, my next may bring you a more welcome account of the lessening of the disease, which God say Amen to.

Dear madam, do me right to my good Lady Slaning, in telling her that I have sent and sent again to Mr. Porter's lodgings, who is in the country, for an answer to my letter about her Ladyship's business, but am yet unable to give her any account of it.

My wife joins with me in ten thousand happy wishes to the young couple, and as many humble services to your Ladyship and them, my Lady Slaning, Lady Scott, and Mr. Sydney, whose return to Scott's Hall, if not burthensome to your Ladyship, will,

I am sure, be as full of content to him as it will ever be of joy and honor to me, to be so esteemed.

Dearest madam, your Ladyship's most affectionate and obedient servant, S. PEPYS.

V.—TRIAL OF THE SEVEN BISHOPS.

From —— *to John Ellis.*

LONDON, June 30th, 1688.

SIR: Yesterday the seven Bishops came to their trial, which held from morning till seven at night. We gave you an account of the jury in our last. The first twelve stood, only Sir John Berry was not there: they did not bring in their verdict last night, and it is said they had not agreed upon it this day at four in the morning.

The counsel, in handling the matter for the Bishops, divided the substance of the information into two parts, whereof the same consisted; the first was that they had maliciously, seditiously, and slanderously made, contrived, and published, a false and seditious libel against the King, which tended to diminish his regal authority and prerogative: the second part of the plea for the Bishops was as to the special matter of their petition, which showed there was no malice or sedition in it.

As to the first point, much time was spent in proving the hands of the Bishops: that of the Archbishop was proved and well known by several, but that of the other Bishops was not otherwise made out than by the belief and supposition of the witnesses, though their own servants were subpœnaed against their masters, so that the Court was of opinion there was not sufficient proof of their handwriting.

As to the Archbishop, it was objected that he could not be within the indictment, for that it was laid in Middlesex, and his Grace had not been out of Surrey in seven or eight months. To this it was answered, that his signing and writing of the petition, and sending of it over to be delivered in Middlesex, was a sufficient publishing of it there. But the Court was divided on this point.

Then the King's counsel alleged that the Bishops had owned their handwriting in the council, and had also confessed the delivery of the petition. It was replied, on the Bishops' side, that they had owned their hands, but after that the Lord Chancellor had required them to do it; and that they had done it, trusting to his Majesty's goodness that no advantage would be made of their confession against themselves. But they denied they had owned the delivery of the petition, much less that they had published it; and there being no other evidence of it than that they had been with the Lord Sunderland, and had offered his lordship a sight of a petition, which he had refused, nor did he see them deliver it to the King, the Court said it was only a presumption, and no proof.

As to the matter of the petition, whether a libel upon the Government or no, the Attorney and Solicitor-General maintained it was, for that it boldly meddled with the acts of the Government, declaring his Majesty's toleration to be illegal, and thereby tending to diminish the King's authority and prerogative royal.

To this the Bishops' counsel replied that they had done but what was the right of every subject, to petition the King, and that in matter of conscience, and upon the account of religion, which they were by their oaths and by the laws of the land to take care of; and quoted several laws and statutes to that purpose. They urged also, that they did not declare the King's declaration of indulgence to be illegal, but said only that the Parliaments of 62, 72, and 89 had declared so; whereupon the journals of Lords and Commons were read.

The Court was also divided in this point. The Chief Justice and Judge Allibone said that it was a libel, but Judges Powell and Holloway were of a contrary opinion.*

The attorney and solicitor were only for the King, and kept their ground against Pemberton, Sawyer, Finch, Pollexfen, Treby, and Sommers, who were for the Bishops.

This morning, between ten and eleven, the jury brought in their verdict, the Bishops attending in Court, not guilty in part or whole, which causes great joy.

VI.—SCOTCH REBELLION IN 1745.

Horace Walpole to Sir Horace Mann.

ARLINGTON STREET, Sept. 13th, 1745.

The rebellion goes on; but hitherto there is no rising in England, nor landing of troops from abroad; indeed, not even of ours or the Dutch. The best account I can give you is, that if the boy has apparently no enemies in Scotland, at least he has openly very few friends. Nobody of note has joined him but a brother of the Duke of Athol, and another of Lord Dunmore.

* "The counsel for the Bishops, the ablest of their profession in all England, produced such arguments in their behalf that the judges were divided, two of them declaring that the proofs did not extend to the making their petition or address a libel, and two of them that they did, which cost Sir Richard Holloway and Sir John Powell their seats on the bench as soon as the term was over."—*Reresby's Memoirs.*

For cannon they have nothing but one-pounders; their greatest resource is money. They have forced Louis-d'ors. The last accounts left them at Perth, making shoes and stockings. It is certain that a sergeant of Cope's, with twelve men, put to flight two hundred, on killing only six or seven. Two hundred of the Monroe clan have joined our forces. Spirit seems to rise in London, though not in the proportion it ought; and then, the person most concerned does every thing to check its progress; when the Ministers propose any thing with regard to the rebellion, he cries, "Pho! don't talk to me of that stuff." Lord Granville has persuaded him that it is of no consequence. Mr. Pelham talks every day of resigning; he certainly will as soon as this is got over!—if it is got over. So, at least we shall see a restoration of Queen Sophia. She has lain-in of a girl, though she had all the pretty boys in town brought to her for patterns.

The young Chevalier has set a reward on the King's head; we are told that his brother is set out for Ireland. However, there is hitherto little countenance given to the undertaking by France or Spain. It seems an effort of despair and weariness of the manner in which he has been kept in France. On the grenadier's caps is written, "a grave or a throne." He stayed some time at the Duke of Athol's, whither old Marquis Tullybardine sent to bespeak dinner, and has since sent his brother word that he likes the alterations made there. The Pretender found pineapples there, the first he ever tasted. Mr. Breton, a great favorite of the Southern Prince of Wales, went the other day to visit the Duchess of Athol, and happened not to know that she is parted from her husband; he asked how the Duke did? "Oh," said she, "he turned me out of his house, and now he is turned out himself." Every now and then a Scotchman comes and pulls the boy by the sleeve: "Prince, here is another mon taken!" Then, with all the dignity in the world, the boy hopes nobody was killed in the action! Lord Bath has made a piece of a ballad, the Duke of Newcastle's speech to the Regency; I have heard but these two lines of it:

"Pray consider, my Lord, how disastrous a thing,
To have two Princes of Wales and never a King!"

The merchants are very zealous, and are opening a great subscription for raising troops. The other day, at the city meeting to draw up the address, Alderman Heathcote proposed a petition for a redress of grievances, but not one man seconded him. In the midst of all this, no Parliament is called? The Ministers say they have nothing ready to offer; but they have nothing to notify!

I must tell you a ridiculous incident: when the magistrates of Edinburgh were searching houses for arms, they came to Mr. Maule's, brother of Lord Panmure, and a great friend of the Duke of Argyle. The maid would not let them go into one room, which was locked, and, as she said, full of arms. They now thought they had found what they looked for, and had the door broke open—where they found an ample collection of coats of arms!

The Deputy Governor of Edinburgh Castle has threatened the magistrates to beat their town about their ears if they admit the rebels. Perth is twenty-four miles from Edinburgh, so we must soon know whether they will go thither, or leave it and come into England. We have great hopes that the Highlanders will not follow him so far. Very few of them could be persuaded, the last time, to go to Preston, and several refused to attend King Charles II. when he marched to Worcester.

The Caledonian "Mercury" never calls them "the rebels," but "the Highlanders."

Adieu, my dear child. Thank Mr. Chute for his letter, which I will answer soon. I don't know how to define my feelings: I don't despair, and yet I expect nothing but bad.

Yours, etc.

P. S. Is not my Princess very happy with the hopes of the restoration of her old tenant?

VII.—TRIAL OF THE REBEL LORDS.

Horace Walpole to Sir Horace Mann.

ARLINGTON STREET, August 1st, 1746.

I am this moment come from the conclusion of the greatest and most melancholy scene I ever yet saw. You will easily guess it was the trials of the rebel lords. As it was the most interesting sight, it was the most solemn and fine; a coronation is a puppet-show, and all the splendor of it idle; but this sight at once feasted one's eyes and engaged all one's passions. It began last Monday. Three parts of Westminster Hall were enclosed with galleries, and hung with scarlet; and the whole ceremony was conducted with the most awful solemnity and decency, except in the one point of leaving the prisoners at the bar amidst the idle curiosity of some crowd, and even with the witnesses who had sworn against them, while the Lords adjourned to their own House to consult. No part of the royal family was there, which was a proper regard to the unhappy men, who were become their victims. One hundred and thirty-nine Lords were present, and made a noble sight on their benches frequent and full! The Chancellor was Lord High Steward; but though a most comely personage with a fine voice, his behavior was mean, curiously searching for occasion to bow to the minister that is no peer, and consequently applying to the other ministers in a manner for their orders; and not even ready at the ceremonial. To the prisoners he was peevish; and instead of keeping up to the humane dignity of the law of England, whose character it is to point out favor to the criminal, he crossed them, and almost scolded at any offer they made toward defence. I had armed myself with all the resolution I could with the thought of their crimes and of the danger past, and was assisted by the sight of the Marquis of Lothian in weepers for his son who fell at Culloden. But the first appearance of the prisoners shocked me; their behavior melted me; Lord Kilmarnock and Lord Cromartie are both past forty, but look younger. Lord Kilmarnock is tall and slender, with an extreme fine person; his behavior a most just mixture between dignity and submission; if in any thing to be reprehended, a little affected, and his hair too exactly dressed for a man in his situation. But when I say this, it is not to find fault with him, but to show how little fault there was to be found. Lord Cromartie is an indifferent figure, appeared much dejected, and rather sullen; he dropped a few tears the first day, and swooned as soon as he got back to his cell. For Lord Balmerino, he is the most natural brave old fellow I ever saw; the highest intrepidity, even to indifference. At the bar, he behaved like a soldier and a man; in the intervals of form, with carelessness and humor. He pressed extremely to have his wife, his pretty Peggy, with him in the Tower. Lady Cromartie only sees her husband through the grate—not choosing to be shut up with him, as she thinks she can serve him better by her intercession without; she is big with child, and very handsome, so are their daughters. When they were to be brought from the Tower in separate coaches, there was some dispute in which the axe must go; old Balmerino cried, "Come, come, put it with me!" At the bar he plays with his fingers upon the axe, while he talks to the gentleman gaoler; and one day, somebody coming up to listen, he took the blade and held it, like a fan, between their faces. During the trial a little boy was near him, but not tall enough to see; he made room for the child, and placed him near himself.

When the trial began, the two Earls pleaded guilty: Balmerino not guilty, saying he could prove his not being at the taking of the castle of Carlisle, as was laid in the indictment. Then the King's counsel opened, and Sergeant Skinner pronounced the most absurd speech imaginable; and mentioned the Duke of Perth, "who," said he, "I see, by the papers, is dead." Then some witnesses were examined, whom, afterwards, the old hero shook cordially by the hand. The Lords withdrew to their House, and returning, demanded of the judges whether, one point not being proved, though all the rest were, the indictment was false? To which they unanimously answered in the negative. Then the Lord High Steward asked the Peers severally whether Lord Balmerino was guilty! All said, "Guilty upon honor," and then adjourned, the prisoner having begged pardon for giving them so much trouble. While the Lords were withdrawn, the Solicitor General Murray (brother of the Pretender's Minister) officiously and insolently went up to Lord Balmerino and asked him how he could give the Lords so much trouble, when his solicitor had informed him that his plea could be of no use to him? Balmerino asked the bystanders who this person was; and being told, he said, "Oh, Mr. Murray! I am extremely glad to see you; I have been with several of your relations; the good lady, your mother, was of great use to us at Perth." Are not you charmed with this speech? How just it was! As he went away, he said, "They call me Jacobite; I am no more a Jacobite than any that tried me; but if the Great Mogul had set up his standard, I should have followed it, for I could not starve." The worst of his case is that, after the battle of Dumblain, having a company in the Duke of Argyle's regiment, he deserted with it to the rebels, and has since been pardoned. Lord Kilmarnock is a Presbyterian with four earldoms in him, but so poor, since Lord Wilmington's stopping a pension that my father had given him, that he often wanted a dinner. Lord Cromartie was receiver of the rents of the King's second son in Scotland, which, it was understood, he should not account for, and by that means had six hundred a year from the government; Lord Elibank, a very prating, impertinent Jacobite, was bound for him in nine hundred pounds, for which the Duke is determined to sue him.

When the Peers were going to vote Lord Foley withdrew, as too well a wisher; Lord Moray, as nephew of Lord Balmerino—and Lord Stair—as I believe, uncle to his great-grandfather. Lord Windsor very affectionately said: "I am sorry I must say, Guilty upon my honor." Lord Stamford would not answer to the name of Henry, having been christened Harry. What a great way of thinking on such an occasion! I was diverted, too, with old Norsa, the father of my brother's concubine, an old Jew that kept a tavern; my brother as auditor of the exchequer has a gallery along one whole side of the court.

I said, "I really feel for the prisoners!" Old Issachar replied, "Feel for them! pray, if they had succeeded, what would have become of all us?" When my Lady Townshend heard her husband vote, she said, "I always thought my Lord was guilty, but I never thought he would own it upon his honor." Lord Balmerino said, that one of his reasons for pleading not guilty was, that so many ladies might not be disappointed of their show.

On Wednesday they were again brought to Westminster Hall, to receive sentence; and being asked what they had to say, Lord Kilmarnock, with a very fine voice, read a very fine speech, confessing the extent of his crime, but offering his principles as some alleviation, having his eldest son (his second unluckily was with him) in the Duke's army, fighting for the liberties of his country at Culloden, where his unhappy father was in arms to destroy them. He insisted much on his tenderness to the English prisoners; which some deny, and say that he was the man who proposed their being put to death, when General Stapleton urged that he was come to fight, and not to butcher; and that if they acted any such barbarity, he would leave him with all his men. He very artfully mentioned Van Hoey's letter, and said how much he should scorn to owe his life to such intercession. Lord Cromartie spoke much shorter, and so low that he was not heard but by those who sat very near him; but they prefer this speech to the other. He mentioned his misfortune in having drawn in his eldest son, who is prisoner with him; and concluded with saying, "If no part of this bitter cup must pass from me, not mine, O Lord, but thy will be done!" If he had pleaded not guilty, there was ready to be produced against him a paper signed with his own hand, for putting the English prisoners to death. Lord Leicester went up to the

Duke of Newcastle, and said, "I never heard so great an orator as Lord Kilmarnock; if I was your grace, I would pardon him, and make him paymaster." That morning a paper had been sent to the lieutenant of the Tower for the prisoners; he gave it to Lord Cornwallis, the governor, who carried it to the House of Lords. It was a plea for the prisoners, objecting that the late act for regulating the trial of rebels did not take place till after their crime was committed. The Lords very tenderly and rightly sent this plea to them, of which, as you have seen, the two Earls did not make use; but old Balmerino did, and demanded council on it. The High Steward, almost in a passion, told him that when he had been offered council, he did not accept it. Do but think on the ridicule of sending them the plea, and then denying them council on it! The Duke of Newcastle, who never lets slip an opportunity of being absurd, took it up as a ministerial point, in defence of his creature the Chancellor; but Lord Granville moved, according to order, to adjourn, to debate in the Chamber of Parliament, where the Duke of Bedford and many others spoke warmly for their having council; and it was granted. I said their, because the plea would have saved them all, and affected nine rebels who had been hanged that very morning; particularly one Morgan, a poetical lawyer. Lord Balmerino asked for Forester and Wilbraham; the latter a very able lawyer in the House of Commons, who the Chancellor said privately he was sure would as soon be hanged as plead such a cause. But he came as council to-day (the third day), when Lord Balmerino gave up his plea as invalid, and submitted without any speech. The High Steward then made his, very long and very poor, with only one or two good passages, and then pronounced sentence!

Great intercession is made for the two Earls: Duke Hamilton, who has never been to court, designs to kiss the King's hand, and ask Lord Kilmarnock's life. The King is much inclined to some mercy; but the Duke, who has not so much of Cæsar after a victory, as in gaining it, is for the utmost severity. It was lately proposed in the city to present him with the freedom of some company, one of the aldermen said aloud, "Then let it be of the Butchers!" The Scotch and his Royal Highness are not at all guarded in their expressions of each other. When he went to Edinburgh, in his pursuit of the rebels, they would not admit his guards, alleging that it was contrary to their privileges; but they rode in sword in hand, and the Duke, very justly incensed, refused to see any of the magistrates. He came with the utmost expedition to town, in order for Flanders; but found that the Court of Vienna had already sent Prince Charles thither, without the least notification, at which both King and Duke are greatly offended. When the latter waited on his brother, the Prince carried him into a room that hangs over the wall of St. James's Park, and stood there with his arm about his neck, to charm the gazing mob.

Murray, the Pretender's secretary, has made ample confessions. The Earl of Traquair, and Mr. Barry, a physician, are apprehended, and more warrants are out. So much for rebels! Your friend Lord Sandwich is instantly going ambassador to Holland, to pray the Dutch to build more ships. I have received yours of July 19th, but you see have no more room left, only to say that I conceive a good idea of my eagle, though the seal is a bad one. Adieu!

P. S. I have not room to say any thing to the Tesi till next post; but, unless she will sing gratis, would advise her to drop this thought.

VIII.—EXECUTION OF THE SCOTCH LORDS.

Horace Walpole to Sir Horace Mann.

WINDSOR, Aug. 21st, 1746.

You will perceive by my date that I am got into a new scene, and that I am retired hither like an old summer-dowager, only that I have no toad-eater to take the air with me in the back part of my lozenge coach, and to be scolded. I have taken a small house here within the castle, and propose spending the greatest part of every week here till the Parliament meets; but my jaunts to town will prevent my news from being quite provincial and marvellous. Then I promise you I will go to no races nor assemblies, nor make comments upon couples that come in chaises to the White Hart.

I came from town (for take notice, I put this place upon myself for the country) the day after the execution of the rebel lords; I was not at it, but had two persons come to me directly who were at the next house to the scaffold; and I saw another who was upon it, so that you may depend upon my accounts.

Just before they came out of the Tower, Lord Balmerino drank a bumper to King James's health. As the clock struck ten they came forth on foot, Lord Kilmarnock all in black, his hair unpowdered in a bag, supported by Forster, the great Presbyterian, and by Mr. Home, a young clergyman, his friend. Lord Balmerino followed, alone, in a blue coat turned up with red, his rebellious regimentals, a flannel waistcoat, and his shroud beneath; their hearses following. They were conducted to a house near the scaffold; the room forwards had benches for spectators; in the second Lord Kilmarnock was put, and in the third backwards Lord Balmerino; all three chambers hung with black. Here they parted! Balmerino embraced the other and said, "My Lord, I wish I could suffer for both!" He had scarce left him before he desired again to see him, and then asked him, "My Lord Kilmarnock do you know any thing of the resolution taken in our army, the day before the battle of Culloden, to put the English prisoners to death?" He replied, "My Lord, I was not present; but since I came hither I have had all the reason in the world to believe that there was such order taken; and I hear the Duke has the pocket-book with the order." Balmerino answered, "It was a lie raised to excuse their barbarity to us." Take notice that the Duke's charging this on Lord Kilmarnock (certainly on misinformation) decided this unhappy man's fate! The most now pretended is, that it would have come to Lord Kilmarnock's turn to have given the word for the slaughter, as lieutenant-general, with the patent for which he was immediately drawn into the rebellion after having been staggered by his wife, her mother, his own poverty, and the defeat of Cope. He remained an hour and a half in the house, and shed tears. At last he came to the scaffold, certainly much terrified, but with a resolution that prevented his behaving in the least meanly or unlike a gentleman. He took no notice of the crowd, only to desire that the baize might be lifted up from the rails, that the mob might see the spectacle. He stood and prayed some time with Forster, who wept over him, exhorted and encouraged him. He delivered a long speech to the sheriff, and with a noble manliness stuck to the recantation he had made at his trial, declaring he wished that all who embarked in the same cause might meet the same fate. He then took off his bag, coat, and waistcoat with great composure, and, after some trouble, put on a napkin cap, and then several times tried the block, the executioner, who was in white, with a white apron, out of tenderness concealing the axe behind himself. At last the Earl knelt down, with a visible unwillingness to depart, and after five minutes, dropped his handkerchief, the signal, and his head was cut off at once, only hanging by a bit of skin, and was received in a scarlet cloth by four of the undertaker's men kneeling, who wrapped it up and put it into the coffin with the body; orders having been given not to expose the heads, as used to be the custom.

The scaffold was immediately new-strewed with sawdust, the block new-covered, the executioner new-dressed, and a new axe brought. Then came old Balmerino, treading with the air of a general. As soon as he mounted the scaffold he read the inscription on his coffin, as he did again afterwards; he then surveyed the spectators, who were in amazing numbers, even upon masts of ships in the river; and pulling out his spectacles, read a treasonable speech, which he delivered to the sheriff, and said the young Pretender was so sweet a prince, that flesh and blood could not resist following him; and lying down to try the block, he said, "If I had a thousand lives I would lay them all down here in the same cause." He said if he had not taken the sacrament the day before, he would have knocked down Williamson, the lieutenant of the Tower, for his ill-usage of him. He took the axe and felt it, and asked the headsman how many blows he had given Lord Kilmarnock, and gave him three guineas. Two clergymen, who attended him, coming up, he said, "No, gentlemen, I believe you have already done me all the service you can." Then he went to the corner of the scaffold and called very loud to the warder to give him his periwig, which he took off and put on a night-cap of Scotch plaid, and then pulled off his coat and waistcoat and lay down; but being told he was on the wrong side, vaulted round, and immediately gave the sign by tossing up his arm, as if he were giving the signal for battle. He received three blows, but the first certainly took away all sensation. He was not a quarter of an hour on the scaffold; Lord Kilmarnock above half a one. Balmerino certainly died with the intrepidity of a hero, but with the insensibility of one too. As he walked from his prison to execution, seeing every window and top of the houses filled with spectators, he cried out, "Look, look, how they are all piled up like rotten oranges!"

My Lady Townshend, who fell in love with Lord Kilmarnock at his trial, will go nowhere to dinner, for fear of meeting with a rebel pie; she says everybody is so bloody-minded that they eat rebels! The Prince of Wales, whose intercession saved Lord Cromartie, says he did it in return for old Sir W. Gordon, Lady Cromartie's father, coming down out of his death-bed to vote against my father in the Chippenham election. If his Royal Highness had not countenanced inveteracy like that of Sir W. Gordon, he would have no occasion to exert his gratitude now in favor of rebels. His brother has plucked a very useful feather out of the cap of the ministry, by forbidding any application for posts in the army to be made to anybody but himself; a resolution, I dare say, he will keep as strictly and minutely as he does the discipline and dress of the army. Adieu!

P. S. I have just received yours of August 9th. You had

not then heard of the second great battle of Placentia, which has already occasioned new instructions, or, in effect, a recall being sent after Lord Sandwich.

IX.—BATTLE OF FONTENOY.

Hon. Philip Yorke to Horace Walpole.

LONDON, May 16th, 1745.

DEAR SIR: I should not have thought of replying upon you so soon had you not invited me to it, by saying you expected from me a further account of the action; and had I done it sooner, it would not have been easy to have added any thing material or explicit to the first advices, which resemble always the confusion of the battle itself. One must stay till the smoke is a little cleared away before one can take a distinct view of any object. I think you very right in your judgment, that the French were only *not beat.* Our repulse was owing, not to their bravery, but their advantageous situation and the number of their batteries, from which they had an hundred pieces of cannon or upwards playing upon us without intermission. Nay, even under these difficult circumstances, the opinion of the most intelligent is, that had Ingoldsby done his duty, and the Dutch infantry behaved as gallantly as ours, there was the greatest probability of our carrying the day. I wonder the former was not superseded on the spot, and that Lastrow, who was sent to him with orders, did not take the command of his brigade and march directly to the fort, which the enemy were beginning to desert. We might then have turned their infernal engines of death upon the artificers themselves. The Duke's behavior was by all accounts the most heroic and gallant imaginable. He was the whole day in the thickest of the fire. When he saw the ranks breaking he rode up and encouraged the soldiers in the most moving and expressive terms; called them countrymen; that it was his highest glory to be at their head; that he scorned to expose them to more danger than he would himself; put them in mind of Blenheim and Ramillies; in short, I am convinced his presence and intrepidity greatly contributed to our coming off so well. Nor must I omit doing justice to Ligonier, who, the Duke writes, fought like a grenadier, and commanded like a general. His Royal Highness seems determined to keep up strict discipline, and drew out a pistol upon an officer whom he saw running away. Konigseck was run over and bruised by the Dutch cavalry in their flight, insomuch that when the army marched to Lessines, he was left at Ath. I have not heard as yet, that the French plume themselves much upon their victory. Their accounts run in a modester strain than usual. It was certainly a dear-bought advantage. You see by the "Gazette" they have a great number of general officers killed and wounded; their loss of private men is said to be from five thousand to ten thousand. Ligonier writes that they confess it to be the latter, but whether he means the reports of deserters, or intelligence from the French camp, I cannot tell. We may thank Count Saxe for our ill-fortune. It was he advised them to erect so many batteries and to throw up entrenchments along part of their line, against the opinion of the rest of the council of war, who were for giving us battle *en rase campagne*. Perhaps you may not have heard that the French, who are generally reckoned a polite enemy, used the prisoners whom they took at Bruffoel with great brutality, stripping the wounded, driving away the surgeons, and taking from them their instruments and medical apparatus. Sir James Campbell died in their hands the next day. Doctor Wintringham was sent to visit him by the Duke, and found him lying in a cottage, within the enemy's quarters, who had not been humane enough to give him any assistance. This has occasioned a pretty warm expostulation between the Duke and Marshal Saxe, who denies knowing or authorizing the behavior of their irregular troops at Bruffoel; but, by way of recrimination, accuses us of having first violated the cartel by detaining Belleisle.

The orders which the States have despatched for their corps de reserve to join the army, and for trying the delinquents, alleviate the clamor which would otherwise be raised against them on account of the bad behavior of several regiments, both horse and foot, in their service. One Appias, Colonel commandant of the regiment of Hesse Homburg, rode off upon the spur to Ath, with the greatest part of his men, in the very beginning of the action, and, with an impudent folly equal to his cowardice, wrote from thence to his masters, that the allied army had engaged the French, and been totally cut to pieces, except that part which he had prudently brought off safe. I hope, after the loss of so much gallant blood, exemplary justice will be done upon the guilty.

Lord Chesterfield returned last Saturday from Holland, and looks much better in his health than when he left us; eating, negotiating, and the fat air of the country agree with him. He has concluded a treaty regulating the contingents of force and expense for this campaign. I wish it could have been for the whole war. The States agree to bring 52,000 men into the field (including their corps on the Lower Rhine) to our 40,000.

In sieges they are to furnish one-third, and we the rest. The expense of the land carriage of artillery is to be borne by the government in Flanders. I take it for granted they could be brought to no more, though it is a most unaccountable thing that we should be at so much trouble to persuade them into what is absolutely requisite, for their own security and independence. Have you seen my Lord's speech at taking leave? It is quite calculated for the language it is writ in, and makes but an indifferent figure in English. The thoughts are common, and yet he strains hard to give them an air of novelty, and the quaintness of the expression is quite *à la Francaise.* You may observe it is intended to steer wide of the alert, and military, and invective turn which reigns through Lord Stair's harangue, and so far was prudent.

Besides the three regiments of Mordaunt, Rice, and Handasyde, there is a draft of 540 men, fifteen per company, made out of the Guards, which embarked on Sunday for Flanders. With these reënforcements, and what the Dutch are sending, we hope to look the enemy once more in the face; and if Tournay does but hold out, some attempt will be made, either by diversion or attack, to raise the siege.

Martin is returned as usual, *re infecta.* People imagined he was gone to the Leeward Islands in search of Caylus, who threatens to invade Nevis and St. Kitts, where I doubt we are weak. There is an expectation that the Elector of Cologne will join his troops to D'Aremberg. If he does, and Bathiany's come down to the Rhine, we trust Monsieur le Prince must leave the coast clear, and that Smessart's corps at least may be detached for Flanders. You see, sir, we follow the Roman *ne cede malis sed contra audentior ito*, and really people are less dispirited with this than I expected, and full of encomiums on the gallant spirit which has shown itself in our officers and private men. And now, sir, I must heartily beg your pardon for this long letter—I should rather call it despatch. This I promise you, not to trouble you with one so long in haste, for I am naturally a lazy correspondent; but when the scribbling fit is upon me, it is as difficult to leave off, as it was uneasy to begin. One question let me put to you, and then I have done. Why are you quite immersed in *re rustica?* Put your papers in order, write some memoirs for the instruction of your friends, or if you will, posterity, of your own negotiations and Lord Oxford's ministry. Methinks I should be loath to go down to future times, either portrayed with all the features of deformity which Lord Bolingbroke's pen can give, or what is as bad, daubed over with the sign-post coloring of the Gazetteers. But I run on insensibly, and you will excuse my freedom as the strongest proof that I can give you of the regard wherewith I am, etc.,

P. YORKE.

X.—WILKES, AND THE MIDDLESEX ELECTIONS.*

William Strahan to David Hume.

LONDON, April 1st, 1768.

Mr. Wilkes (the hero of our tale) made his appearance here some weeks ago, gave notice of his intention to surrender himself at the bar of the King's Bench next term, and walked

* The memorable transactions growing out of the imprisonment of Wilkes, and which made him a popular hero, terminated in securing to the British subject a most valuable muniment of liberty. Lord Halifax, one of the Secretaries of State, issued a roving commission, directing his messengers to search for the authors, printers, and publishers of No. 45 of the "North Briton;" to apprehend and seize them, together with their papers, and to bring them in

the streets as publicly as he could well do, to evade the attempts of his private creditors to secure him.

When *the election for the city* drew near, he, an outlaw and a beggar, without a shilling in his pocket, offered himself as a candidate; and, contrary to all expectation, a spirit was quickly infused into the lowest class of people, which must have ensured him success, had the livery of London been composed in any great measure of such. The appearance for him at Guildhall on the day of election was considerable, not of livery-men, however, but of real mob. I was there upon the hustings and very near the candidates, so that I distinctly heard every word that was spoken.

Wilkes' address (which you must have read in the papers) was delivered with more coolness and presence of mind than could have been expected, from one who was acting so bold a part. Harley, the Lord Mayor, spoke last and best. He said he did not stand up to make apologies for his conduct in Parliament, because he was not conscious it needed any; that no man

safe custody before him. Under this warrant no less than forty-nine persons were arrested on suspicion in three days; many as innocent as Lord Halifax himself. The messengers at length discovered that Wilkes was the culprit of whom they were in search, and received verbal directions to arrest him under the general warrant. Wilkes refused to obey, declaring it "a ridiculous warrant against the whole English nation." The messengers, after removing him, ransacked his drawers, and carried off all his private papers. He was committed as a close prisoner to the Tower, from which, by reason of his privilege as a member of the House of Commons, he was shortly released on habeas corpus. Actions were brought against the messengers and the Secretaries of State, and notwithstanding obstinate and vexatious resistance by the Government, heavy damages were recovered. The illegality of general warrants was affirmed in the strongest terms from the Bench, and afterwards in declaratory resolutions by the House of Commons. For fuller history of this case, the reader is referred to the recent and valuable "Constitutional History of England," by J. E. May.—H.

was a firmer friend to liberty, or would go farther in its defence than himself, but he was for liberty bounded by law, the only basis of true liberty; that in the high office he had now the honor to hold, it behoved him above all things to attend to the preservation of the public peace of the city; he therefore begged that, in their choice of representatives, they would put him entirely out of the question, and fix upon those whom they thought best able to discharge so important a trust. Upon holding up of hands the choice fell upon Mr. Wilkes to be one; but one-fourth of those in the hall were not of the livery. From that moment his consequence began, though the poll ended against him; and yet greatly beyond what was expected. During its continuance he appeared every day on the hustings, though he was more than once arrested there, at the instance of his private creditors. But he found bail for his appearance, braved it out to the last, and was attended by a considerable mob every day.

When he found the poll going against him, he publicly gave out he would stand for Middlesex. There he was likely to stand a better chance. An incredible number of petty freeholders of that county, from Wapping and its environs, immediately declared for him; and, on the day of election, he carried it with ease, and with very little disturbance at Brentford, though the whole road thither was lined with mob, who insulted every one who would not join in the cry of *Wilkes and liberty*. This success immediately reached London, and occasioned such an intoxication in the mob—men, women, and children—that they spread themselves from Hyde Park Corner to Wapping, and broke everybody's windows who refused to illuminate their houses; among the rest, those of the mansion-house of the Lord Mayor, who happened that night to sleep in the country, were quite demolished; and though a party of soldiers were at length sent for by the Mayoress, from the Tower, they, when they came (so general was the infatuation), seemed more disposed to assist the mob than to disperse them.

You will not easily believe it, but it is true, that the Dukes of Grafton and Northumberland, and many others of the first nobility, nay, some of the royal family itself (viz., the Princess Amelia, and the Dukes of Gloucester and Cumberland), were mean enough to submit to illuminate their windows upon this infamous occasion, in obedience to the orders of a paltry mob, which a dozen of their footmen might easily have dispersed. If you ask me why was not Wilkes secured on his arrival, and before he had acquired his present consequence? the answer is plain; the ministry were part of them timid, and part of them secretly his friends. The outlawry, says the present Attorney-General, cannot be defended because of some informalities in the passing of it, and his predecessor who did pass it, is in opposition. The Duke of Grafton, though then in town, is now at Newmarket; the Chancellor at Bath; the rest electioneering in different parts of the country, or skulking in town; but not one of them disposed to prevent the insult to their master, or to issue orders for a party of the Guards (and a small one would have been sufficient) to clear the streets.

The next night the same illuminations were again insisted on, and the same insolence, with the same impunity, was repeated. Strange, in truth, must it appear to friends and to enemies at home and abroad, that a criminal, an outlaw, a man in every sense a wretch, should be chosen by men who call themselves loyal, to represent the very county honored with the royal residence; and this attended, too, with many marks of insolence, brutality, and disaffection. But after all, I do not think there is much to be apprehended from all this; there is actually no real disaffection existing here. We want nothing earthly to keep every thing in order but a firm and spirited ministry. This we are certainly not blessed with, and what the continuance of this want may at length lead to, is indeed justly to be dreaded.

I will now offer some probable conjectures on what is likely to follow upon all this. On the 20th of this month, the first day of term, Wilkes is to surrender himself, and will certainly be attended by a considerable mob. Lord Mansfield, I am assured, will act with becoming spirit, and will be properly supported by the military; of course Wilkes will be committed to the Tower, for he has no privilege; and I really think if this matter is rightly conducted, and the ministry mean that the law should take its course, his sentence may easily be carried into execution. On the 10th of May, the meeting of the Parliament, the farce will be resumed, and will probably have great effects: perhaps no less than the total overthrow of the present ministry and the banishment of Lord Bute from this part of the kingdom. The case of this nobleman is really singular; divested of power, he retains all the odium of Prime Minister. Having long since most injudiciously pushed into office, and as injudiciously retired from the political theatre, he hath ever since exercised the power of recommending or rather nominating every succeeding ministry. These have, by turns, spurned at and renounced their maker; and, what is truly remarkable, though he has had no influence in their councils, though he has all along never dared to interpose, even so far as to occasionally serve an humble retainer or dependent, yet, being well known to have named the *men*, he has made himself, in the public opinion, ultimately responsible for their *measures;* and will ere long, if I am not mistaken, be made the scapegoat of all their misconduct; so that in the end his master's favor, of which he appears to have little known how to avail himself, will cost him dear.

XI.—DEATH OF LORD CHATHAM.

Lord Camden to the Duke of Grafton.

April, 1778, N. B. Street.

MY DEAR LORD: I cannot help considering the little illness which prevented your grace from attending the House of Lords last Tuesday, to have been a piece of good fortune, as it kept you back from a scene that would have overwhelmed you with grief and melancholy, as it did me and many others that were present. I mean Lord Chatham's fit, that seized him as he was attempting to rise and reply to the Duke of Richmond. He fell back upon his seat, and was, to all appearance, in the agonies of death. This threw the whole House into confusion; every person was upon his legs in a moment, hurrying from one place to another—some sending for assistance, others producing salts, and others reviving spirits. Many crowding about the Earl to observe his countenance—all affected—most part really concerned; and even those who might have felt a secret pleasure at the accident, yet put on the appearance of distress, except only the Earl of M.,* who sat still, almost as much unmoved as the senseless body itself. Dr. Brocklesby was the first physician that came; but Dr. Addington, in about an hour, was brought to him. He was carried into the Prince's chamber, and laid upon the table, supported by pillows. The first motion of life

* Either the Earl of Marchmont or Earl of Mansfield.

that appeared was an endeavor to vomit; and after he had discharged the load from his stomach that probably brought on the seizure, he revived fast. Mr. Strutt prepared an apartment for him at his house, where he was carried as soon as he could with safety be removed. He slept remarkably well, and was quite recovered yesterday, though he continued in bed. I have not heard how he is to-day, but will keep my letter open till the evening, that your grace may be informed how he goes on. I saw him in the Prince's chamber before he went into the House, and conversed a little with him; but such was the feeble state of his body, and indeed the distempered agitation of his mind, that I did forebode his strength would certainly fail him before he had finished his speech. In truth, he was not in a condition to go abroad, and he was earnestly requested not to make the attempt; but your grace knows how obstinate he is, when he is resolved. He had a similar fit to this, this summer—like it in all respects in the seizure, the retching, and the recovery; and after that fit, as if it had been the crisis of the disorder, he recovered fast, and grew to be in better health than I had known him for many years. Pray heaven that this may be attended with no worse consequences! The Earl spoke, but was not like himself; his speech faltered, his sentences broken, and his mind not master of itself. He made shift with difficulty to declare his opinion, but was not able to enforce it by argument. His words were shreds of unconnected eloquence, and flashes of the same fire which he, Prometheus-like, had stolen from heaven, and were then returning to the place from whence they were taken. Your grace sees even I, who am a mere prose man, am tempted to be poetical while I am discoursing of this extraordinary man's genius. The Duke of Richmond answered him, and I cannot help giving his grace the commendation he deserves for his candor, courtesy, and liberal treatment of his illustrious adversary. The debate was adjourned till yesterday, and then the former subject was taken up by Lord Shelburne in a speech of one hour and three-quarters. The Duke of Richmond answered; Shelburne replied; and the Duke, who enjoys the privilege of the last word in that House, closed the business, no other Lord, except our friend, Lord Ravensworth, speaking one word; the two other noble Lords consumed between three and four hours. And now, my dear Lord, you must, with me, lament this fatal accident. I fear it is *fatal*, and this great man is now lost forever to his country; for, after such a public and notorious exposure of his decline, no man will look up to him, even if he should recover. France will no longer fear him, nor the King of England court him; and the present set of ministers will finish the ruin of the State, because he being in effect superannuated, the public will call for no other men. This is a very melancholy reflection. The opposion, however, is not broken, and this difference of opinion will wear off; so far, at least, the prospect is favorable. I think I shall not sign the protest, though, in other respects, I shall be very friendly. I have troubled your grace with a deal of stuff, but the importance of the subject will excuse me.

Your grace's, etc., CAMDEN.

P. S. I understand the Earl has slept well last night, and is to be removed to-day to Downing street. He would have gone into the country, but Addington thinks he is too weak.*

* The death of Lord Chatham is the subject of a great historical painting by Copley. The moment chosen for the picture is when Lord Chatham, after vain efforts to speak, presses his hand on his heart, and sinking into convul-

XII.—COMMUNICATION BETWEEN THE AMERICAN COLONIES.

Rev. Dr. Jonathan Mayhew to Hon. James Otis, Jr.

LORD'S DAY MORNING, June 8th, 1766.

SIR: To a good man all time is holy enough, and none too holy to do good, or to think upon it.

Cultivating a good understanding and hearty friendship between these colonies and their several Houses of Assembly, appears to me to be so necessary a part of prudence and good policy, all things considered, that no favorable opportunity for that purpose ought to be omitted. I think such an one now presents. Would it not be very proper and decorous for our Assembly to send circular congratulatory letters to all the rest without exception, on the *repeal*, and the present favorable aspect of things? Letters conceived at once in terms of warm friendship and regard to them, of loyalty to the King, of filial affection toward the mother country, and intimating a desire to cement and perpetuate a union among ourselves by all practicable and laudable methods. A good foundation is already laid for this latter, by the late Congress, which, in my poor opinion, was a wise measure, and contributed not a little to our obtaining a redress of grievances, however some may affect to disparage it.

sions, is caught in the arms of those who stand near, whilst his son, William Pitt, then a youth of seventeen, who had been standing without the bar, springs forward to support him. "History," says an able writer, "has no nobler scene to show than that which now occupied the House of Lords. The unswerving patriot, whose long life had been devoted to his country, had striven to the last. The aristocracy of the land stood around, and even the brother of the sovereign thought himself honored in being one of his supporters; party enmities were remembered no more; every other feeling was lost in admiration of the great spirit which seemed to be passing away from among them." After lingering a few days, he died on the 11th of May, 1778, aged seventy.

Pursuing this track, and never losing sight of it, may be of the utmost importance to the colonies on some future occasions, perhaps the only means of perpetuating their liberties; for what may be hereafter, we cannot tell, how favorable soever present appearances may be. It is not safe for the colonies to *sleep*, since they will probably always have some *wakeful* enemies in Britain; and if they should be such children as to do so, I hope there are, at least, some persons too much of men and friends to them to rock the cradle, or sing lullaby to them. You have heard of the *communion of churches*, and I am, very early to-morrow morning, to set out for Rutland, to assist at an ecclesiastical council. Not expecting to return this week, while I was thinking of this in my bed, with the dawn of day, the great use and importance of a *communion of colonies* appeared to me in a very strong light, which determined me immediately to set down these hints in order to transmit them to you. Not knowing but that the House may be prorogued or dissolved before my return, or having an opportunity to speak to you, you will make such a use of them as you think proper, or none at all.

I have had a sight of the answer to the last extraordinary *speech*,* with which I was much pleased. It appears to me solid and judicious, and though spirited, not more so than the case absolutely required, unless we could be content to have an absolute and uncontrollable, instead of a limited and constitutional Governor. I cannot think the man will have one wise and good, much less one truly great man at home, to stand by him, in so open and flagrant an attack upon our charter right and privileges. But the less asperity in language the better, provided there is

* Speech of Governor Bernard.

firmness in adhering to our rights in opposition to all encroachments.

I am, sir, your most obedient, humble servant,

JONATHAN MAYHEW.

XIII.—CORRESPONDENCE BETWEEN LORD HOWE AND DR. FRANKLIN AS TO PEACE.

Lord Howe to Dr. Franklin.

EAGLE, June 20th, 1776.

I cannot, my worthy friend, permit the letters and parcels which I have sent (in the state I received them), to be landed, without adding a word upon the subject of the injurious extremities in which our unhappy disputes have engaged us.

You will learn the nature of my mission from the official despatches which I have recommended to be forwarded by the same conveyance. Retaining all the earnestness I ever expressed to see our differences accommodated, I shall conceive, if I meet with the disposition in the colonies which I was once taught to expect, the most flattering hopes of proving serviceable in the objects of the king's paternal solicitude, by promoting the establishment of lasting peace and union with the colonies. But, if the deep-rooted prejudices of America, and the necessity of preventing her trade from passing into foreign channels, must keep us still a divided people, I shall, from every private as well as public motive, most heartily lament that this is not the moment wherein those great objects of my ambition are to be attained, and that I am to be longer deprived of an opportunity to assure you, personally, of the regard with which I am your sincere and faithful humble servant,

HOWE.

P. S. I was disappointed of the opportunity I expected for sending this letter at the time it was dated, and have ever since been prevented, by calms and contrary winds, from getting here to inform General Howe of the commission with which I have the satisfaction to be charged, and of his being joined in it.

Off of Sandy Hook, 12th of July.

XIV.—IN REPLY.

Dr. Franklin to Lord Howe.

Philadelphia, July 30th, 1776.

My Lord: I received safe the letters your Lordship so kindly forwarded to me, and beg you to accept *my* thanks.

The official despatches to which you refer me contain nothing more than what we had seen in the act of Parliament, viz.: "Offers of pardon upon submission," which I was sorry to find, as it must give your Lordship pain to be sent so far on so hopeless a business.

Directing pardons to be offered to the colonies, who are the very parties injured, expresses, indeed, that opinion of our ignorance, baseness, and insensibility which your uninformed and proud nation has long been pleased to entertain of us; but it can have no other effect than that of increasing our resentments. It is impossible we should think of submission to a government that has, with the most wanton barbarity and cruelty, burned our defenceless towns in the midst of winter, excited the savages to massacre our (peaceful) farmers, and our slaves to murder their masters; and is even now bringing foreign mercenaries to deluge our settlements with blood. These atrocious injuries have extinguished every spark of affection for that parent country we once held so dear; but were it possible for *us* to forget and forgive them, it is not possible for *you* (I mean the British nation) to forgive the people you have so heavily injured; you can never confide again in those as fellow-subjects, and permit them to enjoy equal freedom, to whom you know you have given such just causes of lasting enmity; and this must impel you, were we again under your government, to endeavor the breaking our spirit by the severest tyranny, and obstructing, by every means in your power, our growing strength and prosperity.

But your Lordship mentions "the king's paternal solicitude for promoting the establishment of lasting peace and union with the colonies." If, by *peace*, is here meant a peace to be entered into by distinct States now at war, and his Majesty has given your Lordship powers to treat with us of such a peace, I may venture to say, though without authority, that I think a treaty for that purpose not quite impracticable, before we enter into foreign alliances. But I am persuaded you have no such powers. Your nation though, by punishing those American governors who have fomented the discord, rebuilding our burnt towns, and repairing, as far as possible, the mischiefs done us, she might recover a great share of our regard, and the greatest share of our growing commerce, with all the advantages of that additional strength to be derived from a friendship with us; yet I know too well her abounding pride and deficient wisdom to believe she will ever take such salutary measures. Her fondness for conquest, as a warlike nation, her lust of dominion, as an ambitious one, and her thirst for a gainful monopoly, as a commercial one (none of them legitimate causes of war), will join to hide from her eyes every view of her true interest, and continually goad her on in these ruinous, distant expeditions, so destructive both of lives and of treasure, that they must prove as pernicious to her, in the end, as the Crusades formerly were to most of the nations of Europe.

I have not the vanity, my Lord, to think of intimidating, by thus predicting the effects of this war, for I know it will in England have the fate of all my former predictions—not to be believed till the event shall verify it.

Long did I endeavor, with unfeigned and unwearied zeal, to preserve from breaking that fine and noble porcelain vase—the British empire; for I knew that, being once broken, the separate parts could not retain even their *share* of the strength and value that existed in the whole; and that a perfect *reunion* of those parts could scarce ever be hoped for. Your Lordship may possibly remember the tears of joy that wetted my cheek when, at your good sister's in London, you once gave me expectations that a reconciliation would soon take place. I had the misfortune to find these expectations disappointed, and to be treated as the cause of the mischief I was laboring to prevent. My consolation, under that groundless and malevolent treatment, was, that I retained the friendship of many wise and good men in that country; and, among the rest, some share in the regard of Lord Howe.

The well-founded esteem, and, permit me to say, affection, which I shall always have for your Lordship, make it painful to me to see you engaged in conducting a war, the great ground of which (as described in your letter) is "the necessity of preventing the American *trade* from passing into foreign channels." To me, it seems that neither the obtaining nor retaining any trade, how valuable soever, is an object for which men may justly spill each other's blood; that the true and sure means of extending and securing commerce are the goodness and cheapness of commodities; and that the profits of no trade can ever be equal to the expense of compelling it, and holding it by fleets and armies. I consider this war against us, therefore, as both unjust and unwise; and I am persuaded that cool and dispassionate posterity will condemn to infamy those who advised it; and that even success will not save from some degree of dishonor those who have voluntarily engaged to conduct it.

I know your great motive in coming hither was the hope of being instrumental in a reconciliation; and I believe, when you find that to be impossible on any terms given you to propose, you will then relinquish so odious a command, and return to a more honorable private station.

With the greatest and most sincere respect, I have the honor to be, my Lord, your Lordship's most obedient humble servant,

B. Franklin.

XV.—REBUKING A SUGGESTION FOR ESTABLISHING A MONARCHY, AND PLACING HIM AT ITS HEAD.

General Washington to Col. Lewis Nicola.

Newburg, May 22d, 1782.

Sir: With a mixture of great surprise and astonishment, I have read with attention the sentiments you have submitted to my perusal. Be assured, sir, no occurrence during the course of the war has given me more painful sensations, than your information of there being such ideas existing in the army as you have expressed, and I must view with abhorrence and reprehend with severity. For the present the communication of them will rest in my own bosom, unless some further agitation of the matter shall make a disclosure necessary.

I am much at a loss to conceive what part of my conduct could have given encouragement to an address, which to me seems big with the greatest mischiefs that can befall my country. If I am not deceived in the knowledge of myself, you could not have found a person to whom your schemes are more disagreeable. At the same time, in justice to my own feelings, I must add, that no man possesses a more sincere wish to see ample justice done to the army than I do; and as far as my powers and influence in a constitutional way extend, they shall be employed to the utmost of my abilities to effect it, should there be any occasion. Let me conjure you then, if you have any regard for your country, concern for yourself or your posterity, or respect for me, to banish these thoughts from your mind, and never communicate as from yourself or any one else, a sentiment of the like nature. I am, sir, etc.,

GEO. WASHINGTON.

XVI.—RECEPTION OF FIRST AMERICAN MINISTER BY GEORGE THE THIRD.*

John Adams to Secretary Jay.

BATH HOTEL, WESTMINSTER, June 2d, 1785.

DEAR SIR: During my interview with the Marquis of Carmarthen, he told me that it was customary for every foreign minister, at his first presentation to the King, to make his

* It will be interesting to compare with this narrative of Mr. Adams, contained in the fourth volume of his works, the account given by Mr. Rush, in his Memoranda of his residence at the Court of St. James's, of his own recent reception. "February 12th:—Had my reception. A competant knowledge of the world may serve to guide any one in the com-

Majesty some compliments conformable to the spirit of his letter of credence; and when Sir Clement Cottrell Dormer, the master of the ceremonies, came to inform me that he should accompany me to the Secretary of State at Court, he said that every foreign

mon walks of life, wherever he may be thrown; more especially if he carry with him the cardinal maxim of good breeding everywhere, a wish to please, and an unwillingness to offend. But if, even in private society, there are rules not to be known but by experience, and if these differ in different places, I could not feel wholly insensible to the approach of an occasion so new to me. My first desire was, not to fail in the public duties of my mission; the next, to pass properly through the scenes of official and personal ceremony, to which it exposed me. At the head of them was my introduction to the Sovereign. I desired to do all that full respect required, but not more; yet—the external observances of it—what where they? They defy exact definition beforehand, and I had never seen them. From the restraints too, that prevail in these spheres, lapses, if you fall into them, are little apt to be told to you; which increases your solicitude to avoid them. I had, in some of my intercourse, caught the impression that simplicity was considered best adapted to such an introduction; also, that the Prince Regent was not thought to be fond of set speeches. This was all that I could collect. But simplicity, all know, is a relative idea, and often attainable, in the right sense, only through the highest art, and on full experience.

"I arrived before the hour appointed. My carriage having the entré, or right to the private entrance, I went through St. James's Park, and got to Carlton House by the paved way, through the gardens. Even this approach was already filled with carriages. I was set down at a side door, where stood servants in the Prince's livery. Gaining the hall, persons were seen in various costumes. Among them were yeomen of the Guard with halberds in their hands; they had velvet hats with wreaths round them, and rosettes in their shoes. From the court-yard, which opened through the columns of a fine portico, bands of music were heard. Carriages, as in a stream, were approaching by this access, through the double gates that separated the royal residence from the street. The company arriving by this access entered through the portico, and turned off to the right. I went to the left, through a vestibule leading to other rooms, into which none went but those having the entré. These consisted of cabinet ministers, the diplomatic corps, persons in chief employment about the Court, and a few others, the privilege being in high esteem. Knights of the Garter appeared to have it, for I observed their insignium round the knee of several. There was the Lord Steward with his minister whom he had attended to the Queen had always made a harangue to her Majesty, and he understood, though he had not been present, that they always harangued the King.

On Tuesday evening, the Baron de Lynden called upon me,

badge of office; the Lord Chamberlain, with his gold stick and silver stick. The foreign ambassadors and ministers wore their national costumes; the cabinet ministers, such as we see in old portraits, with bag and sword; the Lord Chancellor and other functionaries of the law, had black silk gloves with full wigs; the bishops and dignitaries of the Church had aprons of black silk. The walls were covered with paintings. If these were historical, so were the rooms. As I looked through them I thought of the scenes described by Doddington; of the Pelhams, the Bolingbrokes, the Hillsboroughs; of the anecdotes and personalities of the English Court and Cabinet in those days. The company stood conversing; here you saw an ambassador and cabinet minister engaged—there a couple of the latter; in the recess of a window a bishop and the Lord Chancellor, and so on. The Prince had not yet left his apartment. Half an hour went by, when Sir Robert Chester, master of ceremonies, said to me that in a few minutes he would conduct me to the Prince. The Spanish ambassador had gone in, and I was next in turn. When he came out, the master of ceremonies advanced with me to the door. Opening it he left me. I entered alone. The Prince was standing, with Lord Castlereagh by him. No one else was in the room. Holding in my hand the letter of credence, I approached, as to a private gentleman, and said, in the common tone of conversation, that it was 'from the President of the United States, appointing me their Envoy Extraordinary and Minister Plenipotentiary at the Court of his Royal Highness; and that I had been directed by the President to say, that I could in no way better serve the United States, or gain his approbation, than by using all my endeavors to strengthen and prolong the good understanding that happily subsisted between the two countries.' The Prince took the letter and handed it to Lord Castlereagh. He then said that he would 'ever be ready, on his part, to act upon the sentiments I had expressed; that I might assure the President of this; for that he sincerely desired to keep up and improve the friendly relations which he regarded as so much to the advantage of both.' I replied I would do so. The purpose of the interview seeming to be accomplished, I had supposed it would here end, and was about withdraw; but the Prince prolonged it. He congratulated me on my arrival. He inquired for the health of Mr. Adams, and spoke of others who had preceded me in the mission; going back as far as the first Mr. Pinckney. Of him, and Mr. King, his inquiries were minute. He made and said he came from the Baron de Nolken, and they had been conversing upon the singular situation I was in, and they agreed in opinion that it was indispensable that I should make a speech, and that that speech should be as complimentary as possible.

others, which it gave me still more pleasure to answer. He asked if I knew the ladies from my country, then in England, who had made such favorable impressions in their society, naming Mrs. Patterson, since Marchioness of Wellesley, and her sisters, the Miss Catons, of Maryland. I replied that I did, and responded to his gratifying notice of these my fair countrywomen. A few more remarks on the climate of the two countries closed the audience. It would be out of place in me to portray the exterior qualities of this monarch. The commanding union of them has often been a theme in his own dominions. He was then in his fifty-sixth year; but in fine health, and maintaining the erect ambitious carriage of early life. I will only say, that he made his audience of foreign ministers a pleasurable duty to them, instead of a repulsive ceremony. The envoy extraordinary and minister plenipotentiary from Sicily and Naples, Count Ludolf, had his reception immediately after mine.

"When the Prince came from his apartments, called, in the language of palaces his closet, into the entré rooms, I presented to him Mr. John Adams Smith, as Public Secretary of the Legation, and Mr. Ogle Tayloe, as attached to it personally. Other special presentations took place; amongst them that of the Prince of Hesse Homberg, by Lord Stewart, both distinguished in the then recent battles of the continent. The Prince Regent moved about these rooms until he had addressed everybody; all waiting his salutation. Doors hitherto shut, now opened, when a new scene appeared. You beheld, in a gorgeous mass, the company that had turned off to the right. The opening of the doors was the signal for the commencement of the general levee. I remained, with others, to see it. All passed, one by one, before the Prince; each receiving a momentary salutation. To a few he addressed conversation, but briefly; as it stopped the line. All were in rich costume. Men of genius and science were there; the nobility were numerous; so were the military. There were from forty to fifty generals; perhaps as many admirals; with throngs of officers of rank inferior. I remarked upon the number of wounded. 'Who is that,' I asked, 'pallid, but with a countenance so animated?' 'That is General Walker,' I was told, 'who was pierced with bayonets whilst leading on the assault at Badajos;' and he, close by, tall but limping? 'Colonel Ponsonby; he was left for dead at Waterloo; the cavalry, it was thought, had trampled upon him.' Then came one of the like port, but deprived of a leg, and as he moved slowly onward, the whisper went 'That's Lord An-

All this was conformable to the advice lately given by the Count de Vergennes to Mr. Jefferson; so that, finding it was a custom established at both these great Courts, and that this Court and the foreign ministers expected it, I thought I could not avoid it, although my first thought and inclination had been to deliver my credentials silently and retire.

At one on Wednesday, the master of ceremonies called at my house and went with me to the Secretary of State's office, in Cleveland Row, where the Marquis of Carmarthen received me, and introduced me to his under secretary, Mr. Fraser, who has been, as his Lordship told me, uninterruptedly in that office, through all the changes of administration, for thirty years, having first been appointed by the Earl of Holderness. After a short conversation upon the subject of importing my effects from Holland and France free of duty, which Mr. Fraser himself introduced, Lord Carmarthen invited me to go with him in his coach to Court. When we arrived in the antechamber, the *œil de beuf* of St. James's, the master of the ceremonies met me and attended me, while the Secretary of State went to take the commands of the King. While I stood in this place, where it seems all ministers stand upon such occasions, always attended by the master of ceremonies, the room very full of ministers of state, lords, and bishops, and all sorts of courtiers, as well as the next room, which is the King's bedchamber, you may well sup-

glesea.' A fourth had been wounded at Seringapatam; a fifth at Talavera; some had suffered in Egypt—some in America. There were those who had received scars on the deck with Nelson; others who carried them from the days of Howe. One, yes, one had fought at Saratoga. It was so that my inquiries were answered. All had 'done their duty;' this was the favorite praise bestowed. They had earned a right to come before their sovereign, and read in his recognition their country's approbation."—H.

pose I was the focus of all eyes. I was relieved, however, from the embarrassment of it by the Swedish and Dutch ministers, who came to me and entertained me in a very agreeable conversation during the whole time. Some other gentlemen, whom I had seen before, came to make their compliments too, until the Marquis of Carmarthen returned and desired me to go with him to his Majesty. I went with his Lordship through the levée-room into the King's closet. The door was shut, and I was left with his Majesty and the Secretary of State alone. I made the three reverences—one at the door, another about half-way, and a third before the presence—according to the usage established at this and all the northern courts of Europe, and then addressed myself to his Majesty in the following words:

"SIR: The United States of America have appointed me their Minister Plenipotentiary to your Majesty, and have directed me to deliver to your Majesty this letter, which contains the evidence of it. It is in obedience to their express commands that I have the honor to assure your Majesty of their unanimous disposition and desire to cultivate the most friendly and liberal intercourse between your Majesty's subjects and their citizens, and of their best wishes for your Majesty's health and happiness, and for that of your royal family. The appointment of a Minister from the United States to your Majesty's court will form an epoch in the history of England and of America. I think myself more fortunate than all my fellow-citizens, in having the distinguished honor to be the first to stand in your Majesty's royal presence in a diplomatic character; and I shall esteem myself the happiest of men if I can be instrumental in recommending my country more and more to your Majesty's royal benevolence, and of restoring an entire esteem, confidence, and affection, or, in better words, the old good nature and the old good humor between people who, though separated by an ocean and under different governments, have the same language, a similar religion, and kindred blood.

"I beg your Majesty's permission to add, that although I have sometimes before been intrusted by my country, it was never in my whole life in a manner so agreeable to myself."

The King listened to every word I said with dignity, but with an apparent emotion. Whether it was the nature of the interview, or whether it was my visible agitation—for I felt more than I did or could express—that touched him, I cannot say. But he was much affected, and answered me with more tremor than I had spoken with, and said:

"Sir: The circumstances of this audience are so extraordinary, the language you have now held is so extremely proper, and the feelings you have discovered so justly adapted to the occasion, that I must say that I not only receive with pleasure the assurance of the friendly dispositions of the United States, but that I am very glad the choice has fallen upon you to be their Minister. I wish you, sir, to believe, and that it may be understood in America, that I have done nothing in the late contest but what I thought myself indispensably bound to do, by the duty which I owed to my people. I will be very frank with you. I was the last to consent to the separation; but the separation having been made, and having become inevitable, I have always said, as I say now, that I would be the first to meet the friendship of the United States as an independent power. The moment I see such sentiments and language as yours prevail, and a disposition to give to this country the preference, that moment I shall say, let the circumstances of language, religion, and blood have their natural and full effect."

I dare not say that these were the King's precise words, and it is even possible that I may have in some particular mistaken his meaning; for, although his pronunciation is as distinct as I ever heard, he hesitated some time between his periods, and between the members of the same period. He was, indeed, much affected, and I confess I was not less so, and therefore I cannot be certain that I was so cool and attentive, heard so clearly and understood so perfectly, as to be confident of all his words or sense; and I think that all which he said to me should at present be kept secret in America, unless his Majesty or his Secretary of State, who alone was present, should judge proper to report it. This I do say, that the foregoing is his Majesty's meaning as I then understood it, and his own words as nearly as I can recollect them.

The King then asked me whether I came last from France, and upon my answering in the affirmative, he put on an air of familiarity, and smiling, or rather laughing, said: "There is an opinion among some people that you are not the most attached of all your countrymen to the manners of France." I was surprised at this, because I thought it an indiscretion, and a departure from the dignity. I was a little embarrassed, but determined not to deny the truth on one hand, nor leave him to infer from it any attachment to England on the other. I threw off as much gravity as I could, and assumed an air of gayety and a tone of decision, as far as was decent, and said: "That opinion, sir, is not mistaken; I must avow to your Majesty I have no attachment but to my own country." The King replied, as quick as lightning, "An honest man will never have any other." The King then said a word or two to the Secretary of State, which, being between them, I did not hear, and then turned round and bowed to me, as is customary with all kings and princes when they give the signal to retire. I retreated, stepping backward, as is the etiquette, and, making my last reverence at the door of the chamber, I went my way. The master of the ceremonies joined me the moment of my coming out of the King's closet, and accompanied me through the apartments down to my carriage, several stages of servants, gentlemen-porters, and under-porters, roaring out like thunder as I went along, "Mr. Adams's servants, Mr. Adams's carriage," etc. I have been thus minute, as it may be useful to others hereafter to know.

The conversation with the King, Congress will form their own judgment of. I may expect from it a residence less painful than I once expected, as so marked an attention from the King will silence many grumblers: but we can infer nothing from all this concerning the success of my mission. There are a train of other ceremonies yet to go through, in presentations to the Queen, and visits to and from ministers and ambassadors, which will take up much time, and interrupt me in my endeavors to obtain all that I have at heart—the objects of my instructions. It is thus the essence of things is lost in ceremony in every country of Europe. We must submit to what we cannot alter; patience is the only remedy.

With great respect, etc.,

JOHN ADAMS.

XVII.—GEN. WASHINGTON'S FIRST ADDRESS TO THE TWO HOUSES OF CONGRESS.*

Fisher Ames to George Richards Minot.

NEW YORK, May 3d, 1789.—Sunday.

DEAR GEORGE: I would very cheerfully comply with the wishes expressed in your last, and pursue my sour commentary upon great folks and public bodies, but haste will not permit. I was present in the pew with the President, and must assure you that, after making all deductions for the delusions of one's fancy in regard to characters, I still think of him with more veneration than for any other person. Time has made havoc upon his face. That, and many other circumstances not to be reasoned about, conspire to keep up the awe I brought with me. He addressed the two Houses in the Senate chamber; it was a touching scene, and quite of the solemn kind. His aspect grave, almost to sadness; his modesty, actually shaking; his voice deep, a little tremulous, and so low as to call for close attention, added to the series of objects presented to the mind, and overwhelming it, produced emotions of the most affecting kind upon the members. I, Pilgarlic, sat entranced. It seemed to me an allegory, in which Virtue was personified, and addressing those whom she would make her votaries. Her power over the heart was never greater, and the illustration of her doctrine by her own example was never more perfect.

* It was the custom, for some time after the organization of the Government, in analogy to English usage, for the President, instead of sending a message to the two Houses of Congress, to meet them in person and deliver an address.—H.

24

XVIII.—APPLICATION FOR RELEASE OF LA FAYETTE.

*General Washington to the Emperor of Germany.**

PHILADELPHIA, May 15th, 1796.

It may readily occur to your Majesty that occasions may sometimes exist on which official considerations may constrain the chief of a nation to be silent and passive, in relation even to objects which affect his sensibility and claim his interposition as a man. Finding myself precisely in this situation at present, I take the liberty of writing this private letter to your Majesty, being persuaded that my motives will also be my apology for it. In common with the people of this country, I retain a strong and cordial sense of the services rendered them by the Marquis

* In connection with this letter an interesting incident may be recalled, which is related by Mr. Rush ("Occasional Productions," p. 99). "One evening Mr. Bradford, the Attorney-General, had called on General Washington. None were present but the family circle, consisting of the General and Mrs. Washington, his Private Secretary, with young Custis and his accomplished sisters. The conversation going on with the wonted ease and dignity of that illustrious circle, the sufferings of La Fayette became, as was frequent, the theme. Washington, as he dwelt upon them in contrast with the former fortunes and splendid merits of La Fayette, and recalling scenes that woke anew the warmth of his friendship for him, became greatly affected. His whole nature seemed melted; his eyes were suffused with tears. If the great Condé, at the representation of one of Corneille's tragedies, wept at the part where Cæsar is made to utter a fine sentiment, what was that in its power to stir the soul, in comparison with the spectacle of Washington shedding tears over the real woes of La Fayette?" It is a warning illustration of the power of prejudice to warp alike the understanding and the heart, that a man so wise and good as Edmund Burke, should have resisted General Fitzpatrick's motion beseeching the King to intercede for the deliverance of this illustrious captive, and have concluded his argument by declaring, that "he would not debauch his humanity by supporting an application like the present in behalf of such a horrid ruffian."

The letter of General Washington was never answered. La Fayette remained in the Castle of Olmutz until his release was peremptorily demanded by Napoleon in the conferences at Leoben, which preceded the treaty of Campo Formio. He was finally set at liberty on the 23d Sept., 1797.—H.

de La Fayette, and my friendship for him has been constant and sincere. It is natural, therefore, that I should sympathize with him and his family in their misfortune, and endeavor to mitigate the calamities they experience, among which his present confinement is not the least distressing.

I forbear to enlarge on this delicate subject. Permit me only to suggest to your Majesty's consideration whether his long imprisonment, and the confiscation of his estate, and the indigence and dispersion of his family, and the painful anxieties incident to all these circumstances, do not form an assemblage of sufferings which recommend him to the mediation of humanity? Allow me, sir, on this occasion to be its organ, and to entreat that he may be permitted to come to this country, on such conditions as your Majesty may think it expedient to prescribe.

As it is a maxim with me not to ask, what under similar circumstances I would not grant, your Majesty will do me the justice to believe, that this request appears to me to correspond with those great principles of magnanimity and wisdom which form the basis of sound policy and durable glory.

May the Almighty and Merciful Sovereign of the Universe keep your Majesty under His protection and guidance.

XIX.—ON THE DAY THAT HIS ELECTION TO THE PRESIDENCY OF THE UNITED STATES WAS OFFICIALLY DECLARED.*

Mrs. John Adams to her Husband.

QUINCY, Feb 8th, 1797.

" The sun is dressed in brightest beams,
To give thy honors to the day."

And may it prove an auspicious prelude to each ensuing season. You have this day to declare yourself the head of a nation.

* The editor of the " Letters of Mrs. Adams," a volume which should be

"And now, O Lord, my God, thou hast made thy servant ruler over the people. Give unto him an understanding heart, that he may know how to go out and to come in before this great people; that he may discern between good and bad. For who is able to judge this thy so great a people?" were the words of a royal sovereign; and not less applicable to him who is invested with the chief magistracy of a nation, though he wear not a crown nor the robes of royalty.

My thoughts and my meditations are with you, though personally absent; and my petitions to Heaven are, that "the things which make for peace, may not be hidden from your eyes." My feelings are not those of pride or ostentation upon the occasion. They are solemnized by a sense of the obligations, the important trusts, and the numerous duties connected with it. That you may be enabled to discharge them with honor to yourself, with justice and impartiality to your country, and with satisfaction to this great people, shall be the daily prayer of your A. A.

XX.—ON THE DAY AFTER HIS INAUGURATION AS PRESIDENT OF THE UNITED STATES.

John Adams to his Wife.

PHILADELPHIA, March 5th, 1797.

MY DEAREST FRIEND: Your dearest friend never had a more trying day than yesterday. A solemn scene it was, in-

read by every American lady, speaks of this letter as the "gem of the collection, for the exalted feeling of the moment shines out with all the lustre of ancient patriotism. Perhaps there is not one among the whole number of her letters which in its spirit brings so strongly to mind as this does the celebrated Roman lady (Portia) whose signature she at one time assumed, whilst it is chastened by a sentiment of Christian humility of which ancient history furnishes no example."—H.

deed; and it was made more affecting to me by the presence of the General (Washington), whose countenance was as serene and unclouded as the day. He seemed to me to enjoy a triumph over me. Methought I heard him say, "Ay! I am fairly out, and you fairly in! See which of us will be happiest." When the ceremony was over, he came and made me a visit, and cordially congratulated me, and wished my administration might be happy, successful, and honorable.

It is now settled that I am to go into his house. It is whispered that he intends to take French leave to-morrow. I shall write you as fast as we proceed. My chariot is finished, and I made my first appearance in it yesterday. It is simple, but elegant enough. My horses are young, but clever.

In the chamber of the House of Representatives was a multitude as great as the space could contain, and I believe scarcely a dry eye but Washington's. The sight of the sun setting full-orbed, and another rising, though less splendid, was a novelty. Chief-Justice Ellsworth administered the oath, and with great energy. Judges Cushing, Wilson, and Iredell were present; many ladies. I had not slept well the night before, and did not sleep well the night after. I was unwell, and did not know whether I should go through or not. I did, however. How the business was received, I know not; only I have been told that Mason, the treaty publisher, said we should lose nothing by the change, for he never heard such a speech in public in his life.

All agree that, taken altogether, it was the sublimest thing ever exhibited in America.

I am, my dearest friend, most affectionately and kindly yours,

JOHN ADAMS.

XXI.—BOMBARDMENT OF COPENHAGEN.

B. George Niebuhr to Madame Hensler.

COPENHAGEN, 3d April, 1801.

The report of our unsuccessful defence will no doubt have reached you before you receive this letter.

On Wednesday afternoon, about five o'clock, the alarm was given on account of the movements of the English fleet.* . . .

When, yesterday morning, about eleven o'clock, the cannonade suddenly commenced with great violence, which was the only thing that could give us notice of what impended, we were excited, but still in good spirits. We had fancied that it would sound much more terrific when so close, and did not therefore believe the attack would be so furious or so general as was really the case. I went to my office to see that the archives were all packed up. On the way, and when there, I heard various reports that two, three, or more English ships had got aground, and that they were firing with such vehemence in order to escape being boarded. Meanwhile, the firing went on with redoubled violence: toward half-past two it quite died away, and only single shots fell from time to time. I went out then to gain intelligence. The streets had become perfectly silent, and only single hollow shots were to be heard. By chance, I overheard an officer telling a citizen of a bomb that had fallen and burst by his side. At the next corner, some people were crowding forward to read a placard from the head of the police, containing directions how to act in case of a bombardment. I now return home considerably startled; I hear the single shots which

* Here follows the account of the manner in which the English fleet advanced, which is sufficiently well known from other histories.

I now know to be throwing bombs. I go out again, go at last to Countess Schimmelman, who had just spoken with some one of the Admiralty, and was full of terror. Soon Count S. comes with the tidings, that our block-ships on the right wing are annihilated. I had never before been so dismayed. I return home and tell Milly only a part of the calamity. I soon went back once more, learnt that the arrival of a cartel-ship from Nelson's fleet was the cause of the sudden, incomprehensible silence of the enemy's guns; and then heard details of the fight, that were touching to the last degree. The whole city was in consternation, and the streets deserted.

4th.—Since we have not sufficient intelligence to be able to give you a connected narrative of the battle, and, besides, our situation will interest you still more than the events of the never-to-be-forgotten day, I meant to write to you yesterday about the former in the first place, and to get more information about the latter against to-day. The regular history of the action you shall have, as soon as I know enough about it myself; to-day I can only write you some unconnected particulars. We cannot deny it—we are quite beaten; our line of defence is destroyed, and all is at stake, as far as we can see, without a chance of our winning any thing—without our being able to do much injury to the enemy, as long as he contents himself with bombarding the city, or especially the docks and the fleet; because we have been deceived in the plan of attack.

But while we look with sorrowful anxiety on our peril, with indignation on the authors of our mistakes, our spirit rises at beholding the unexampled heroism of our people, which gives us a melancholy joy full of affection, that does not indeed comfort us about the State, nor suffice to deceive us as to our true position, yet fills and warms our hearts, binds us closely to our nation, and makes us rejoice to suffer with it. Such a resistance was never seen. Nelson himself has confessed that never, in all the battles in which he has taken part, has he witnessed any thing that could be compared to it. His loss is greater than at Aboukir. It is a battle that can only be compared to Thermopylæ; but Thermopylæ, too, laid Greece open to devastation. . . . .

The appearance of the city [after all was over] was terrible. Every place was desolate; there was nothing to be seen in the streets but wagons loaded with goods to be carried to some place of safety, a silence as of the grave, faces covered with tears, the full expression of the bleeding wound given us by our defeat. The bringing home of the dead and wounded, and the wretched scenes that took place then, I can scarcely allude to. Milly burst into a flood of tears, when she heard of the fate of the crew of the Proevesteen,* which was the first news we received. She was again overpowered by her grief when a false report was spread abroad, that our defences had been deserted: she only feared a too hasty, inglorious truce.

The negotiations have been continued; but I cannot tell you any thing about them, except that nothing had been decided yesterday, though Nelson himself was on shore. The truce will last at least till to-morrow morning. We must at all events be prepared for a bombardment. The worst is, the Crown batteries can be held no longer, and the enemy will scarcely expose his ships-of-the-line, while he can bombard our docks, fleet, and city. Do not be alarmed about us in case of a bombardment.

* Of which only thirty men came ashore out of a crew of between 300 and 400 men.

Our house is in a distant quarter, and it would be impossible really to take the city. . . . . .

XXII.

Same to same.

COPENHAGEN, 6th April, 1801.

. . . . The truce has been prolonged since I wrote till the present time, and may last a few days longer, even though no arrangement should be concluded; which, if it could be brought to pass without exposing us to other dangers, must be earnestly desired, when we reflect calmly on our position after the battle of the 2d. You will not ascribe this wish to any motives of personal fear. Milly is indescribably calm; the reverence for our dead heroes is ever present to elevate our thoughts; the whole nation gives us an example of courage, of unmoved self-possession, than which nothing can be nobler. Danger is the best instructress; you must not, therefore, think of fear. But the risk to which the fleet, docks, marine arsenal, all the most important buildings of the city, that is, of the whole kingdom, would be exposed in case of a bombardment from the side of the scene of combat, is most serious. It is not inevitable, I know: we have hitherto found by experience, that the English bombs are very bad, and when preparations have been made for extinguishing them, the devastation caused even by the best, may be confined within certain limits; at least so we hope. But accident may be against us; and where order and dexterity must be our safeguards, I do not expect so much from our people, as when all depends on Spartan courage. We must not shut our eyes to this; nor to the condition of the remaining half of our defences, which, owing to the short-sightedness of their constructor, are useless, now that the right wing is broken—a defect over which I have many a time, since last summer, fruitlessly meditated. Providence has now brought us a man whose position is sufficiently high to enable him to carry out his projects; and these few days have certainly been employed in repairing the evil as far as possible. But is this enough? and if not, what slaughter must be caused by a new attack, and without our being able to revenge ourselves!

Tuesday. The negotiation is still far from settled, and I can tell you nothing further without abusing confidence.

It is still possible that a fresh attack may be averted; if not, it will be much more dreadful for us in the city than the first. You may be certain that Milly strives to retain her self-possession. It is the sorrow for our people, and the wounds with which the State is threatened, that weigh us down: we fear a violent attack upon the remains of our fleet; not so much a bombardment. O that they would content themselves with that!

I am so depressed that I cannot now give you a full account of the battle. As soon as we are quiet you shall have it.

Adieu, you best beloved of our friends! Shall we soon be able to correspond in peace again? Will not the time come when these hours will be scarred over, and we shall return to our accustomed sphere of occupation, in which alone we can be happy and of use? This time will indeed leave a deep impression on the whole of our lives.

XXIII.

Same to same.

COPENHAGEN, 11th April.

My last letter was written in a state of depression that I would willingly have concealed from you. But that was impossible, and the circumstances of our position only rendered such feelings too unavoidable. We were expecting (which I did not tell you) a bombardment that evening: we only reckoned on a delay from the wind, which was high, and against the enemy. It appeared as if the negotiations would come to nothing. While this, and the general flight in the city toward our quarter and the other less exposed parts, depressed us, and filled us with grief at the fate of our country, even the gloomy turbulence of the elements contributed to our dejection.

My heart is heavy with what I have to tell you, or should have, if we could speak to each other.

The English changed their minds quite unexpectedly. The truce was renewed, and Nelson came on shore the next day to see the Crown Prince. A truce of longer extent was agreed to, and finally fixed for fourteen weeks. We shall thereby gain the opportunity of sending succor to Norway, where the people are almost dying of hunger. We shall not disarm. The militia are disbanded, to attend to their farming operations.

The loss of the enemy is placed beyond a doubt by this convention. It is not very favorable to him. The utmost he could do would be to sail away, if he wished it. They will scarcely take all their ships home. Parker's son is said to have fallen. Nelson has lost three captains, two who had been at Aboukir; on the Elephant, his own ship, the captain, two lieutenants, and one hundred and seventeen men. It is said that in another English ship two hundred and thirty were killed. Two English ships-of-the-line struck their flag, but could not be taken.

Thus we have, I think, won honor and consideration throughout Europe; likewise a firmer hold on the reverence and affection of all classes of the realm. . . . .

XXIV.—BATTLE OF WATERLOO.

Sir Walter Scott to the Duke of Buccleuch.

My dear Lord Duke: I promised to let you hear of my wanderings, however unimportant; and have now the pleasure of informing your Grace that I am at this present time an inhabitant of the Premier Hotel de Cambrai, after having been about a week upon the Continent. We landed at Helvoet, and proceeded to Brussels, by Bergen-op-Zoom and Antwerp, both of which are very stongly fortified. The ravages of war are little remarked in a country so rich by nature; but every thing seems at present stationary, or rather retrograde, where capital is required. The châteaux are deserted, and going to decay; no new houses are built, and those of older date are passing rapidly into the possession of a class inferior to those for whom we must suppose them to have been built. Even the old gentlewoman of Babylon has lost much of her splendor, and her robes and pomp are of a description far subordinate to the costume of her more magnificent days. The dresses of the priests were worn and shabby, both at Antwerp and Brussels, and reminded me of the decayed wardrobe of a bankrupt theatre; yet, though the gentry and priesthood have suffered, the eternal bounty of

Nature has protected the lower ranks against much distress. The unexampled fertility of the soil gives them all, and more than they want; and could they but sell the grain which they raise in the Netherlands, nothing else would be wanting to render them the richest people (common people, that is to say) in the world.

On Wednesday last I rode over the field of Waterloo, now forever consecrated to immortality. The more ghastly tokens of the carnage are now removed, the bodies both of men and horses being either burned or buried; but all the ground is still torn with the shot and shells, and covered with cartridges, old hats, and shoes, and various relics of the fray which the peasants have not thought worth removing. Besides, at Waterloo, and all the hamlets in the vicinity, there is a mart established for cuirasses; for the eagles worn by the imperial guard on their caps; for casques, swords, carabines, and similar articles. I have bought two handsome cuirasses, and intend them, one for Bowhill, and one for Abbotsford, if I can get them safe over, which Major Pryse Gordon has promised to manage for me. I have also, for your Grace, one of the little memorandum-books, which I picked up on the field, in which every French soldier was obliged to enter his receipts and expenditure, his services, and even his punishments. The field was covered with fragments of these records. I also got a good MS. collection of French songs, probably the work of some young officer, and a cross of the Legion of Honor. I enclose, under another cover, a sketch of the battle made at Brussels. It is not, I understand, strictly accurate, but sufficiently so to give a good notion of what took place. In fact, it would require twenty separate plans to give an idea of the battle at its various stages. The front, upon which the armies engaged, does not exceed a long mile. Our line, indeed, originally extended half a mile farther toward the village of Brain-la-Leude; but, as the French indicated no disposition to attack in that direction, the troops which occupied this space were gradually concentrated by Lord Wellington, and made to advance till they had reached Hougomont—a sort of château, with a garden and wood attached to it, which was powerfully and effectually maintained by the Guards during the action. This place was particularly interesting. It was a quiet-looking, gentleman's house, which had been burned by the French shells. The defenders, burnt out of the house itself, betook themselves to the little garden, where, breaking loop-holes through the brick walls, they kept up a most destructive fire on the assailants, who had possessed themselves of a little wood which surrounds the villa on one side. In this spot vast numbers had fallen; and, being hastily buried, the smell is most offensive at this moment. Indeed, I felt the same annoyance in many parts of the field; and, did I live near the spot, I should be anxious about the diseases which this steaming carnage might occasion. The rest of the ground, excepting this château and a farm-house called La Hay Sainte, early taken, and long held, by the French, because it was too close under the brow of the descent on which our artillery was placed to admit of the pieces being depressed so as to play into it—the rest of the ground, I say, is quite open, and lies between two ridges, one of which (Mont St. Jean) was constantly occupied by the English; the other, upon which is the farm of La Belle Alliance, was the position of the French. The slopes between are gentle and varied; the ground everywhere practicable for cavalry, as was well experienced on that memorable day. The cuirassiers, despite their arms of proof, were quite inferior to our heavy dragoons. The meeting of the two bodies occasioned a noise not unaptly compared to the tinkering and hammering of a smith's shop. Generally, the cuirassiers came on stooping their heads very low, and giving point; the British frequently struck away their casques while they were in this position, and then laid at the bare head. Officers and soldiers all fought, hand to hand, without distinction; and many of the former owed their lives to dexterity at their weapon, and personal strength of body. Shaw, the milling Life-Guards' man, whom your Grace may remember among the champions of The Fancy, maintained the honor of the fist, and killed or disabled upwards of twenty Frenchmen with his single arm, until he was killed by the assault of numbers. At one place, where there is a precipitous sand or gravel pit, the heavy English cavalry drove many of the cuirassiers over pell-mell, and followed over themselves like fox-hunters. The conduct of the infantry and artillery was equally, or, if possible, more distinguished, and it was all fully necessary; for, besides that our army was much outnumbered, a great part of the sum total were foreigners. Of these, the Brunswickers and Hanoverians behaved very well; the Belgians but sorrily enough. On one occasion, when a Belgic regiment fairly ran off, Lord Wellington rode up to them, and said: "My lads, you must be a little blown; come, do take your breath for a moment, and then we'll go back, and try if we can do a little better;" and he actually carried them back to the charge. He was, indeed, upon that day, everywhere, and the soul of every thing; nor could less than his personal endeavors have supported the spirits of the men through a contest so long, so desperate, and so unequal. At his last attack, Buonaparte brought up

15,000 of his Guard, who had never drawn trigger during the day. It was upon their failure that his hopes abandoned him.

I spoke long with a shrewd Flemish peasant, called John de Costar, whom he had seized upon as his guide, and who remained beside him the whole day, and afterwards accompanied him in his flight as far as Charleroi. Your Grace may be sure that I interrogated Mynheer very closely about what he heard and saw. He guided me to the spot where Buonaparte remained during the latter part of the action. It was in the highway from Brussels to Charleroi, where it runs between two high banks, on each of which was a French battery. He was pretty well sheltered from the English fire; and, though many bullets flew over his head, neither he nor any of his suite were touched. His other stations during that day were still more remote from all danger. The story of his having an observatory erected for him is a mistake. There is such a thing, and he repaired to it during the action; but it was built or erected some months before, for the purpose of a trigonometrical survey of the country, by the King of the Netherlands. Bony's last position was nearly fronting a tree, where the Duke of Wellington was stationed; there was not more than a quarter of a mile between them; but Bony was well sheltered, and the Duke so much exposed that the tree is barked in several places by the cannon-balls levelled at him. As for Bony, De Costar says he was very cool during the whole day, and even gay. As the cannon-balls flew over them, De Costar ducked; at which the Emperor laughed, and told him they would hit him all the same. At length, about the time he made his grand and last effort, the fire of the Prussian artillery was heard upon his right, and the heads of their columns became visible pressing out of the woods. Aide-de-camp after aide-de-camp came with the tidings of their advance, to which Bony only replied, *Attendez, attendez, un instant*, until he saw his troops, *fantassins et cavaliers*, return in disorder from the attack. He then observed hastily to a general beside him, *Je crois qu'ils sont mêlés.* The person to whom he spoke hastily raised the spyglass to his eye; but Bony, whom the first glance had satisfied of their total discomfiture, bent his face to the ground, and shook his head twice, his complexion being then as pale as death. The general then said something, to which Buonaparte answered, *C'est trop tard—sauvons nous.* Just at that moment the allied troops, cavalry and infantry, appeared in full advance on all hands; and the Prussians, operating upon the right flank of the French, were rapidly gaining their rear. Bony, therefore, was compelled to abandon the high-road, which, besides, was choked with dead, with baggage, and with cannon; and, gaining the open country, kept at full gallop, until he gained, like Johnny Cope, the van of the flying army. The marshals followed his example; and it was the most complete *sauve qui peut* that can well be imagined. Nevertheless, the prisoners who were brought into Brussels maintained their national impudence, and boldly avowed their intention of sacking the city with every sort of severity. At the same time they had friends there. One man of rank and wealth went over to Bony during the action, and I saw his hotel converted into a hospital for wounded soldiers. It occupied one-half of one of the sides of the Place Royale, a noble square, which your Grace has probably seen. But, in general, the inhabitants of Brussels were very differently disposed; and their benevolence to our poor wounded fellows was unbounded. The diffi culty was to prevent them from killing their guests with kindness, by giving them butcher's meat and wine during their fever. As I cannot put my letter into post until we get to Paris, I shall continue it as we get along.

12*th August, Roye, in Picardy.* I imagine your Grace about this time to be tolerably well fagged with a hard day on the moors. If the weather has been as propitious as with us, it must be delightful. The country through which we have travelled is most uncommonly fertile, and skirted with beautiful woods; but its present political situation is so very uncommon, that I would give the world your Grace had come over for a fortnight. France may be considered as neither at peace nor war. Valenciennes, for example, is in a state of blockade; we passed through the posts of the allies, all in the utmost state of vigilance, with patrols of cavalry, and videttes of infantry, up to the very gates, and two or three batteries were manned and mounted. The French troops were equally vigilant at the gates, yet made no objections to our passing through the town. Most of them had the white cockade, but looked very sulky, and were in obvious disorder and confusion. They had not yet made their terms with the King, nor accepted a commander appointed by him; but as they obviously feel their party desperate, the soldiers are running from the officers, and the officers from the soldiers. In fact, the multiplied hosts which pour into this country, exhibiting all the various dresses and forms of war which can be imagined, must necessarily render resistance impracticable. Yet, like Satan, these fellows retain the unconquered propensity to defiance, even in the midst of defeat and despair. This morning we passed a great number of the disbanded garrison of Condé, and they were the most horrid-looking cut-throats

I ever saw, extremely disposed to be very insolent, and only repressed by the consciousness that all the villages and towns around are occupied by the allies. They began by crying to us, in an ironical tone, *Vive le Roi ;* then followed, *sotto voce*, *Sacre B——*, *Mille diables*, and other graces of French eloquence. I felt very well pleased that we were armed, and four in number ; and still more so that it was daylight, for they seemed most mischievous ruffians. As for the appearance of the country, it is, notwithstanding a fine harvest, most melancholy. The windows of all the detached houses on the road are uniformly shut up ; and you see few people, excepting the peasants who are employed in driving the contributions to maintain the armies. The towns are little better, having for the most part been partially injured by shells or by storm, as was the case both of Cambrai and Peronne. The men look very sulky ; and if you speak three words to a woman, she is sure to fall a-crying. In short, the *politesse* and good humor of this people have fled with the annihilation of their self-conceit ; and they look on you as if they thought you were laughing at them, or come to enjoy the triumph of our arms over theirs. Postmasters and landlords are all the same, and hardly to be propitiated even by English money, although they charge us about three times as much as they durst do to their country folks. As for the Prussians, a party of cavalry dined at our hotel at Mons, ate and drank of the best the poor devils had left to give, called for their horses, and laughed in the face of the landlord when he offered his bill, telling him they should pay as they came back. The English, they say, have always paid honorably, and upon these they indemnify themselves. It is impossible to *marchander*, for if you object, the poor landlady begins to cry, and tells you she will accept whatever *your lordship* pleases, but that she is almost ruined and bankrupt, etc., etc., etc.

This is a long, stupid letter, but I will endeavor to send a better from Paris. Ever your Grace's truly obliged,

WALTER SCOTT.

XXV.—SIEGE OF ROME BY THE FRENCH.*

Madame Ossoli to R. W. Emerson.

ROME, June 10th, 1849.

I received your letter amid the round of cannonade and musketry. It was a terrible battle fought here, from the first to the last light of day. I could see all its progress from my balcony. The Italians fought like lions. It is a truly heroic spirit that animates them. They make a stand here for honor and their rights, with little ground for hope that they can resist, now that they are betrayed by France. Since the 30th of April I go almost daily to the hospitals, and though I have suffered, for I had no idea before how terrible gun-shot wounds and wound fevers are, yet I have taken pleasure, and great pleasure, in being with the men. There is scarcely one who is not moved by a noble spirit. Many, especially among the Lombards, are the flower of the Italian youth. When they begin to get better, I carry them books and flowers; they read, and we talk.

The palace of the Pope, on the Quirinal, is now used for convalescents. In those beautiful gardens I walk with them—one with his sling, another with his crutch. The gardener plays off all his waterworks for the defenders of the country, and gathers flowers for me, their friend. A day or two since we sat

* From "At Home and Abroad," by Madame Ossoli.

in the Pope's little pavilion, where he used to give private audience. The sun was going gloriously down over Monte Mario, where gleamed the white tents of the French light-horse among the trees. The cannonade was heard at intervals. Two bright-eyed boys sat at our feet, and gathered up eagerly every word said by the heroes of the day. It was a beautiful hour stolen from the midst of ruin and sorrow, and tales were told as full of grace and pathos as in the gardens of Boccaccio, only in a very different spirit, with noble hope for man and reverence for woman.

The young ladies of the family, very young girls, were filled with enthusiasm for the suffering, wounded patriots, and they wished to go to the hospitals to give their service. Excepting the three superintendents, none but married ladies were permitted to serve there, but their services were accepted. Their governess then wished to go too, and as she could speak several languages she was admitted to the rooms of the wounded soldiers, as the nurses knew nothing but Italian, and many of these poor men were suffering because they could not make their wishes known. Some are French, some Germans, many Poles. Indeed, I am afraid it is too true that there were comparatively few Romans among them. This young lady passed several nights there.

Should I never return, and sometimes I despair of doing so, it seems so far off—so difficult—I am caught in such a net of ties here; if ever you know of my life here, I think you will only wonder at the constancy with which I have sustained myself; the degree of profit to which, amid great difficulties, I have put the time, at least in the way of observation. Meanwhile, love me all you can. Let me feel that amid the fearful agitations of the world there are pure hands, with healthful, even pulse, stretched out toward me, if I claim their grasp.

I feel profoundly for Mazzini. At moments I am tempted to say, "Cursed with every granted prayer;" so cunning is the demon. Mazzini has become the inspiring soul of his people. He saw Rome, to which all his hopes through life tended, for the first time as a Roman citizen, and to become in a few days its ruler. He has animated, he sustains her to a glorious effort, which, if it fails this time, will not in the age. His country will be free; yet to me it would be so dreadful to cause all this bloodshed, to dig the graves of such martyrs.

Then, Rome is being destroyed; her glorious oaks, her villas, haunts of sacred beauty, that seemed the possession of the world forever; the villa of Raphael, the villa of Albani, home of Winckelmann, and the best expression of the ideal of modern Rome, and so many other sanctuaries of beauty, all must perish, lest a foe should level his musket from their shelter. I could not, could not.*

I know not, dear friend, whether I shall ever get home across that great ocean, but here in Rome I shall no longer wish to live. O Rome, *my* country! could I imagine that the triumph of what I held dear was to heap such desolation on thy head?

Speaking of the Republic you say, "Do you not wish Italy had a great man?" Mazzini is a great man. In mind, a great poetic statesman; in heart, a lover; in action, decisive; and full of resource as Cæsar. Dearly I love Mazzini. He came in

* It is stated, in the Memoirs of De Tocqueville, that almost the whole damage done by the siege was the destruction of the trees and frescoes in the Borghese gardens; and that in order to save those monuments, which are the property of the whole Christian world, the French submitted to some loss of men and much of time.

just as I had finished the first letter to you. His soft, radiant look makes melancholy music in my soul; it consecrates my present life, that like the Magdalen I may at the important hour shed all the consecrated ointment on his head. There is one, Mazzini, who understands thee well; who knew thee no less when an object of popular fear than now of idolatry, and who, if the pen be not held too feebly, will help posterity to know thee too.

BOOK THE FIFTH.

Literary Biography, Anecdote, and Criticism in Letters.

BOOK THE FIFTH.

LITERARY BIOGRAPHY, ANECDOTE, AND CRITICISM IN LETTERS.

I.—ACCOUNT OF HIS LOSS OF SIGHT.

John Milton to Leonard Philara, the Athenian.*

I HAVE been always devotedly attached to the literature of Greece, and particularly to that of your Athens; and have never ceased to cherish the persuasion that that city would one day make me ample recompense for the warmth of my regard. The ancient genius of your renowned country has favored the completion of my prophecy in presenting me with your friendship and esteem. Though I was known to you only by my writings, and we were removed to such a distance from each

* Milton's eyesight began to fail when he was about thirty years of age, but the process of obscuration was so gradual that total blindness did not supervene for nine years. The affection was *gutta serena*, and left his eyes clear, and with no external disfigurement.

"My mind," says Coleridge, in his Biographia Literaria (3d vol. of Works, p. 168), "is not capable of forming a more august conception than arises from the contemplation of this great man in his latter days; poor, sick, old, blind, slandered, persecuted,—

"'Darkness before, and danger's voice behind,'

in an age in which he was as little understood by the party for whom, as by that against whom, he had contended; and among men before whom he other, you most courteously addressed me by letter; and when you unexpectedly came to London and saw me who could no longer see, my affliction, which causes none to regard me with greater admiration, and perhaps many even with feelings of contempt, excited your tenderest sympathy and concern. You would not suffer me to abandon the hope of recovering my sight, and informed me you had an intimate friend at Paris—Dr. Thevenot, who was particularly celebrated in disorders of the eyes, whom you would consult about mine, if I would enable you to lay before him the causes and symptoms of the complaint. I will do what you desire, lest I seem to reject that aid which, perhaps, may be offered me by Heaven. It is now, I think, about ten years since I perceived my vision to grow weak and dull, and, at the same time, I was troubled with pain in my kidneys and bowels, accompanied with flatulency. In the morning, if I began to read, as was my custom, my eyes instantly ached intensely, but were refreshed after a little corporeal exercise. The candle which I looked at seemed as it were encircled with a rainbow. Not long after, the sight in the left part of the left eye (which I lost some years before the other) became quite obscured, and prevented me from discerning any object on that side. The sight in my other eye has now been gradually and sensibly vanishing away for about three years; some months before it had entirely perished, though I stood motionless, every

strode so far as to dwarf himself by the distance; yet still listening to the music of his own thoughts, or, if additionally cheered, yet cheered only by the prophetic faith of two or three solitary individuals, he did nevertheless

> ——— Argue not
> Against Heaven's hand or will, nor bate a jot
> Of heart or hope; but still bore up, and steered
> Right onward."—H.

thing I looked at seemed in motion to and fro. A stiff, cloudy vapor seemed to have settled on my forehead and temples, which usually occasions a sort of somnolent pressure upon my eyes, and particularly from dinner till the evening. So that I often recollect what is said of the poet Phineas in the Argonautics:

> "A stupor deep his cloudy temples bound,
> And when he walked he seemed as whirling round,
> Or in a feeble trance he speechless lay."

I ought not to omit that while I had my sight, as soon as I lay down on my bed and turned on either side, a flood of light used to gush from my closed eyelids. Then, as my sight became daily more impaired, the colors became more faint, and were emitted with a certain inward crackling sound; but at present, every species of illumination being as it were extinguished, there is diffused around me nothing but darkness, or darkness mingled and streaked with an ashy brown. Yet the darkness in which I am perpetually immersed seems always, both night and day, to approach nearer to white than black; and when the eye is rolling in its socket, it admits a little particle of light, as through a chink. And, though your physician may kindle a small ray of hope, yet I make up my mind to the malady as quite incurable; and I often reflect, that as the wise man admonishes, days of darkness are destined to each of us, the darkness which I experience, less oppressive than that of the tomb, is, owing to the singular goodness of the Deity, passed amid the pursuits of literature, and the cheering salutations of friendship. But if, as is written, man shall not live by bread alone, but by every word that proceedeth from the mouth of God, why may not any one acquiesce in the privation of his sight, when God has so amply furnished his mind and his conscience with eyes? While He so tenderly provides for me, while He so graciously leads me by the hand, and conducts me on the way, I will, since it is His pleasure, rather rejoice than repine at being blind. And, my dear Philara, whatever may be the event, I bid you adieu with no less courage and composure than if I had the eyes of a lynx.

II.—JOURNEY TO OXFORD WITH LINTOT.

Alexander Pope to the Earl of Burlington.

My Lord: If your mare could speak, she would give an account of what extraordinary company she had on the road; which, since she cannot do, I will.

It was the enterprising Mr. Lintot, the redoubtable rival of Mr. Tonson, who, mounted on a stone-horse (no disagreeable companion to your Lordship's mare), overtook me in Windsor Forest. He said he heard I designed for Oxford, the seat of the muses, and would, as my bookseller, by all means accompany me thither.

I asked him where he got his horse? He answered he got it of his publisher. "For that rogue, my printer," said he, "disappointed me; I hoped to put him in good humor by a treat at the tavern, of a brown fricassee of rabbits, which cost two shillings, with two quarts of wine, besides my conversation. I thought myself cocksure of his horse, which he readily promised me, but said that Mr. Tonson had just such another design of going to Cambridge, expecting there the copy of a new kind of Horace from Dr. ——, and if Mr. Tonson went, he was pre-engaged to attend him, being to have the printing of the said copy.

"So, in short, I borrowed this stone-horse of my publisher, which he had of Mr. Oldmixon for a debt. He lent me, too, the pretty boy you see after me; he was a smutty dog yesterday, and cost me near two hours to wash the ink off his face; but the devil is a fair-conditioned devil, and very forward in his catechise; if you have any more bags, he shall carry them."

I thought Mr. Lintot's civility not to be neglected, so gave the boy a small bag containing three shirts and an Elzevir Virgil; and, mounting in an instant, proceeded on the road, with my man before, my courteous stationer beside, and the aforesaid devil behind.

Mr. Lintot began in this manner: "Now, damn them! what if they should put it into the newspaper how you and I went together to Oxford? what would I care? If I should go down into Sussex, they would say I was gone to the Speaker. But what of that? If my son were but big enough to go on with the business, by G—d I would keep as good company as old Jacob."

Hereupon I inquired of his son. "The lad," says he, "has fine parts, but is somewhat sickly, much as you are—I spare for nothing in his education at Westminster. Pray, don't you think Westminster to be the best school in England? most of the late ministry came out of it, so did many of this ministry; I hope the boy will make his fortune." Don't you design to let him pass a year at Oxford? "To what purpose?" said he, "the universities do but make pedants, and I intend to breed him a man of business."

As Mr. Lintot was talking, I observed he sat uneasy on his

saddle, for which I expressed some solicitude. "Nothing," says he, "I can bear it well enough; but since we have the day before us, methinks it would be very pleasant for you to rest awhile under the woods." When we were alighted, "See here, what a mighty pretty Horace I have in my pocket! what if you amused yourself in turning an ode, till we mount again? Lord! if you pleased, what a clever miscellany might you make at leisure hours." Perhaps I may, said I, if we ride on; the motion is an aid to my fancy, a round trot very much awakens my spirits; then jog on apace, and I'll think as hard as I can.

Silence ensued for a full hour; after which Mr. Lintot lugged the reins, stopped short, and broke out: "Well, sir, how far have you gone?" I answered, seven miles. "Zounds, sir," said Lintot, "I thought you had done seven stanzas. Oldsworth, in a ramble round Wimbleton Hill, would translate a whole ode in half this time. I'll say that for Oldsworth (though I lost by his Timothy's), he translates an ode of Horace the quickest of any man in England. I remember Dr. King would write verses in a tavern three hours after he could not speak; and there's Sir Richard, in that rumbling old chariot of his, between Fleetditch and St. Giles's pond, shall make you half a Job.

Pray, Mr. Lintot, said I, now you talk of translators, what is your method of managing them? "Sir," replied he, "those are the saddest pack of rogues in the world; in a hungry fit, they'll swear they understand all the languages in the universe; I have known one of them take down a Greek book upon my counter and cry, Ay, this is Hebrew, I must read it from the latter end. By G—d I can never be sure in these fellows, for I neither understand Greek, Latin, French, nor Italian myself.

But this is my way: I agree with them for ten shillings per sheet, with a proviso that I will have their doings corrected by whom I please; so by one or other they are led at last to the true sense of an author; my judgment giving the negative to all my translators." But how are you secure those correctors may not impose upon you? "Why, I get any civil gentleman (especially any Scotchman) that comes into my shop, to read the original to me in English; by this I know whether my first translator be deficient, and whether my corrector merits his money or not.

"I'll tell you what happened to me last month: I bargained with S—— for a new version of Lucretius to publish against Tonson's; agreeing to pay the author so many shillings at his producing so many lines. He made a great progress in a very short time, and I gave it to the corrector to compare with the Latin, but he went directly to Creech's translation, and found it the same, word for word, all but the first page. Now, what d'ye think I did? I arrested the translator for a cheat; nay, and I stopped the corrector's pay, too, upon this proof, that he had made use of Creech instead of the original."

Pray, tell me next how you deal with the critics? "Sir," said he, "nothing more easy. I can silence the most formidable of them; the rich ones for a sheet apiece of the blotted manuscript, which costs me nothing; they'll go about with it to their acquaintance, and pretend that they had it from the author, who submitted to their correction; this has given some of them such an air, that in time they come to be consulted with, and dedicated to as the top critics of the town. As for the poor critics, I'll give you one instance of my management, by which you may guess at the rest. A lean man, that looked like a very good scholar, came to me t'other day; he turned over your Homer, shook his head, shrugged up his shoulders, and pished at every line of it. One would wonder (says he) at the strange presumption of some men; Homer is no such easy talk, that every stripling, every versifier—He was going on, when my wife called to dinner. Sir, said I, will you please to eat a piece of beef with me? Mr. Lintot (said he), I am sorry you should be at the expense of this great book; I am really concerned on your account. Sir, I am obliged to you; if you can dine upon a piece of beef, together with a slice of pudding—Mr. Lintot, I do not say but Mr. Pope, if he would condescend to advise with men of learning—Sir, the pudding is upon the table, if you please to go in—My critic complies, he comes to a taste of your poetry, and tells me in the same breath that the book is commendable, and the pudding excellent. "Now, sir," concluded Mr. Lintot, "in return to the frankness I have shown, pray tell me, is it the opinion of your friends at Court that my Lord Lansdowne will be brought to the bar or not?" I told him I heard he would not, and I hoped it, my Lord being one I had particular obligations to. "That may be," replied Mr. Lintot, "but, by G—d, if he should not, I shall lose the printing of a very good trial."

These, my Lord, are a few traits by which you may discern the genius of Mr. Lintot, which I have chosen for the subject of a letter. I dropped him as soon as I got to Oxford, and paid a visit to my Lord Carleton at Middleton.

The conversations I enjoy here are not to be prejudiced by my pen, and the pleasures from them only to be equalled when I meet your Lordship. I hope in a few days to cast myself from your horse at your feet. I am, etc.

III.—FRIENDLY FEELINGS AND ADVICE.

Dr. Arbuthnot to Alexander Pope.

HAMPSTEAD, July 17, 1734.

I little doubt of your kind concern for me, nor of that of the lady you mention. I have nothing to repay my friends with at present, but prayers and good wishes. I have the satisfaction to find that I am as officiously served by my friends, as he that has thousands to leave in legacies; besides the assurance of their sincerity. God Almighty has made my bodily distress as easy as a thing of that nature can be. I have found some relief, at least sometimes, from the air of this place. My nights are bad, but many poor creatures have worse.

As for you, my good friend, I think, since our first acquaintance, there have not been any of those little suspicions or jealousies that often affect the sincerest friendships; I am sure not on my side. I must be so sincere as to own that, though I could not help valuing you for those talents which the world prizes, yet they were not the foundation of my friendship; they were quite of another sort; nor shall I at present offend you by enumerating them; and I make it my last request, that you will continue that noble disdain and abhorrence of vice which you seem naturally endued with; but still with a due regard to your own safety; and study more to reform than chastise, though the one cannot be effected without the other.

Lord Bathurst I have always honored for every good quality that a person of his rank ought to have; pray, give my respects and kindest wishes to the family. My venison stomach is gone, but I have those about me, and often with me, who will be very glad of his present. If it is left at my house, it will be transmitted safe to me.

A recovery in my case, and at my age, is impossible; the kindest wish of my friends is Euthanasia. Living or dying, I shall always be, Yours, etc.

IV.—IN REPLY.—FUNCTIONS OF SATIRE.

Alexander Pope to Dr. Arbuthnot.

July 26th, 1734.

I thank you for your letter, which has all those genuine marks of a good mind by which I have ever distinguished yours, and for which I have so long loved you. Our friendship has been constant, because it was grounded on good principles, and, therefore, not only uninterrupted by any distrust, but by any vanity, much less any interest.

What you recommend to me with the solemnity of a last request, shall have its due weight with me. That disdain and indignation against vice is (I thank God) the only disdain and indignation I have; it is sincere, and it will be a lasting one. But sure it is as impossible to have a just abhorrence of vice, without hating the vicious, as to bear a true love for virtue, without loving the good. To reform, and not to chastise, I am afraid, is impossible; and that the best precepts, as well as the best laws, would prove of small use, if there were no examples to enforce them. To attack vices in the abstract, without touching persons, may be safe fighting indeed; but it is fighting with shadows. General propositions are obscure, misty, and uncertain, compared with plain, full, and home examples. Precepts only apply to our reason, which, in most men, is but weak; examples are pictures, and strike the senses; nay, raise the passions, and call in those (the strongest and most general of all motives) to the aid of reformation. Every vicious man makes the case his own; and that is the only way by which such men can be affected, much less deterred; so that to chastise is to reform. The only sign by which I found my writings ever did any good, or had any weight, has been that they raised the anger of bad men; and my greatest comfort and encouragement to proceed has been to see that those who have no shame, and no fear of any thing else, have appeared touched by my satires.

As to your kind concern for my safety, I can guess what occasions it at this time. Some characters * I have drawn, are such that, if there be any who deserve them, 'tis evidently a service to mankind to point those men out; yet such as, if all the world gave them, none, I think, will own they take to themselves; but if they should, those of whom all the world think in such a manner, must be men I cannot fear. Such, in particular, as have the meanness to do mischiefs in the dark, have seldom the courage to justify them in the face of day; the talents that make a cheat or a whisperer, are not the same that qualify a man for an insulter; and as to private villainy, it is not so safe to join in an assassination, as in a libel. I will consult my safety, so far as I think it becomes a prudent man; but not so far as to omit any thing which I think becomes an honest one. As to personal attacks beyond the law, every man is liable to them; as for danger within the law, I am not guilty enough to fear any. For the good opinion of all the world, I know it is not to be had; for that of worthy men, I hope I shall not forfeit it; for that of the great or those in power, I may wish I had it; but if, through misrepresentations (too common about persons in that station), I have it not, I shall be sorry, but not miserable in the want of it.

* The character of Sporus in the Epistle to Dr. Arbuthnot.

It is certain much freer Satirists than I have enjoyed the encouragement and protection of the princes under whom they lived. Augustus and Mæcenas made Horace their companion, though he had been in arms on the side of Brutus; and allow me to remark, it was out of the suffering party too, that they favored and distinguished Virgil. You will not suspect me of comparing myself with Virgil and Horace, nor even with another court-favorite, Boileau. I have always been too modest to imagine my panegyrics were incense worthy of a court; and that I hope will be thought the true reason why I have never offered any. I would only have observed that it was under the greatest princes and best ministers that moral satirists were most encouraged; and that then poets exercised the same jurisdiction over the follies as historians did over the vices of men. It may also be worth considering whether Augustus himself makes the greater figure in the writings of the former or of the latter; and whether Nero and Domitian do not appear as ridiculous for their alse tastes and affectation, in Persius and Juvenal, as odious for their bad government in Tacitus and Suetonius. In the first of these reigns it was that Horace was protected and caressed; and in the latter that Lucan was put to death, and Juvenal banished.

I would not have said so much, but to show you my whole heart on this subject, and to convince you I am deliberately bent to perform that request which you make your last to me, and to perform it with temper, justice, and resolution. As your approbation (being the testimony of a sound head and an honest heart) does greatly confirm me herein, I wish you may live to see the effect it may hereafter have upon me, in something more deserving of that approbation; but if it be the will of God (which, I know, will also be yours) that we may separate, I hope it will be better for you than it can be for me. You are fitter to live, or to die, than any man I know. Adieu, my dear friend! and may God preserve your life easy, or make your death happy.*

V.—CRITICISM OF THE EMPEROR ADRIAN'S VERSES TO HIS SOUL.

Alexander Pope to Mr. Steele.

November 7th, 1712.

I was the other day in company with five or six men of some learning, where, chancing to mention the famous verses which the Emperor Adrian spoke on his death-bed, they were all agreed that it was a piece of gayety unworthy of that Prince in those circumstances. I could not but differ from this opinion; methinks it was by no means a gay, but a very serious soliloquy to his soul at the point of its departure; in which sense I naturally took the verses at my first reading of them, when I was very young, and before I knew what interpretation the world generally put upon them:

Animula, vagula, blandula,
Hospes comesque corporis
Quæ nunc abibis in loca?
Pallidula, rigida, nudula
Nec (ut soles) dabis joca!

"Alas my soul! Thou pleasing companion of this body; thou fleeting thing that art now deserting it! Whither art thou flying? To what unknown scene? All trembling, fearful, and pensive? What now is become of thy former wit and humor? Thou shalt jest and be gay no more."

* This excellent person died Feb. 27, 1734–'5.

I confess I cannot apprehend where lies the trifling in all this. It is the most natural and obvious reflection imaginable to a dying man; and if we consider the Emperor was a heathen, that doubt concerning the future state of his soul will seem so far from being the effect of want of thought, that it was scarce reasonable he should think otherwise, not to mention that here is a plain confession included of its immortality. The diminutive epithets of *vagula*, *blandula*, and the rest appear not to me as expressions of levity, but rather of endearment and concern, such as we find in Catullus and the authors of *hendecasyllabi* after him, where they are used to express the utmost love and tenderness for their mistresses. If you think me right in my notion of the last words of Adrian, be pleased to insert it in the Spectator; if not, to suppress it. I am, etc.

ADRIANI MORIENTIS AD ANIMAM—TRANSLATED.

Ah, fleeting spirit! wandering fire,
That long has warmed my tender breast,
Must thou no more this frame inspire?
No more a pleasing, cheerful guest?
Whither, ah, whither art thou flying?
To what dark, undiscovered shore?
Thou seem'st all trembling, shivering, dying,
And wit and humor are no more.

VI.—REQUESTS AN ODE.

Mr. Steele to Alexander Pope.

This is to desire of you that you will please to make an Ode as of a cheerful dying spirit, that is to say, the Emperor Adrian's *Animula vagula*, put into two or three stanzas for music. If you comply with this, and send me word so, you will very particularly oblige, Yours, etc.

VII.—IN REPLY: SENDS "THE DYING CHRISTIAN TO HIS SOUL."

Alexander Pope to Mr. Steele.

I do not send you word I will do, but have already done the thing you have desired of me. You have it (as Cowley calls it) just warm from the brain. It came to me the first moment I awaked this morning: yet you will see it was not so absolutely inspiration, but that I had in my head not only the verses of Adrian, but the fine fragment of Sappho, etc.

[Then follows the familiar ode, beginning, "Vital spark of heavenly flame."]

VIII.—CORRESPONDENCE BETWEEN SIR ISAAC NEWTON AND JOHN LOCKE.—NOBLE ACKNOWLEDGMENT OF WRONG.

Sir Isaac Newton to John Locke.

September 16th, 1693.

SIR: Being of opinion that you endeavored to embroil me with women, and by other means, I was so much affected with it as that when told me that you were sickly and would not live, I answered, "'Twere better if you were dead." I desire you to forgive this uncharitableness, for I am now satisfied that what you have done is just, and I beg your pardon for my having hard thoughts of you for it; and for representing that you struck at the root of morality, in a principle you laid down in your book of ideas, and designed to pursue in another book, and that I took you for a Hobbist. I beg your pardon, also, for saying or thinking that there was a design to sell me an office or to embroil me.

I am your most humble and unfortunate servant,

ISAAC NEWTON.*

IX.—MAGNANIMOUS FORGIVENESS.

John Locke to Sir Isaac Newton.

OATES, October 5th, 1693.

SIR: I have been, ever since I first knew you, so kindly and sincerely your friend, and thought you so much mine, that I could not have believed what you tell me of yourself, had I had it from anybody else. And though I cannot but be mightily troubled that you should have had so many wrong and unjust thoughts of me, yet next to the return of good offices, such as from a sincere good will I have ever done you, I receive your acknowledgment of the contrary as the kindest thing you could have done me, since it gives me hopes I have not lost a friend I so much valued. After what your letter expresses, I shall not need to say any thing to justify myself to you; I shall always think your own reflection on my carriage both to you and all mankind will sufficiently do that. Instead of that, give me leave to assure you that I am more ready to forgive you, than you can

* The contrition expressed in this letter, with a humility and candor characteristic of its great author, elicited the response in the text from Locke, than which, says Dugald Stewart, "he has left nothing behind him that does more honor to his temper and character. It is written with the magnanimity of a philosopher, and the good-humored forbearance of a man of the world; and it breathes throughout so tender and so unaffected a veneration for the good as well as great qualities of the excellent person to whom it is addressed, as demonstrates at once the conscious integrity of the writer, and the superiority of his mind to the irritation of little passions."—H.

be to desire it; and I do it so freely and fully, that I wish for nothing more than the opportunity to convince you that I truly love and esteem you; and that I still have the same good will for you as if nothing of this had happened. To confirm this to you more fully, I should be glad to meet you anywhere, and the rather because the conclusion of your letter makes me apprehend it would not be wholly useless to you. I shall always be ready to serve you to my utmost, in any way you shall like, and shall only need your commands or permission to do it.

My book is going to press for a second edition; and though I can answer for the design with which I writ it, yet since you have so opportunely given me notice of what you have said of it, I should take it as a favor if you would point out to me the places that gave occasion to that censure, that, by explaining myself better, I may avoid being mistaken by others, or unwillingly doing the least prejudice to truth or virtue. I am sure you are so much a friend to both, that were you none to me, I could expect this from you. But I cannot doubt you would do a great deal more than this for my sake, who, after all, have all the concern of a friend for you, wish you extremely well, and am without compliment, etc.

X.—IN REPLY.

*Sir Isaac Newton to Mr. Locke.**

Sir: The last winter, by sleeping too often by my fire, I got an ill habit of sleeping, and a distemper which this summer has been epidemical put me further out of order, so that when I

* Newton's reply shows that the aberrations into which he had been led, were to be referred to the influence of disordered health on his mental faculties.

wrote to you I had not slept an hour a night for a fortnight, and for five days together not a wink. I remember I wrote to you, but what I said of your book I remember not. If you please to send me a transcript of that passage, I will give you an account of it, if I can. I am your most humble servant,

ISAAC NEWTON.

XI.—GARDENING—FROISSART—TRISTRAM SHANDY.

Thomas Gray to Dr. Wharton.

LONDON, June 22d, 1760.

I am not sorry to hear you are exceeding busy, except as it has deprived me of the pleasure I should have in hearing often from you; and as it has been occasioned by a little vexation and disappointment. To find one's self business I am persuaded is the great art of life; I am never so angry as when I hear my acquaintance wishing they had been bred to some poking profession, or employed in some office of drudgery, as if it were pleasanter to be at the command of other people than at one's own, and as if they could not go unless they were wound up; yet I know and feel what they mean by this complaint; it proves that some spirit, something of genius (more than common), is required to teach a man how to employ himself. I say a man, for women, commonly speaking, never feel this distemper; they have always something to do; time hangs not on their hands (unless they be fine ladies); a variety of small inventions and occupations fill up the void, and their eyes are never open in vain.

As to myself, I have again found rest for the sole of my gouty foot in your old dining-room, and hope that you will find at least an equal satisfaction at Old-Park; if your bog prove as comfortable as my oven, I shall see no occasion to pity you, and only wish you may brew no worse than I bake.

You totally mistake my talents, when you impute to me any magical skill in planting roses. I know I am no conjurer in these things; when they are done I can find fault, and that is all. Now this is the very reverse of genius, and I feel my own littleness. Reasonable people know themselves better than is commonly imagined, and therefore (though I never saw any instance of it) I believe Mason when he tells me that he understands these things. The prophetic eye of taste (as Mr. Pitt calls it) sees all the beauties that a place is susceptible of long before they are born, and when it plants a seedling already sits under the shadow of it, and enjoys the effect it will have from every point of view that lies in prospect. You must therefore invoke Caractacus, and he will send his spirits from the top of Snowdon to Cross-fell or Wardenlaw.

I am much obliged to you for your antique news. Froissart is a favorite book of mine (though I have not attentively read him, but only dipped here and there), and it is strange to me that people who would give thousands for a dozen portraits (originals of that time) to furnish a gallery, should never cast an eye on so many moving pictures of the life, actions, manners, and thoughts of their ancestors, done on the spot, and in strong though simple colors. In the succeeding century Froissart, I find, was read with great satisfaction by everybody that could read, and on the same footing with King Arthur, Sir Tristram, and Archbishop Turpin; not because they thought him a fabulous writer, but because they took them all for true and authentic historians; to so little purpose was it in that age for a man to be at the pains of writing truth. Pray, are you come to the four Irish kings that went to school to King Richard the Second's master of the ceremonies, and the man who informed Froissart of all he had seen in St. Patrick's purgatory?

The town are reading the King of Prussia's poetry (*Le Philosophe Sans Souci*), and I have done like the town; they do not seem so sick of it as I am; it is all the scum of Voltaire and Lord Bolingbroke, the *Crambe recocta* of our worst free-thinkers, tossed up in German-French rhyme. Tristram Shandy is still a greater object of admiration, the man as well as the book; one is invited to dinner, where he dines a fortnight before; as to the volumes yet published, there is much good fun in them, and humor sometimes hit and sometimes missed. Have you read his sermons, with his own comic figure, from a painting by Reynolds, at the head of them? They are in the style I think most proper for the pulpit,* and show a strong imagination and a sensible heart; but you see him often tottering on the verge of laughter, and ready to throw his periwig in the face of the audidience.

* Our author was of opinion that it was the business of the preacher rather to persuade by the power of eloquence to the practice of known duties, than to reason with the art of logic on points of controverted doctrine. Hence, therefore, he thought that sometimes imagination might not be out of its place in a sermon. But let him speak for himself, in an extract from one of his letters to me in the following year: "Your quotation from Jeremy Taylor is a fine one. I have long thought of reading him, for I am persuaded that chopping logic in the pulpit, as our divines have done ever since the revolution, is not the thing; but that imagination and warmth of expression are in their place there as much as on the stage, moderated, however, and chastised a little by the purity and severity of religion."

XII.—ON THE PUBLICATION OF HIS DICTIONARY.

*Dr. Johnson to Lord Chesterfield.**

February, 1755.

My Lord: I have been lately informed by the proprietor of the "World," that two papers, in which my dictionary is recommended to the public, were written by your Lordship. To be so distinguished is an honor which, being very little accustomed to favors from the great, I know not well how to receive, or in what terms to acknowledge.

* When Johnson determined to write an English dictionary, he addressed the prospectus to Lord Chesterfield, who was regarded as the Mæcenas of the age. Many years were spent upon the execution of the work, amid sorrow, want, and disappointment, and with no notice from the distinguished nobleman who had been selected as its patron. As it drew near its completion, it was, however, heralded by Lord Chesterfield to the public, through two numbers of the "World," in terms of graceful and well-merited compliment. He proposed to have recourse to the old Roman expedient in times of confusion, and choose a dictator of the language. "Upon this principle," he proceeds, "I give my vote for Mr. Johnson to fill that great and arduous post. And I hereby declare that I make a total surrender of all my rights and privileges in the English language, as a free-born British subject, to the said Mr. Johnson, during the term of his dictatorship: nay, more; I will not only obey him like an old Roman, as my dictator, but like a modern Roman I will implicitly believe in him as my Pope, and hold him to be infallible whilst in the chair, but no longer." This courtly device did not secure the dedication it has been supposed to have invited. Johnson was deeply offended at the real or apparent neglect of Lord Chesterfield, and repelled his advances in the celebrated letter in the text. It may admit of doubt whether the wounded pride of the great scholar has not led him to do some injustice to Lord Chesterfield. He subsequently qualified the statement that "no assistance had been received" by the acknowledgment of having at one time received ten pounds from that nobleman. The neglect occurred at a period of Lord Chesterfield's life when his deafness had in a great measure banished him from society; and Lord C. declared to Dodsley that "he would have turned off the best servant he ever had if he had known that he had denied him to a man who would have been always more than welcome." For many years Johnson gave no copies of this letter. It was read only by those who saw it on Lord Chesterfield's table, where it lay for any one's perusal.—H.

When, upon some slight encouragement, I first visited your Lordship, I was overpowered, like the rest of mankind, by the enchantment of your address, and could not forbear to wish that I might boast myself *le vainqueur du vainqueur de la terre*—that I might obtain that regard for which I saw the world contending; but I found my attendance so little encouraged that neither pride nor modesty would suffer me to continue it. When I had once addressed your Lordship in public, I had exhausted all the art of pleasing which a retired and uncourtly scholar can possess. I had done all that I could, and no man is well pleased to have his all neglected, be it ever so little.

Seven years, my Lord, have now past since I waited in your outward rooms or was repulsed from your door, during which time I have been pushing on my work through difficulties, of which it is useless to complain, and have brought it at last to the very verge of publication, without one act of assistance, one word of encouragement, or one smile of favor. Such treatment I did not expect, for I never had a patron before.

The shepherd in Virgil grew at last acquainted with Love, and found him a native of the rocks.

Is not a patron, my Lord, one who looks with unconcern on a man struggling for life in the water, and, when he has reached ground, encumbers him with help? The notice which you have been pleased to take of my labors, had it been early, had been kind; but it has been delayed till I am indifferent, and cannot enjoy it; till I am solitary, and cannot impart it; till I am known, and do not want it. I hope it is no very cynical asperity not to confess obligations where no benefit has been received, or to be unwilling that the public should consider me as owing that to a patron which Providence has enabled me to do for myself.

Having carried on my work thus far with so little obligation to any favorer of learning, I shall not be disappointed though I should conclude it, if less be possible, with less, for I have been long wakened from that dream of hope in which I once boasted myself with so much exultation, my Lord, your Lordship's most humble, most obedient servant, S. JOHNSON.

XIII.—ON THE PUBLICATION OF HIS THEORY OF MORAL SENTIMENTS.

David Hume to Adam Smith.

LONDON, 12th April, 1759.

I give you thanks for the agreeable present of your "Theory." Wedderburn and I made presents of our copies to such of our acquaintances as we thought good judges, and proper to spread the reputation of the book. I sent one to the Duke of Argyll, to Lord Lyttleton, Horace Walpole, Soame Jennyns, and Burke, an Irish gentleman who wrote lately a very pretty treatise on the Sublime. Millar desired my permission to send one in your name to Dr. Warburton. I have delayed writing to you till I could tell you something of the success of the book, and could prognosticate, with some probability, whether it should be finally damned to oblivion, or should be registered in the temple of immortality. Though it has been published only a few weeks, I think there appear already such strong symptoms that I can almost venture to foretell its fate. It is, in short, this ———. But I have been interrupted in my letter by a foolish, impertinent visit of one who has lately come from Scotland. He tells me that the University of Glasgow intend to declare Rouet's office vacant, upon his going abroad with Lord Hope.

I question not but you will have our friend Ferguson in your eye, in case another project for procuring him a place in the University of Edinburgh should fail. Ferguson has very much polished and improved his treatise on Refinement,* and with some amendments it will make an admirable book, and discovers an elegant and a singular genius. The Epigoniad, I hope, will do, but it is somewhat up-hill work. As I doubt not but you consult the reviews sometimes at present, you will see in the "Critical Review" a letter upon that poem; and I desire you to employ your conjectures in finding out the author. Let me see a sample of your skill in knowing hands by your guessing at the person. I am afraid of Lord Kames's Law Tracts. A man might as well think of making a fine sauce by a mixture of wormwood and aloes, as an agreeable composition by joining metaphysics and Scotch law. However, the book, I believe, has merit, though few persons will take the pains of diving into it. But, to return to your book and its success in this town. I must tell you——A plague of interruptions! I ordered myself to be denied, and yet here is one who has broke in upon me again. He is a man of letters, and we have had a good deal of literary conversation. You told me that you were curious of literary anecdotes, and therefore I shall inform you of a few that have come to my knowledge. I believe I have mentioned to you already Helvetius's book de l'Esprit. It is worth your reading, not for its philosophy, which I do not highly value, but for its agreeable composition. I had a letter from him a few days ago, wherein he tells me that my name was much oftener in the manuscript, but that the Censor of books at Paris obliged him to strike it out. Voltaire has lately published a small work

* Published as "An Essay on the History of Civil Society."

called *Candide ou l'Optimiste.* I shall give you a detail of it. ——But what is all this to my book? say you. My dear Mr. Smith, have patience; compose yourself to tranquillity. Show yourself a philosopher in practice as well as profession. Think on the emptiness and rashness and futility of the common judgments of men; how little they are regulated by reason in any subject, much more in philosophical subjects, which so far exceed the comprehension of the vulgar.

> ———Non si quid turbida Roma,
> Elevet, accedas; examenve improbum in illa
> Castiges tintina: nec te quæsiveris extra.

A wise man's kingdom is his own breast, or, if he ever looks farther, it will only be to the judgment of a select few, who are free from prejudices, and capable of examining his work. Nothing, indeed, can be a stronger presumption of falsehood, than the approbation of the multitude; and Phocion, you know, always suspected himself of some blunder, when he was attended with the applauses of the populace.

Supposing, therefore, that you have duly prepared yourself for the worst of all these reflections, I proceed to tell you the melancholy news, that your book has been very unfortunate, for the public seem disposed to applaud it extremely. It was looked for by the foolish people with some impatience, and the mob of literati are beginning already to be very loud in its praises. Three bishops called yesterday at Millar's shop in order to buy copies, and to ask questions about the author. The Bishop of Peterborough said he had passed the evening in a company where he heard it extolled above all books in the world. The Duke of Argyll is more decisive than he uses to be in its favor. I suppose he either considers it as an exotic, or thinks the author will be serviceable to him in the Glasgow elections. Lord Lyttleton says that Robertson, and Smith, and Bowyer are the glories of English literature. Oswald protests he does not know whether he has reaped more instruction or entertainment from it. But you may easily judge what reliance can be put on his judgment who has been engaged all his life in public business, and who never sees any faults in his friends. Millar exults and brags that two-thirds of the edition are already sold, and that he is now sure of success. You see what a son of the earth that is, to value books only by the profit they may bring him. In that view, I believe it may prove a very good book.

Charles Townsend, who passes for the cleverest fellow in England, is so taken with the performance, that he said to Oswald he would put the Duke of Buccleuch under the author's care, and would make it worth his while to accept of that charge. As soon as I heard this, I called on him twice, with a view of talking with him about the matter, and of consulting him on the propriety of sending that young nobleman to Glasgow, for I could not hope that he could offer you any terms which would tempt you to renounce your professorship. But I missed him. Mr. Townsend passes for being a little uncertain in his resolution; so perhaps you need not build much on this sally.

In recompense for so many mortifying things, which nothing but truth could have extorted from me, and which I could easily have multiplied to a greater number, I doubt not but you are so good a Christian as to return good for evil, and to flatter my vanity by telling me that all the godly in Scotland abuse me for my account of John Knox and the Reformation. I suppose you are glad to see my paper end, and I am obliged to conclude with

Your humble servant, DAVID HUME.

XIV.—FUTURE SPREAD OF THE ENGLISH LANGUAGE.

*David Hume to Edward Gibbon.**

LONDON, Oct. 24th, 1767.

SIR: It is but a few days ago since Mr. Deyverdun put your manuscript into my hands, and I have perused it with great pleasure and satisfaction. I have only one objection derived from the language in which it is written. Why do you compose in French, and carry fagots into the wood, as Horace says with regard to Romans who wrote in Greek? I grant that you have a like motive to those Romans, and adopt a language much more generally diffused than your native tongue; but have you not remarked the fate of those two ancient languages in following ages? The Latin, though then less celebrated, and confined to more narrow limits, has, in some measure, outlived the Greek, and is now more generally understood by men of letters. Let the French, therefore, triumph in the present diffusion of their tongue. Our solid and increasing establishments in America, where we need less dread the inundations of barbarians, promise a superior stability and duration to the English language.

Your use of the French tongue has also led you into a style more poetical and figurative and more highly colored than our

* Gibbon, before beginning his Decline and Fall of the Roman Empire, composed one book of an historical essay in French, on the liberty of the Swiss. This was submitted to some friends, whose unfavorable judgment induced him to relinquish that design. Mr. Hume's opinion was more favorable. Gibbon's partiality for France was not confined to the language. "His external solicitude," says Mr. Rogers, "to catch the exact tone of French manners and society, was constantly betraying itself. Madame du Deffand, though blind, recognized it, and thus writes to Walpole: 'He sets too much value on our talents for society (*nos agrêments*), shows too much desire of acquiring them; it is constantly on the tip of my tongue to say to him, "Do not put yourself to so much trouble; you deserve the honor of being a Frenchman."' "—H.

language seems to admit of in historical productions; for such is the practice of French writers, particularly the more recent ones, who illuminate their pictures more than custom will permit us. On the whole, your History is written, in my opinion, with spirit and judgment, and I exhort you very earnestly to continue it. The objections that occurred to me, on reading it, were so frivolous, that I shall not trouble you with them, and should, I believe, have a difficulty to recollect them. I am, with great esteem, Your most obedient servant,

David Hume

XV.—ENTERTAINING ACCOUNT OF HIS RECEPTION IN PARIS.

David Hume to Dr. Robertson.

Paris, December 1st, 1763.

Dear Robertson: Among other agreeable circumstances which attend me at Paris, I must mention that of having a lady for a translator, a woman of merit, the widow of an advocate. She was before very poor and known but to few, but this work has got her reputation, and procured her a pension from the Court, which sets her at her ease. She tells me that she has got a habit of industry, and would continue, if I could point out to her any other English book she could undertake, without running the risk of being anticipated by any other translator. Your History of Scotland is translated and is in the press; but I recommended to her your History of Charles V., and promised to write to you, in order to know when it would be printed, and to desire you to send over the sheets from London as they came from the press; I should put them into her hands, and she would, by that means, have the start of every other translator. My two volumes last published are at present in the press. She has a very easy, natural style; sometimes she mistakes the sense, but I now correct her manuscript, and should be happy to render you the same service, if my leisure permit me, as I hope it will. Do you ask me about my course of life? I can only say that I eat nothing but ambrosia, drink nothing but nectar, breathe nothing but incense, and tread on nothing but flowers. Every man I meet, and still more every lady, would think they were wanting in the most indispensable duty, if they did not make to me a long and elaborate harangue in my praise. What happened last week, when I had the honor of being presented to the Dauphin's children, at Versailles, is one of the most curious scenes I ever yet passed through. The Duc de B., the eldest, a boy of ten years old, stepped forth and told me how many friends and admirers I had in this country, and that he reckoned himself in the number from the pleasure he had received from the reading of many passages in my works. When he had finished, his brother, the Count of P., who is two years younger, began his discourse, and informed me that I had been long and impatiently expected in France, and that he, himself, expected soon to have great satisfaction from the reading of my fine History. But, what is more curious, when I was carried thence to the Count de A., who is but four years of age, I heard him mumble something, which, though he had forgot it in the way, I conjectured, from some scattered words, to have been also a panegyric dictated to him. Nothing could more surprise my friends, the Parisian philosophers, than this incident. * * *

It is conjectured that this honor was paid me by express order from the D., who, indeed, is not, on any occasion, sparing in my praise. All this attention and panegyric was at first oppressive to me, but now it fits more easy. I have recovered, in some measure, the use of the language, and am falling into friendships which are very agreeable, much more so than silly, distant admiration. They now begin to banter me and tell droll stories of me, which they have either observed themselves or have heard from others, so that you see I am beginning to be at home. It is probable that this place will be long my home. I feel little inclination to the factious barbarians of London, and have ever desired to remain in the place where I am planted. How much more so, when it is the best place in the world! I could here live in great abundance on the half of my income, for there is no place where money is so little requisite to a man who is distinguished either by his birth or by personal qualities. I could run out, you see, in a panegyric on the people, but you would suspect that this was a mutual convention between us. However, I cannot forbear observing on what a different footing learning and the learned are here, from what they are among the factious barbarians above mentioned.

I have here met with a prodigious historical curiosity; the Memoirs of King James II., in fourteen volumes, all wrote with his own hand, and kept in the Scots College. I have looked into it, and have made great discoveries. It will be all communicated to me; and I have had an offer of access to the Secretary of State's office, if I want to know the despatches of any French Minister that resided in London. But these matters are much out of my head. I beg of you to visit Lord Marischal, who will be pleased with your company. I have little paper remaining and less time, and, therefore, conclude abruptly, by assuring you that I am, dear doctor,

Yours sincerely, DAVID HUME.*

* "Hume," says Mr. Rogers in his biographical sketch, Encyclopædia

XVI.—ON THE RECEIPT OF HIS HISTORY OF AMERICA.*

Edmund Burke to Dr. William Robertson.

I am perfectly sensible of the very flattering description I have received in your thinking me worthy of so noble a present as that of your History of America. I have, however, suffered my gratitude to live under some suspicion by delaying my ac-

Britannica, "was not only welcome in Paris, he was the rage. Some of the scenes in which fashionable society doomed him to enact a part must have been exquisitely comic, and, had his friends intended to ridicule, not to honor him, they could hardly have devised any thing better adapted to the purpose." 'The celebrated David Hume,' writes Madame D'Epinay, 'the great fat English historian, known and esteemed for his writings, has not equal talents for the social amusements for which all our pretty women had decided him to be fit. He made his début at the house of Madame de T——. They had destined him to act the part of a Sultan seated between two slaves, employing all his eloquence to make them fall in love with him; finding them inexorable, he was to seek the cause of their obstinacy; he is placed on the sofa between the two prettiest women in Paris, he looks at them attentively, keeps striking his hands on his stomach and knees, and finds nothing else to say to them than 'Eh bien! mes demoiselles. . . . . . Eh bien! vous voilà donc! . . . . . Eh bien! vous voilà ici?' This lasted for a quarter of an hour, without his being able to get any further. One of them at last rose impatiently. . . . . . Since then he has been doomed to the part of a spectator, and is not less welcomed and flattered. In truth, the part he plays here is most amusing. Unfortunately for him, or rather for philosophic dignity (for he seems to accommodate himself very well to this mode of life), there was no ruling mania in this country when he came here; under these circumstances, he was looked upon as a new-found treasure, and the enthusiasm of our young heads turned toward him. All the pretty women are mad about him; he is at all the fine suppers, and there is no good fête without him; in a word, he is amongst our fashionables what the Genevese are to me!' Since the exhibition of the old Fabliaux of Aristotle, in love, down upon all fours and his mistress riding on his back, there has been no representation of philosophy so out of character, as it is shown us in the portrait of Hume by Madame D'Epinay." *Ed. Rev.*, Jan., 1847.—H.

* Mr. Burke, in a letter to Mr. Murphy on his Translation of Tacitus, makes some critical reflections on Dr. Robertson's style, which, whether just

knowledgment of so great a favor. But my delay was only to render my obligation to you more complete, and my thanks, if possible, more merited. The close of the session brought a good deal of very troublesome, though not important, business on me at once. I could not go through your work with one breath at that time, though I have done it since. I am now enabled to thank you, not only for the honor you have done me, but for the great satisfacton, and infinite variety and compass of instruction

or not in reference to that historian, are entitled in themselves to great consideration. "There is a style," says he, "which daily gains amongst us, which I should be sorry to see further advanced by a writer of your just reputation. The tendency of the mode to which I allude, is to establish two very different idioms amongst us, and to introduce a marked distinction between the English that is written and the English that is spoken. This practice, if grown a little more general, would confirm this distemper, such I must think it in our language, and render it incurable. From this feigned manner of *falsetto*, as I think the musicians call something of the same sort in singing, no one modern historian, Robertson only excepted, is perfectly free. It is assumed, I know, to give dignity and variety to the style. But whatever success the attempt may sometimes have, it is always obtained at the expense of purity and of the graces that are natural and appropriate to our language. It is true that when the exigence calls for auxiliaries of all sorts, and common language becomes unequal to the demands of extraordinary thoughts, something ought to be conceded to the necessities which make 'ambition virtue.' But the allowance to necessities ought not to grow into a practice." Mr. Dugald Stewart, in commenting upon this letter (Life of Dr. Robertson), adds a very just warning to young writers. "May I," says he, "be permitted to remark, that in the opposite extreme to that fault which Mr. Burke has censured, there is another, originating in too close an adherence to what he recommends as the model of good writing, the ease and familiarity of colloquial discourse? In the productions of his more advanced years, he has occasionally fallen into it himself, and has sanctioned it by his example, in the numerous herd of his imitators, who are incapable of atoning, by copying the exquisite and inimitable beauties which abound in his compositions. For my own part, I can much more easily reconcile myself, in a grave and dignified argument, to the *dulcia vitia* of Tacitus and of Gibbon, than that affectation of *cant* words and allusions which so often debases Mr. Burke's eloquence, and which was long ago stigmatized by Swift 'as the most ruinous of all the corruptions of a language.'"

I have received from your incomparable work. Every thing has been done which was so naturally to be expected from the author of the History of Scotland, and of the age of Charles the Fifth. I believe few books have done more than this toward clearing up dark points, correcting errors, and removing prejudices; you have, too, the rare secret of rekindling an interest on subjects that had so often been treated, and in which every thing that could feed a vital flame appeared to have been consumed. I am sure I read many parts of your History with that fresh concern and anxiety which attend those who are not previously apprised of the event. You have besides thrown quite a new light on the present state of the Spanish provinces, and furnished both materials and hints for a rational theory of what may be expected from them in future.

The part which I read with the greatest pleasure is the discussion on the manners and character of the inhabitants of that new world. I have always thought, with you, that we possess at this time very great advantages toward the knowledge of human nature. We need no longer go to history to trace it in all its stages and periods. History, from its comparative youth, is but a poor instructor. When the Egyptians called the Greeks children in antiquities, we may well call them children; and so we may call all those nations which were able to trace the progress of society only within their own limits. But now the great map of mankind is unrolled at once, and there is no state or gradation of barbarism, and no mode of refinement, which we have not at the same moment under our view: the very different civility of Europe and of China; the barbarism of Persia and of Abyssinia; the erratic manners of Tartary and of Arabia; the savage state of North America and of New Zealand. Indeed, you have made a noble use of the advantages you have had. You have employed philosophy to judge on manners, and from manners you have drawn new resources for philosophy. I only think that, in one or two points, you have hardly done justice to the savage character.

There remains before you a great field.

"Periculosæ plenum opus aleæ
Tractas, et incedis per ignes
Suppositos cineri doloso."

When even those ashes are spread over the present fire, God knows. I am heartily sorry that we are now supplying you with that kind of dignity and concern which is purchased to history at the expense of mankind. I had rather, by far, that Dr. Robertson's pen were only employed in delineating the humble scenes of political economy, than the great events of a civil war. However, if our statesmen had read the book of human nature instead of the Journals of the House of Commons, and history instead of Acts of Parliament, we should not by the latter have furnished out so ample a page for the former. For my part, I have not been, nor am I very forward in my speculations on this subject. All that I have ventured to make have hitherto proved very fallacious. I confess I thought the colonies, left to themselves, could not have made any thing like the present resistance to the whole power of this country and its allies. I did not think it could have been done without the declared interference of the house of Bourbon. But I looked on it as very probable that France and Spain before this time would have taken a decided part. In both these conjectures I have judged amiss. You will smile when I send you a trifling temporary production, made for the occasion of a day, and to perish with it, in return for your immortal work. But our exchange resembles the politics of the times. You send out solid wealth, the accumulation of ages, and in return you get a few flying leaves of poor American paper. However, you have the mercantile comfort of finding the balance of trade infinitely in your favor; and I console myself with the snug consideration of uninformed natural acuteness, that I have my warehouse full of goods at another's expense.

Adieu, sir: continue to instruct the world; and whilst we carry on a poor unequal conflict with the passions and prejudices of our day, perhaps with no better weapons than other prejudices and passions of our own, convey wisdom at our expense to future generations.

XVII.—VISIT OF DR. ROBERTSON TO LONDON—HIS CONTEMPLATED HISTORY OF KING WILLIAM.

Horace Walpole to Rev. Wm. Mason.

1778.

The purport of Dr. Robertson's visit was to inquire where he could find materials for the reigns of King William and Queen Anne, which he means to write as a supplement to David Hume. I had heard of his purpose, but did not own I knew it, that the discouragement might seem the more natural. I do not care a straw what he writes about the Church's wet-nurse, Goody Anne, but no Scot is worthy of being the historian of William, but Dr. Watson.*

When he told me his object, I said: "Write the reign of King William, Dr. Robertson! That is a great task! I look

* Historian of Philip the Second of Spain.

on him as the greatest man of modern times, since his ancestor, Prince William of Orange." I soon found the Doctor had very little idea of him, or had taken upon trust the pitiful partialities of Dalrymple and Macpherson. I said: "Sir, I do not doubt but that King William came over with a view to the crown; nor was he called upon by patriotism, for he was not an Englishman, to assert our liberties. No, his patriotism was of a higher rank. He aimed not at the crown of England from ambition, but to employ its forces and wealth against Louis the Fourteenth, for the common cause of the liberties of Europe. The Whigs did not understand the extent of his views, and the Tories betrayed him. He has been thought not to have understood us; but the truth was, he took either party as it was predominant, that he might sway the Parliament to support his general plan." The Doctor, suspecting I doubted his principles being enlarged enough to do justice to so great a character, told me he himself had been born and bred a Whig, though he owned he was now a moderate one—I believe a very moderate one. I said Macpherson had done great injustice to another hero, the Duke of Marlborough, whom he accuses of betraying the design on Brest to Louis the Fourteenth. The truth was, as I heard often in my youth from my father, my uncle, and old persons who had lived in those times, that the Duke trusted the Duchess with the secret, and she her sister, the Popish Duchess of Tyrconnell, who was as poor and as bigoted as a church mouse. A corroboration of this was the wise and sententious answer of King William to the Duke, whom he taxed with having betrayed the secret. "Upon my honor, sir," said the Duke, "I told it to nobody but my wife." "I did not tell it to mine," said the King.

I added, that Dalrymple's and Macpherson's invidious scandals really serve but to heighten the amazing greatness of the King's genius; for, if they say true, he maintained the crown on his head, though the nobility, the Churchmen, the country gentlemen, were against him; and though almost all his own ministers betrayed him. "But," said I, "nothing is so silly as to suppose that the Duke of Marlborough and Lord Godolphin ever meant seriously to restore King James. Both had offended him too much to expect forgiveness, especially from so remorseless a nature. Yet a re-revolution was so probable, that it is no wonder they kept up a correspondence with him, at least to break their fall if he returned. But as they never did effectuate the least service in his favor when they had the fullest power, nothing can be inferred but King James's folly in continuing to lean on them. To imagine they meant to sacrifice his weak daughter, whom they governed absolutely, to a man who was sure of being governed by others, one must have as little sense as James himself had."

The precise truth I take to be this: Marlborough and Godolphin both knew the meanness and credulity of James's character. They knew that he must be ever dealing for partisans; and they might be sure, if he could hope for support from the General and the Lord Treasurer, he must be less solicitous for mere impotent supporters. "Is it impossible," said I to the Doctor, "but they might correspond with the King, even by Anne's own consent? Do not be surprised, sir," said I, "such things have happened. My own father often received letters from the Pretender, which he carried to George the Second, and had them endorsed by his Majesty. I myself have seen them countersigned by the King's own hand."

In short, I endeavored to impress him with proper ideas of

his subject, and painted to him the difficulties, and the want of materials. But the booksellers will out-argue me, and the Doctor will forget his education. *Panem et circenses*, if you will allow me to use the latter for those who are captivated by favor in the *circle*, will decide his writing and give the color. I once wished he should write the History of King William, but his Charles the Fifth, and his America, have opened my eyes, and the times have shut his. Adieu.

XVIII.—DAY WITH MR. BURKE.—CONVERSATION, ETC.

Miss Burney to Samuel Crisp, Chesington.

My dear Mr. Crisp: At the Knight of Plympton's house, on Richmond Hill, next to the Star and Garter, we were met by the Bishop of St. Asaph, who stands as high in general esteem for agreeability as for worth and learning; and by his accomplished and spirited daughter, Miss Shipley. My father was already acquainted with both; and to both I was introduced by Miss Palmer.

No other company was mentioned; but some smiling whispers passed between Sir Joshua, Miss Palmer, and my father, that awakened in me a notion that the party was not yet complete; and with that notion, an idea that Mr. Burke might be the awaited chief of the assemblage; for, as they knew I had long had as much eagerness to see Mr. Burke, as I had fears of meeting his expectations, I thought they might forbear naming him, to save me a fit of fright.

Sir Joshua, who, though full of kindness, dearly loves a little innocent malice, drew me soon afterwards to a window to look at the beautiful prospect below ; the soft meandering of the Thames, and the brightly picturesque situation of the elegant white house which Horace Walpole had made the habitation of Lady Diana Beauclerk and her fair progeny ; in order to gather, as he afterwards laughingly acknowledged, my sentiments of the view, that he might compare them with those of Mr. Burke on the same scene. However, I escaped, luckily, falling, through ignorance, into such a competition, by the entrance of a large, though unannounced, party in a mass. For, as this was only a visit of a day, there were very few servants ; and those few, I suppose, were preparing the dinner apartment, for this group appeared to have found its own way up to the drawing-room with an easiness as well suited to its humor, by the gay air of its approach, as to that of Sir Joshua, who holds ceremony almost in horror, and who received them without any form or apology.

He quitted me, however, to go forward and greet with distinction a lady who was in the set. They were all familiarly recognized by the Bishop and Miss Shipley, as well as by Miss Palmer ; and some of them by my father, whose own face wore an expression of pleasure, that helped to fix a conjecture in my mind that one among them, whom I peculiarly signalized, tall, and of fine deportment, with an air of courtesy and command, might be Edmund Burke.

Excited as I felt by this idea, I continued at my picturesque window, as all the company were strangers to me, till Miss Palmer gave her hand to the tall, suspected, but unknown personage, saying, in a half whisper, " Have I kept my promise at last? " and then, but in a lower tone still, and pointing to the window, she pronounced " Miss Burney."

As this seemed intended for private information, previously

to an introduction, be the person whom he might, though accidentally it was overheard, I instantly bent my head out of the window, as if not attending to them. Yet I caught, unavoidably, the answer, which was uttered in a voice most emphatic, though low, "Why did you tell me it was Miss Burney? Did you think I should not have known it?"

An awkward feeling now, from having still no certainty of my surmise, or of what it might produce, made me seize a spy-glass and set about re-examining the prospect, till a pat on my arm soon after, by Miss Palmer, turned me round to the company, just as the still unknown, to my great regret, was going out of the room with a footman, who seemed to call him away upon some sudden summons of business. But my father, who was at Miss Palmer's elbow, said, "Fanny, Mr. Gibbon!" This, too, was a great name; but of how different a figure and presentation! Fat and ill-constructed, Mr. Gibbon has cheeks of such prodigious chubbiness that they envelop his nose so completely as to render it, in profile, absolutely invisible. His look and manner are placidly mild, but rather effeminate; his voice—for he was speaking to Sir Joshua at a little distance—is gentle, but of studied precision of accent. Yet, with these Brobdignatious cheeks, his neat little feet are of a miniature description; and with these, as soon as I turned round, he hastily described a quaint sort of circle, with small quick steps, and a dapper gait, as if to mark the alacrity of his approach, and then stopping short, when full face to me, he made so singularly profound a bow that—though hardly able to keep my gravity—I felt myself blush deeply at its undue, but palpably intended, obsequiousness.

This demonstration, however, over, his sense of politeness, or project of flattery, was satisfied; for he spoke not a word, though his gallant advance seemed to indicate a design of bestowing upon me a little rhetorical touch of a compliment. But, as all eyes in the room were suddenly cast upon us both, it is possible he partook a little himself of the embarrassment he could not but see that he occasioned; and was, therefore, unwilling, or uprepared, to hold forth so publicly upon—he scarcely, perhaps, knew what! for, unless my partial Sir Joshua should just then have poured it into his ears, how little is it likely Mr. Gibbon should have heard of Evelina!

But at this moment, to my great relief, the unknown again appeared; and with a spirit, an air, a deportment that seemed to spread around him the glow of pleasure with which he himself was visibly exhilarated. But speech was there none, for dinner, which I suppose had awaited him, was at the same instant proclaimed; and all the company, in a mixed, quite irregular, and even confused manner, descended, *sans ceremonie*, to the eating parlor.

The unknown, however, catching the arm and the trumpet of Sir Joshua, as they were coming down stairs, murmured something in a rather reproachful tone in the knight's ear; to which Sir Joshua made no audible answer. But when he had placed himself at his table, he called out smilingly, "Come, Miss Burney, will you take a seat next mine?" adding, as if to reward my very alert compliance, "and then, Mr. Burke shall sit on your other side!"

"O no, indeed!" cried the sprightly Miss Shipley, who was also next to Sir Joshua; "I shan't agree to that. Mr. Burke must sit next to me; I won't consent to part with him. So pray come, and sit down quiet, Mr. Burke."

Mr. Burke—for Mr. Burke, Edmund Burke it was—smiled and obeyed.

"I only proposed it to make my peace with Mr. Burke," said Sir Joshua, passively, "by giving him that place, for he has been scolding me all the way down stairs for not having introduced him to Miss Burney; however, I must do it now. Mr. Burke—Miss Burney!"

We both half rose to reciprocate a little salutation, and Mr. Burke said: "I have been complaining to Sir Joshua that he left me wholly to my own sagacity, which, however, did not here deceive me!"

Delightedly as my dear father, who had never before seen Mr. Burke in private society, enjoyed this encounter, I, my dear Mr. Crisp, had a delight in it that transcended all comparison. No expectation that I had formed of Mr. Burke, either from his works, his speeches, his character, or his fame, had anticipated to me such a man as I now met. He appeared, perhaps, at this moment, to the highest possible advantage, in health, vivacity, and spirits. Removed from the impetuous aggravations of party contentions that, at times, by inflaming his passions, seem, momentarily at least, to disorder his character, he was lulled into gentleness by the grateful feelings of prosperity; exhilarated, but not intoxicated, by sudden success, and just risen, after toiling years of failures, disappointments, fire, and fury, to place, affluence, and honors, which were brightly smiling on the zenith of his powers. He looked, indeed, as if he had no wish but to diffuse philanthropy, pleasure, and genial gayety all around.

His figure, when he is not negligent in his carriage, is noble, his air commanding, his address graceful; his voice clear, penetrating, sonorous, and powerful; his language copious, eloquent, and changefully impressive; his manners are attractive; his conversation is past all praise!

You will call me mad, I know; but if I wait till I see another Mr. Burke, for such another fit of ecstasy, I may be long enough in my very sober good senses.

Sir Joshua next made Mrs. Burke greet the new-comer into this select circle, which she did with marked distinction. She appears to be pleasing and sensible, but silent and reserved.

Sir Joshua went through the same introductory etiquette with Mr. Richard Burke, the brother; Mr. William Burke, the cousin; and young Burke, the son of *the* Burke. They all, in different ways, seem lively and agreeable, but at miles and myriads of miles from the towering chief.

How proud should I be to give you a sample of the conversation of Mr. Burke! But the subjects were in general so fleeting, his ideas so full of variety, of gayety, and of matter; and he darted from one of them to another with such rapidity, that the manner, the eye, the air, with which all was pronounced, ought to be separately delineated, to do any justice to the effect that every sentence, nay, that every word, produced upon his admiring hearers and beholders.

Mad again, says my Mr. Crisp; stark, staring mad!

Well, all the better; for "there's pleasure in being mad," as I have heard you quote from Nat Lee, or some other old playwright, "that none but madmen know."

I must not, however, fail to particularize one point of his discourse, because 'tis upon your own favorite hobby, politics; and my father very much admired its candor and frankness.

In speaking of the great Lord Chatham, while he was yet Mr. Pitt, Mr. Burke confessed his Lordship to have been the only person whom he (Mr. Burke) did not name in Parliament without caution. But Lord Chatham, he said, had obtained so preponderating a height of public favor that, though occasionally he could not concur in its enthusiasm, he would not attempt to oppose its cry.

He then, however, positively, nay solemnly, protested that this was the only subject upon which he did not talk with exactly the same openness and sincerity in the House, as at the table.

He bestowed the most liberal praise upon Lord Chatham's second son, the *now* young William Pitt, with whom he is acting; and who had not only, he said, the most truly extraordinary talents, but who appeared to be immediately gifted by nature with the judgment which others acquire by experience.

"Though judgment," he presently added, "is not so rare in youth as is generally supposed, I have commonly observed that those who do not possess it early are apt to miss it late."

But the subject on which he most enlarged and most brightened, was Cardinal Ximenes; which was brought forward accidentally by Miss Shipley.

That young lady, with the pleasure of youthful exultation in a literary honor, proclaimed that she had just received a letter from the famous Dr. Franklin.

Mr. Burke, then, to Miss Shipley's great delight, broke forth into an eulogy of the abilities and character of Dr. Franklin, which he mingled with a history the most striking, yet simple, of his life, and a veneration the most profound for his eminence in science, and his liberal sentiments and skill in politics.

This led him imperceptibly to a dissertation upon the beauty but rarity of great minds sustaining great powers to great old age; illustrating his remarks by historical proofs and biographical anecdotes of antique worthies, till he came to Cardinal

Ximenes, who lived to his ninetieth year. And here he made a pause. He could go, he said, no further. Perfection rested there!

His pause, however, producing only a general silence, that indicated no wish of speech but from himself, he suddenly burst forth again into an oration so glowing, so flowing, so noble, so divinely eloquent, upon the life, conduct, and endowments of this Cardinal, that I felt as if I had never before known what it was to listen. I saw Mr. Burke, and Mr. Burke only. Nothing, no one else, was visible any more than audible. I seemed suddenly organized into a new intellectual existence that was wholly engrossed by one single use of the senses of seeing and hearing, to the total exclusion of every object but of the figure of Mr. Burke, and of every sound but of that of his voice. All else, my dear father alone excepted, appeared but amalgamations of the chairs on which they were seated, and seemed placed around the table merely as furniture.

I cannot pretend to write you such a speech; but such sentences as I can recollect with exactitude, I cannot let pass. "The Cardinal," he said, "gave counsel and admonition to princes and sovereigns with the calm courage and dauntless authority with which he might have given them to his own children; yet to such noble courage he joined a humility still more magnanimous, in never desiring to disprove or to disguise his own lowly origin, but confessing at times, with openness and simplicity, his surprise at the height of the mountain to which, from so deep a valley, he had ascended. And, in the midst of all his greatness, he personally visited the village in which he was born, where he touchingly recognized what remained of his kith and kin."

Next he descanted upon the erudition of this exemplary prelate; his scarce collection of bibles; his unequalled mass of rare manuscripts; his charitable institutions; his learned seminaries; and his stupendous university at Alcala. "Yet so untinged," he continued, "was his scholastic lore with the bigotry of the times, and so untainted with its despotism, that, even in its most forcible acts for securing the press from licentiousness, he had the enlargement of mind to permit the merely ignorant, or merely needy instruments of its abuse, when detected in promulgating profane works, from being involved in their destruction; for though on such occasions he caused the culprits' shops or warehouses to be strictly searched, he let previous notice of his orders be given to the owners, who then privily executed judgment themselves upon the peccant property, while they preserved what was sane, as well as their personal liberty. But, if the misdemeanor was committed a second time, he manfully left the offenders, unaided and unpitied, to its forfeiture."

"To a vigor," Mr. Burke went on, "that seemed never to calculate upon danger, he joined a prudence that seemed never to run a risk. Though often the object of aspersion—as who, conspicuous in the political world, is not?—he always refused to prosecute; he would not even answer his calumniators. He held that all classes had a right to stand for something in public life!" "We," he said, "who are at the head, act; in God's name let those who are at the other end talk! If we are right, we may be content enough with our superiority to teach unprovoked malice its impotence, by leaving it to its own fester." "So elevated, indeed," Mr. Burke continued, "was his disdain of detraction, that instead of suffering it to blight his tranquillity, he taught it to become the spur to his virtues."

Mr. Burke again paused—paused as if overcome by the

warmth of his own emotion of admiration, and presently he gravely protested that the multifarious perfections of Cardinal Ximenes were beyond human delineation.

Soon, however, afterwards, as if fearing he had become too serious, he rose to help himself to some distant fruit, for all this had passed during the dessert, and then, while standing in the noblest attitude, and with a sudden smile full of radiant ideas, he vivaciously exclaimed: "No imagination—not even the imagination of Miss Burney—could have invented a character so extraordinary as that of Cardinal Ximenes; no pen—not even the pen of Miss Burney!—could have described it adequately!"

Think of me, my dear Mr. Crisp, at a climax so unexpected! my eyes at the moment being openly riveted upon him; my head bent forward with excess of eagerness; my attention exclusively his own. But now, by this sudden turn, I myself became the universally absorbing object; for instantaneously I felt every eye upon my face, and my cheeks tingled as if they were the heated focus of stares that almost burnt them alive.

And yet, you will laugh when I tell you that, though thus struck, I had not time to be disconcerted. The whole was momentary; 'twas like a flash of lightning in the evening, which makes every object of a dazzling brightness for a quarter of an instant, and then leaves all again to a twilight obscurity.

Mr. Burke, by his delicacy as much as by his kindness, reminding me of my opening encouragement from Dr. Johnson, looked now everywhere rather than at me, as if he had made the allusion by mere chance; and flew from it with a velocity that quickly drew back to himself the eyes which he had transitorily employed to see how his superb compliment was taken; though not before I had caught from kind Sir Joshua a look of congratulatory sportiveness, conveyed by a comic nod. My dear Mr. Crisp will be the last to want to be told that I received this speech as the mere effervescence of chivalrous gallantry in Mr. Burke; yet, to be its object, even in pleasantry—oh! my dear Mr. Crisp, how could I have foreseen such a distinction? My dear father's eyes glistened; I wish you could have had a glimpse of him.

"There has been," Mr. Burke then smilingly resumed, "an age for all excellence; we have had an age for statesmen, an age for heroes, an age for poets, an age for artists; but this," bowing down with an air of obsequious gallantry, his head almost upon the table-cloth, "this is the age for women."

"A very happy modern improvement!" cried Sir Joshua, laughing, "don't you think so, Miss Burney? But that's not a fair question to put to you; so we won't make a point of your answering it. However," continued the dear, natural knight, "what Mr. Burke says is very true now. The women begin to make a figure in every thing; though I remember, when I first came into the world, it was thought but a poor compliment to say a person did any thing like a lady."

"Ay, Sir Joshua," cried my father, "but, like Molière's physician, *nous avons changê tout cela!*"

"Very true, Dr. Burney," replied the Knight, "but I remember the time—and so, I dare say, do you—when it was thought a slight, if not a sneer, to speak any thing of a lady's performance; it was only in mockery to talk of painting like a lady, singing like a lady, playing like a lady."

"But now," interrupted Mr. Burke, warmly, "to talk of writing like a lady is the greatest compliment that need be wished for by a man."

Would you believe it, my daddy, everybody now—myself and my father excepted—turned about, Sir Joshua leading the way, to make a little playful bow to—can you ever guess to whom?

Mr. Burke then, archly shrugging his shoulders, added: "What is left now, exclusively, for *us*, and what we are to devise in our defence, I know not. We seem to have nothing for it but assuming a sovereign contempt, for the next most dignified thing to possessing merit is an heroic barbarism in despising it."

I can recollect nothing else; so adieu!

One word more, by way of my last speech and confession on this subject: Should you demand, now that I have seen, in their own social circles, the two first men of letters of our day, how, in one word, I should discriminate them, I answer that I think Dr. Johnson the first discourser, and Mr. Burke the first converser, of the British empire. FANNY BURNEY.

XIX.—DR. JOHNSON—LORD MONBODDO.

Hannah More to her Sister.

LONDON, 1782.

Thursday I spent the evening at the Bishop of Llandaff's. Mrs. Barrington is so perfectly well bred, and the Bishop so delightful, that it is impossible not to be happy in their company. Mitred Chester and all the favorites were there. Good Friday I went to hear the Bishop of Llandaff preach; he is extremely sensible and deeply serious. Mrs. Carter and I met at a little breakfast party with a French lady who writes metaphysical books. We got into great disgrace for saying that a little common sense and a little Scripture would lead one much further and safer than volumes of metaphysics. She forgave us, however, on condition that we would promise to read two huge quartos which she had just translated. What Mrs. Carter will do I know not, but I certainly never shall fulfil my part of the compact. It is a terrible fetter upon the liberty of free-born English conversation, to have so many foreigners as this town now abounds with, imposing their language upon us.

It has affected me very much to hear of our King's being obliged to part with all his confidential friends, and his own personal servants, in the late general sweep. Out of a hundred stories I will only tell you one, which concerns your old acquaintance, Lord Bateman; he went to the King, as usual, overnight, to ask if his Majesty would please to hunt the next day. "Yes, my Lord," replied the King, "but I find with great grief that I am not to have the satisfaction of your company." This was the first intimation he had had of the loss of his place; and I really think the contest with France and America might have been settled, though the buck-hounds retained their old master.

I dined very pleasantly one day last week at the Bishop of Chester's. Johnson was there, and the Bishop was very desirous to draw him out, as he wished to show him off to some of the company who had never seen him. He begged me to sit next him at dinner, and to devote myself to making him talk. To this end I consented to talk more than became me, and our stratagem succeeded. You would have enjoyed seeing him take me by the hand in the middle of dinner and repeat, with no small enthusiasm, many passages from the "Fair Penitent," etc. I urged him to take a little wine; he replied: "I can't drink a little, child, therefore I never touch it. Abstinence is as easy to me as temperance would be difficult." He was very good-humored and gay. One of the company happened to say a word about poetry. "Hush, hush," said he, "it is dangerous to say a word of poetry before her; it is talking of the art of war before Hannibal." He continued his jokes, and lamented that I had not married Chatterton, that posterity might have seen a propagation of poets.

The metaphysical and philological Lord Monboddo breakfasted with us yesterday; he is such an extravagant adorer of the ancients, that he scarcely allows the English language to be capable of any excellency, still less the French. He has a hearty contempt for that people and their language; he said we moderns are entirely degenerated. I asked in what. "In every thing," was his reply. "Men are not so tall as they were, women are not so handsome as they were, nobody can now write a long period, every thing dwindles." I ventured to say that, though long periods were fine in oratory and declamation, yet that such was not the language of passion. He insisted that it was. I defended my opinion by many passages from Shakspeare—among others, those broken bursts of passion in Constance: "Gone to be married!"—"Gone to swear a truce!"—"False blood with false blood joined!" Again, "My name is Constance! I am Geoffrey's wife—young Arthur is my son, and he is slain!"

We then resumed our old quarrel about the slave-trade: he loves slavery upon principle. I asked him how he could vindicate such an enormity. He owned it was because Plutarch justified it. Among much just thinking and some taste, especially in his valuable third volume on the "Origin and Progress of Language," he entertains some opinions so absurd, that they would be hardly credible if he did not deliver them himself, both in writing and conversation, with a gravity which shows that he is in earnest, but which makes the hearer feel that to be grave exceeds all power of face. He is so wedded to system that, as Lord Barrington said to me the other day, rather than sacrifice his favorite opinion that men were born with tails, he would be contented to wear one himself.

XX.—LIFE AT LAUSANNE.

Edward Gibbon to Mrs. Partens.

LAUSANNE, December 27th, 1783.

* * * From this base subject I descend to one which more strongly and seriously engages your thoughts, the consideration of my health and happiness. And you will give me credit when I assure you with sincerity, that I have not repented a single moment of the step I have taken, and that I only regret the not having executed the same design two, or five, or even ten years ago. By this time I might have returned independent and rich to my native country; I should have escaped many disagreeable events that have happened in the meanwhile, and I should have avoided the parliamentary life which experience has proved to be neither suitable to my temper nor conducive to my fortune. In speaking of the happiness I enjoy, you will agree with me in giving the preference to a sincere and sensible friend; and though you cannot discern the full extent of his merit, you will easily believe that Deyverdun is the man. Perhaps two persons so perfectly fitted to live together, were never formed by nature and education. We have both read and seen a great variety of objects; the lights and shades of our different characters are

happily blended, and a friendship of thirty years has taught us to enjoy our mutual advantages, and to support our unavoidable imperfections. In love and marriage some harsh sounds will sometimes interrupt the harmony, and in the course of time, like our neighbors, we must expect some disagreeable moments; but confidence and freedom are the two pillars of our union, and I am much mistaken if the building be not solid and comfortable. One disappointment I have indeed experienced, and patiently supported. The family who were settled in Deyverdun's house started some unexpected difficulties, and will not leave it till the spring, so that you must not yet expect any poetical or even historical description of the beauties of my habitation. During the dull months of winter we are satisfied with a very comfortable apartment in the middle of the town, and even derive some advantage from this delay, as it gives us time to arrange some plans of alteration and furniture, which will embellish our future and more elegant dwelling. In this season I rise (not at four in the morning), but a little before eight; at nine I am called from my study to breakfast, which I always perform alone in the English style; and with the aid of Caplin, I perceive no difference between Lausanne and Bentinck street. Our mornings are usually passed in separate studies; we never approach each other's door without a previous message, or thrice knocking, and my apartment is already sacred and formidable to strangers. I dress at half-past one, and at two (an early hour, to which I am not perfectly reconciled) we sit down to dinner. We have hired a female cook, well-skilled in her profession, and accustomed to the taste of every nation; as, for instance, we had excellent mince-pie yesterday. After dinner, and the departure of our company, one, two, or three friends, we read together some amusing book, or play at chess, or retire to our rooms, or make visits, or go to the coffee-house. Between six and seven the assemblies begin, and I am oppressed only with their number and variety. Whist at shillings or half-crowns is the game I generally play, and I play three rubbers with pleasure. Between nine and ten we withdraw to our bread and cheese, and friendly converse, which sends us to bed at eleven; but these sober hours are too often interrupted by private or numerous suppers, which I have not the courage to resist, though I practise a laudable abstinence at the best-furnished tables. Such is the skeleton of my life; it is impossible to communicate a perfect idea of the vital and substantial parts, the characters of the men and women with whom I have very easily connected myself in looser and closer bonds, according to their inclination and my own. If I do not deceive myself, and if Deyverdun does not flatter me, I am a general favorite; and as our likings and dislikes are commonly mutual, I am equally satisfied with the freedom and elegance of manners, and (after proper allowances and exceptions) with the worthy and amiable qualities of many individuals. The autumn has been beautiful, and the winter hitherto mild, but in January we must expect some severe frost. Instead of rolling in a coach, I walk the streets, wrapped up in a fur cloak; but this exercise is wholesome, and, except an accidental fit of the gout for a few days, I never enjoyed better health. I am no longer in Pavillard's house, where I was almost starved with cold and hunger, and you may be assured that I now enjoy every benefit of comfort, plenty, and even decent luxury. You wish me happy; acknowledge that such a life is more conducive to happiness than five nights in the week passed in the House of Commons, or five mornings spent at the Custom House. Send me in return a fair account of your own situation in mind and body. I am satisfied your own good sense would have reconciled you to inevitable separation; but there never was a more suitable diversion than your visit to Sheffield Place. Among the innumerable proofs of friendship I have received from that family, there are none which affect me more sensibly than their kind civilities to you. Though I am persuaded they are at least as much on your own account as on mine. * * *

XXI.—VISIT TO THE RESIDENCE OF MILTON.

Sir William Jones to Lady Spencer.

September 7th, 1769.

MADAM: The necessary trouble of correcting the first sheets of my History,* prevented me to-day from paying respect to the memory of Shakspeare, by attending his jubilee. But I was resolved to do all the honor in my power to as great a poet; and I set out in the morning, in company with a friend, to visit a place where Milton spent some part of his life, and where, in all probability, he composed several of his earliest productions. It is a small village, situated on a pleasant hill, about three miles from Oxford, called Forest Hill, because it formerly lay contiguous to a forest, which has since been cut down. The poet chose this place of retirement after his first marriage, and he describes the beauties of his retreat in that fine passage of his "L'Allegro":

"Sometimes walking, not unseen,
By hedge-row elms on hillocks green,
* * * * *

* His translation, from the Persian, of the Life of Nidar Shah.

When the ploughman, near at hand,
Whistles o'er the furrowed land,
And the milkmaid singeth blithe,
And the mower whets his sithe;
And ev'ry shepherd tells his tale,
Under the hawthorne in the dale.
Straight mine eye hath caught new pleasures,
Whilst the landscape round it measures
Russet lawns and fallows gray,
Where the nibbling flocks do stray;
Mountains, on whose barren breast
The lab'ring clouds do often rest;
Meadows trim, with daisies pied;
Shallow brooks, and rivers wide;
Towers and battlements it sees,
Bosom'd high in tufted trees.
* * * * *
Hard by, a cottage-chimney smokes
From betwixt two aged oaks," &c.

It was neither the proper season of the year nor the time of the day to hear all the rural sounds, and to see all the objects mentioned in this description; but, by a pleasing concurrence of circumstances, we were saluted, on our approach to the village, with the mower and his sithe; we saw the ploughman intent upon his labor, and the milkmaid returning from her country employment.

As we ascended the hill, the variety of beautiful objects, the agreeable stillness and natural simplicity of the whole scene, gave us the highest pleasure. At length we reached the spot whence Milton, undoubtedly, took most of his images; it is on the top of the hill, from which there is a most extensive prospect on all sides. The distant mountains that seemed to support the clouds; the villages and turrets, partly shaded with trees of the finest verdure, and partly raised above the groves that surrounded them; the dark plains and meadows of a grayish color, where the sheep were feeding at large; in short, the view of the streams and rivers, convinced us that there was not a single useless or idle word in the above-mentioned description; but that it was a most exact and lively representation of nature. Thus will this fine passage, which has always been admired for its elegance, receive an additional beauty for its exactness. After we had walked, with a kind of poetical enthusiasm, over this enchanted ground, we returned to the village.

The poet's house was close to the church; the greatest part of it has been pulled down, and what remains belongs to an adjacent farm. I am informed that several papers, in Milton's own hand, were found by the gentleman who was last in possession of the estate. The tradition of his having lived there is current among the villagers; one of them showed us a ruinous wall that made part of his chamber; and I was much pleased with another, who had forgotten the name of Milton, but recollected him by the title of "The Poet."

It must not be omitted that the groves near this village are famous for nightingales, which are so elegantly described in "Il Penseroso." Most of the cottage-windows are overgrown with sweetbriers, vines, and honeysuckles: and that Milton's habitation had the same rustic ornament, we may conclude from his description of the lark bidding him good-morrow:

> Through the sweet-brier, or the vine,
> Or the twisted eglantine;

for it is evident that he meant a sort of honeysuckle by the eglantine, though that word is commonly used for the sweet-brier, which he could not mention twice in the same couplet.

If I ever pass a month or six weeks at Oxford in the summer, I shall be inclined to hire and repair this venerable mansion, and to make a festival for a circle of friends in honor of Milton, the greatest scholar, as well as the sublimest poet, that our country ever produced. Such an honor will be less splendid, but more sincere and respectful, than all the pomp and ceremony on the banks of the Avon.

I have the honor to be, etc., WILLIAM JONES.

XXII.—REMINISCENCES OF FRANKLIN.

Thomas Jefferson to Dr. Smith.

PHILADELPHIA, February 19th, 1791.

DEAR SIR: I feel both the wish and the duty to communicate, in compliance with your request, whatever, within my knowledge, might render justice to the memory of our great countryman, Dr. Franklin, in whom philosophy has to deplore one of its principal luminaries extinguished. But my opportunities of knowing the interesting facts of his life have not been equal to my desire of making them known. I could, indeed, relate a number of those bon mots with which he used to charm every society, as having heard many of them. But these are not your object. Particulars of greater dignity happened not to occur during his stay of nine months, after my arrival in France.

A little before that, Argand had invented his celebrated lamp, in which the flame is spread into a hollow cylinder, and thus brought into contact with the air within as well as without.

Dr. Franklin had been on the point of the same discovery. The idea had occurred to him; but he had tried a bulrush as a wick, which did not succeed. His occupations did not permit him to repeat and extend his trials to the introduction of a larger column of air than could pass through the stem of a bulrush.

The animal magnetism, too, of the maniac Mesmer had just received its death-wound from his hand, in conjunction with his brethren of the learned committee appointed to unveil that compound of fraud and folly. But, after this, nothing very interesting was before the public, either in philosophy or politics, during his stay; and he was principally occupied in winding up his affairs there.

I can only therefore testify, in general, that there appeared to me more respect and veneration attached to the character of Doctor Franklin in France, than to that of any other person of the same country, foreign or native. I had opportunities of knowing how far these sentiments were felt by the foreign ambassadors and ministers at the court of Versailles. The fable of his capture by the Algerines, propagated by the English newspapers, excited no uneasiness, as it was seen at once to be a dish cooked up to the palate of the readers. But nothing could exceed the anxiety of his diplomatic brethren on a subsequent report of his death, which, though premature, bore some marks of authenticity.

I found the ministers of France equally impressed with the talents and integrity of Dr. Franklin. The Count de Vergennes particularly gave me repeated and unequivocal demonstrations of his entire confidence in him.

When he left Passy, it seemed as if the village had lost its patriarch. On taking leave of the court, which he did by letter, the King ordered him to be handsomely complimented, and furnished him with a litter and mules of his own, the only kind of conveyance the state of his health could bear.

No greater proof of his estimation in France can be given than the late letters of condolence on his death, from the National Assembly of that country, and the community of Paris, to the President of the United States and to Congress, and their public mournings on that event. It is, I believe, the first instance of that homage having been paid by a public body of one nation to a private citizen of another.

His death was an affliction which was to happen to us at some time or other. We have reason to be thankful he was so long spared; that the most useful life should be the longest also; that it was protracted so far beyond the ordinary span allotted to man, as to avail us of his wisdom in the establishment of our freedom, and to bless him with a view of its dawn in the east, where they seemed, till now, to have learned every thing but how to be free.

The succession to Dr. Franklin, at the court of France, was an excellent school of humility. On being presented to any one as the minister of America, the commonplace question used in such cases was, "C'est vous, monsieur, qui remplace le Docteur Franklin?" "It is you, sir, who replace Doctor Franklin?" I generally answered, "No one can replace him, sir: I am only his successor."

These small offerings to the memory of our great and dear friend, whom time will be making greater while it is sponging us from its records, must be accepted by you, sir, in that spirit of love and veneration for him, in which they are made; and not according to their insignificance in the eyes of a world, who did not want this mite to fill up the measure of his worth.

I pray you to accept, in addition, assurances of the sincere esteem and respect with which I have the honor to be, sir, your most obedient and most humble servant.

XXIII.—CRITICISM ON GARRICK IN HAMLET.

Hannah More to her Sister.

ADELPHI, 1776.

I imagine my last was not so ambiguous but that you saw well enough I stayed in town to see Hamlet, and I will venture to say that it was such an entertainment as will probably never again be exhibited to an admiring world. But this general panegyric can give you no idea of *my* feelings; and particular praise would be injurious to his excellences.

In every part he filled the whole soul of the spectator, and transcended the most finished idea of the poet. The requisites for Hamlet are not only various but opposed. In him they are all united, and, as it were, concentrated. One thing I must particularly remark, that, whether in the simulation of madness, in the sinking of despair, in the familiarity of friendship, in the whirlwind of passion, or in the meltings of tenderness, he never once forgot he was a prince; and in every variety of situation and transition of feeling, you discovered the highest polish of fine breeding and courtly manners.

Hamlet experiences the conflict of many passions and affections, but filial love ever takes the lead; *that* is the great point, from which he sets out, and to which he returns; the others are all contingent and subordinate to it, and are cherished or renounced, as they promote or obstruct the operations of this leading principle. Had you seen with what exquisite art and skill

Garrick maintained the subserviency of the less to the greater interests, you would agree with me, of what importance to the perfection of acting is that consummate good sense which always pervades every part of his performances.

To the most eloquent expression of the eye, to the handwriting of the passions on his features, to a sensibility which tears to pieces the hearts of his auditors—to powers so unparalleled, he adds a judgment of the most exquisite accuracy, the fruit of long experience and close observation, by which he preserves every gradation and transition of the passions, keeping all under the control of a just dependence and natural consistency. So naturally, indeed, do the ideas of the poet seem to mix with his own, that he seemed himself to be engaged in a succession of affecting situations; not giving utterance to a speech, but to the instantaneous expressions of his feelings, delivered in the most affecting tones of voice, and with gestures that belong only to nature. It was a fiction as delightful as fancy, and as touching as truth. A few nights before I saw him in "Abel Drugger," and had I not seen him in both, I should have thought it as possible for Milton to have written "Hudibras," and Butler "Paradise Lost," as for one man to have played "Hamlet" and "Drugger" with such excellence. I found myself not only in the best place, but with the best company in the house, for I sat next the orchestra, in which were a number of my acquaintance (and those no vulgar names), Edmund and Richard Burke, Dr. Warton, and Sheridan.

Have you seen an ode to Mr. Pinchbeck, by the author of the "Heroic Epistle"? There is a little slight sarcasm on Cumberland, the Dean of Gloucester, and Dr. Johnson. There is something of wit in it, but I think it is by no means worthy of the author of the "Heroic Epistle," which is, in my opinion, the best satire, both for matter and versification, that has appeared since the "Dunciad." I do not include Johnson's two admirable imitations of "Juvenal," which are more in the manner of Pope's other satires.

XXIV.—ORIGIN OF "SCOTS WHA HAE WI' WALLACE BLED."

Robert Burns to Mr. Thompson.

Sept., 1793.

You may readily trust, my dear sir, that any exertion in my power is heartily at your service. But one thing I must hint to you: the very name of Peter Pindar is of great service to your publication, so get a verse from him now and then, though I have no objection as well as I can to bear the burden of the business. You know that my pretensions to musical taste are merely a few of Nature's instincts, untaught and untutored by art. For this reason many musical compositions, particularly where much of the merit lies in counterpoint, however they may transport and ravish the ears of your connoisseurs, affect my simple lug no otherwise than melodious din. On the other hand, by way of amends, I am delighted with many little melodies, which the learned musician despises as silly and insipid. I do not know whether the old air "Hey tuttie taitie," may rank among this number, but well I know that, with Fraser's hautboy, it has often filled my eye with tears. There is a tradition which I have met with in many places of Scotland, that it was Robert Bruce's march at the battle of Bannockburn. This thought in my solitary wanderings, warmed me to a pitch of enthusiasm on the theme of liberty and independence, which I threw into a kind of Scottish ode, fitted to the air, that one might suppose to be the gallant Royal Scot's address to his heroic followers on that eventful morning.

"Scots wha hae wi' Wallace bled," etc.*

So may God ever defend the cause of truth and liberty as he did that day! Amen.

P. S. I showed the air to Urbani, who was highly pleased with it, and begged me to make soft verses for it; but I had no idea of giving myself any trouble on the subject, till the accidental recollection of that glorious struggle for freedom, *associated with the glowing ideas of some other struggles of the same nature, not quite so ancient*, roused my rhyming mania. Clark's set of the tune, with his bass, you will find in the museum, though I am afraid that the air is not what will entitle it to a place in your elegant selection.

* This noble lyric was conceived by the poet during a storm, among the wilds of Glenken in Galloway. The first two stanzas, as they stood in the poet's manuscript, were suppressed by the advice of some critical friends. As they are not found in many editions, they are reproduced here:

"At Bannockburn the English lay;
The Scots they wer na far away,
But waited for the break of day
That glinted in the east.

"But the sun broke through the heath,
And lighted up that field of death;
When Bruce wi' saul-inspiring breath
His heralds thus addressed:
'Scots, wha hae,'" etc.

XXV.—AN INTERVIEW WITH HERSCHEL, THE ASTRONOMER.

Thomas Campbell to ———

September 15th, 1813.

I wish you had been with me the day before yesterday, when you would have joined me I am sure deeply, in admiring a great, simple, good old man, Dr. Herschel. Do not think me vain, or at least put up with my vanity, in saying that I almost flatter myself I have made him my friend. I have an invitation, and a pressing one, to go to his house; and the lady who introduced me to him, says he spoke of me as if he would be really happy to see me. I spent all Sunday with him and his family. His son is a prodigy in science, and fond of poetry, but very unassuming.

Now for the old astronomer himself. His simplicity, his kindness, his anecdotes, his readiness to explain, and make perfectly conspicuous, too, his own sublime conceptions of the universe, are indescribably charming. He is seventy-six, but fresh and stout; and there he sat nearest to the door, at his friend's house, alternately smiling at a joke, or contentedly sitting without share or notice in the conversation. Any train of conversation he follows implicitly; any thing you ask, he labors with a sort of boyish earnestness to explain.

I was anxious to get from him as many particulars as I could about his interview with Buonaparte. The latter, it was reported, had astonished him by his astronomical knowledge. "No," he said, "the First Consul did surprise me by his quickness and versatility on all subjects; but in science he seemed to know little more than any well-educated gentleman; and of astronomy much less, for instance, than our own King. His general air was something like affecting to know more than he did know." He was high, and tried to be great with Herschel, I suppose, without success. "And I remarked," said the astronomer, "his hypocrisy in concluding the conversation on astronomy by observing how all these glorious views gave proofs of an Almighty wisdom." I asked him if he thought the system of La Place to be quite certain with regard to the total security of the planetary system, from the effects of gravitation losing its present balance. He said, "No; he thought by no means that the universe was secured from the chance of sudden losses of parts." He was convinced that there had existed a planet between Mars and Jupiter, in our own system, of which the little Asteroids, or planetkins lately discovered, are indubitably fragments; and "Remember," said he, "that though they have discovered only four of those parts, there will be thousands, perhaps thirty thousand more yet discovered." This planet he believed to have been lost by explosion.*

With great kindness and patience he referred me, in the course of my attempts to talk with him, to a theorem in Newton's "Principles of Natural Philosophy," in which the time that light takes to travel from the sun is proved with a simplicity which requires but a few steps in reasoning. In talking of some inconceivably distant bodies, he introduced the mention of this plain theorem, to remind me that the progress of light could be measured in the one case as well as the other. Then, speaking of himself, he said, with a modesty of manner which quite overcame me, when taken together with the greatness of the

* Dr. Beattie states that the opinion here attributed to Herschel, as to the number of fragments of the destroyed planet, was never advanced except as an hypothesis, having some probability.

assertion, "*I have looked farther into space than ever human being did before me.* I have observed stars of which the light, it can be proved, must take two millions of years to reach this earth!" I really and unfeignedly felt at the moment as if I had been conversing with a supernatural intelligence. "Nay, more," said he, "if those distant bodies had ceased to exist two millions of years ago, we should still see them, as the light would travel after the body was gone." * * * * These were Herschel's words; and if you had heard him speak them, you would not think he was apt to tell more than truth.

After leaving Herschel, I felt elevated and overcome; and have, in writing to you, made only the memorandum of the most interesting moments of my life. T. C.

XXVI.—THE PASSION OF FEAR.

Sir Walter Scott to Miss Joanna Baillie.

My dear Friend: * * * It is too little to say I am enchanted with the said third volume, especially with the first two plays, which in every point not only sustain, but even exalt, your reputation as a dramatist. The whole character of Orra is exquisitely supported as well as imagined, and the language distinguished by a rich variety of fancy which I know no instance of excepting in Shakspeare. After I had read Orra twice to myself, Jerry read it over to us a third time aloud, and I have seldom seen a little circle so much affected as during the whole fifth act. I think it would act charmingly, omitting, perhaps, the baying of the hounds, which could not be happily imitated, and retaining only the blast of the horn and the halloo of the huntsman at a distance. Only I doubt if we have now an actress that could carry through the mad scene in the fifth act, which is certainly one of the most sublime that ever was written. Yet I have a great quarrel with this beautiful drama, for you must know you have utterly destroyed a song of mine, precisely in the turn of your outlaw's ditty, and sung by persons in somewhat the same situation. I took out my unfortunate manuscript to look at it, but, alas! it was the encounter of the iron and the earthen pitchers in the fable. I was clearly sunk, and the potsherds not worth gathering up. But only conceive that the chorus should have run thus verbatim:

> "'Tis mirk midnight with peaceful men,
> With us 'tis dawn of day."

And again:

> "Then boot and saddle, comrades boon,
> Nor wait the dawn of day."

I think the dream extremely powerful indeed, but I am rather glad we did not hazard the representation. It rests so entirely on Osterloo that I am almost sure we must have made a bad piece of work of it. By-the-bye, a story is told of an Italian buffoon who had contrived to give his master, a petty prince of Italy, a good, hearty ducking, and a fright to boot, to cure him of an ague; the treatment succeeded, but the potentate, by way of retaliation, had his audacious physician tried for treason and condemned to lose his head. The criminal was brought forth, the priest heard his confession, and the poor jester knelt down to the block. Instead of wielding his axe, the executioner, as he had been instructed, threw a pitcher of water on the bare neck of the criminal; here the jest was to have terminated, but poor Gonella was found dead on the spot. I believe the catastrophe is very possible. The latter half of the volume I have not perused with the same attention, though I have devoured both the Comedy and the Beacon in a hasty manner. I think the approbation of the public will make you alter your intention of taking up the knitting-needle, and that I shall have as much to seek for my purse as for the bank-notes which you say are to stuff it, though I have no idea where they are to come from. But I shall think more of the purse than the notes, come when or how they may.

To return, I really think fear the most dramatic passion you have hitherto touched, because capable of being drawn to the most extreme paroxysm on the stage. In Orra you have all gradations, from a timidity excited by a strong and irritable imagination, to the extremity which altogether unhinges the understanding. The most dreadful fright I ever had in my life (being neither constitutionally timid, nor in the way of being exposed to real danger) was in returning from Hampstead the day which I spent so pleasantly with you. Although the evening was nearly closed, I foolishly chose to take the short cut through the fields; and in that enclosure, where the path leads close by a thick and high hedge—with several gaps in it, however—did I meet one of your very thorough-paced London ruffians, at least, judging from the squalid and jail-bird appearance, and blackguard expression of countenance. Like the man that met the devil, I had nothing to say to him if he had nothing to say to me; but I could not help looking back to watch the movements of such a suspicious figure, and, to my great uneasiness, saw him creep through the hedge on my left hand. I instantly went to the gap to watch his motions, and saw him stooping, as I thought, either to lift a bundle or to speak to some person who seemed to be lying in the ditch. Immediately after he came cowering back up the opposite side of the hedge, as returning toward me under cover of it. I saw no weapons he had except a stick but as I moved on to gain the stile which was to let me into the free field—with the idea of a wretch springing upon me from the covert at every step I took—I assure you I would not wish the worst enemy I ever had to undergo such a feeling as I had for about five minutes; my fancy made him of that description which usually combines murder with plunder, and though I was well armed with a stout stick and a very formidable knife, which, when open, becomes a sort of *skenedhu* or dagger, I confess my sensations, though those of a man much resolved not to die like a sheep, were vilely short of heroism; so much so, that when I jumped over the stile, a sliver of the wood run a third of an inch between my nail and flesh, without my feeling the pain or being sensible such a thing had happened. However, I saw my man no more, and it is astonishing how my spirits rose when I got into the open field; and when I reached the top of the little mount, and all the bells in London (for aught I know) began to jingle at once, I thought I had never heard any thing so delightful in my life—so rapid are the alternations of our feelings. This foolish story, for perhaps I had no rational grounds for the horrible feeling which possessed my mind for a little while, came irresistibly to my pen when writing to you on this subject of terror.

Poor Graham, gentle and amiable, and enthusiastic, deserves all you can say of him. His was really a hallowed harp, as he was himself an Israelite without guile. How often have I teased him, but never out of his good humor, by praising Dundee and laughing at the Covenanters! but I beg your pardon, you are a Westland Whig too, and will perhaps make less allowance for a descendant of the persecutors. I think his works should be collected and published for the benefit of his family. Surely the wife and orphans of such a man have a claim on the generosity of the public.

Pray make my remembrance to the lady who so kindly remembers our early intimacy. I do perfectly remember being an exceedingly spoiled, chattering monkey, whom indifferent health and the cares of a kind Grandmamma and Aunt had made, I suspect, extremely abominable to everybody who had not a great deal of sympathy and good nature, which I dare say was the case of my quondam bedfellow, since she recollects me so favorably. Farewell, and believe me faithfully and respectfully

Your sincere friend, WALTER SCOTT.

XXVII.—THE LAUREATESHIP.*

Sir Walter Scott to Robert Southey.

EDINBURGH, Nov. 13th, 1813.

I do not delay, my dear Southey, to say my gratulor. Long may you live, as Paddy says, to rule over us, and to redeem the crown of Spenser and of Dryden to its pristine dignity. I am only discontented with the extent of your royal revenue, which I thought had been £400, or £300 at the very least. Is there no

* The Leaureateship, although associated with the glorious names of Ben Jonson and Dryden, had been, prior to this period, degraded in popular estimation by being conferred upon unworthy incumbents. Southey, Wordsworth, and Tennyson have revived the pristine lustre of the office. It is now understood that the Laureate may write only when and what he pleases.—H.

30

getting rid of that ridiculous modus, and requiring the *butt* in kind? I would have you think of it: I know no man so well entitled to Xeres sack as yourself, though many bards would make a better figure at drinking it. I should think that in due time a memorial might get some relief in this part of the appointment—it should be at least £100 wet and £100 dry. When you have carried your point of discarding the ode, and my point of getting the sack, you will be exactly in the situation of Davy in the farce, who stipulates for more wages, less work, and the key of the ale-cellar. I was greatly delighted with the circumstances of your investiture. It reminded me of the porters at Calais with Dr. Smollett's baggage, six of them seizing one small portmanteau and bearing it in triumph to his lodgings. You see what it is to laugh at the superstitions of a gentleman usher, as I think you do somewhere. "The whirligig of time brings about his revenge."

Adieu, my dear Southey; my best wishes attend all that you do, and my best congratulations every good that attends you—yea, even this, the very least of Providence's mercies, as a poor clergyman said when pronouncing grace over a herring. I should like to know how the Prince received you; his address is said to be excellent, and his knowledge of literature far from despicable. What a change of fortune ever since the short time when we met! The great work of retribution is now rolling onward to consummation, yet am I not fully satisfied—*pereat iste*—there will be no permanent peace in Europe till Buonaparte sleeps with the tyrants of old. My best compliments attend Mrs. Southey and your family. Ever yours,

WALTER SCOTT.

XXVIII.—MADAME DU DEFFAND'S LETTERS.

William Roscoe to Miss Berry.

ALLERTON, Dec. 30th, 1810.

DEAR MADAM: It was not possible that your obliging note of the 26th could have arrived at a more welcome moment; in fact, I may almost be said to have passed the last ten or twelve days in your society, for having been confined to the house by indisposition, my chief pleasure has been the perusal of Madam du Deffand's letters, with the notes, together with Lord Orford's correspondence, which, of all the books in our language, is the best calculated for the study of a convalescent, and I really believe is better than most of the physic in the pharmacopœia. On the table before me lay the beginning of a letter, intended to thank you for the four elegant volumes which I some time since received, although I have scarcely, till this interval of leisure, had time to look into them. These letters seem to me to be curious and interesting, but they open the way to other reflections than the author himself was ever aware of. What these are I need not inform you. The judicious and excellent notes which accompany them show that you have considered them in their proper light, and that you are as well aware as I am, that the horrible depravity, selfishness, insincerity, and licentiousness, which, under the example of the French monarchs, had infected all the higher ranks of society, and impoverished and enslaved the nation at large, could have no other result than that which has actually taken place.

As to Madame du Deffand herself, I have some doubts whether we shall so nearly agree. She is a true Frenchwoman, with great penetration and shrewdness, but little discretion; great pretence to sentiment, but wholly without a heart; witness her conduct with respect to Voltaire, whom she professed to esteem and admire above all her other friends, but whose death she has noticed with the utmost indifference, and whose yet warm ashes she insulted with a wretched witticism.

Madame du Deffand was sick in mind all her life, and could never discover the cause. Mr. Walpole, her true friend, seems from time to time to have given her some good advice, which she had the philosophy to take in good part, as a patient receives a bottle of physic, the contents of which he resolves never to swallow. This disease was vanity; her opiate admiration; and as this, like other opiates, requires an increased dose, she became miserable when she could not obtain it. How happy it would have been for her if, instead of depending on the opinion of others, she had relied on herself; chastised her mind; improved her understanding—naturally so capable of it; viewed the present and the future, not through the glass of fashion, but with the eye of reason; and whilst she enjoyed the calm and temperate pleasures which even her situation afforded, have looked forward with hope and confidence to a better state. But retirement was not fashionable; good sense was not fashionable; sincerity was not fashionable; religion was not fashionable, and morality still less so; in short, it was the fashion to turn every thing that is truly estimable in public and private life into ridicule; and Madame du Deffand had the assurance to sing in the presence of the King of Sweden her *Chanson des Philosophes*, little thinking that such outrages on decency were only the dreadful notes of preparation for those horrible calamities which were so shortly to ensue.

It would, however, be unjust to Madame du D. not to acknowledge that the easy and unaffected style of her letters, must insure the approbation of the admirers of the best models of French composition, and that the succession of important personages who pass in review before her, will amuse those who like to contemplate the shadows of fallen greatness.

If I have been pleased with your notes on Madame du Deffand, I am delighted with the favorable opinion you have so kindly expressed of my collection of tracts on the war. In proportion as those who avow such opinions are few, the approbation they express is nearer to the feelings of an author; besides, the ladies of the present day are so warlike, that it is really extraordinary to find one who has retained the clear and unprejudiced use of her understanding amidst the attempts that are made on all hands to confound right and wrong, and to persuade us that no other nations have either a right to think for themselves, or to be happy in their own way.

To talk over these subjects with you, and for once in my life to visit the real "Castle of Ortanto" before I go to meet its late possessor, would, I assure you, give me great pleasure. Lord Orford's character improves upon me every time I read his works. His wit is universally acknowledged; of his political sagacity and foresight he has left many very striking proofs; but, above all, there are so many instances of a kind and beneficent disposition, and such an enlarged and impartial solicitude for the good of others, without the least affectation or pretence, that I cannot but venerate his memory, and in this sentiment find an additional motive of assuring you how truly I am,

Dear Madam, your obliged and faithful friend, and very obedient servant,

W. ROSCOE.

XXIX.—WHAT IS INDELICATE IN A FEMALE AUTHOR?

Joanna Baillie to Miss Berry.

HAMPSTEAD, June 9th, 1828.

MY DEAR FRIEND: The mention of one friend's book naturally tends to another's. I have read your "View of the Social Life, etc.," twice, and it has lost nothing, but rather gained on the second perusal. The style is clear and scholar-like, in the *good* sense of the word; it is written in a good spirit of liberality and rectitude, and it abounds in excellent observations, concisely and cleverly expressed. For my own part I should have liked it better had you given us less of court anecdote, and more of illustration of the manners of the middling classes of society, though I am aware that such illustrations would have been more difficult to come at. There is another thing which I could have wished otherwise, but perhaps the general run of readers may not feel it: the account given of Voltaire's mistress, Madame de Chatelet, rather offends as to that delicacy which is expected in the writings of a woman. The mention, too, of Lady M. W. Montagu's poem on Lady Murray's disagreeable adventure, though very justly reprobated by you, falls a little under the same condemnation; and these I notice because they have been felt by others whose judgment and feelings I respect, though, as I said before, the generality of readers may not see them in the same light. I also mention them because I know you expect my sincere opinion, and the work itself has sufficient merit to afford such exceptions to its praise.

I am expecting every day the publication of my Cingalese drama, the last proof-sheet of which I corrected some days ago —I believe nearly a week. It is a little cockboat to be launched upon a wide ocean, bound on a distant voyage; I hope it will not prove a castaway. I don't know whether you saw it in MS. When we return from Devon, where we shall probably remain two months, I shall be anxious to know what sale it had in Colburn's hands, who is the bookseller to whom Sir A. Johnstone has given it, for the profits of this little work may be of more consequence than itself.

Your friend Miss A. Turner called on me last Saturday, and was very kind in coming, for she knew I was anxious to hear particularly concerning the illness of our poor friend, which could not so well be detailed in a note. What a cheerful, useful person Miss Turner is! She is one of those easy, well-conditioned beings who gathers no thorns in the world for herself, and has both time and inclination to clear them away from the paths of other people. If you are a reader of Jeremy Taylor, perhaps you will recollect a passage where he says: "How many people are busy in this world in gathering together a handful of thorns to sit upon!" I confess myself to be somewhat a gatherer of thorns, and fain would I get the better of this foolish propensity, but I am, as we say in Scotland, o'er auld to mend.

Always affectionately yours,

J. BAILLIE.

XXX.—THE SAME SUBJECT.

Miss Berry to Joanna Baillie.

BADEN, June 19th, 1828.

MY DEAR JOANNA: I am much flattered by your praises of my book, and almost as much by what you blame. Had I professed writing a comparative view of the *manners*, instead of the "*social life*" of England and France, I should have found, and so would you, that the *manners* of the "middling classes of society" in both countries were always a bad imitation of the upper. I must have gone down to the manners of the *people* for any difference, and that would have led me into a larger field of disquisition than I felt myself equal to, and involved discussions out of the pale of my personal knowledge.

On the charge of "offending the delicacy which is expected in the writings of a woman," the two instances marked by you have been passed over by others, who have observed on a note of which you take no notice. I have only to observe that, if women treat of *human* nature and *human* life in *history*, and not in *fiction* (which perhaps they had better not do), human nature and human life are very often indelicate; and if such passages in them are treated always with the gravity and the reprobation they deserve, it is all a reasonable woman can do, and (not writing for children) all she can think necessary.

I shall be very curious to see how you treat a *new world* both of men and things; as it can't be very bulky, if you will order one to be sent to Mrs. Anne Turner, directed to me, she will contrive to send it to me, if any possible opportunity offers. The merits of the said Anne Turner you will only admire the more when I tell you, instead of being blessed with the happy, easy disposition you suppose, hers is a very anxious mind, and therefore she has a double merit in forgetting her own anxieties to soothe those of her friends.

Farewell, dear Joanna. Let me hear from you again in the leisure of the country, and believe me always your

Sincerely attached friend,

M. Berry.

XXXI.—CONSOLATIONS AND PLEASURES OF LITERATURE.

Thomas Hood to the Secretary of the Manchester Athenæum.

ST. JOHNSWOOD, July 18th, 1843. (From my bed.)

If my humble name can be of the least use for your purpose, it is heartily at your service, with my best wishes for the prosperity of the Manchester Athenæum, and my warmest approval of the objects of that institution.

I have elsewhere recorded my own deep obligations to literature: that a natural turn for reading and intellectual pursuits probably preserved me from the moral shipwreck so apt to befall those who are deprived in early life of the paternal pilotage. At the least my books kept me from the ring, the dog-pit, the tavern, the saloon, with their degrading orgies. For the closet associate of Pope and Addison, the mind accustomed to the noble though silent discourse of Shakspeare and Milton, will hardly seek or put up with low company and slang. The reading animal will not be content with the brutish wallowings that satisfy the unlearned pigs of the world.

Later experience enables me to depose to the comfort and blessing that literature can prove in seasons of sickness and sorrow—how powerfully intellectual pursuits can help in keeping the head from crazing, and the heart from breaking—nay, not to be too grave, how generous mental food can even atone for too meagre diet—rich fare on the paper for short commons on the cloth.

Poisoned by the malaria of the Dutch marshes, my stomach for many months resolutely set itself against fish, flesh, or fowl; my appetite had no more edge than the German knife set before me. But luckily the mental palate and digestion were still sensible and vigorous; and whilst I passed untasted every dish at the Rhenish *table d'hôte*, I could yet enjoy my Peregrine Pickle, and the feast after the manner of the ancients. There was no yearning toward calf's head *à la tortue*, or sheep's heart; but I could still relish Head *à la Brunnen*, and the Heart of Mid Lothian.

Still more recently it was my misfortune, with a tolerable appetite, to be condemned to lenten fare, like Sancho Panza, by my physician; to a diet, in fact, lower than any prescribed by the poor-law commissioners, all animal food from a bullock to a rabbit being strictly interdicted; as well as all fluids stronger than that which lays dust, washes pinafores, and waters polyanthus. But "the feast of reason and the flow of soul" were still mine. Denied beef, I had *Bul*wer and *Cow*per*;* forbidden mutton, there was *Lamb;* and in lieu of pork, the great *Bacon* or *Hog*.

Then as to beverage, it was hard doubtless for a Christian to set his face like a Turk against the juice of the grape. But, eschewing wine, I had still my *Butler*, and in the absence of liquor all the *choice spirits* from Tom Browne to Tom Moore.

Thus, though confined physically to the drink that drowns kittens, I quaffed mentally, not merely the best of our own home-made, but the rich, racy, sparkling growths of France and Italy, of Germany and Spain; the champagne of Molière, and the Monte Palciano of Boccaccio; the hock of Schiller, and the sherry of Cervantes. Depressed bodily by the fluid that damps every thing, I got intellectually elevated with Milton, a little merry with Swift, or rather jolly with Rabelais, whose Pantagruel, by the way, is quite equal to the best gruel with rum in it.

So far can literature palliate or compensate for gastronomical privations. But there are other evils, great and small, in this world, which try the stomach less than the head, the heart, and the temper—bowls that will not roll right—well-laid schemes that will "gang aglee," and ill winds that blow with the pertinacity of the monsoon. Of these, Providence has allotted me a full share; but still, paradoxical as it may sound, my *burden* has been greatly lightened by a *load of books*. The manner of this will be best understood from a feline illustration. Everybody has heard of the two Kilkenny cats who devoured each other; but it is not so generally known that they left behind them an orphan kitten, which, true to the breed, began to eat itself up, till it was diverted from the operation by a mouse. Now, the human mind, under vexation, is like that kitten, for it is apt to prey upon itself, unless drawn off by a new object, and none better for the purpose than a book; for example, one of Defoe's; for who, in reading his thrilling history of the Great Plague, would not be reconciled to a few little ones?

Many, many a dreary, weary hour have I got over—many a gloomy misgiving postponed—many a mental or bodily annoyance forgotten, by help of the tragedies and comedies of our dramatists and novelists! Many a trouble has been soothed by the still small voice of the moral philosopher—many a dragon-like care charmed to sleep by the sweet song of the poet; for all which I cry incessantly; not aloud, but in my heart. Thanks and honor to the glorious masters of the pen, and the great inventors of the press!

Such has been my own experience of the blessing and comfort of literature and intellectual pursuits; and of the same mind doubtless was Sir Humphrey Davy, who went for "consolations in *Travel,*" not to the inn or the posting-house, but to his library and his books. I am yours, truly,

THOMAS HOOD.*

XXXII.—THE BOY MACAULAY.

Hannah More to Zachary Macaulay.

MY DEAR SIR: I wanted Tom to write to-day, but as he is likely to be much engaged with a favorite friend, and I shall have no time to-morrow, I scribble a line. This friend is a sensible youth at Woolwich; he is qualifying for the artillery. I overheard a debate between them on the comparative merits of Eugene and Marlborough as Generals. The quantity of reading that Tom has poured in, and the quantity of writing he has poured out, is astonishing. It is in vain I have tried to make him subscribe to Sir Harry Savile's notion that the poets are the best writers next to those who write prose. We have poetry for breakfast, dinner, and supper. He recited *all* "Palestine," † while we breakfasted, to our pious friend Mr. Whalley, at my desire, and did it incomparably. I was pleased with his delicacy in one thing. You know the Italian poets, like the French, too much indulge in the profane habit of attesting the Supreme Be-

* In a still higher and more eloquent strain does Hood acknowledge his obligations to men of genius, in his "Copy right and copy wrong." "They were my interpreters in the House Beautiful of God, and my guide among the Delectable Mountains of Nature. They reformed my prejudices, chastened my passions, tempered my heart, purified my tastes, elevated my mind, directed my aspirations. I was lost in a chaos of undigested problems, false theories, crude fancies, obscure impulses, and bewildering doubts, when these bright intelligences called my mental world out of darkness like a new creation, and gave it 'two great lights,' Hope and Memory, the past for a moon, and the future for a sun."—H.

† Heber's poem of that name.

ing; but without any hint from me, whenever he comes to the sacred name he reverently passes it over. I sometimes fancy I observe a daily progress in the growth of his mental powers. His fine promise of mind expands more and more, and, what is extraordinary, he has as much accuracy in his expression as spirit and vivacity in his imagination. I like, too, that he takes a lively interest in all passing events, and that the *child* is still preserved; I like to see him as boyish as he is studious, and that he is as much amused with making a pat of butter as a poem. Though loquacious, he is very docile, and I don't remember a single instance in which he has persisted in doing any thing when he saw we did not approve it. Several men of sense and learning have been struck with the union of gayety and rationality in his conversation. It was a pretty trait of him yesterday; being invited to dine abroad, he hesitated, and then said, "No; I have so few days, that I will give them all to you." And he said to-day at dinner, when speaking of his journey, "I know not whether to think on my departure with most pain or pleasure—with most kindness for my friends, or affection for my parents."

Sometimes we converse in ballad rhymes, sometimes in Johnsonian sesquipedalians; at tea we condescend to riddles and charades. He rises early, and walks an hour or two before breakfast, generally composing verses. I encourage him to live much in the open air; this, with great exercise on these airy summits, I hope will invigorate his body; though this frail body is sometimes tired, the spirits are never exhausted. He is, however, not sorry to be sent to bed soon after nine; and seldom stays to our supper.

A new poem is produced less incorrect than its predecessors; it is an excellent satire on radical reform, under the title of

"Clodpole and the Quack Doctor." It is really good. I am glad to see that they are thrown by as soon as they have been once read, and he thinks no more of them. He has very quick perceptions of the beautiful and the defective in composition. I received your note last night, and Tom his humbling one.* I tell him he is incorrigible in the way of tidiness. The other day, talking of what were the symptoms of a gentleman, he said with some humor, and much good humor, that he had certain infallible marks of one, which were neatness, love of cleanliness, and delicacy in his person. I know not when I have written so long a scrawl, but I thought you and his good mother would feel an interest in any trifles which related to him. I hope it will please God to prosper his journey, and restore him in safety to you. Let us hear of his arrival.

Yours, my dear sir, very sincerely, H. MORE.

* Mr. Roberts informs us that in 1814 Zachary Macaulay set his son to make the index to vol. xiii. of the *Christian Observer;* and the "humbling" note received by Tom at Barley Wood, may have been the order for this task, accompanied by a paternal lecture on tidiness and exactitude.

BOOK THE SIXTH.

Letters of Moral and Devotional Reflection.

BOOK THE SIXTH.

LETTERS OF MORAL AND DEVOTIONAL REFLECTION.

I.—ON THE DEATH OF A CHRISTIAN SOLDIER.

To my Loving Brother, Colonel Valentine Walton.

"LEAGUER BEFORE YORK," July 5th, 1644.

DEAR SIR: It's our duty to sympathize in all mercies, and to praise the Lord together in chastisements or trials, so that we may sorrow together. Truly England and the Church of God hath had a great favor from the Lord in this great victory given unto us, such as the like never was since this war began. It had all the evidences of an absolute victory, obtained by the Lord's blessing upon the godly party principally. We never charged but we routed the enemy. The left wing, which I commanded, being our iron horse, saving a few Scots in our rear, beat all the Prince's horse. God made them as stubble to our swords. We charged their regiments of foot with our horse, and routed all we charged. The particulars I cannot relate now, but I believe of twenty thousand, the Prince hath not four thousand left. Give glory, all the glory, to God. Sir, God hath taken away your eldest son by a cannon-shot. It broke his leg. We were necessitated to have it cut off, whereof he died. Sir, you know my own trials this way, but the Lord supported me with this: that the Lord took him into the happiness we all pant for and live for. There is your precious child, full of glory, never to know sin or sorrow any more. He was a gallant young man, exceedingly gracious. God give you His comfort. Before his death he was so full of comfort he could not express it: "It was so great above his pain." This he said to us; indeed, it was admirable. A little after, he said one thing lay upon his spirits. I asked him what that was. He told me it was that God had not suffered him to be any more the executioner of His enemies. At his fall, his horse being killed with the bullet, and, as I am informed, three horses more, I am told he bid them open to the right and left, that he might see the rogues run. Truly he was exceedingly beloved in the army of all that knew him. But few knew him, for he was a precious young man, fit for God. You have cause to bless the Lord. He is a glorious saint in heaven, wherein you ought exceedingly to rejoice. Let this drink up your sorrow; being these are not feigned words to comfort you, but the thing is so real and undoubted a truth. You may do all things by the strength of Christ. Seek that, and you shall easily bear your trial. Let this public mercy to the Church of God make you to forget your private sorrow. The Lord be your strength; so prays your truly faithful and loving brother,

OLIVER CROMWELL.

My love to your daughter, and my Cousin Percival, Sister Desbrow, and all friends with you.

II.—HAPPINESS FLOWING FROM RELIGION.

Dr. Philip Doddridge to Mrs. Doddridge.

NORTHAMPTON, October, 1742.

I hope, my dear, you will not be offended when I tell you that I am, what I hardly thought it possible, without a miracle, I should have been, very easy and happy without you. My days begin, pass, and end in pleasure, and seem short because they are so delightful. It may seem strange to say it, but really so it is. I hardly feel that I want any thing. I often think of you, and pray for you, and bless God on your account, and please myself with the hope of many comfortable days, and weeks, and years with you. Yet I am not at all anxious about your return, or indeed about any thing else. And the reason, the great and sufficient reason, is, that I have more of the presence of God with me than I ever remember to have enjoyed in any one month of my life. He enables me to live for Him, and to live with Him. When I awake in the morning, which is always before it is light, I address myself to Him, and converse with Him, speak to Him while I am lighting my candle and putting on my clothes, and have often more delight before I come out of my chamber, though it be hardly a quarter of an hour after my awaking, than I have enjoyed for whole days, or perhaps weeks of my life. He meets me in my study, in secret, in family devotions. It is pleasant to read; pleasant to compose; pleasant to converse with my friends at home; pleasant to visit those abroad—the poor and the sick; pleasant to write letters of necessary business by which any good can be done; pleasant to go out and preach the Gospel to poor souls, of which some are thirsting for it, and others dying without it; pleasant in the week-day to think how near another Sabbath is; but, oh! how much more pleasant to think how near eternity is, and how short the journey through this wilderness, and that it is but a step from earth to heaven! I cannot forbear, in these circumstances, pausing a little, and considering whence this happy scene just at this time arises, and whither it tends. Whether God is about to bring upon me any peculiar trial, for which this is to prepare me; whether He is shortly about to remove me from earth, and so is giving me more sensible prelibations of heaven, to prepare me for it; or whether He intends to do some peculiar services by me just at this time, which many other circumstances leads me sometimes to hope; or whether it be that, in answer to your prayers, and in compassion to that distress which I must otherwise have felt in the absence and illness of her who has been so exceedingly dear to me, and never was more sensibly dear to me than now, He is pleased to favor me with this teaching experience, in consequence of which I freely own I am less afraid than ever of any event which can possibly arise, consistent with His nearness to my heart, and the tokens of His paternal and covenant love. I will muse no further on the cause. It is enough, the effect is so blessed.

III.—THE USES OF SICKNESS.

Alexander Pope to Richard Steele.

July 15, 1742.

Dear Sir: You formerly observed to me, that nothing makes a more ridiculous figure in a man's life than the disparity we often find in him sick and well; thus one of an unfortunate constitution is perpetually exhibiting a miserable example of the alternate weakness of his mind and of his body. I have had frequent opportunities of late to consider myself in these different views, and I hope I have received some advantage by it. If what Waller says be true, that

> "The soul's dark cottage, batter'd and decay'd,
> Lets in new light through chinks that time has made" —

then surely sickness, contributing not less than old age to shake down this scaffolding of the body, may discover the inward structure more plainly. Sickness is a sort of early old age. It teaches us a diffidence in our earthly state, and inspires us with the thoughts of a future, better than a thousand volumes of philosophers and divines. It gives so warning a concussion to those props of our vanity, our strength and youth, that we think of fortifying ourselves within, when there is so little dependence upon our outworks. Youth, at the very best, is but a betrayer of human life, in a gentler and smoother manner than age. It is like a stream that nourishes a plant upon its bank, and causes it to flourish and blossom to the sight, but at the same time is undermining it at the root in secret. My youth has dealt more fairly and openly with me. It has afforded several prospects of my danger, and given me an advantage not very common to young men, that the attractions of the world have not dazzled me very much; and I begin, where most people end, with a full conviction of the emptiness of all sorts of ambition, and the unsatisfactory nature of all human pleasures.

When a smart fit of sickness tells me that this poor tenement of my body will fall in a little time, I am even as unconcerned as was that honest Hibernian, who, being in bed in the great storm some years ago, and told the house would tumble over his head, made answer: "What care I for the house? I am only a lodger." I fancy it is the best time to die when one is in the best humor; and so excessively weak as I now am, I may say with conscience that I am not at all uneasy at the thought that many men, whom I never had any esteem for, are likely to enjoy this world after me. When I reflect what an inconsiderable little atom every single man is, with respect to the whole creation, I think it is a shame to be concerned at the removal of so trivial an animal as I am. The morning after my exit the sun will rise as bright as ever, the flowers smell as sweet, the plants spring as green; the world will proceed in its old course; people will laugh as heartily, and marry as fast, as they were used to do. "The memory of man" (as it is elegantly expressed in the book of wisdom) "passeth away as the remembrance of a guest that tarrieth but one day." There are reasons enough, in the fourth chapter of the same book, to make a young man contented with the prospect of death. "For honorable age is not that which standeth in length of time, or is measured by number of years. But wisdom is the gray hair to men; and an unspotted life is old age.—He was taken away speedily, lest wickedness should alter his understanding, or deceit beguile his soul."

I am your, etc., ALEXANDER POPE.

IV.—GRATITUDE FOR THE MUSIC OF NATURE.

William Cowper to Rev. John Newton.

September 18th, 1784.

Following your good example, I lay before me a sheet of my largest paper. It was this moment fair and unblemished, but I have begun to blot it, and having begun, am not likely to cease till I have spoiled it. I have sent you many a sheet that, in my judgment of it, has been very unworthy of your acceptance; but my conscience was in some measure satisfied by reflecting that, if it were good for nothing, at the same time it cost you nothing but the trouble of reading it. But the case is altered now. You must pay a solid price for frothy matter; and though I do not absolutely pick your pocket, yet you lose your money, and as the saying is, are never the wiser—a saying literally fulfilled to the reader of my epistles.

My greenhouse is never so pleasant as when we are just upon the point of being burned out of it. The gentleness of the autumnal suns, and the calmness of this latter season, make it a much more agreeable retreat than we ever find it in summer, when, the winds being generally brisk, we cannot cool it by admitting a sufficient quantity of air, without being at the same time incommoded by it. But now I sit with all the windows and the door wide open, and am regaled with the scent of every flower in a garden as full of flowers as I have known how to make it. We keep no bees; but if I lived in a hive, we should hardly hear more of their music. All the bees in the neighborhood resort to a bed of mignonette opposite to the window, and pay me for the honey they get out of it by a hum, which, though rather monotonous, is as agreeable to my ear as the whistling of my linnets. *All* the sounds that Nature utters are delightful—at least in this country. I should not, perhaps, find the roaring of lions in Africa, or of bears in Russia, very pleasing; but I know no beast in England whose voice I do not account musical, save and except always the braying of an ass. The notes of all our birds and fowls please me without one exception. I should not, indeed, think of keeping a goose in a cage, that I might hang him up in the parlor for the sake of his melody; but a goose upon a common, or in a farm-yard, is no bad performer; and as to insects, if the black beetle, and beetles indeed of all hues, will keep out of my way, I have no objection to any of the rest; on the contrary, in whatever key they sing, from the gnat's fine treble to the bass of the humble-bee, I admire them all. Seriously, however, it strikes me as a very observable instance of Providential kindness to man that such an exact accord has been contrived between his ear and the sounds with which, at least in a rural situation, it is almost every moment visited. All the world is sensible of the uncomfortable effect that certain sounds have upon the nerves, and consequently upon the spirits; and if a sinful world had been filled with such as would have curdled the blood, and have made the sense of hearing a perpetual inconvenience, I do not know that we should have had a right to complain. But now the fields, the woods, the gardens, have each their concerts, and the ear of man is forever regaled by creatures who seem only to please themselves. Even the ears that are deaf to the Gospel, are continually entertained, though without knowing it, by sounds for which they are solely indebted to its Author. There is, somewhere within infinite space, a world that does not roll within the precincts of mercy, and, as it is reasonable, and even scriptural, to suppose that there is music in heaven, in those dismal regions perhaps the reverse of it is found; tones so dismal as to make woe itself more insupportable, and to acuminate even despair. But my paper admonishes me in good time to draw the reins, and to check the descent of my family into deeps with which she is but too familiar.

Our best love attends you both, with yours, *Sum ut semper, tui studiosissimus.* W. C.

V.—DYING REQUESTS MADE BY DR. JOHNSON, OF SIR JOSHUA REYNOLDS.

Hannah More to her Sister.

HAMPTON, December, 1784.

Poor dear Johnson! he is past all hope. The dropsy has brought him to the point of death. His legs are scarified; but nothing will do. I have, however, the comfort to hear that his dread of dying is in a great measure subdued; and now he says, "The bitterness of death is past." He sent the other day for Sir Joshua; and after much serious conversation, told him he had three favors to beg of him, and hoped he would not refuse a dying friend, be they what they would. Sir Joshua promised. The first was, that he never would paint on Sunday; the second, that he would forgive him thirty pounds that he had lent him, as he wanted to leave them to a distressed family; the third was, that he would read the Bible whenever he had an opportunity, and that he would never omit it on a Sunday. There was no difficulty but upon the *first* point; but at length Sir Joshua promised to gratify him in all. How delighted should I be to hear the dying discourse of this great and good man, especially now that faith has subdued his fears! I wish I could see him.

VI.—ON THE DEATH OF HIS WIFE.*

Thomas Gray to Mr. Mason.

March 28th, 1767.

I break in upon you at a moment when we least of all are permitted to disturb our friends, only to say that you are daily

* This and the two following letters have been placed together without regard to date, from the kindred character of their subject matter.—H.

and hourly present to my thoughts. If the worst* be not yet past, you will neglect and pardon me; but if the last struggle be over; if the poor object of your long anxieties be no longer sensible to your kindness, or to her own sufferings, allow me (at least in idea, for what could I do, were I present, more than this?) to sit by you in silence, and pity from my heart, not her who is at rest, but you who lose her. May He who made us, the Master of our pleasures and of our pains, preserve and support you! Adieu.

I have long understood how little you had to hope.

VII.—ON THE DEATH OF MRS. ADAMS.

Thomas Jefferson to John Adams.

MONTICELLO, Nov. 13th, 1818.

The public papers, my dear friend, announce the fatal event of which your letter of October 20th had given me ominous forebodings. Tried myself in the school of affliction, by the loss of every form of connection which can rive the human heart, I know full well and feel what you have lost, what you have suffered, are suffering, and have yet to endure. The same trials have taught me that for ills so immeasurable, time and silence are the only medicine. I will not, therefore, by useless condolences, open afresh the sluices of your grief, nor, although mingling sincerely my tears with yours, will I say a word more where words are vain, but that it is some comfort to us both

* "As this little billet (which I received at the Hot-Wells at Bristol) then breathed, and still seems to breathe, the very voice of friendship in its tenderest and most pathetic note, I cannot refrain from publishing it in this place. I opened it almost at the precise moment when it would necessarily be the most affecting."—*Note of Mason, to Gray's Letters.*

that the time is not very distant at which we are to deposit in the same cerement our sorrows and suffering bodies, and to ascend in essence to an ecstatic meeting with the friends we have loved and lost, and whom we shall still love and never lose again. God bless and support you under your heavy affliction.

THOMAS JEFFERSON.

VIII.—" LOVE IS ABOVE ALL."

A. Humboldt to Varnhagen.

BERLIN, Sunday, 6 o'clock A. M., April 5th, 1855.

You, my dear Varnhagen, who are not afraid of grief, but who trace its phases through the depths of sentiment, you should receive at this sorrowful time a few words expressing the love which both brothers feel for you. The release has not yet come. I left him * last night at eleven o'clock, and I hasten to him again. The day yesterday was less distressing. A half lethargic condition, frequent though not restless slumber, and after each waking words of love, of comfort, but always the clearness of the great intellect, which penetrates and distinguishes every thing, and examines its own condition. The voice was very feeble, hoarse, and thin like a child's; leeches were therefore applied to the throat. Full consciousness! " Think of me," he said the day before yesterday, " but always with cheerfulness. I was very happy, and this day also was a beautiful one for me, for ' love is above all.' I will soon be with mother, and have an insight into a higher order of things." I have no shadow of hope. I never thought my old eyes had so many tears! It has lasted near eight days.

* William Humboldt, then on his dying bed.

IX.—ON HIS RECOVERY FROM TEMPORARY INSANITY.

Sir James Mackintosh to Robert Hall.

BOMBAY, 21st Sept., 1805.

MY DEAR HALL: I believe that, in the hurry of leaving England, I did not answer the letter which you wrote to me in December, 1803. I did not, however, forget your interesting young friend, from whom I have had one letter from Constantinople, and to whom I have twice written at Cairo, where he now is. No request of yours could, indeed, be lightly esteemed by me.

It happened to me a few days ago, in drawing up (merely for my own use) a short sketch of my life, that I had occasion to give a faithful statement of my recollection of the circumstances of my first acquaintance with you. On the most impartial survey of my early life, I could see nothing which tended so much to excite and invigorate my understanding, and to direct it toward high, though perhaps scarcely accessible objects, as my intimacy with you. Five-and-twenty years are now past since we first met; yet hardly any thing has occurred since, which has left a deeper or more agreeable impression on my mind. I now remember the extraordinary union of brilliant fancy with acute intellect, which would have excited more admiration than it has done, if it had been dedicated to the amusement of the great and learned, instead of being consecrated to the far more noble office of consoling, instructing, and reforming the poor and the forgotten. It was then too early for me to discover that extreme purity, which, in a mind preoccupied with the low realities of life, would have been no natural companion of so much activity and ardor, but which thoroughly detached you from the world, and made you the inhabitant of regions where alone it is possible to be always active, without impurity, and where the ardor of your sensibility had unbounded scope, amid the inexhaustible combinations of beauty and excellence.

It is not given to us to preserve an exact medium. Nothing is so difficult as to decide how much ideal models ought to be combined with experience; how much of the future should be let into the present, in the progress of the human mind. To ennoble and purify, without raising us above the sphere of our usefulness—to qualify us for what we ought to seek, without unfitting us for that to which we must submit—are great and difficult problems, which can be but imperfectly solved.

It is certain the child may be too manly, not only for his present enjoyments, but for his future prospects. Perhaps, my good friend, you have fallen into this error of superior natures. From this error has, I think, arisen that calamity with which it has pleased Providence to visit you, which, to a mind less fortified by reason and religion, I should not dare to mention, but which I really consider in you as little more than the indignant struggles of a pure mind with the low realities which surround it—the fervent aspirations after regions more congenial to it—and a momentary blindness, produced by the fixed contemplation of objects too bright for human vision. I may say, in this case, in a far grander sense than that in which the words were originally spoken by our great poet:

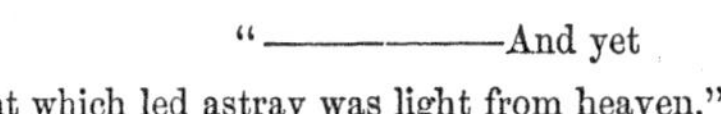

> "————And yet
> The light which led astray was light from heaven."

On your return to us you must surely have found consolation in the only terrestrial produce which is pure and truly exquisite;

in the affections and attachments you have inspired, which you were most worthy to inspire, and which no human pollution can rob of their heavenly nature. If I were to prosecute the reflections and indulge the feelings which at this moment fill my mind, I should soon venture to doubt whether for a calamity derived from such a source, and attended with such consolations, I should so far yield to the views and opinions of men as to seek to condole with you. But I check myself, and I exhort you, my most worthy friend, to check your best propensities, for the sake of attaining their object. You cannot live for men without living with them. Serve God, then, by the active service of men. Contemplate more the good you *can* do, than the evil you can only lament. Allow yourself to see the loveliness of virtue amid all its imperfections; and employ your moral imagination, not so much by bringing it into contrast with the model of ideal perfection, as in gently blending some of the fainter colors of the latter with the brighter hues of real experienced excellence, thus heightening their beauty, instead of broadening the shade which must surround us till we awaken from this dream in other spheres of existence.

My habits of life have not been favorable for this train of meditation. I have been too busy, or too trifling. My nature, perhaps, would have been better consulted, if I had been placed in a quieter station, where speculation might have been my business, and visions of the fair and good my chief recreations. When I approach you I feel a powerful attraction toward this which seems the natural destiny of my mind; but habit opposes obstacles, and duty calls me off, and reason frowns on him who wastes that reflection on a destiny independent of him, which he ought to reserve for actions of which he is the master.

In another letter I may write to you on miscellaneous subjects; at present I cannot bring my mind to speak of them. Let me hear from you soon and often.

Farewell, my dear friend.

Yours ever most faithfully,

JAMES MACKINTOSH.

X.—ON HIS RECOVERY FROM A SECOND ATTACK OF INSANITY.

Robert Hall to W. Hollick.

February 1st, 1806.

MY DEAR FRIEND: Accept my sincere thanks for your kind letter. Every assurance of respect from old friends, and especially from one whose friendship has been so long tried, and evinced on so many occasions, must afford much satisfaction to a person in any situation. Though Providence has produced a separation, which will probably be of long continuance (and, in one sense, final), nothing I am certain can efface from my mind those impressions of gratitude and esteem with which I shall ever look back upon my connections at Cambridge and its vicinity. With the deepest submission, I wish to bow to the mandate of that awful, yet I trust paternal Power, which, when it pleases, confounds all human hopes, and lays us prostrate in the dust. It is for Him to dispose of His creatures as he pleases; and, if they be willing and obedient, to work out their happiness, though by methods the most painful and afflictive. His plans are infinitely extended, and His measures determined by views of that ultimate issue, that final result which transcends our comprehension. It is with the sincerest gratitude I would acknowledge the goodness of God in restoring me. I am, as far as I can judge, as remote from any thing wild and irregular in the state of my mind, as I ever was in my life; though I think, owing probably to the former increased excitation, I feel some abatement of vigor. My mind seems inert. During my affliction I have not been entirely forsaken of God, nor left destitute of that calm trust in His providence which was left to support me; yet I have not been favored with that intimate communion, and that delightful sense of His love, which I have enjoyed on former occasions. I have seldom been without a degree of composure, though I have had little consolation or joy. Such, with little variation, has been my mental state, very nearly from the time of my coming to the Fish-ponds; for I had not been here more than a fortnight before I found myself perfectly recovered, though my pulse continued too high. It has long subsided, and exhibits, the doctor assures me, every indication of confirmed health.

With respect to my future prospects and plans, they are necessarily in a state of great uncertainty. I am fully convinced of the propriety of relinquishing my pastoral charge at Cambridge, which I shall do in an official letter to the Church, as soon as I leave Dr. Cox, which I believe will be at the expiration of the quarter from my coming. My return to Cambridgeshire was extremely ill-judged, I am convinced; nor had I the smallest intention of doing it, until I was acquainted with the generous interposition of my friends, to which it appeared to me that my declining to live among them would appear a most ungrateful return. I most earnestly request that they will do me the justice to believe the intention I have named, of declining the pastoral charge, does not proceed from any such motive, but from the exigencies of my situation and a sense of duty. I propose to lay aside preaching for at least a twelvemonth.

Please to remember me affectionately and respectfully to your cousin, and all inquiring friends, as if named.

I am, my dear sir, your affectionate and obliged friend,

ROBERT HALL.

P. S. Please to present my best respects to Mrs. Hollick and your daughter.

XI.—TRANSMITTING A PRAYER FOUND AMONGST THE PAPERS OF HIS DECEASED WIFE.

John Sheppard to Lord Byron.

FROME, SOMERSET, Nov. 21st, 1821.

MY LORD: More than two years since a lovely and beloved wife was taken from me by lingering disease, after a very short union. She possessed unvarying gentleness and fortitude, and a piety so retiring as rarely to disclose itself in words, but so influential as to produce uniform benevolence of conduct. In the last hour of life, after a farewell look on a lately born and only infant, for whom she had evinced inexpressible affection, her last whispers were, "God's happiness! God's happiness!" Since the second anniversary of her decease, I have read some papers which no one had seen during her life, and which contain her most secret thoughts. I am induced to communicate to your Lordship a passage from these papers, which there is no doubt refers to yourself, as I have more than once heard the writer mention your agility on the rocks at Hastings.

"Oh, my God, I take encouragement from the assurance of Thy Word, to pray to Thee in behalf of one for whom I have lately been much interested. May the person to whom I allude (and who is now, we fear, as much distinguished for his neglect of Thee, as for the transcendent talent Thou hast bestowed on him) be awakened to a sense of his own danger, and led to seek that peace of mind, in a proper sense of religion, which he has found this world's enjoyments unable to procure! Do Thou grant that his future example may be productive of far more extensive benefit than his past conduct and writings have been of evil; and may the Sun of righteousness, which we trust will, at some future period, arise on him, be bright in proportion to the darkness of those clouds which guilt has raised around him, and the balm which it bestows healing and soothing in proportion to the keenness of that agony which the punishment of his vices has inflicted on him! May the hope that the sincerity of my own efforts for the attainment of holiness, and the approval of my own love to the Great Author of religion, will render the prayer, and every other for the benefit of mankind, more efficacious. Cheer me in the path of duty; but let me not forget, that, while we are permitted to animate ourselves to exertion by every innocent motive, these are but the lesser streams which may serve to increase the current, but which, deprived of the grand fountain of good (a deep conviction of inborn sin, and firm belief in the efficacy of Christ's death for the salvation of those who trust in Him, and really wish to serve Him), would soon dry up, and leave us barren of every virtue as before.

"HASTINGS, July 31st, 1814."

There is nothing, my Lord, in this extract, which, in a literary sense, can at all interest you; but it may, perhaps, appear to you worthy of reflection how deep and expansive a concern for the happiness of others, the Christain faith can awaken in youth and prosperity. Here is nothing poetical and splendid, as in the expostulatory homage of M. De Lamartine; but here is the *sublime*, my Lord; for this intercession was offered, on your account, to the Supreme source of happiness. It sprang from a faith more confirmed than that of the French poet, and from a charity which, in combination with faith, showed its power unimpaired amid the languors and pains of approaching dissolution. I will hope that a prayer, which I am sure was deeply sincere, may not be always unavailing.

It would add *nothing*, my Lord, to the fame with which your genius has surrounded you, for an unknown and obscure individual to express his admiration of it. I had rather be numbered with those who wish and pray that "wisdom from above," and "peace," and "joy," may enter such a mind.

JOHN SHEPPARD.

XII.—ANSWER TO PRECEDING LETTER.

Lord Byron to Rev. Mr. Sheppard.

PISA, December 3d, 1821.

SIR: I have received your letter. I need not say that the extract which it contains has affected me, because it would imply a want of all feeling to have read it with indifference. Though I am not quite *sure* that it was intended by the writer for *me*, yet the date, the place where it was written, with some other circumstances that you mention, render the allusion probable. But for whomsoever it was meant, I have read it with all the pleasure which can arise from so melancholy a topic. I say *pleasure*, because your brief and simple picture of the life and demeanor of the excellent person, whom I trust you will again meet, cannot be contemplated without the admiration due to her virtues and her pure and unpretending piety. Her last moments were particularly striking, and I do not know that, in the course of reading the story of mankind, and still less in my observations upon the existing portion, I ever met with any thing so unostentatiously beautiful. Indisputably, the firm believers in the Gospel have a great advantage over all others, for this simple reason: that, if true, they will have their reward hereafter; and if there be no hereafter, they can be but with the infidel in his eternal sleep, having had the assistance of an exalted hope, through life, without subsequent disappointment, since (at the worse for them) "out of nothing, nothing can arise," not even sorrow. But a man's creed does not depend upon *himself; who* can say I will believe this, that, or the other? and, least of all, that which he least can comprehend? I have, however, observed those who have begun life with extreme faith, have in the end greatly narrowed it, as Chillingworth, Clarke (who ended as an Arian), Bayle, and Gibbon (once a Catholic), and some others; while, on the other hand, nothing is more common than for the early sceptic to end in a firm belief, like Maupertius and Henry Kirke White. But my business is to acknowledge your letter, and not to make a dissertation. I am obliged to you for your good wishes, and more than obliged by the extracts from the papers of the beloved object whose qualities you have so well described in a few words. I can assure you, that all the fame which ever cheated humanity into higher notions of its own importance, would never weigh in my mind against the pure and pious interest which a virtuous being may be pleased to take in my welfare. In this point of view, I would not exchange the prayer of the deceased in my behalf, for the united glory of Homer, Cæsar, and Napoleon, could such be accumulated upon a living head. Do me at least the justice to suppose that "*Video meliora proboque*," however the "*deteriora sequor*" may have been applied to my conduct. I have the honor to be your obliged and obedient servant,

BYRON.

P. S. I do not know that I am addressing a clergyman, but I presume that you will not be affronted by the mistake (if it is one) on the address of this letter. One who has so well explained and deeply felt the doctrines of religion, will excuse the error which led me to believe him its minister.

XIII.—BISHOP PORTEUS AND THE PRINCE OF WALES.

Mrs. Grant to Mrs. Brown.

EDINBURGH, 25th January, 1811.

MY DEAR MRS. BROWN: I lose no time in telling you how glad I am to hear of you, and to know, by added experience, how good and kind you are in thinking of, and acting for me. How happy for a poor mortal like me, tossed from one exigency to another, to have friends so attached and attentive as all mine, in different ways, have been!

My time is at present very much occupied, but I shall avail myself of a short interval of leisure to tell you what I am sure you will be interested in hearing—the particulars of the final interview between the Prince of Wales and the late Bishop of London,* which have lately been communicated to me from a source which appears to me quite authentic. Among other good people with whom my informant is intimate is Mr. Owen, minister of Fulham, who was in a manner the Bishop's parish clergyman,

* Dr. Porteus.

and long his chaplain. Mr. Owen gave my friend an account of this interview, as the Bishop gave it to him two days before his death.

It seems his Royal Highness had sent out a summons for a great military review, which was to take place on a Sunday. The Bishop had been confined, and did not hope nor, I suppose, wish ever in this world to go out again. He ordered his carriage, however, upon hearing this, proceeded to Carlton House, and waited on the Prince, who received him very graciously. He said, "I am come, sir, urged by my regard to you, to your father, and to this great nation, who are anxiously beholding every public action of yours. I am on the verge of time; new prospects open to me; the favor of human beings or their displeasure, is as nothing to me now. I am come to warn your Royal Highness of the awful consequences of your breaking down the very little that remains of distinction to the day that the Author of all power has hallowed and set apart for himself." He went on in pathetic terms to represent the awful responsibility to which the Prince exposed himself, and how much benefit or injury might result to the immortal souls of millions by his consulting or neglecting the revealed will of the King of kings; and, after much tender and awful exhortation, concluded with saying, "You see how your father, greatly your inferior in talent and capacity, has been a blessing to all around him and to the nation at large, because he made it the study and business of his life to exert all his abilities for the good of his people, to study and to do the will of God, and to give an example to the world of a life regulated by the precepts of Christian morality; he has been an object of respect and veneration to the whole world for so doing. If he has done much, you, with your excellent abilities and pleasing and popular manners, may do much more. It is impossible for you to remain stationary in this awful crisis; you must rise to true glory and renown, and lead millions in the same path by the power of your example, or sink to sudden and perpetual ruin, aggravated by the great numbers whom your fall will draw with you to the same destruction. And now, were I able to rise, or were any one here who would assist me, I should, with the awful feeling of a dying man, give my last blessing to your Royal Highness." The Prince, upon this, burst into tears, and fell on his knees before the Bishop, who bestowed upon him, with folded hands, his dying benediction; the Prince then, in the most gracious and affecting manner, assisted him himself to go down, and put him into his carriage. The Bishop went home, never came out again, and died the fifth day after. On hearing of his death, the Prince shut himself up, and was heard by his attendants to sob as under deep affliction.

I think I have now given you a brief but faithful account of this transaction as I heard it. * * * * *

I can easily believe that a mind so well regulated as yours, has in itself resources that make "quiet, though sad, the remnant of your days." But I think that a life somewhere balanced between your pensive tranquillity and my ever-during bustle would be preferable to either. Such is that of our dear friend and sister at Jordanhill, whose felicities I have been celebrating ever since I returned here. Remember me in all kindness to your mother and aunt, and believe me, most affectionately, dear old friend, yours always,

Anne Grant.

XIV.—DUTY OF THE CLERGY TOWARD THE TWO ORDERS OF SOCIETY.

Dr. Thomas Arnold to Rev. Augustus Hare.

December 24th, 1830.

I have longed very much to see you, over and above my general wish that we could meet oftener, ever since the fearful state of our poor has announced itself even to the blindest. My dread is that when the Special Commissioners shall have done their work (necessary and just I most cordially agree with you that it is), the richer classes will relapse into their old callousness, and the seeds be sown of a far more deadly and irremediable quarrel hereafter. If you can get Arthur Young's "Travels in France," I think you will be greatly struck with their applicability to our own times and country. He shows how deadly was the hatred of the peasantry toward their lords, and how in 1789 the chateaux were destroyed and the families of the gentry insulted, from a common feeling of hatred to all who had made themselves and the poor *two orders*, and who were now to pay the penalty of having put asunder what God had joined. At this moment, Carlyle tells the poor that they and the rich are enemies, and that to destroy the property of an enemy, whether by fire or otherwise, is always lawful in war. A devil's doctrine certainly, and devilishly applied; but unquestionably, our aristocratical manners and habits have made us and the poor two distinct and unsympathizing bodies, and from want of sympathy I fear the transition to enmity is but too easy, when distress embitters the feelings, and the sight of others in luxury makes that distress still more intolerable. This is the plague spot, to my mind, in our whole state of society, which must be removed or the whole must perish. And, under God, it is for the clergy to come forward boldly and begin to combat it. If you read Isaiah, ch. v., 3–32 v.; Jeremiah, ch. v., 22–30 v.; Amos, ch. iv.; Habakkuk, ch. ii.; and the Epistle of St. James, written to the same people, a little before the second destruction of Jerusalem, you will be struck, I think, with the close resemblance of our own state to that of the Jews; while the state of the Greek churches to whom St. Paul wrote is wholly different, because, from their thin population and better political circumstances, poverty among them is hardly noticed, and our duties to the poor are consequently much less prominently brought forward. And unluckily, our Evangelicals read St. Paul more than any other part of the Scriptures, and think very little of consulting most those parts of Scripture which are addressed to persons circumstanced most like ourselves. I want to get up a real "Poor Man's Magazine," which should not bolster up abuses, nor veil iniquities, nor prose to the poor as children; but should address them in the style of Cobbett, plainly, boldly, and in sincerity, excusing nothing, concealing nothing, misrepresenting nothing, but speaking the very whole truth in love, Cobbett-like in style, but Christian in spirit. Now you are the man, I think, to join with me in such a work, and most earnestly do I wish that you would think of it. * * * I should be for putting my name to whatever I wrote of this nature, for I think it is of great importance our addresses should be those of substantive and tangible persons, and not of anonymous shadows.

XV.—MORAL USES OF A POOR CLASS.

Alexander Knox to Bishop Jebb.

December 28th, 1802.

MY DEAR MR. JEBB: I received your letter on Christmas day, in my bed; not being able to rise, in consequence of bilious sickness, until after the post hour.

As to your charity sermon, I fear the text in Isaiah would be too far about. I happened to be looking into a pamphlet, sent me a day or two before from London, and I thought I saw some topics which would furnish a good body for such a discourse.

"No large community can long subsist without a considerable part of its members being destined to laborious situations and dependent circumstances; it cannot long subsist without food and clothing; and these cannot be attained without labor; and men generally will not labor but upon the urgency of necessity. If every man was provided with a stock of the necessaries of life, and had wealth to purchase them, we should see few shuttles in motion, and few ploughs turning up the soil, till the time came when, having wasted their resources, distress would compel some to the loom, others to the field."

"In a civilized state, besides food and clothing, much domestic service is necessary; of which a great part being neither elegant nor unlaborious, will not commonly be performed by those who can avoid it, which all may do who are under no immediate pressure or fear of want. Therefore, without such a degree of indigence in society as may dispose some to undergo the daily drudgery of life, and such a degree of affluence as may enable others to reward them for it, we could expect to find but little either of domestic neatness or comfort. Want, in the political machine, is the weight necessary to keep it in motion; and all that can or ought to be done is duly to regulate it."

"Hence, it will follow, that, to preserve society from sinking into its savage state, in which every man must be content to fish and hunt for himself, and to wear the skin of the beast he has slain, a large proportion of the people must depend for their subsistence on the toils of husbandry or useful manufactures and domestic service; which implies the relation of master and servant, * * of those who have nothing but their labor to bring to market; and of those who come with a price in their hands to purchase it."

Now, I cannot help thinking that the above paragraphs contain a very satisfactory view of at least the political final cause of poverty. And, I conceive, it might be expanded into a much larger detail of the benefits arising to the higher classes from this providential arrangement. In short, to this arrangement the higher classes, as such, owe their civil existence.

The text, then, out of which such remarks might best grow, would, perhaps, be Deut. xv., 11: "The poor shall never cease out of the land. Therefore, I command thee, saying, Thou shalt open thy hands wide unto thy brother, to thy poor, and to thy needy in thy land."

"The poor shall never cease," etc. * * Why? because the ceasing of poverty would be taking the weight off the great machine; and because the ceasing of the poor would be the annihilation of all the instrumental agency subserving to civil comfort. Is not, then, such an appointment worthy of eternal wisdom?

The luxuries of the great, as to personal comfort, might be dispensed with; but, in a civil and political light, they too have their use; yea, and in a moral light also. But even those conveniences which we must all value, the accommodations of our houses and our persons, of our sedentary and our active hours, the food we eat, the clothes we wear, every thing, in short, which forms our extrinsic comfort, flows to us from that providential adjustment of continued poverty.

But this is not all; from the same source arose our fathers' leisure as our own; and, hence, how infinite our intellectual blessings! Who, of an enlarged mind, would willingly relinquish the happiness of an improved and exercised understanding? What lover of science, what admirer of classic elegance and simplicity, what inquirer into the moral relations between man and man, and between man and his God, would be willing to have all at once swept from his mind by a dark, vacant, and everlasting oblivion? Yet, if these are blessings, they also are chiefly owing to the same cause, which, by the permanent stimulation of want, has roused mankind from indolence into that series of exertions which has given rise to all the rest.

> Pater ipse colendi
> Haud facilem esse viam voluit, primúsque per artem
> Movit agros, curis acuens mortalia corda.

With what just and gracious fitness, then, is the subsequent command given? How becoming the source of goodness and happiness? Every humane mind hears with pleasure that other injunction, "Thou shalt not muzzle the ox that treadeth out the corn;" but this, resting on the same ground of justice, rises far above it in importance. The very terms are exquisitely suitable. "Therefore, I command thee:" in no instance is the language more authoritative. As if he had said, * * * The existence of poverty is my direct and special appointment, as being indispensable to your civil welfare. Therefore, on the fairest principle, I enjoin a just acknowledgment of that benefit. You are to be the daily objects of my bounty; and the chief of that bounty shall be conveyed to you through the instrumentality of the poor. You owe me a return for this bounty, and they who are my instruments in giving, are my appointed agents for receiving: "Therefore, I command thee."

But there is, in addition to this, a natural tie. It is not for one of another nature or other feelings I am solicitous; it is *thy brother* to whom I enjoin thee to open thy hand, * * * to whom thou oughtest to be kind, if for this reason only, because you are "of one blood," * * * creatures of like passions. Thy own weaknesses and wants, therefore, are so many advocates within thee for his. But he is "thy poor, and thy needy, in thy land." This returns to the main argument, the civil connection between the rich and poor. He is an appendage to thy civil existence, * * * a necessary part of the great body. "The body is not one member, but many. If the whole body were an eye, where were the hearing? if the whole body were hearing, where were the smelling? and if they were all one member, where were the body? The eye, therefore, cannot say unto the hand, I have no need of thee; nor, again, the head to the feet, I have no need of you. Nay, much more, those members of the body which seem to be more feeble, are more necessary." The poor, then, being as it were the hands and feet of the body politic, it is most fitly said, "thy poor and thy needy." They are one with their superiors as to unity of action. They should be one, therefore, in just sustenance; in sympathetic tenderness; and in every instance, of requisite care. This is the voice of reason, of interest, of nature, and of God. "Thou shalt open thine hand wide unto thy brother."

Various are the duties which this command embraces. But none more peculiarly or distinctly than in meeting their opening wants and weaknesses, and fitting them betimes for sustaining their lot with credit and comfort. It is the great end of all the divine dispensations to diffuse and heighten happiness. But, in this lower world, God has been pleased, as it were, to abridge His own power as to direct exercise, and to commit in a great degree to man's agency the executing of His beneficial purposes; as if every blessing here were to be conveyed in the way of mediation. What, therefore, must be the divine complacency when He beholds His adorable design in progress, in consequence of an harmonious coöperation of all the different agencies. To supply physical wants is, as has been stated, the function of the poor. To manufacture and distribute mental, intellectual, and moral comfort, is the high allotment of superior classes. God has so ordered matters that the former function is steadily performed. But what a reckoning will the rich and great have if they do not perform theirs! What are God's final designs as to human society He has not fully revealed. But universality of moral happiness is intimated. The progress, however, is awfully committed, in a great degree as already hinted, to society itself. We have made some progress, doubtless. Two thousand years ago, what were these islands? who, then, can say how far civilization might be carried? But we do not *yet* know and feel, in this less happy island particularly, what the evils of barbarism are; and how can we so remove them as by the very duty of this day? To multiply moral and religious mechanists, servants, and laborers, is the only way we can at present leaven the lump. And, so sure as we faithfully endeavor, God will bless.

Such, my good friend, are the crude hints of a less common kind which have occurred to me. Use or not just as suits. Whatever I send you, is always yours to throw by, just as much as to take up. What you say of my little work is gratifying to me. I did not forget you, but there has been an omission either at the post-office or the castle.

Most truly yours, ALEXANDER KNOX.

XVI.—COURSE TO BE PURSUED ON RECEIVING A CHALLENGE.

Rev. Dr. J. M. Mason to Capt. ——, *U. S. Army.*

NEW YORK, Jan. 10th, 1814.

MY DEAR SIR: I deeply sympathize with you in the trial to which your public duty and Christian virtue have been put by a challenge from one of your brother officers; and am rejoiced and consoled by the triumph, thus far, of all that is good and holy, of all that is rational and true, of all that is magnanimous and brave, in refusing from principle to fight a duel; in which fools and atheists, madmen and cut throats, and cowards, have courage enough to engage on the slightest provocation, but which it requires that rare virtue, *moral heroism*, to decline on the greatest. At the same time, I doubt the propriety of the course which in this *stage* of the business you seem inclined to take. Direct appeals to the public ought to be the last resort. It is hardly military to adopt, without *final* necessity, an unmilitary mode of defence. You have a regular military form of redress, which by all means ought to be tried, before you present yourself at the bar of the public.

I take it for granted that you have given no plausible reason of dissatisfaction to the challenger. Be *very sure* on this head; and be not fastidious. If you have in any way been so unfortunate as to injure him, honor and generosity combine with justice and religion to enforce the utmost extent of reparation consistent with their united claims. If you have done no wrong, then the process is short; have the challenger and his second immediately arrested and tried by a court-martial, under the "Rules and Articles of War." You may prefer solid charges, and touch no others. You will, of course, be certain of your proofs; and will not fail to keep for inspection the *written* challenge, if such an one was sent.

I trust you will keep yourself perfectly cool; but insist on a court-martial. Provided you can fairly make out your case, and should the court not do you justice, appeal to a general court-martial. Should you fail there, appeal to God and your country, and resign a sword which you cannot wear without crime. I pray you to put it fully to the test, whether the "Articles of War" are an unmeaning letter or not. Reap the honor of arraying public principle against private depravity. But as you love your country, as you would not be a perjured soldier, as you fear God, as you look for reward to *that* eternity, as you would not break the hearts of your best friends, as you would not scandalize the wise and good, and be cast away from the Church of Jesus Christ in the present life—persist, inflexibly persist in refusing the challenge. My prayers are for you in this time of need. Affectionately yours,

J. M. MASON.

XVII.—PASTORAL EXHORTATION.

*Bishop of Exeter to Lord Eldon.**

My dear Lord: I take blame to myself for having, as I fear, obtruded on you some important matters of consideration at a time when you were not prepared to admit them; or in a manner which may have been deemed too earnest and importunate.

* Dr. Philpotts, Bishop of Exeter, who was connected with Lord Eldon by marriage, hearing of his extreme indisposition, called upon him, and prayed with him. Not having touched on any topic that was distasteful, this visit passed off most satisfactorily. The next time Mr. Pennington appeared, the patient said, "I have had another doctor since I saw you." "I am glad of it," said the worthy apothecary. "Oh, but," said Lord Eldon, "he was a spiritual doctor, not a medical. The Bishop of Exeter paid me a visit, and after setting a little by me, and observing me look very ill, he got up and bolted the door, and knelt down by me. 'Let us pray,' he said. He did pray, and such a prayer! I never heard such a prayer." A few days subsequently, as was gathered from Lord Eldon's own statement, the Bishop repeated his visit, and after some religious conversation with him, was alarmed by finding the entire self-satisfaction with which he looked back on the whole of his past life, and his great seeming reliance upon his own merits. In the true spirit of a faithful Christian pastor, who must not regard the rank or station of a dying man, the Bishop tried in mild terms to remind him that we have all followed too much the devices and desires of our own hearts; and that, confessing our faults, we ought to look elsewhere for pardon than to the recollection of the good works which we may rashly impute to ourselves. The old peer thereupon became very refractory, thinking that some personal disrespect was shown to him, and that a slur was meant to be cast upon his conduct as a public man, which he had ever regarded as most spotless, as well as consistent. He was particularly indignant at the thought of such a charge coming from one whom, notwithstanding a show of outward civility he had regarded with some secret suspicion, from the part at last taken by the right Reverend Prelate respecting Catholic emancipation; and he considered it particularly hard to bear taunts from such a quarter. As the ex-Chancellor displayed some impatience and even resentment, the pious divine in vain strove to make him understand that the only object of this conference was to call his attention to spiritual things; and having exhausted all the means which the acutest intellect, the deepest knowledge, and the most win-

That you pardon the intrusion I have no doubt, and that you ascribe what may have been ill-timed or ill considered to the true cause—an anxious wish to lead a highly-gifted mind like yours to those thoughts which alone can satisfy it. Before I leave this place, instead of again trespassing on you in person, I have resolved to commit to paper a few considerations which your own powerful mind will know how to improve, and which I humbly pray the Holy Spirit of God to impress, so far as they accord with His truth, on the hearts of both of us. I contemplate in you, my dear Lord, an object of no ordinary interest. I see a man, full of years and honors, honors richly earned (ay, were they tenfold greater than they are) by a life which, protracted long beyond the ordinary age of man, has been employed during all the period of service in promoting, strengthening, and securing the best and most sacred interests of your country. I see in you the faithful, zealous, and most able advocate of the connection of true religion with the Constitution and Government of England. I see in you one who has largely benefited the generation of which you have been among the most distinguished ornaments. Seeing and feeling this, I am sure you will pardon me if I exhibit a little even of undue eagerness to perform to you the only service which I can hope to render—that of exciting such a mind to those reflections by which, after serving others, it can now do the best and surest service to itself. In truth, those reflections are few and brief, but most pregnant. In short, my dear Lord, I would seek most

ning manners could supply, was obliged to retire without, in any degree, making the impression he desired. Next day Lord Eldon received the above beautiful letter, which, no doubt, brought him to a right frame of mind, and which may be perused with advantage by persons of all ages and conditions of life, whether in health or sickness.—*Lord Campbell's Lives of the Chancellors.*

earnestly to guard you against the danger which arises from the very qualities which we most admire in you, and from the actions for which we are most grateful to you. That danger is, lest you contemplate these matters with too much satisfaction—lest you rest upon them as the grounds of your hope of final acceptance with God. Oh! my dear Lord, the best of the sons of men must be content, or rather must be most anxious, to look out of themselves, and above themselves, for any sure hope, I will not say of justification, but of mercy. Consider the infinite holiness and purity of God, and then say whether any man was ever fit to appear at His tribunal. Consider the demands of His law, extending to the most secret thoughts, and wishes, and imaginations of the heart; and then say whether you, or any one, can stand before Him in your own strength, when He cometh to judgment. No: it is as sinners, as grievous sinners, we shall, we must appear; and the only plea which will be admitted for us is the righteousness and the merits of our crucified Redeemer. If we place any reliance on our own poor doings or fancied virtues, those very virtues will be our snares, our downfall.

Above all things, therefore, it is our duty, and preëminently the duty of the purest and best among us, to cast off all confidence in ourselves, and thankfully to embrace Christ's most precious offer on the terms on which He offers it. He will be our Saviour only if we know, and feel, and humbly acknowledge that we need His salvation. He will be more and more our Saviour in proportion as we more and more love and rely upon Him. But surely, the more we feel and deplore our own sinfulness, the more earnest will be our love, the firmer our reliance on Him who alone is mighty to save. Therefore it is that in preparing ourselves to appear before Him, the less we think of what we may fondly deem our good deeds and good qualities, and the more rigidly we scrutinize our hearts, and detect and deplore our manifold sinfulness, the fitter shall we be, because the more deeply sensible of the absolute necessity and of the incalculable value of His blessed undertaking and suffering for us. One word only more: of ourselves, we cannot come to this due sense of our own worthlessness; and the devil is always ready to tempt our weak hearts with the bait which is most taking to many among us—confidence in ourselves. It is the Holy Spirit who alone can give us that only knowledge which will be useful to us at the last—the knowledge of our own hearts, of their weakness, their wickedness, and of the way of God's salvation, pardon of the faithful and confiding penitent for His dear Son's sake. Oh! my dear Lord, may you and I be found among the truly penitent, and then we shall have our perfect consummation and bliss among the truly blessed.

I am, my dear Lord, with true veneration and regard, your Lordship's most faithful servant, and affectionate brother in Christ, H. Exeter.

XVIII.—ADVICE TO A GOD-CHILD.

Samuel Taylor Coleridge to Adam Steinmitz K——

My dear God-child: I offer up the same fervent prayer for you now, as I did, kneeling before the altar, when you were baptized into Christ, and solemnly received as a living member of His spiritual body, the Church.

Years must pass before you will be able to read with an

understanding heart what I now write; but I trust that the all-gracious God, the Father of our Lord Jesus Christ, the Father of mercies, who, by His only begotton Son (all mercies in one sovereign mercy!), has redeemed you from the evil ground, and willed you to be born out of darkness, but into light—out of death, but into life—out of sin, but into righteousness—even into the Lord our righteousness; I trust that He will graciously hear the prayers of your dear parents, and be with you as the spirit of health and growth in body and mind.

My dear God-child, you received from Christ's minister at the baptismal fount, as your Christian name, the name of a most dear friend of your father's, and who was to me even as a son, the late Adam Steinmitz, whose fervent aspiration and ever paramount aim, even from early youth, was to be a Christian in thought, word, and deed—in will, mind, and affections.

I too, your God-father, have known what the enjoyments and advantages of this life are, and what the more refined pleasures which learning and intellectual power can bestow; and with all the experience which more than threescore years can give, I now, on the eve of my departure, declare to you (and earnestly pray that you may hereafter live and act on the conviction), that health is a great blessing—competence obtained by honorable industry is a great blessing—and a great blessing it is to have kind, faithful, honest relatives; but that the greatest of all blessings, as it is the most ennobling of all privileges, to be, indeed, a Christian. But I have been likewise, through a large portion of my later life, a sufferer, sorely afflicted with bodily pains, languors, and bodily infirmities, and for the last three or four years have, with few and brief intervals, been confined to a sick room, and at this moment, in great weakness and heaviness, write from a sick-bed, hopeless of a recovery; * and I thus, on the very brink of the grave, solemnly bear witness to you that the Almighty Redeemer, most gracious in His promises to them that truly seek Him, is faithful to perform what He hath promised, and hath preserved, under all my pains and infirmities, the inward peace that passeth all understanding, with the supporting assurance of a reconciled God, who will not withdraw His Spirit from me in the conflict, and in His own time will deliver me from the evil one.

O, my dear God-child! eminently blessed are those who begin early to seek, fear, and love their God, trusting wholly in the righteousness and mediation of their Lord, Redeemer, Saviour, and everlasting High Priest, Jesus Christ!

O, preserve this as a legacy and bequest from your unseen God-father and friend, S. T. COLERIDGE.

July 13th, 1834.

XIX.—CONSOLATIONS OF RELIGION—BISHOP HORNE.

Sir W. W. Pepys to Hannah More.

WIMPOLE STREET, May 12th, 1808.

MY DEAR FRIEND: To have written to me at all so kindly and so spontaneously as you did, excited my warmest gratitude; but to follow it up by another most friendly and delightful letter, convinces me that you will not be sorry, during the short space before "we go hence and are no more seen," to hear now and then from your old and sincere friend. I am aware, however, that such kindness demands some discretion on my part, and

* He died on the 25th day of the same month.

that I must not alarm you by too quick a succession of letters, but encourage you to resume the habit of writing to me now and then, not as a task, but as one of those many occupations in which your whole life has been passed, the object of which has always been to afford comfort and satisfaction to somebody.

The day is not long enough for what I find to do, now that I am supposed to do nothing; and if I can but so employ the short remainder of my time as to be able to render a good account of it hereafter, I have no apprehension of not passing it to my own satisfaction, while it shall please God to continue my health. "*Thou upholdest me in my health*," are the words in which I daily acknowledge my dependence on God's goodness for the continuance of it; and I humbly hope, as I do not trust in my own strength, but look up to Him with the deepest sense of gratitude for all His mercies, that they will be continued to me. But I "rejoice with trembling," when I hear of such disasters as the loss of Lord Royston, and ask myself how would it indeed have been possible for me to bear the stroke! Indeed, my good friend, I am thoroughly sensible that if religion is so necessary to keep us temperate in prosperity, it is our only support in adversity. I can safely say that the most delightful moments of my life have been those in which I have raised my heart toward heaven in thankfulness for the innumerable blessings which I have enjoyed. If devotion be, therefore, my greatest delight in the time of my health, what other comfort can I look to in the time of my tribulation, and in the hour of my death! How strangely unacquainted with the delights of religion are those who consider it only as a system of hard duties to be performed, which afford here nothing but labor and sorrow, though hereafter they may attended with their reward.

I am persuaded, on the contrary, that as Bishop Horne says beautifully on our Saviour's caution against too great anxiety for the morrow, that he has consulted in his precepts our happiness here as well as hereafter. By the way, did you ever see those beautiful applications of passages from the classics of Bishop Horne, published by Mr. Jones? One of them was peculiarly pleasing to me from Terence's Phormio, act 1, scene 3.

Poor Mrs. Ord! she is, I think, the last of those we used so often to meet; how few old friends left! *Apparent rari nantes in gurgite vasto.* You see how profuse I am of my Latin, but I have great pleasure in communicating any classical allusion where I know it will be relished. As to the common intercourse of life, it seems to me that I might have walked up and down St. James's street all my life with Florio, for any use that literature is of in *conversation;* but it is my great delight when alone, and *that* is much more important.

As my time is now more at my command, it has occurred to me that I could not make a better use of it than to take an active part in soliciting the assistance of the public to prevent the Middlesex Hospital from being shut up; for, as people bestow their charity upon *new* institutions, they are apt to let the old ones shift for themselves, till, by degrees, our finances have become so inadequate to the relief of the many poor wretches who apply, that we have been obliged to appeal to the public for immediate assistance. I mention this because I think it not improbable that you may know some persons who have much to give, and would not be sorry to know where their money might be best applied.

Have you read Shee's "Rhymes on Art"? Some parts are excellent, particularly those on the French Revolution, where he speaks of new experiments in government, made with the same apathy as if they were performing some operation in chemistry.

"What shapes of social order rise refined,
From speculation's crucible combined,
While cool state chemists watch the boiling brim,
And life's low dregs upon the surface swim:
What though midst passion's fiery tumults tost,
A generation's in the process lost,
The calm philosopher pursues his plan,
Regardless of his raw material, man."

Did I tell you how much my son and I were struck with a work of Madame de Staël, "Sur la Literature"? We both thought it excellent, though possibly in some places too refined. As to "Marmion," I do not know such powers of representation in very modern poetry; but there are no lines which one wishes to get by heart like those in the "Last Lay," and so many of them bear such marks of haste and idleness, that he who could do so much better ought to be whipped for them. The battle is the best I remember since old Homer. You see the banners stoop and rise again. It has been upon every table this winter.

And now, my good friend, have you had enough of my politico-prosaic epistle? or shall I tell you that, at the age of sixty-eight I am sitting for my picture, at the earnest request of my dear children? Could I but show you the letter in which my son conveyed his own and his sister's request, you would say that you never saw a *picture* of filial attachment which gave you more pleasure; what then must it have afforded me! * People used to threaten me, when I first undertook to educate my sons,

* The son afterwards became one of the most distinguished of the High Chancellors who have held the seal of Great Britain.

that they would hate me as their schoolmaster; but, thank God, I am daily receiving marks of the sincerest attachment from them.

Do not fail to cherish the remembrance of me, as of one who has never ceased to entertain the most cordial attachment to you, mixed up with a great degree of veneration for your piety, virtue, and talents; and if you ever do permit yourself to offer up a prayer for your friends, let me hope that you will join with me in supplication that we may meet in heaven!

Ever yours, W. W. PEPYS.

XX.—HEALTH—COWPER, CORINNE—SUPPORT FROM RELIGION UNDER TRIALS.

Hannah More to Sir W. W. Pepys.

BARLEY WOOD, April 5th.

MY DEAR SIR WILLIAM: No! I cannot express to you a tenth part of the pleasure which I felt on reading your most kind and interesting letter. The delightful family picture was so pleasing to my mind, that I was never weary of contemplating it, and I am in love with all the portraits individually and aggregately. Every change of this very capricious season brings on a fresh attack of fever; and though the calendar tells us it is April, my own feelings corroborate the testimony of the leafless shrubs and the brown grass, that it is December. I confess I have had intervals in which I *could* have written, but it is so unpleasant to be always speaking ill of one's self, that I deferred my letter from one week to another, in the hope of being able to tell you that I was emancipated from my long imprisonment. I thank God, however, that I continue to bear it cheerfully; and when the *rigors of the month of May* are past, I trust I shall again experience the blessings of fresh air.

> "He does not scorn it who has long endured
> A fever's agonies, and fed on drugs."

How have I felt, how have I *tasted* these lines of Cowper. I remember it was said more than twenty years ago, that I was the only one of the old school who strongly relished Cowper; but then he had not published the "Task," which I am sure must have converted *you*, though I think our friends Mrs. Montagu and Lord Orford were never brought over to the faith. Beattie came over but slowly, and I took the credit of his conversion to myself; I believe I rather frightened him into it. And so you agree with me that conversation is absolutely extinct. The classic spirit has, I think, declined with it; and I should think poetry extinct also, did it not in Walter Scott give signs of life. I have not read "Marmion," but hear it is not unworthy the author of the "Lay."

I would have given something if I *could* have drank tea with your family party the evening after I had finished "*Corinne*," which your account led me to read. There never *was* such a book! such a compound of genius and bad taste! such a fermentation of sense and nonsense! The descriptions of Italy are the best; and the descriptions of love the worst I ever met with. There are no shades. As there is little nature, it excites little interest; and the virtuous hero is to me a gloomy specimen of frigid sentimentality. Corinne herself gave me too much the idea of Dr. Graham's Goddess of Health, or the French Goddess of Reason, or the English Attitudinarian of Naples, for me to take a very lively interest in her. Yet let me acknowledge that, though like Pistol I swallowed and execrated, yet I went on swallowing; and I must own it is a book which requires great knowledge and very considerable powers of mind to produce. She never stumbles so much as when she attempts to introduce Christianity, as there is no subject on which she appears so completely ignorant. You see, evidently, that she drags it into play as a creditable novelty, having, I am told, tried Atheism without success in Delphine, which I have never read.

I have been reading through two books sent me by the authors, my friends, both clergymen of Bristol. One the Life of Thuanus. One felt glad to be introduced into such respectable company as the authors and statesmen of the days of Henri Quartre, the Sullys, the l'Hôpitals, the Casaubons, the Heinsiuses and the Grotiuses. I counselled the author to translate the huge works of Thuanus, but he says the irreclaimable prolixity must ever prevent their being popular. The other is a pamphlet, "Latium Redivivum." The object is to repress the universality of the French language, that provoking criterion of the ascendency of France, and to restore the popular usage of the language of Rome; at least to make it the colloquial tongue of schools and universities, and the medium of our communication with foreigners; and especially that ambassadors shall negotiate in Latin. And why not as well now as in the days of our once "right-learned" Queen? Though I fear some of our corps diplomatique would not be very Ciceronian.

But it is time to revert to your kind letter; and allow me to say, that from no part of it did I derive such heartfelt satisfaction as from the evidence it afforded me of the pious feelings of your heart, and your devout recognition of the merciful hand whence your multiplied blessings flow. O, my good friend! there is no other stable foundation for solid comfort but the Christian religion; not barely acknowledged as a truth from the conviction of external evidence (strong and important as that is), but from embracing it as a principle of hope, and joy, and peace, and from feeling its suitableness to the wants and necessities of our nature, as well as its power to alleviate and even sanctify our sorrows. Little as has been my own progress in this school, yet that little was an unspeakable support to me on the bed of sickness; and in my weak and helpless state, I often thought what would have become of me if I had then had to begin to learn the elements of religion!

You have doubtless heard that I have had far greater trials than any which sickness could inflict. I will only say, in a few words, that two Jacobin and infidel curates, poor and ambitious, formed the design of attracting notice and getting preferment by attacking some charity schools (which, with no small labor, I have carried on in this county for near twenty years), as seminaries of vice, sedition, and disaffection. At this distance of time, for it is now ended in their disgrace and shame, it will make you smile when I tell you a few of the charges brought against me, viz.: that I hired two men to assassinate one of these clergymen; that I was actually taken up for seditious practices; that I was with Hadfield in his attack on the King's life. One of them strongly insinuated this from the pulpit, and then caused the newspaper which related the attack to be read at the church door. At the same time, mark the consistency! they declared that I was in the pay of Mr. Pitt, and the grand instigator (poor I) of the war, by mischievous pamphlets; and to crown the whole, that I was concerned with Charlotte Corday in the murder of Marat!!! That wicked and needy men should invent this is not so strange, as that they should have found magazines, reviews, and pamphleteers to support them. My declared resolution never to defend myself, certainly encouraged them to go on. How thankful am I that I kept that resolution; though the grief and astonishment excited by this combination nearly cost me my life. I can now look, not only without emotion, to this attack, but it has been even matter of *thankfulness* to me; it helped to break my too strong attachment to the world, it showed me the vanity of human applause, and has led me, I hope, to be *more* anxious about the motives of my actions, and *less* anxious about their consequences.

I am happy in the esteem of neighbors, and my schools flourish. I have a sister whose associated labors supply my lack of service. I had intended to have said more in answer to your letter. Your two eldest sons I well remember, and Miss Pepys. I rejoice they are all such blessings to you and their excellent mother.

I beg my affectionate respects to Lady Pepys. How glad I am at your honorable and profitable retreat from your professional labors. May God bless your clerical son, and make him an instrument to His glory!

Yours very sincerely,

H. More.

XXI.—NO DISPENSATION FROM THE DUTIES OF RELIGION TO GENIUS.

Hannah More to Mr. and Mrs. Huber.

1820.

My dear Friends: It is only a few days ago that I could prevail on Messrs. T. & Co. to let me have *the book.* Imprisoned in my chamber for three weeks, it was only yesterday that I could finish it. I have read it with mingled feelings; pain and pleasure had by turns the upper hand. But first let me, through you, thank the admirable author, not only for her kind present, but for the elegant and delicate hand with which she has reproved me. As to the work, it indicates a kindred genius with the subject it celebrates; a similarity of striking thoughts, brilliancy of style, and happy turn of expression, the same ardor in feeling, the same generosity of sentiment. I wish my sacred regard to truth would allow me to stop here, but you *insist* on knowing my sentiments. I really feel myself so *entirely* inferior to both ladies, that I am not worthy to offer them, and I feel, also, that I am going to expose myself to the charge of want of taste, of want of candor, or of envy of such eclipsing merits. It appears to me, then, that from the excess of her affection and the warmth of her generosity, Madame Necker, not content with making the eloge of Madame de Staël, has made her *apotheosis*. It would be a satire on my own judgment and feelings not to allow that I am one among the innumerable admirers of Madame de Staël. Corinne, as an exhibition of genius, is a *chef-d'œuvre*; of Delphine I have no right to speak, as I have never read it; but, having been assured that it was offensive to morality, I was sorry to observe that Madame Necker's warm heart had led her pure mind to defend it. I am at present too unwell to look over the passages on the admirable work "de l'Allemagne," on which I took the liberty to hazard a remark or two, in my essay on St. Paul. A passage in Madame Necker's book serves to recall the substance of it to my mind; the passage is, "*Le Juge suprême sera clement envers le génie.*" I humbly conceive this is a dangerous sentiment; Voltaire, Rousseau, Bolingbroke, Lord Byron, and a hundred others, would be happy to take shelter, for the use to which they applied their talents, under the wing of so admirable a woman as Madame Necker. Perhaps, had I as much personal interest in defending genius as she has, I might have been tempted to treat it with greater lenity. Again, I am a passionate admirer of whatever is beautiful in nature, or exquisite in art. These are the gifts of God, but no part of His essence; they proceed from God's goodness, and should kindle our gratitude to Him; but I cannot conceive that the most enchanting beauties of nature, or the most splendid productions of the fine arts, have any necessary connexion with religion. You will observe that I mean the religion of Christ, not that of Plato; the religion of reality, and not of the beau ideal. Adam sinned in a garden too beautiful for us to have any conception of it. The Israelties selected fair groves and pleasant mountains for the peculiar scenes of their idolatry. The most exquisite pictures and statues have been produced in those parts of Europe where true religion has made the least progress. These decorate religion, but they neither produce nor advance it. They are the enjoyments and refreshments of life, and very compatible with true religion, but they make no part of religion. Athens was at once the most learned and the most polished city in the world—so devoted to the fine arts, that it is said to have contained more statues than men; yet in this city the eloquent apostle's preaching made but one proselyte in the whole Areopagus.

I am happy to learn from her elegant biographer, that the close of life of her illustrious cousin was so eminently pious. The best Christians must look with envy at the passage in which she describes herself as not spending a quarter of an hour without thinking of God.

Though I have already said too much, I cannot help adding a word on what appears to me to be the distinctive character of Christianity. I mean a deep and abiding sense in the heart of our fallen nature; of our actual and personal sinfulness; of our lost state, but for the redemption wrought for us by Jesus Christ; and of the universal necessity of a change of heart, and the conviction that this change can only be effected by the influence of the Holy Spirit. This is not a splendid, but it is a saving religion; it is humbling now that it may be elevating hereafter. It appears to me, also, that the requisition which the Christian religion makes of the most highly gifted, as well as of the most meanly endowed, is, that after the loftiest and most successful exercise of the most brilliant talents, the favored possessor should lay his talents and himself at the foot of the Cross with the same deep abasement and self-renunciation as his more illiterate neighbor, and this from a conviction of who it is that hath made them to differ. I give Madame Necker high credit for the exact pencil with which she has drawn Madame Necker *la mère*. It is precisely the picture I drew in my own mind more than forty years ago. I saw much of both these distinguished parents, as they were in familiar intimacy with Mr. Garrick, at whose house I was then staying; with great abilities, I thought her too studiously ingenious to be agreeable, and too *recherchée* to seem uneasy; in short, she seemed to have been formed to be the admiration of Mr. Gibbon.

I am sorry you insisted so much on my real opinion of the excellently written volume in question. I feel that I have exposed myself to the charge of injustice to distinguished merit, and of ingratitude for the entertainment I have received from the living lady, as well as from *her* to whom human opinion, even of much higher order than mine, is now of no value. I have no room for other subjects. May the Almighty grant us all the benefits and consolations of the late gracious season!

H. MORE.

I must add, that in sallies of imagination and happiness of illustration, Madame Necker is frequently not inferior to her admirable relative.

XXII.—SPIRIT OF PRAYER—SAYING OF BOWDLER—FEELINGS AND STUDIES OF THE OLD.

Sir W. W. Pepys to Hannah More.

POTTERELLS, January 7th, 1825.

MY DEAR FRIEND: I have just finished your "Spirit of Prayer," for which I give you my sincerest thanks. I have told my family what, if said only to you, might savor too much of compliment, that I do not recollect to have ever risen from a book which gave me greater *pleasure;* I said actual *pleasure*, not merely instruction or useful exhortation, but positive delight. There is such an animated spirit of piety running through the whole of it, that not to have greatly relished it would have impeached one's taste even more than one's principles. Mrs. Montagu and I used always to agree that you had more wit in your serious writings than other people had when they meant to be professedly witty; and I used to tell her that whenever I should see you, I should plague you by complimenting you upon the wit of your writings, and not upon the good which I thought they would do. As to this last treatise, I hope to have it always upon my table, and to read it over and over again, as long as I shall wish to cherish the spirit of piety; which I pray to God may be as long as I live.

Mrs. H. Bowdler writes me word that she saw you lately, and you were still in your chamber. She says: "I left her with feelings of respect and admiration which I cannot describe. I never saw her more agreeable or more animated than on this last visit." Though you have long since been raised above the praise of us poor mortals, yet if any such can give you pleasure, it must be when it comes from such a person as Mrs. Bowdler.

We are just now reading of an evening a "Memoir of Mr. John Bowdler," her brother, written by his son, which shows him to have been worthy of that excellent family to which he belonged. I have long known and highly respected Thomas Bowdler, but of John I knew nothing, except an admirable saying which I remember was attributed to him some years ago, when the fashion was to lament over the state of this unhappy country. "If," said he, "a man were to go from the northern to the southern extremity of this island, with his eyes shut and his ears open, he would think that this country was sinking into an abyss of destruction; but if he were to return with his ears shut and his eyes open, he would be satisfied that he had the greatest reason to be thankful for our prosperity." As we have not finished the "Memoir," I can only hope that this observation has been preserved in it. What would he have said had he lived to see the *present* state of this country?

We hope to return to our winter quarters on Friday next, the 14th, and, blessed be God, in the same state of health and spirits as though Tuesday next would not complete my eighty-fifth year. I will not fill my paper with any effusions of that gratitude which the most obdurate heart must feel for such unmerited kindness. I wonder whether I shall ever see that young lady in whose favor you have so highly prepossessed me by the account which you gave of her kindness and attentions to you. If that false sentiment be so applauded,

"My friend must hate the man who injures me,"

surely it is equally fair that your friend should like (I suppose I must not say *love*) the young lady who has shown such attachment to you; pray remember me to her, and tell her that I think she has much more reason to value herself upon the conquest of an old man who has never seen her than of any young man who has.

We have been of late very much pleased on an evening by the "Memoirs of the Life of Dr. Clarke," the traveller, which we thought an acquisition, as it is so difficult to find any book that will suit equally the taste and ages of a whole family circle. For my part, when I am alone I feel that I have so little concern with this world, and so much with the next, that I am apt to reproach myself if I bestow much time on any book that has not some *tendency* at least to prepare me for the awful change I must expect soon to undergo. Dr. Doddridge, on the words, "Wist ye not that I must be about my Father's business?" recommends that answer to those who lose their time on the curiosities of literature, and quotes the last words of a great scholar: "*Heu! vitam perdidi operose nihil agendo*," instead of being about their heavenly "Father's business." This, my dear friend, will never rise up, I trust, as a just accusation against you, who have employed those brilliant talents which God has bestowed on you so much to His glory and the good of your fellow-creatures. I sometimes compare you with those who have attained the summit of earthly renown, and ask myself which I had rather be at this period of my life? I need not tell you the answer, which would be attended with still more self-reproach than it is, did I not feel that the mediocrity of my own talents exempts me in some degree from much of that responsibility which is attached to such as yours. But this is too fearful a subject to dwell upon, for we have all so much to be forgiven that it is idle to compare the quantities. May God in His mercy receive us both, through our only Mediator and Advocate.

XXIII.—A CHRISTIAN VIEW OF THE LOT OF WOMAN.

Rev. F. W. Robertson to a Lady.

My dear ——: A woman's position is one of subjection, mythically described as a curse in the Book of Genesis. Well, but I ween that all curses are blessings in disguise. Labor among thorns and thistles—man's best health. Woman's subjection? What say you to His? "Obedient," a "servant"; *wherefore* God also hath highly exalted Him. Methinks a thoughtful, high-minded woman would scarcely feel degraded by a lot which assimilates her to the divinest Man. "He came not to be ministered unto, but to minister." I have always conceived that you had learned to count that ministry the sublimest life which the world has seen, and its humiliation and subjection precisely the features which were most divine. The Greeks at Corinth wanted that part to be left out, and it was exactly that part which Paul would not leave out—Jesus Christ, but Jesus Christ *crucified*, which the Evangelicals rob of all its beauty.

Trust me, a noble woman laying on herself the duties of her sex, while fit for higher things—the world has nothing to show more like the Son of Man than that. Do you remember Wordsworth's beautiful lines to Milton?

> Thy soul was as a star, and dwelt apart;
> Thou hadst a voice whose sound was like the sea:
> Pure as the naked heavens, majestic, free,
> So didst thou travel on life's common way,
> In cheerful godliness: *and yet thy heart*
> *The lowliest duties on itself did lay.*

I do not know any thing of Alfieri's "Life." By whom is it written? The misfortunes of genius, its false direction, its misery, I suppose rise partly from the fact of the life of genius being that which is chiefly given to the world. Many a soldier died as bravely and with as much suffering as Sir John Moore at Corunna; but every soldier had not a Wolfe to write his death-song. Many an innocent victim perished—yes, by hundreds of thousands—on the scaffolds of France, and in the dungeons of the robber barons, but they died silently. A few aristocrats whose shriek was loud have filled the world with pity at the tale of their suffering. Many a mediocre boy have I seen spoilt at school—many a commonplace destiny has been marred in life: only these things are not matters of history. Peasants grow savage with domestic troubles, and washerwomen pine under brutal treatment; but the former are locked up for burying their misery in drunkenness—the latter die of a broken heart, with plenty of unwritten poetry lost among the soapsuds. I fancy the *inarticulate* sorrows are far more pitiable than those of an Alfieri, who has a tongue to utter them. Carlyle in this respect seems to me to hold a tone utterly diverse from that of the Gospel. The worship of the hero, that is his religion: condescension to the small and unknown, that was His!

A little plan which I have found serviceable in past years, is to put down every night the engagements and duties of the next day, arranging the hours well. The advantages of this are several. You get more done than if a great part of each day is spent in contriving and considering "what next?" A healthful feeling pervades the whole of life. There is a feeling of satisfaction at the end of the day on finding that, generally, the greater part of what is planned has been accomplished. This is the secret of giving dignity to trifles. As units they are insignificant; they rise in importance when they become parts of a plan. Besides this—and I think the most important thing of all—there is gained a consciousness of Will, the opposite of that which is the sense of impotency. The thought of time, to me at least, is a very overpowering and often a very annihilating one for energy: Time rushing on, unbroken, irresistible, hurrying the worlds and the ages into being, and out of it, and making our "noisy years seem moments in the *being* of the eternal Silence." The sense of powerlessness which this gives is very painful. But I have felt that this is neutralized by such a little plan as that. You feel that you do not control your own course; you are borne on, but not resistlessly. Down the rapids you go, certainly, but you are steering and trimming your own raft, and making the flood of Time your vassal, and not your conqueror. I first, I think, began this plan after reading a valuable little book, and a sunny, cheerful one, Abbott's "Way to do Good." It has been omitted for years, but I have begun it again these last few days.

"There is nothing in the drudgery of domestic duties to

soften"—you quote that. No, but a great deal to strengthen with the sense of duty done, self-control and power. Besides, you cannot calculate how much corroding rust is *kept off*—how much of disconsolate, dull despondency is hindered. Daily use is not the jeweller's mercurial polish: but it will keep your little silver pencil from tarnishing.

I have been interrupted by the visit of a lady of my congregation, who came to take leave; one, it appears, who has been warmly attached to the instruction given there. She told me the delight, the tears of gratitude, which she had witnessed in a poor girl to whom, in passing, I gave a kind look on going out of church on Sunday. What a lesson! How cheaply happiness can be given! What opportunities we miss of doing an angel's work! I remember doing it, full of sad feelings, passing on, and thinking no more about it; and it gave an hour's sunshine to a human life, and lightened the load of life to a human heart—for a time!

THE END.

www.ingramcontent.com/pod-product-compliance
Lightning Source LLC
LaVergne TN
LVHW021302110826
845150LV00003B/458